PRAISE FOR *SUPPLY CHAIN NETWORK DESIGN*

"With the recent disruptions that tested traditional supply chain strategies fresh in our rearview mirror, we can all benefit from a new, innovative approach to network design that supports supply chains that are resilient, agile, and sustainable. *Supply Chain Network Design* offers practitioners and academics alike the insight and tools they need to develop supply chain strategies that meet the risks and challenges of today's and tomorrow's global supply chain. This insight will help to inform and transform the global supply chain."
Dr Noel Hacegaba, Chief Operating Officer, Port of Long Beach

"This book provides a road map for developing agile and sustainable supply chains in the face of global disruptions. *Supply Chain Network Design* is an excellent resource for supply chain professionals looking to optimize their networks and improve customer-centric workflows—a must-read!"
Jeff McDonald, EVP, NNR Global Logistics USA

"This is a relevant and timely book addressing both the fundamentals of supply chain network design and the realities of the decade we are living in with global risks we need to manage"
Chris Richard, Managing Director and Partner, The Boston Consulting Group

"A great, engaging read with a lot of practical application. Supply chain networks have never been more complex and challenging with several variables to solve for. While cost and service pressures continue on supply chain executives, additional factors such as agility, resilience, and sustainability also need to be considered. This book does a great job of articulating modern techniques in designing and optimizing networks as well as the emerging technologies in this space."
Dheera Anand, Partner of Supply Chain Consulting, Bain

"In *Supply Chain Network Design*, Nick Vyas, Greys Sošić and Das Dasgupta, tackle the urgent need for resilient, agile, and sustainable supply chains. With backgrounds in supply chain management, sustainability, and data analytics, this trio offers a cutting-edge perspective on redesigning supply networks in the face of global disruptions. Their book is a rich resource of innovative strategies, analytics, and real-world examples aimed at professionals and students alike. It provides a roadmap for creating supply chains that are efficient and prepared to meet future geopolitical challenges sustainably. A concise manifesto for transforming global supply chains, this work is essential for those ready to lead in evolving supply chain practices."
Randy Kenrick, CEO, Xebec Realty

Supply Chain Network Design showcases cutting-edge thought leadership in action. Nick Vyas, Das Dasgupta, and Greys Sošić have meticulously navigated into the complexities of our supply chains. The book covers an in-depth study of global supply chain networks, exploring strategies to mitigate disruptions by embracing innovative technologies, all while prioritizing sustainability. This book aims to revolutionize the global supply chain industry."
Joe Schofield, Chief Operations Officer, Port of Tanjung Pelepas, Malaysia

"This book delivers profound insights, invaluable case studies, and pioneering thought leadership on establishing resilient supply chain networks in an era marked by geopolitical shifts and rapid technological progress. Readers will gain essential tools for navigating evolving supply chain landscapes, harnessing cutting-edge technologies, and prioritizing sustainability in supply chain design optimization."
Dr K Ravi Kumar, Emeritus Professor, Marshall School of Business, University of Southern California

"In this book, Nick Vyas, Das Dasgupta, and Greys Sošić present key examples of how to re-imagine forward-thinking supply chains and emphasize why fostering resilience and agility are pivotal in overcoming challenges faced by industry leaders today and in the future."
Markus Mau, President, European Logistics Association

“In *Supply Chain Network Design* Nick Vyas, Das Dasgupta, and Greys Sošić, delve into geopolitical disruptions, digital transformation, and sustainability in the supply chain sector. This book is not just for supply chain professionals. It serves as an eye-opener and a service for humanity, shedding light on what goes on behind the scenes and the essence of building resilience.”
Bob Trebilcock, Editorial Advisor, *Supply Chain Management Review*

“For those seeking a thorough and detailed comprehension of supply chain network design, this is a valuable resource. This book provides clear explanations and excellent case studies on the successful integration of supply chain network design with the Triple Bottom Line framework, circular economy, and sustainability. Leaders will be better equipped to implement the best practices for their organizations amidst complex business and geopolitical landscapes. Recommended for all business leaders and entrepreneurs.”
Divya Modi, Investor & Entrepreneur

“Over the past few years, business leaders have witnessed volatility, uncertainty, complexity, and ambiguity become the new normal. Building resilient supply chain networks that benefit from AI/ML and digital twin technologies is becoming an increasing necessity. Nick Vyas, Das Dasgupta, and Greys Sošic successfully walk through the steps necessary to redesign and digitally transform supply chains to not only meet the challenges we face today, but to embrace the future possibilities to come.”
Chakri Gottemukkala, CEO, o9 Solutions

We’ve witnessed in the world today how uncertainty and change can especially impact supply chains. The solution is to build a resilient, agile, and sustainable supply chain that can deliver in spite of these disruptions. Nick Vas, Das Dasgupta, and Greys Sošić’s new book *Supply Chain Network Design* is a great guide to help you deliver for your organization. The authors bring decades of real-time, hands-on experience that will help you understand and deliver that ideal supply chain to your constituencies.
John Quinn II, Former EVP of Global Supply Chain, Warner Brothers

Supply Chain Network Design

How to Create Resilient, Agile and Sustainable Supply Chains

Dr Das Dasgupta, Dr Greys Sošić, and Dr Nick Vyas

KoganPage

First published in Great Britain and the United States in 2024 by Kogan Page Limited

2nd Floor, 45 Gee Street
London
EC1V 3RS
United Kingdom

8 W 38th Street, Suite 902
New York, NY 10018
USA

www.koganpage.com

Kogan Page books are printed on paper from sustainable forests.

ISBNs

Hardback 978 1 3986 1493 2
Paperback 978 1 3986 1491 8
Ebook 978 1 3986 1492 5

British Library Cataloguing-in-Publication Data

A CIP record for this book is available from the British Library.

Library of Congress Cataloging-in-Publication Data

A CIP record for this book is available from the Library of Congress

Typeset by Integra Software Services, Pondicherry
Print production managed by Jellyfish
Printed and bound by CPI Group (UK) Ltd, Croydon CR0 4YY

CONTENTS

PREFACE

In the intricately woven fabric of our post-pandemic, globally interconnected economy, the strategic importance of supply chain network design has never been more pronounced. Our publication, *Supply Chain Network Design*, represents a carefully curated synthesis of academic rigor and practical wisdom designed to offer a sophisticated balance of theoretical insights and tangible applications.

Authored by distinguished academicians and seasoned corporate leaders in supply chain management, this book presents a rich, multidimensional narrative. The authors' varied backgrounds enrich the content, making it an invaluable resource for newcomers and experienced supply chain management professionals, thought leaders, policymakers, and concerned citizens.

With this book, we aim to bridge the divide between academic theory and corporate practice, providing readers with a profound understanding of the nuances and complexities inherent in supply chain network design. We hope this text will serve as both a navigational tool and a source of inspiration for those embarking on or advancing within this vital and dynamic sector.

ACKNOWLEDGEMENTS

The journey to bringing *Supply Chain Network Design* to fruition has been an enriching experience, one that has been made possible through the collaborative efforts and unwavering support of numerous individuals. The enduring support of our families, friends, and loved ones has been a cornerstone of strength, enabling us to balance our academic, personal, professional, and writing commitments.

We extend our profound gratitude to our academic peers, whose insightful contributions and rigorous standards have greatly enhanced the depth of this work. The support and expertise of our publisher have been essential in transforming this vision into reality, ensuring the book's high quality and broad accessibility.

Our heartfelt thanks go to our corporate colleagues, whose practical perspectives have significantly enriched the academic content of this book.

Special recognition is due to the Kendrick Global Supply Chain Institute team (Marvi, Michelle, Jean, Ruth, Katy, Morgan, and Aanand/Dilmini) at USC Marshall School of Business for their steadfast support in cultivating innovative, critical-thinking, and resilient student leaders in a digitally transformative data-driven supply chain ecosystem. We also applaud our colleagues at Marshall's Data Science and Operations Department for their ongoing commitment to driving excellence in research and creating global impact.

Lastly, we acknowledge the worldwide community of supply chain professionals, policymakers, students and thought leaders. Your unwavering dedication to excellence is a constant source of motivation. We trust this book will significantly contribute to your professional journey, spurring growth, innovation, and success.

With sincere appreciation,
Dr. Nick Vyas
Dr. Greys Sošić
Dr. Das Dasgupta

Introduction: The Supply Chain Landscape: Disruptions, Threats, and Key Trends to Watch

01

Every supply chain management practice is built, studied, and improved upon by academics and practitioners with a singular aim: Deduce the best possible configuration of cost, service, and sustainability for a supply chain organization. Viewed from this perspective, the subject of Supply Chain Network Design (SCND), sometimes also referred to by researchers as network modelling[1] or strategic supply chain planning[2] is among the most crucial supply chain planning processes. We will come across a more descriptive definition of the subject in the following chapters. Still, at its simplest, SCND is a network architecture building process that best optimizes the use of all the supply chain facilities, operators, and resources including plants, warehouses, ports, suppliers, and distributors to bring goods to the market. A growing body of research continues to bring up different supply chain design approaches. All of them can be grouped under or seen to be relative to three primary queries: What is the network footprint?[3] What is the capacity of the network (determined by capital and technology)?, and What are the vital flows (of products, information, financials, regulatory, and contracts, etc.) that bring the network to life?

A common belief about SCND among academics and practitioners is that about 80 percent of a supply chain's total cost is "fixed" based on its network design. Supply Chain Digest founder and columnist Dan Gilmore noted this in a 2014 column and described how this had been shown to hold somewhat true during a Unilever network modelling exercise. The exercise took an exciting approach to network modelling, showing why SCND is a vital planning practice. In the exercise, Unilever executives imagined a perfect supply chain network, built in an unconstrained environment, calculated its logistics costs, and then added real-life complexities, inefficiencies, and constraints to the ideal model, and calculated the additional cost incurred due to the latter. The sum of it came out to be uncomfortably close to 81 percent. Then, Unilever did the same program in other geographies and found out that the percentage of costs of inefficiencies differed considerably.

The Unilever exercise reveals two important aspects of the discipline of SCND. One is SCND's crucial importance to the supply-chain organization. The second is the significance of the real-life complexities, such as constraints imposed upon it by socio-economic environments and inefficiencies that vary across geographies, often related to the former. Further, these real-life factors influence every single one of the aforestated elements, such as network footprint, capacity, flows, capital, technology, and geography that go into designing and forming supply chain networks. For students and practitioners of supply chains, a studied understanding of these real-life constraints and enablers is crucial to understanding the concept of SCND. Any such understanding must begin from a knowledge of the evolution of supply chain networks throughout history, with a keen eye on the impact of socio-economic and technological constraints and enablers. This chapter aims to provide a comprehensive overview of trade history, significant supply chain innovations, and the evolution of supply chain networks. It explores vital historical examples to highlight notable trade routes, transportation, communication, and technology developments.

How we got Here: A Historical Perspective of SCND

The evolution of Supply Chain Network Design is intertwined with the evolution of trade occurring throughout much of documented human history. Even more, trade has played a structural role in shaping the world and driving economic development. Numerous civilizations and regions have emerged as critical players in global trade. It has been a fundamental aspect of human society, enabling the exchange of goods, services, and ideas across regions and cultures. It has shaped economies, driven technological advancements, and fostered cultural interaction throughout history. As trade expanded, supply chains emerged to facilitate the flow of goods from producers to consumers. Over the years, numerous innovations and developments have revolutionized supply chain networks, increasing efficiency and globalization.

By examining historical milestones, we can understand how trade and supply chains have evolved and anticipate future trends. Various historical periods and regions have been considered to provide a comprehensive perspective on the evolution of trade and supply chain networks. Key examples have been selected to illustrate significant innovations and developments in each era. By examining key events, we trace the development of trade routes, transportation methods, and logistical strategies that have shaped global commerce. From the ancient Silk Road to modern global supply chains, this chapter presents a comprehensive overview of how trade evolved, and the pivotal role that supply chains played in facilitating economic growth and cultural exchange. Traditional supply chains can be viewed as flows of physical goods, information, financial transactions, and regulatory requirements. According to the World Trade Organization (WTO), global trade has grown over 45 times by volume and almost 400 times by value in the last 70 years, as recorded by the organization (see Figure 1.1).[4] However, like with everything else in this world, there is always a beginning.

Figure 1.1 Evolution of World Trade, 1950–2022

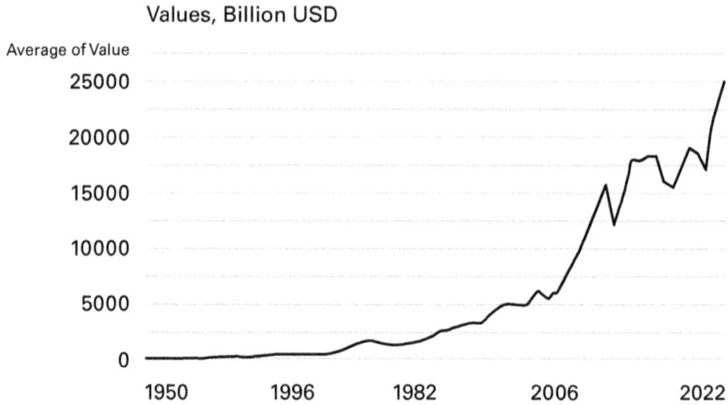

SOURCE WTO
NOTE Trade is calculated as average of exports and imports, and excludes significant re-exports or imports for re-exports.

3000–500 BCE: Ancient Trade Goes Long Distance

Evidence of long-distance trade dates back to 3000 BCE.[5] The ancient civilization of Mesopotamia (the area between Euphrates and Tigris Rivers), particularly the merchants of Sumer and Babylon, developed complex supply chain networks to trade grain, textiles, and precious metals with their counterparts living in the Indus Valley Civilization, also known as the Harappan Civilization, located in the northwestern region of the Indian subcontinent.

The Silk Road, the world's first major network of (geographically shifting) routes linking Europe to the Far East originated around 130 BCE.[6] The Silk Road facilitated the exchange of silk, spices, and other luxury goods, fostering cultural interactions and economic growth. Stretched across 4,000 miles of some of the world's most daunting terrains between North-Central China and ancient Anatolia (modern-day Turkey), the Silk Road brought silk, porcelain, and precious stones to Europe; and horses, glassware, Nestorian Christianity, and Buddhism to China. The Silk Road continued to function for more than a millennium under an epiphenomenal cover of protection provided by numerous empires in return for heavy customs duties.[7]

The period between 1550 and 600 BCE witnessed the emergence of the Phoenicians. Inhabitants of the city-states of ancient Phoenicia situated on the Mediterranean coastline, Phoenicians, were expert seafarers and traders who established a vast trading network in the region. They introduced innovations such as standardized weights and measures, currency, and bills of exchange, which streamlined trade and influenced subsequent civilizations.

It makes an interesting study that even the limited information available on the ancient trade networks reveals the presence of the constituent factors of SCNDs as we know them today. The flow of products between the Mesopotamian and Egyptian civilizations comprised grain, metals, and textiles with each other, giving rise to supply routes between them. The Indus Valley Civilization engaged in trade with Mesopotamia and the Persian Gulf, exporting goods like cotton, ivory, and spices.

The Roman Empire expanded trade routes, mainly through the Mediterranean, connecting Europe, Asia, and Africa. Establishing a vast road network and using ships for maritime trade enabled the efficient movement of goods, including agricultural products, metals, and luxury items. The Roman advancements in infrastructure and logistics set the stage for future trade developments. The next chapter will delve into how these empires and kingdoms were the earliest signs of supply chain network designs and how they evolved into what we have today.

During this period, network design decisions that determined the sourcing strategies or the contractual relationships were carried out under the constraints set by the powers that provided military coverage to their parts of the trade network. The Silk Road, for example, functioned for many millennia under the respective governance mechanisms, across time, provided by the Holy Roman Empire, the Byzantine Empire, China's imperial dynasties including the Han and Tang Dynasties, the Mongol Empire, and the Kushan Empire.

500–1500 CE: Trade and Markets Become Specialized

As we move forward from the age of ancient trade, we enter the era of the Hanseatic League, and Medieval European Trade, which lasted from 500 CE to 1500 CE. The Hanseatic League emerged as a prominent trading alliance in Northern Europe during this era, facilitating trade through a network of cities, promoting economic cooperation, standardization of trade practices, and the development of specialized markets. This network contributed significantly to the growth of European commerce and the exchange of goods such as timber, furs, and grain.

At the same time, the exchange of goods and ideas flourished between the countries and cities bordering the Indian Ocean region. Indian merchants sailed to various regions, including Southeast Asia, China, Arabia, and East Africa, exchanging commodities like textiles, spices such as pepper, precious gems, and indigo. Coastal cities such as Kilwa and Mombasa on East Africa's Swahili Coast became important trading hubs, showcasing the influence of cultural diversity on the trade flows. This period witnessed the flourishing of Indian empires such as the Gupta and Vijayanagara Empires, and a marked rise in trade and cultural exchange between India and the rest of the world. India's exquisite textiles, including fine cotton and silk fabrics, were in high demand in foreign markets. Arab traders, particularly those from the Abbasid Caliphate (750–1258), established significant trade links with India. They introduced new crops like cotton and introduced the concept of credit, leading to the growth of commercial centers such as the port of Calicut.

The Silk Road also contributed to the global flow of goods and ideas, with the Mongol Empire, that lasted from 1206 to 1368, facilitating safe passage and encouraging commerce across their vast empire. This period also saw the introduction of paper money, which revolutionized trade transactions—the Mongols' infrastructure developments, including the Yam system, expedited communication, and the movement of goods.

1500 to 1800s: The Age of Exploration and Exploitation

The Silk Road met its abrupt end in 1453 CE following the fall of the Byzantine Empire to the Turks. It also set the stage for new trade routes and networks. The European Maritime Expansion and the Age of Exploration marked a significant turning point in global trade, which spanned from 1500–1800. European nations, including Portugal,

Spain, the Netherlands, and England, embarked on voyages to discover new trade routes and establish colonies (see Table 1.1).

The discovery of new lands in the Americas and Asia led to the integration of previously isolated regions into global trade networks. The so-called Columbian exchange, which resulted from Christopher Columbus's voyages, initiated a massive transfer of plants, animals, and diseases between the Old and New World. It transformed agriculture, diet, and economies, with crops like maize, potatoes, and tomatoes becoming integral to food production and trade.

Triangular trade and the transatlantic slave trade triangular trade routes emerged during the 16th to 19th centuries, linking Europe, Africa, and the Americas. This system involved the exchange of goods, including raw materials, manufactured goods, and enslaved Africans. The transatlantic slave trade, a tragic chapter in history, profoundly impacted the development of global supply chains. The magnitude of international trade during this period remained relatively modest, constituting merely a fraction, approximately 5 percent,[8] of the global Gross Domestic Product (GDP). The primary factor impeding its exponential growth was the restricted nature of trade, largely confined to exchanges between European powers and their colonies, predominantly enforced through coercive and exploitative measures.

Table 1.1 Major political forces that shaped global trade routes

European voyages	European powers, including Portugal, Spain, the Netherlands, France, and Britain, embarked on voyages of exploration. They sought direct sea routes to Asia to bypass intermediaries and secure control over valuable trade networks.
Portuguese in India	The Portuguese established a maritime empire in India, with Goa as their headquarters. They monopolized the spice trade, including pepper, cinnamon, and cloves.
British East India Company	The British East India Company, granted a royal charter in 1600, expanded its presence in India. It gradually gained control over regions like Bengal, Madras, and Bombay, establishing trade outposts and exploiting local resources.

Industrial Revolution and Later: Events and Ideas that Shaped Today's Supply Chain Networks

The Industrial Revolution and Early Supply Chain Innovations (1800–1900 CE)

The Industrial Revolution brought significant advancements in transportation. The invention of the steam engine and the subsequent development of steamships and railways revolutionized the movement of goods over long distances. These innovations significantly reduced transportation costs and accelerated trade. The expansion of railways during the 19th century facilitated the transportation of goods within countries and across continents. Railways connected production centers to ports, enabling efficient supply chain networks and the growth of international trade. The development of telegraph lines further improved communication and coordination. The invention of the telegraph revolutionized communication during the 19th century. It allowed for the near-instantaneous transmission of messages over long distances, enhancing coordination between trading partners, improving supply chain visibility, and enabling faster decision-making.

Mass Production and Global Supply Chains (1900–2000)

The mass production concept pioneered by Henry Ford transformed manufacturing processes and supply chains. The assembly line allowed for the efficient production of standardized goods, such as automobiles, at lower costs. While Henry Ford did not invent the automobile, he forever revolutionized factory production with his assembly-line methods, transforming American lives by making transportation affordable to the common man/woman (see Figure 1.2). Ford was inspired by the continuous-flow production methods used by flour mills, breweries, canneries, industrial bakers, and in

Chicago's meat-packing plants, so Ford installed moving lines for bits and pieces of the manufacturing process. For example, factory workers built motors and transmission on rope-and-pulley powered conveyer belts. This eventually led to the unveiling of the moving-chassis assembly line in December of 1913.

In 1914, the Panama Canal officially opened, allowing for trade between the Atlantic and Pacific Oceans. Due to these shipping developments, the cost of transporting goods dropped significantly by 70 per cent between 1840 and 1910. This approach influenced supply chain management practices worldwide. The introduction of containerization in the mid-20th century revolutionized the shipping industry. Standardized containers enable the easy transfer of goods between different modes of transportation, reducing handling costs and time. This innovation spurred the growth of global supply chains, facilitating the movement of goods across continents. Japanese manufacturing principles, such as Just-in-Time (JIT) manufacturing and lean production, gained prominence in the latter half of the 20th century. These approaches aim to minimize waste, reduce inventory, and improve efficiency throughout the supply chain. JIT practices became widespread, influencing global supply chain management strategies.

Figure 1.2 Industrial Revolution evolution

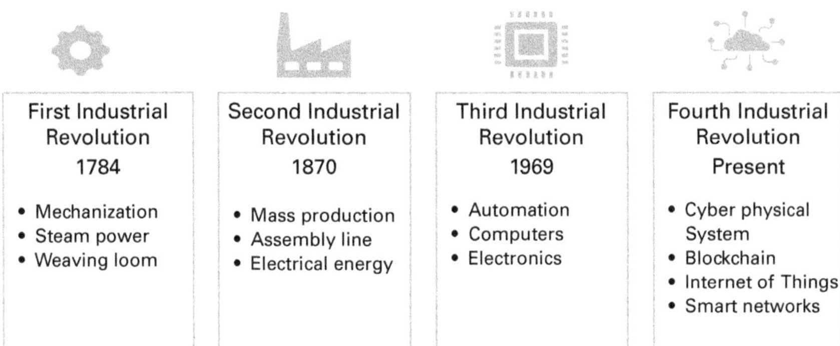

SOURCE USC Marshall-Randall R. Kendrick Global Supply Chain Institute

The factory system: The factory system's rise centralized production and profoundly impacted supply chains. Mass production in factories enabled economies of scale, streamlined processes, and reduced costs. This transformation required efficient supply chain management to coordinate raw material procurement, production, and distribution.

Interchangeable parts: The concept of interchangeable parts pioneered by Eli Whitney in the late 18th century revolutionized manufacturing and supply chains. Standardized parts allowed for the mass production of goods, and simplified repairs and replacements. This innovation improved efficiency, reduced costs, and accelerated supply chain operations.

The invention of the telegraph and Morse code in the 19th century enhanced communication and coordination in supply chains. Real-time messaging facilitated coordination between suppliers, manufacturers, and distributors. The telegraph accelerated decision-making, improved supply chain visibility, and reduced response times.

Decolonization and regional trade: Following World War II, many countries gained independence, including India, in 1947. During this period, we have witnessed the rise of regional trade blocs, such as the European Union, ASEAN, and SAARC, aiming to enhance economic cooperation and reduce trade barriers.

Globalization and technological advancements: The latter half of the 20th century witnessed significant advancements in transportation, communication, and information technology. These developments, along with the liberalization of trade policies, propelled globalization, and increased interconnectivity between nations.

Containerization: The development of containerization revolutionized global trade in the 20th century. Standardized containers and container ships simplified goods loading, unloading, and transportation. This innovation reduced shipping costs, improved efficiency, and enabled the global expansion of supply chains, which we'll explore a bit further below.

Just-in-Time (JIT) manufacturing: Just-in-time manufacturing emerged in the 20th century, pioneered by companies like Toyota. JIT principles focused on minimizing inventory and waste, with a tight synchronization of supply and demand. JIT manufacturing transformed supply chains, reducing storage costs and improving responsiveness to customer needs.

Globalization and outsourcing: The advent of globalization facilitated the outsourcing of manufacturing and supply chain activities to low-cost regions. Supply chains have become increasingly global, involving complex networks of suppliers, manufacturers, and distributors across different countries. This globalization of supply chains led to increased interconnectivity and economic interdependence.

Containerization

The introduction of standardized shipping containers revolutionized global trade in the 20th century. This innovation, pioneered by Malcolm McLean, transformed how goods were transported and handled in supply chains. Shipping containers provided a uniform and efficient means of packaging, protecting, and securing goods during transportation. They could be seamlessly transferred between different modes of transportation, including ships, trains, and trucks. Containerization significantly improved supply chain efficiency, reducing shipping costs, improving inventory management, and facilitating the globalization of trade.

Ocean shipping remains the primary mode of global trade transit (almost 90% of traded goods are moved by water). Container ships are a vital part of the global economy, and their size is only increasing. With increased worldwide demand for commodities from major export countries such as the United States, Germany, China, Japan, and Hong Kong, the need for these future vessels to transport more in a single voyage will grow. Prior to international containerization in 1961, ocean freight costs alone were 12% of the value of U.S. exports and 10% of the value of U.S. imports, with the average U.S. import tariff at 7%. For example, it would cost a pharmaceutical company about $2,400 to ship a truckload of medicines from the Midwest to Europe. At the time, trading costs were so high, it didn't make sense for companies to trade overseas. In contrast, the typical pre-pandemic price of transporting a 20-foot container carrying over 20 tons of cargo from Asia to Europe was about the same as an economy ticket to fly the same journey. World

GDP in 1952 was $10.52 trillion, tripled by the 1990s, and the world GDP today now stands at 112.6 trillion. While the standardized container wasn't created until the 1950s, the Vietnam War catapulted the use of the container during the 1960s and 1970s. Along with various agreements and geopolitical conflicts, containerization allowed for rising living standards around the world, especially as more developing countries played integral roles in world trade. Developing countries now account for about 33% of world trade, especially with increased exports of manufacturers and services, which now account for 40% of their exports going to other developing countries (Fig 1.3). Along with trade liberalization and the creation of the standard container, people in absolute poverty declined by 14% between 1993 and 1998, and countries such as Singapore and South Korea saw immense increases in wealth where there had previously been extreme poverty until the 1970s. Shipping contributes 2.9% of total world greenhouse gas emissions. Marine trade volumes are predicted to triple by 2050 as global freight demand rises. However, this presents both opportunities and challenges, which will be discussed further in Chapter 6.

The widespread adoption of containerization led to the development of specialized container terminals at ports worldwide. These terminals were equipped with cranes, container storage yards, and advanced handling equipment to accommodate the efficient movement of containers. The need for larger vessels and deeper harbors prompted significant investments in port infrastructure. Mega-container ships, capable of carrying thousands of containers, emerged. This port infrastructure and vessel size transformation has profoundly impacted supply chain networks and global trade flows.

Containerization facilitated the growth of intermodal transportation, where goods are transported using multiple modes of transport. The seamless transfer of containers between ships, trains, and trucks reduced handling costs, improved transportation efficiency, and shortened transit times. Intermodal transportation networks have become critical components of modern supply chains, enabling goods to be transported over long distances, connecting global markets and regions. Containerization has altered the way we think about

Figure 1.3 Speed of change in history

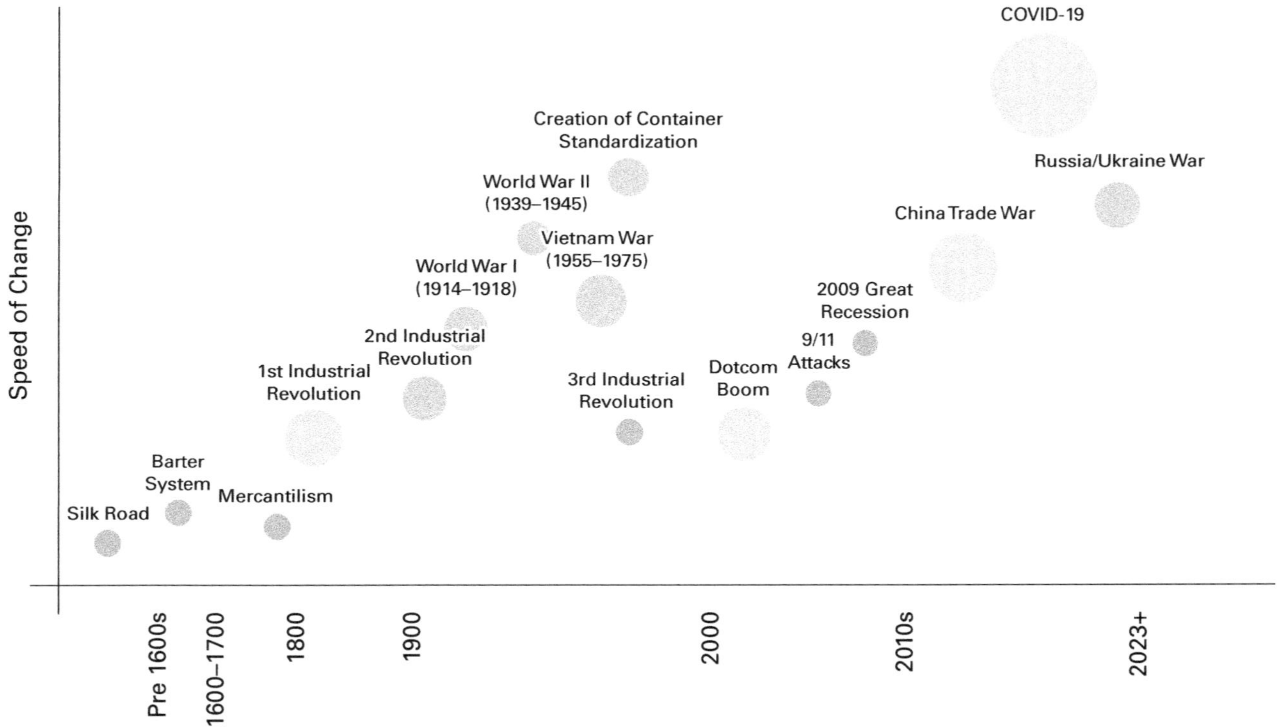

SOURCE USC Marshall-Randall R. Kendrick Global Supply Chain Institute

transportation and has been driven by digital technologies and data analysis. As the world becomes more interconnected, the future of multimodal transportation becomes clearer. To accomplish this, businesses must maximize their resources in both the physical and digital worlds. Intermodal transportation has become a critical component for businesses looking to increase production and efficiency. It has also helped to minimize transportation expenses, environmental impact, carbon footprint, and gridlock in traffic.

2000-Present: The Age of Information

As we come out of the time of exponential growth in global trade along international supply chain networks, we head into the modern era, which has witnessed remarkable advancements in supply chain management and network design. With the rise of globalization, rapid technological progress, and shifting consumer demands, supply chains have evolved to meet the challenges of a rapidly changing world. What we are seeing in this period and evidence leads us to think beyond corporate profit and that we are at an inflection point where we must approach supply chains and how we operate more holistically. This section provides a comprehensive overview of supply chain innovations in the modern era, spanning the 20th and 21st centuries. Additionally, recent events and facts are explored to highlight the current state and emerging trends in supply chain management.

E-commerce and Online Marketplaces: The rise of the internet and e-commerce transformed retail and supply chains. Online marketplaces, such as Amazon and Alibaba, revolutionized how goods are bought and sold, enabling direct connections between buyers and sellers, and offering a vast array of products globally.

RFID and Supply Chain Visibility: Radio Frequency Identification (RFID) technology has improved supply chain visibility and traceability. RFID tags allow real-time tracking of goods throughout the supply chain, enhancing inventory management, reducing stockouts, and enabling efficient logistics operations.

Blockchain and Smart Contracts in Supply Chain Management: Blockchain technology has the potential to revolutionize supply chains by providing secure, transparent, and immutable records of transactions. Smart contracts enable automated and trustless agreements, streamlining procurement, payment, and provenance tracking processes.

Today, technology has become a vital component of the transportation sector because of e-commerce and globalization, and the use of such innovative technology is critical to ensuring that goods are safe and accounted for at every point of the route. Because roughly 90% of global trade occurs via sea and 60% of goods are packed into containers, technology plays a crucial role now more than ever. Visibility across the end-to-end process will ensure efficiency and accuracy. Several significant technological advances that are influencing the future of intermodal shipping are autonomous vehicles, Internet of Things (IoT), blockchain, weather intelligence, big data, and artificial intelligence (AI)/machine learning (ML), to name a few.

Following are the important principles and practices that have defined the way we operate both in manufacturing and in supply chain management processes in the 21st century.

Supplier Relationship Management

JIT manufacturing emphasized strong supplier relationships and collaboration. Close coordination with suppliers was crucial to ensuring a continuous flow of materials to support production schedules. Companies implemented supplier development programs, fostering long-term partnerships and shared goals. Effective supplier relationship management significantly optimized supply chain efficiency, reduced lead times, and improved overall quality.

Kanban System and Pull Production

The Kanban system, a key element of JIT manufacturing, introduced a visual signaling system to manage inventory levels and control production. It relied on "pull" production, where production time was by actual customer demand rather than forecasting. Kanban cards or electronic signals communicated the need for replenishment, triggering the production of additional units. This approach minimized excess inventory, reduced stockouts, and improved production efficiency.

Globalization and Offshoring

Offshoring and nearshoring provided the foundation of modern-day globalization through complex manufacturing and supply chain network activities to low-cost regions. Companies sought to leverage cost advantages and access new markets by establishing global supply chains. Offshoring involved relocating production to distant countries, while nearshoring focused on transferring operations to geographically closer regions. These strategies allowed companies to take advantage of lower labor costs, specialized expertise, and favorable regulatory environments. However, they also introduced cultural differences, supply chain complexity, and risk management challenges.

Sustainability: Ethical and Environmental Imperatives

Globalization brought heightened awareness of ethical and environmental issues in supply chains. Companies faced growing pressure to ensure responsible sourcing, fair labor practices, and sustainable manufacturing processes. Stakeholders, including consumers, investors, and regulatory bodies, demanded transparency and accountability throughout the supply chain. Ethical and environmentally conscious practices became critical for companies seeking to build trust and maintain a positive brand image.

E-commerce and Digitalization

The rise of e-commerce and digitalization has transformed supply chain management in the 21st century. Online retail platforms, advanced analytics, and real-time tracking systems have improved supply chain visibility, demand forecasting, and customer experiences. Digital technologies have accelerated the speed and efficiency of supply chain operations. E-commerce has transformed consumer behavior and supply chain dynamics. Online retail platforms have enabled direct-to-consumer sales, bypassing traditional distribution channels. E-commerce has empowered consumers with more excellent choices, convenience, and access to a global marketplace. Companies have responded by developing sophisticated supply chain strategies to meet the demands of e-commerce, including last-mile delivery optimization, reverse logistics for returns, and real-time inventory management. For last-mile delivery, only 25% of sellers truly rely on traditional carriers such as UPS, FedEx, and USPS, but they have faced issues with on-time delivery. In a recent survey, 5% of organizations are crowdsourcing last-mile delivery as it will ensure timely delivery by relying on various providers. The only possible disadvantage is the potential lack of visibility for sellers (Brown, 2023).

In the past, sellers typically only used one provider. There has been a shift to decentralized fulfillment—retailers typically rely on a centralized model where product will be fulfilled by a single fulfillment center and only use one of the traditional carrier networks, severely limiting retailers from reaching more customers faster. In a recent Gartner analysis of 50 retailers within the apparel and footwear space, only 8% of them offer same-day delivery. When Target, a chain of US-based discounted department stores, recognized that a decentralized approach fulfills more and faster, they also saw a serious decline in expenses as well. The fulfillment from store model for their last-mile cost efficiency helped them reduce costs by 40%, with more than 75% of orders being fulfilled from their store network. The buy online, pick-up instore, or fulfilling orders from the store inventory not only helps reduce fulfillment center costs, but by allowing a store to be another provider for products to reach customers, it paves the way for that omnichannel experience; therefore, an improved customer experience (O'Connor, 2022).

Digitalization has revolutionized supply chain operations through advanced technologies and data analytics. IoT devices, such as sensors and RFID tags, enable real-time tracking and monitoring of goods throughout the supply chain. Data analytics and AI algorithms provide actionable insights for demand forecasting, inventory optimization, and supply chain risk management. Digital technologies have enhanced supply chain visibility, responsiveness, and decision-making capabilities. A new host of software vendors allow for better information flow. This allows sellers to evaluate various fulfillment provider rates in real time, thus allowing them to find the most cost-efficient or quickest delivery time. Having multi-cloud service providers has two major benefits: one is the ability to view geographic coverage models, and another is that it brings solutions to market faster, since the technology and implementing cloud services is more recent. Additionally, about 79 per cent of 500 senior cloud-decision makers surveyed said they use more than one software provider (Rockel, 2022). Additionally, many tech-enabled third-party logistics (3PL) companies also create their own version of warehouse management and transportation management systems, to not only stay competitive, but to ensure that there is more high-tech visibility for customers through the end-to-end process, and better ability to integrate with so many different e-commerce platforms. Companies include Advatix-XPDEL, ShipBob, ShipMonk, and Seko Logistics.

In a lot of these tech-enabled 3PLs, the technology enables sellers (who are the clients of the 3PL companies) to use the lowest-cost options across sellers, or even use the 3PL pre-negotiated shipping rates across different carriers to get the best rates. These rates are typically housed in the in-house technology of the respective 3PL companies. One of the supply chain trends for 2023 and beyond is the plethora of globally supply chain software that are arising, which leads to greater focus on leveraging data that helps sellers understand pricing, more visibility of the last mile and entire end-to-end process (Sethuraman, 2023).

Sustainability, Circular Economy, Social Responsibility

E-commerce and digitalization have also facilitated the emergence of sustainable supply chain practices. The circular economy concept has gained traction, focusing on reducing waste and promoting resource efficiency. Companies are adopting product lifecycle extension, recycling, and remanufacturing strategies. Supply chains are being redesigned to minimize environmental impact, promote sustainable sourcing, and reduce carbon footprints. Integrating sustainability into supply chain strategies has become a crucial aspect of corporate social responsibility and a driver of long-term competitiveness (see Figure 1.4). This will be further discussed in Chapter 6, but a great example of sustainability and a circular economy is how companies are recycling lithium-ion batteries (LIBs). Lithium-ion batteries have emerged as a promising alternative for powering portable electronic devices and electric vehicles, as well as serving as an energy storage solution (see Figure 1.5). However, their integration into the sustainability-focused economies of the future hinges on the efficiency of their recycling and re-introduction processes. According to a recent study, "recycling processes are the only option to re-introduce end-of-life (EOL) batteries and their components into the economic cycle, reducing the need for primary raw materials and promoting an improved acceptance of pure and hybrid electric vehicles." This alone shows us the promise that comes with the use of LIB as a renewable energy source.

Let's look at how a Tesla EV battery is recycled and reused. Tesla lithium-ion batteries are fully recycled. None go to landfill and are all returned to a Tesla service to be reused. Hydrometallurgy goes through three stages. The first step is the leaching process where liquid solutions are introduced to the black mass to help dissolve the different metal components in the aqueous phase. The next phase is that the 'leach liquor', a term used in the context of hydrometallurgy and mining, undergoes precipitation to remove impurities and certain compounds, while froth flotation can be used to separate materials. After processing, metal recovery begins. This is the final step and results in the recovery of the raw materials. Once they're back in their raw form, they can go back into manufacturing to be created into new products. This allows Tesla batteries to have a closed-loop recycling process. This is just one of the ways that companies can adopt circular economy processes into their supply chain in the hope of achieving more sustainable business practices.

The focus on sustainability and circular economy also leads the way for greater focus on social responsibility in supply chains. Stakeholders, including consumers, investors, and governments, demand greater transparency and accountability. Companies incorporate

Figure 1.4 Example of a circular economy

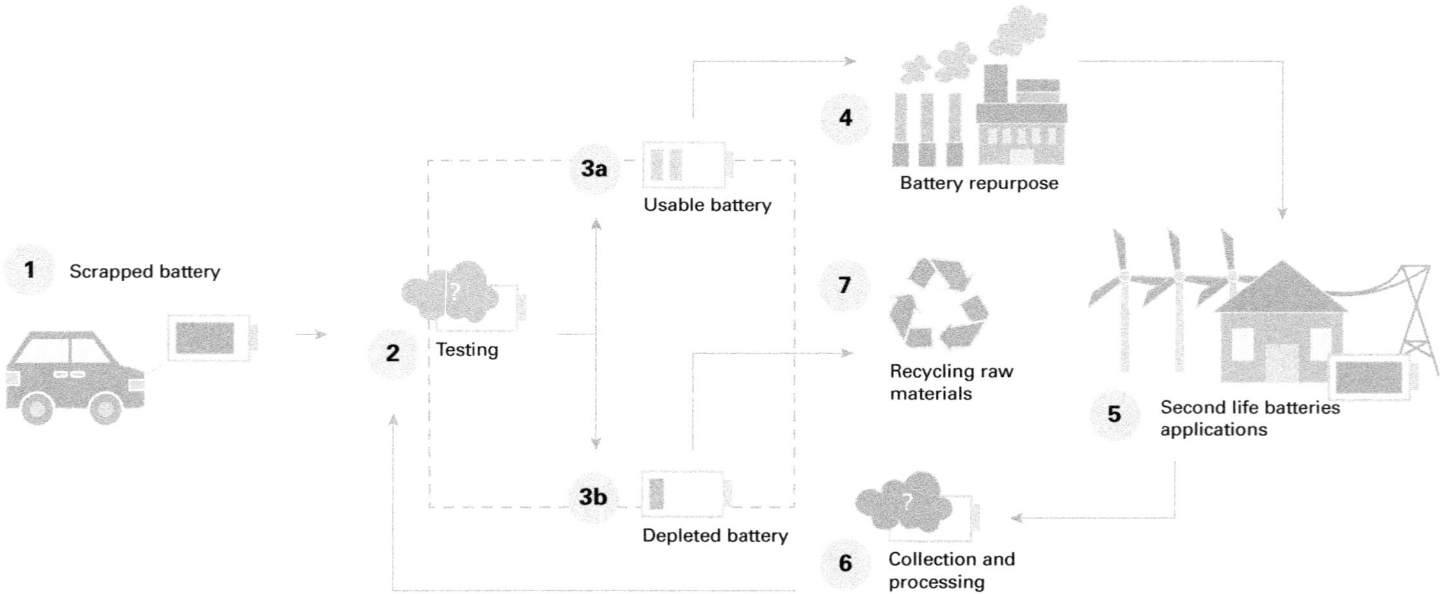

SOURCE USC Marshall-Randall R. Kendrick Global Supply Chain Institute

Figure 1.5 Circular energy storage

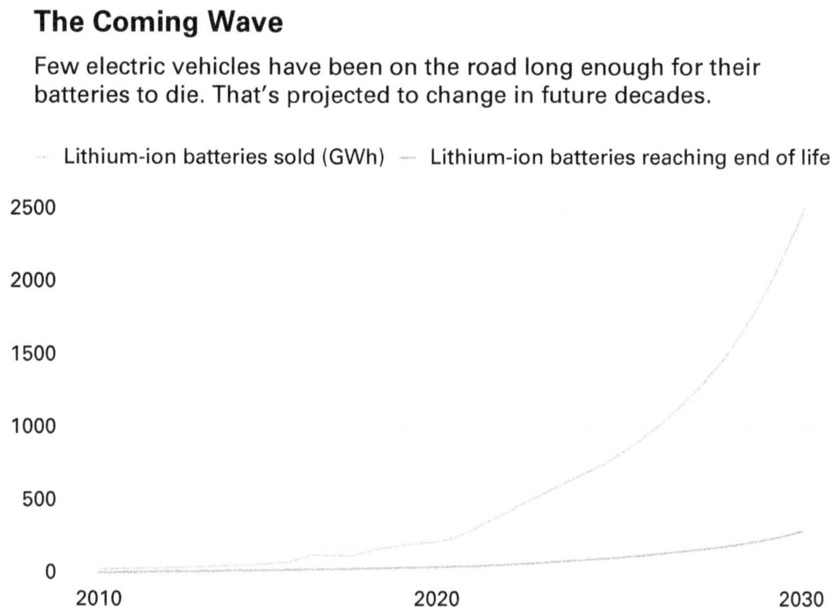

SOURCE USC Marshall-Randall R. Kendrick Global Supply Chain Institute

sustainability practices into their supply chains, such as responsible sourcing, reduced greenhouse gas emissions, and fair labor practices. Certification programs, standards, and industry initiatives are being developed to promote sustainable supply chain practices.

Global Supply Chain Network

The globalization of supply chains led to the establishment of complex global networks of suppliers, manufacturers, and distributors. It allowed companies engaged in global sourcing to seek the best suppliers from different regions to optimize cost, quality, and availability. These intricate supply chain networks enhanced resilience by diversifying sourcing and reducing dependency on single regions. However, they also increased the vulnerability to disruptions, such as natural disasters, geopolitical events, and trade conflicts. The purpose of this book is to understand how all these disruptions have eventually led us to believe in the vital importance of a resilient supply chain, and how that can be put into practice as we continue to deep dive into supply chain networks further.

Chasmic Disruptions

COVID-19 Pandemic: As we are aware, the COVID-19 pandemic, starting in late 2019, profoundly impacted global supply chains. Lockdowns, travel restrictions, and disruptions to manufacturing and transportation caused significant disruptions. Supply chain vulnerabilities were exposed, such as reliance on single sourcing and limited inventory buffers. Companies had to rapidly adapt to changing consumer demands, implement new safety measures, and diversify sourcing strategies. The pandemic highlighted the importance of supply chain resilience, agility, and risk management. Sean Harapko, EY Americas Supply Chain Transformation and Global Supply Chain RPA leader, in a January 2022 article, highlighted the impact of COVID-19 shutdowns that disrupted both the flows of raw material and finished goods. Fewer people were working, and less time was spent working due to these closures. This exposed an existing supply chain issue of worker shortages.

Trade Wars and Protectionism: Recent years have increased trade tensions and protectionist measures. Trade conflicts between major economies, such as the United States and China, have led to the imposition of tariffs and trade barriers.

In 1949, the People's Republic of China (PRC) was founded under Mao Zedong, with his desire to reform society and increase industrial output in a short period, by focusing on putting the residents of the countryside of China into large communes that would produce both food, iron, and steel. This was considered the "Great Leap," which failed, causing famines across the country, and plummeting the Chinese economy. It wasn't until Deng Xiaoping came into power that there were full diplomatic relations between China and the United States. During Carter's administration, the United States recognized the PRC as the sole government of China and affirmed that Taiwan was part of China. This eventually led to Deng's visit in 1979, where the two countries signed a trade agreement that enabled Chinese products to receive temporary most favored nation (MFN) tariff status. This was just the beginning of China's economic growth to becoming a powerhouse nation. In 1980, to launch economic reform and improve the lives of Chinese people, Deng's major focus was opening the doors to foreign investment and business.

During this time China also joined the International Monetary Fund (IMF) and World Bank. China joined the World Trade Organization (WTO) in 2001 and the Clinton administration ended the debate of China's trading status when Clinton granted China permanent Normal Trade Relations (NTR, formerly MFN). Because China was able to join the WTO, it brought 400 million people in China out of extreme poverty. The US had championed China's accession because it would have to adhere to WTO rules, reducing tariffs and guaranteeing intellectual property rights. The US had hoped that China joining the WTO would act as a check on China's communist government. The United States had hoped that, economically, the United States would profit. However, there have been both some benefits and drawbacks. With China entering the WTO, consumers pay cheaper prices for imported Chinese goods, corporations' profits increased from access to the largest market in the world, and industries like manufacturing experienced job losses because of Chinese competition (see Figure 1.6). Labor unions in manufacturing and factory work opposed granting China Non-fungible token (NTF), worried that it would cost jobs in the United States. Between 1999 and 2011, almost 6 million US manufacturing jobs were lost. While manufacturing in China has opened the doors for trading and has made trading with Asia more accessible, it has also made many in the industry question how much of that negatively affected manufacturing jobs in the US. In terms of China's economy, it skyrocketed. Four hundred million Chinese people were lifted out of poverty since 1999, China's economy is now the second biggest in the world and is eight times larger than in 2001. China now exports about five times more than in 2001 and has become the world's largest exporting nation.

Figure 1.6 Impact of China entering the WTO

SOURCE USC Marshall-Randall R. Kendrick Global Supply Chain Institute

Today, the trade war with China continues. These developments have disrupted global supply chains, impacting sourcing strategies and creating uncertainties for companies. Organizations have been compelled to reevaluate supply chain strategies, diversify sourcing, and explore regionalization to mitigate the risks associated with trade wars. For example, in 2020, the rise of US tariffs on Chinese imports led to increasing supply chain costs for companies, which ultimately led to decreased profits for companies. With the trade war, it was the sharpest decline in imports from China since the 2009 financial crisis. Additionally, the trade wars forced companies to diversify their networks, to which countries such as Vietnam, Taiwan, and India benefited. This directly impacted supply chain networks because now companies aren't relying on a single source, but multiple ones, which would benefit the companies in the long run, and in turn allow them to be agile and resilient to any future disruptions.

Supply Chain Digital Transformation: The acceleration of digitalization has led to widespread digital transformations in supply chains. Companies leverage cloud computing, blockchain, and AI technologies to enhance visibility, improve efficiency, and enable data-driven decision-making. Digital platforms facilitate collaboration among supply chain partners, enabling real-time information sharing and streamlined processes. Supply chain professionals are increasingly skilled in data analytics, digital tools, and cybersecurity to navigate the digital landscape effectively. The modern era has witnessed significant supply chain innovations driven by globalization, technological advancements, and evolving consumer demands. Containerization, JIT manufacturing, globalization, outsourcing, e-commerce, and digitalization have reshaped supply chains and revolutionized trade. Recent events, such as the COVID-19 pandemic, trade wars, and the focus on sustainability, have further highlighted the importance of resilience, agility, and responsible practices in supply chain management. Supply chain professionals must continue to embrace innovation, adapt to changing market dynamics, and prioritize sustainability to navigate the complexities of the modern supply chain landscape.

Decoupling of Supply Chains without Deglobalization: If there is one thing that COVID-19 taught the world, it's the importance of supply chain and that those are not words to take lightly. There was global disruption in the end-to-end global supply chain when COVID-19 hit. Each product you use entails many elements before it reaches you: the raw material, the manufacturing, packaging, transportation, and distribution. Each element takes a journey using ocean, rail, air, and road before it goes to the end consumer's doorstep. Imagine each of these steps having a complex supply chain network connected globally. When you take one of the nodes out of commission, it impacts the entire process. This is exactly what happened when COVID-19 hit, affecting all the nodes connected through the China-centric network. Typically, times of crisis lead to "deglobalization," which is a reversal of globalization. This usually leads to removal of cross-border trade flows and the rise of protectionism for the nation, as we had seen both in the aftermath of the Great Depression and the 2008 financial crisis. This leads to the question of how to keep our supply chains global without reducing footprint and minimizing disruptions across the board. Generally, decoupling is widely used for inventory management where it plays a vital role in centralizing distribution

Figure 1.7 Supply Chain Process Flow

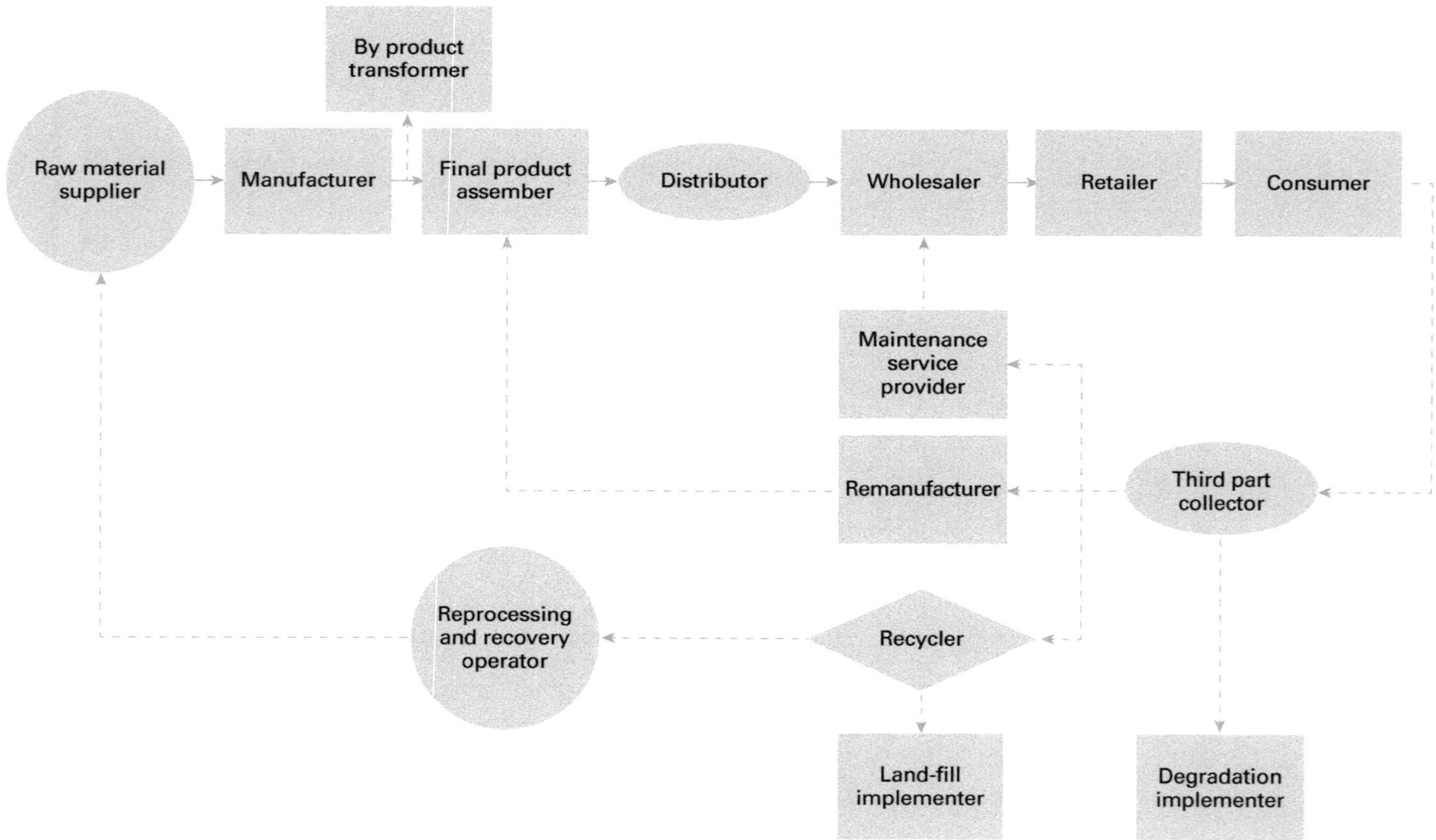

SOURCE USC Marshall-Randall R. Kendrick Global Supply Chain Institute

networks. A decoupling point, established close to the operational zone, acts as both a strategic distribution hub and a safety buffer that protects the supply chain network from demand shocks.

For global supply chain management, decoupling points or nodes also connect supply chain pathways to customers. For example, a customer base can be divided into different regions, with each region having its own supply chain network that is independent and, at the same time, interdependent with other network clusters (see Figure 1.8). In the event of a global crisis like COVID-19, regional decoupling nodes can help organizations react and effectively redistribute production and sourcing to unaffected areas. This ensures that operations in other parts of the world are not affected, thus mitigating supply chain risks. What we are seeing long term, coming out of the pandemic, is a decoupling from long-term supply chain dependencies from the China-centric supply chain network, and the trade war really set the stage for this process to begin. We are shifting to a regional, customer-centric supply chain cluster forming globally. We are starting to see more appetite to bring the supply chain close to customer demand with onshore or nearshore, especially for key items such as pharmaceuticals, batteries, and computer chips. For US manufacturers, Mexico is likely to play a significant role, but that will likely be contingent upon if they can stabilize the government and deal with the drug violence and political corruption issues. As another example, Intel announced in March 2021 that it would commit $20 billion to build two new microchip factories in Arizona. If there was more diversification of supply chain nodes across the globe, we would not see the impact of disruption we saw during the pandemic. Building a successful decoupled supply chain will not happen overnight. It takes time to shift manufacturing facilities and get distribution operations running to be set up for success (see Figure 1.7).

When we think about the future, we must shift our mindsets to the Triple Bottom Line (TBL) philosophy, which focuses on profit, the planet, and people, versus just on profit. Decoupling is a solution to getting away from the thought of cheaper and fast is better, to reasonably priced, sustainable, and agile. Many companies know they must do this to stay agile and relevant, but most don't know how, or are waiting for someone to show them the way. Throughout this book, we will continue to uncover how we can design agile, resilient, and

Figure 1.8 With and Without Decoupling Point

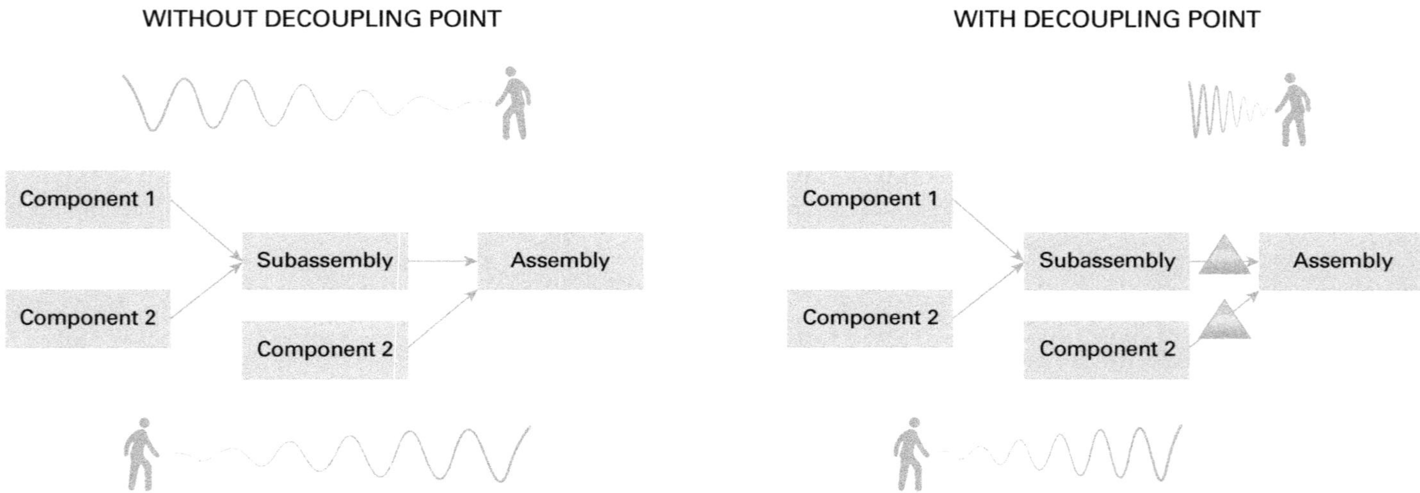

SOURCE Adapted for USC Marshall-Randall R. Kendrick Global Supply Chain Institute

sustainable supply chain networks to do just this. For example, Chapter 2 examines the shift required in supply chain management, considering social, environmental, and economic impacts for a more holistic and responsible approach; and Chapter 6 explores the measures being devised to integrate sustainability into the supply chain DNA.

Endnotes

1 Bookbinder. Watson, Michael, Sara Lewis, Peter Cacioppi, Jay Jayaraman. 2012. Supply Chain Network Design: Applying Optimization and Analytics to the Global Supply Chain. *Interfaces* 44, no. 3(2014): 348+.

2 K Govindan, M Fattahi and E Keyvanshokooh. Supply chain network design under uncertainty: A comprehensive review and future research directions. *European Journal of Operational Research* 263, no. 1 (2017): 108–141. doi.org/10.1016/j.ejor.2017.04.009 (archived at https://perma.cc/N4PN-DESH).

3 D Torkornoo, OPS Rules Blog: Insights into Supply Chain and Operations Strategy When is it a good time for supply chain network design? OPS Rules Blog, August 2014, web.archive.org/web/20160925195356/http:/www.opsrules.com/supply-chain-optimization-blog/bid/342858/When-is-it-a-good-time-for-supply-chain-network-design (archived at https://perma.cc/5NEF-GG55).

4 Evolution of trade under the WTO, World Trade Organization, https://www.wto.org/english/res_e/statis_e/trade_evolution_e/evolution_trade_wto_e.htm (archived at perma.cc/2VUT-GRZA).

5 H Whipps, How Ancient Trade Changed the World, Livescience, 8 February, 2008, www.livescience.com/4823-ancient-trade-changed-world.html (archived at perma.cc/5Y4C-LX3U).

6 The Silk Road, National Geographic Society, 20 May 2022, https://education.nationalgeographic.org/resource/silk-road/ (archived at https://perma.cc/K759-2E5E).

7 D F Graf (2017) The Silk Road between Syria and China, in *Trade, Commerce, and the State in the Roman World*, Oxford Studies on the Roman Economy, eds. Andrew Wilson and Alan Bowman (Oxford: Publisher, 2017; online edn: Oxford Academic, December 21, 2017).

8 P Vanham, A brief history of globalization, Weforum.org January 17, 2019. (archived at https://perma.cc/7MNE-Q6N7)

The Principles of Network Design and How to Optimize Supply Chains 02

The previous chapter outlined the history of supply chain networks. It examined the forces that brought these networks to life and sustained them, and the different moments in time that transformed and propelled supply chain networks to their present state as they continue to evolve.

This chapter examines the study and practice of the modern Supply Chain Network Design (SCND) field, where it existed in history, and how it continues to evolve today. It starts with understanding the reasons why the subject of SCND has drawn broad interest not only within academia but also in global trade.

SCND: Gaining Significance

We first examined how traditional supply chains have evolved, predominantly driven by cost and speed optimization, aiming to maximize efficiency and profitability. This means that supply chain managers have focused on minimizing the costs of production, transportation, and inventory while ensuring that the products and services are delivered to the customers as quickly as possible. Supply chains have adopted lean manufacturing, Just-in-Time delivery, outsourcing, offshoring, and global sourcing to achieve this.

Pandemic Disruption to Supply Chain Networks

In several ways, some of which are still unfolding, the COVID-19 pandemic has had a defining impact on the fields of SCND.

Acute shortages of lifesaving drugs and daily essentials at the peak of the pandemic, followed by sustained hits to supply chains of large consumer goods and automotive companies, made analysts and consumers look askance at the stability of global supply chains.

Industry surveys such as CSCMP's 2021 Third-Party Logistics Study showed that a good percentage of executives felt that supply chains were too lean. The sentiment has persisted. "We went way too far," said a McKinsey partner in an October 2021 NYT article exploring the seemingly causative role of Just-in-Time manufacturing practices.[1]

While the upcoming chapters will explore the solidity of these claims, it has become evident that the traditional supply chain model based on cost and speed optimization is no longer sufficient or sustainable in the post-pandemic era. Supply chains must adapt and transform to cope with the new challenges and opportunities. Digitalization, diversification, localization, collaboration, and circularity are emerging trends and practices that can help supply chains become more resilient, agile, and responsible. These trends and practices can help supply

Figure 2.1 Supply Chain Disruptions Make a Comeback

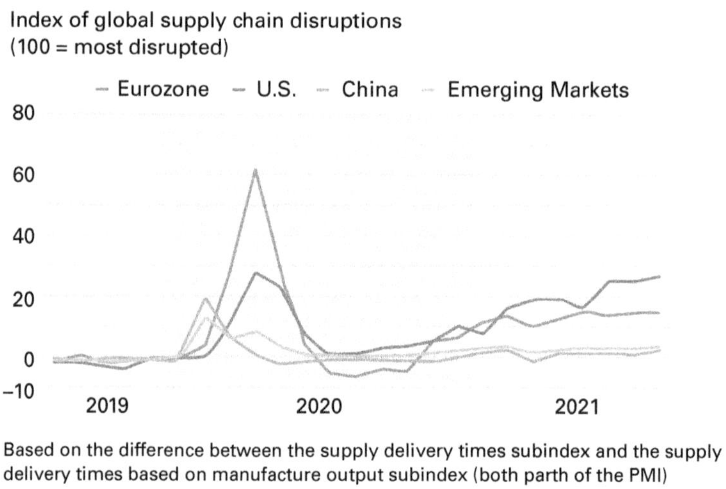

SOURCE Statista

chains improve visibility, flexibility, responsiveness, innovation, and sustainability.

The challenges posed by the pandemic have brought to light the need for a profound transformation in supply chain models. Moving beyond the cost and speed optimization paradigm, businesses must integrate social, environmental, and economic considerations into their supply chain strategies (see Figure 2.1). Heightened awareness of geopolitical, environmental, and national security concerns is essential for building resilient and responsible supply chains. Organizations can build agile and adaptive supply chains that improve society, the environment, and economies worldwide by prioritizing sustainability, fostering collaboration, and embracing technology.

Following is an account of the major pandemic-engendered supply chain disruptions that continue to afflict global trade.

Manufacturing and Production Disruptions

The pandemic forced the closure of factories and manufacturing plants in several countries, particularly in China, which plays a significant role in the global supply chain. As the "factory of the world," China's extensive network of manufacturers faced delays, labor shortages, and transportation bottlenecks. Disruptions in production lines led to shortages of essential goods and components worldwide, affecting various industries. COVID-19 struck the core of global value chain hub regions, including China, Europe, and the US. Industrial production in China had fallen by 13.5 per cent in January and February of 2021, combined with the previous year. The pandemic had severe implications for international production networks and may leave its legacy for years to come. Unlike previous significant disruptions, COVID-19 has adversely affected global supply chains throughout all their stages, with major turbulences in manufacturing, processing, transport, logistics and significant shifts in demand.

The pandemic has also exposed the fragility of global supply chains. Unscheduled closures of manufacturing and distribution facilities, bottlenecks at borders, and sick workers caused congestion points in supply lines, while people being cooped up in their homes for months on end drove up demand for a host of products.

Transportation and Logistics Challenges

The pandemic severely impacted transportation and logistics operations, with significant air and sea freight disruptions. The grounding of flights and reduced container shipping capacity had an impact on the movement of goods globally. Countries implementing strict border controls and quarantine measures further compounded delays, leading to a backlog of shipments and increased freight costs. There have also been other disruptors during the height of the COVID-19 pandemic, like the massive winter storm in Texas in February, the six-day blockage of the Suez Canal due to the grounded ship the Ever Given in March 2021, and the six-day closure of the colonial gasoline pipeline in the US after a cyberattack in May. Also, shipping containers were lost in record amounts for various reasons, with more than 3,000 going overboard in 2020 and the 2021 number already hitting 1,000 by the end of April.

Demand and Supply Imbalances

The pandemic significantly altered consumer behavior, resulting in unpredictable fluctuations in demand for certain products. Panic buying and stockpiling led to a surge in demand for essential goods like medical supplies, personal protective equipment (PPE), and food items. Simultaneously, demand for non-essential items dropped significantly, causing inventory buildup and wastage in various industries.

Dependency on Single-Sourcing

In pursuit of cost efficiencies, many businesses have become overly dependent on single-sourcing strategies, primarily from China. The pandemic exposed the vulnerability of such strategies, as disruptions in one region could disrupt entire supply chains. As a result, there has been a growing emphasis on diversification and reshoring of supply chains to mitigate risks.

Events of the pandemic years have only added to the prevailing state of uncertainty. Supply chains have this known tendency to respond to risks of any kind or degree exaggeratedly. This phenomenon is very aptly called the "bullwhip effect." Also called the "whiplash effect," the concept was introduced by the MIT Sloan School of Management professor Jay W. Forrester in *Industrial Dynamics* (1961), a classic in systems thinking. The bullwhip effect is a well-documented phenomenon occurring in forecast-driven supply chains when crisis events have an unexpected, amplified impact along the supply chains due to the suppliers' precautionary response to variations in market demand. Bullwhip effects *almost always* lead to undesirable situations like stockouts or inventory buildups, as it happened with supply chains of various essential products and commodities like lifesaving drugs, food supplies, and semiconductors in the aftermath of the pandemic. *Almost always*, because some tools and strategies act like bulwarks at the critical supply chain nodes against these effects; the coming chapters will focus on such strategies to be adopted under the practice of SCND. Alarmed by the recurrence and the deep value-destroying propensity of these events, academics and corporate strategists have homed in on disciplines that improve the resiliency of supply chains. The encouraging realization, referenced in the book's first chapter, that a judicious SCND policy can lock in a large part of the value of supply chains, has helped create a good amount of interest in this subject.

One more factor that has increased the interest is the growing realization on the part of governments and global organizations that supply chains must be more humanitarian and sustainable in their make and orientation. Spurred by changing consumer preferences, environmental concerns, and economic necessities, universities, corporations, and democratic governments worldwide have accelerated efforts to revamp supply chains in humanitarian and sustainable ways. A heightened awareness of supply chains' social and environmental impact, driven by increased media coverage and public pressure, has compelled corporations to demonstrate a commitment to responsible sourcing and manufacturing processes.

Governments, on their part, are responding to the pressing need for sustainable supply chains by enacting regulations that encourage responsible business practices. These regulations often include incentives for eco-friendly practices, labor rights protection, and transparent reporting mechanisms. Further, governments understand that resilient and ethical supply chains are essential for national security, as demonstrated by disruptions caused by the COVID-19 pandemic.

Moreover, both governments and corporations realize the economic advantages of sustainable supply chains. Resilient supply chains reduce the risk of disruptions, ensuring a steady flow of goods and services. Additionally, embracing sustainable practices can lead to long-term cost savings, improved brand reputation, and enhanced stakeholder relationships. Older SCND paradigms need to change and be broken to achieve this objective. The new generational leaders must learn to reprogram the DNA of supply chains so that concepts and practices like environmental, social, and corporate governance (ESG) and TBL thinking become an inextricable part of global supply chains. Ensuring this will require empathy, awareness, and a new, bold way of thinking for leaders and organizations.

First Signs of Modern Network Design

The study of SCND and processes, much like its parent field of supply chain management, can be traced back to the development of operations research (OR). OR, which is the application of scientific methods to the management and administration of organized military, governmental, commercial, and industrial processes,[2] has had network analysis and design as an integral and vital part since the early 20th century[3] when, for industry and military purposes, researchers began developing mathematical models to optimize complex systems and decision-making processes. The first documented instance[4] of the use of OR for network analysis is believed to be during the initial months of the Second World War, when Britain's Royal Air Force put to use a technique developed two years earlier by A.P. Rowe, superintendent of Bawdsey Research Station, known in the popular imagination as the birthplace of radar.[5]

The Royal Air Force employed OR to assess physical machinery and communication system networks. The findings from these studies uncovered methods for enhancing operators' strategies and shed light on previously unrecognized constraints within their network. The Second World War cemented the role and significance of network design in solving intricate logistical challenges, such as efficiently deploying troops, allocating resources, and managing supply chains. This prompted the application of network design principles to tackle these problems effectively. Following the wars, the evolution of network design continued as it found new applications for civilian work. Modeling city infrastructure, communication networks, and product supply chains became crucial in urban planning, telecommunications, and business operations. Researchers could analyze and optimize the flow of information, goods, and services by representing these systems as interconnected nodes and edges. This approach revolutionized how cities were designed, information was disseminated, and products reached consumers.

Today, the field of network design remains integral to the study of OR, with applications spanning diverse domains. From designing efficient transportation networks and improving emergency response systems, to optimizing global supply chains and enhancing communication networks' resilience, network design plays a vital role in shaping the modern world's infrastructure and interconnected systems. For example, in city infrastructure, network design plans and structures an IT network's physical, virtual, and logical infrastructure arrangement.[6] In mobile network companies, network design is used to determine the best location and optimal size of facilities to be included in the supply chain, and to ensure an optimal flow of products using advanced mathematical modelling. For product supply chains, network design is used to optimize inventory, working capital, and logistics costs while increasing visibility, identifying opportunities for cost savings, and reducing potential risks. This is the area of application that has grown into a widely researched and technologically advanced field of SCND.

The Evolution of Modern Methods in Supply Chain Network Design

The discipline of SCND branched out from the supply chain management practice in the early 2010s. This coincided with—and was seemingly driven by—a marked shift in the warehousing developmental pattern away from the cities, as observed in and around significant consumption centers like Los Angeles, California, and Seattle, Washington. Scholars from the University of Washington[7] called it the phenomenon of "logistics sprawl." Such observations have been made in the past, as in the case of a 2010 *Journal of Transport Geography* research paper that conducted a spatial analysis of the Economic Census Data to find that most US metropolitan areas witnessed "decentralization in the spatial distribution of freight-related activity."[8]

The decentralization of logistics and supply chain activities during this period prompted organizations like Unilever (as noted in Chapter 1), FedEx, and a nascent Amazon to utilize SCND to strategically map out a path toward sustained profitability and continuous expansion.

In recent years, big data and analytics have further galvanized SCND. More companies have begun to use big data and advanced analytics to provide more actionable insights into their supply chain strategy, processes, and operations. For example, the concept of digital twins, in which digital representation of a physical object, person, or process, contextualized in a digital version of its environment, has enabled companies to create virtual representations of their supply chains, allowing for real-time monitoring, optimization, and scenario testing.

Notably, there has been a growing emphasis on sustainability and environmental considerations in SCND. Researchers like Luk Van Wassenhove and Aurélie Charles[9] have highlighted the significance of integrating eco-friendly practices into network design. Methods for evaluating carbon emissions, energy consumption, and other environmental factors have become essential components of modern SCND approaches. Today, machine learning and artificial intelligence are poised to redefine SCND again. Academics are exploring how reinforcement learning, neural networks, and optimization algorithms can work in tandem to create self-learning and adaptive supply chain networks. These technologies can potentially automate SCND processes and optimize network performance in real time.

The following section will review how models used in supply chain network designs needed to be reworked, embracing the TBL for sustainability, and tie the geopolitical, environmental, and national security concerns to heighten awareness.

Cost and speed-focused models—how they developed

Computer programs were written as early as the 1960s to generate purchasing and production scheduling. Spearheaded by Joseph Orlicky, Oliver Wight, and others, the American Production and Inventory Control Society (APICS, as known at the time) launched a "Material Requirements Planning" (MRP) campaign in 1972 to promote MRP. The essential logic of MRP was the concept of "dependent demand"; if one thousand cars are to be built, one needs to procure or make five thousand wheels (including a spare). Several methods of estimating material requirements are presented in Figure 2.2.

The basic premise of using a computer for computing these numbers was scalability. Simple multiplications could be done by hand; but with hundreds of products and thousands of dependent raw materials and work-in-progress (WIP), the computations provided cost savings from reduced dependence on humans, and increasing speed and accuracy. The requirements for effective use of dependent demand inventory models were a Master Production Schedule (MPS), a Bill of Materials (BOM), inventory "Available to Promise (ATP), Purchase Orders Outstanding (PO), and Lead Times (LT).

Since the seventies, MRP has leveraged computer information systems to determine the quantity and timing of dependent demand items. Mainly for discrete products, MRP depends on an accurate bill of material, inventory accuracy, and stable lead times. The benefits were many: increased customer service due to meeting delivery schedules, faster response to market changes, improved labor and equipment utilization, better inventory planning and scheduling, and finally, reduced inventory levels without compromising customer service levels.

Inputs to the production plan involved data and strategy from the divisions of an organization, as shown in Figure 2.3.

An aggregate production plan requires a forecasted or confirmed demand from marketing (top-down estimates) as well as sales (bottom-up, or account-based forecasted sales), finance data for cash flow and appetite for additional investment, human resources data for labor planning, engineering data for product lifecycle, new part

Figure 2.2 Dependent vs Independent Demand

Item	Materials with Independent Demand	Materials with Dependent Demand
Demand Source	Company Customers	Parent Items
Material Type	Finished Goods	WIP and Raw Materials
Method of Estimating Demand	Forecast & Booked Customer Orders	Calculated
Planning Technology	Economic Order Quantity (EOQ) and Reorder Point (ROP)	Materials Requirement Planning (MRP)

SOURCE USC Marshall-Randall R. Kendrick Global Supply Chain Institute

or product specs, production data with capacity and inventory, procurement data for supplier capacity, lead times and rates, and finally management data on their expected return on invested capital (ROIC). Notice that at least two of these areas require the firm to go "outside the four walls of an organization," which involves suppliers, customers, and markets.

As we have seen over the last two decades with the evolution of the Supply Chain Operational Reference (SCOR) model, it has been a common practice for organizations to go a level (or more) beyond one's customers and suppliers. As the SCOR model in its earliest forms started showing during the nineties and beyond, one needs to understand the trends and requirements of demand for one's customers' customers and be able to leverage data for one's suppliers' suppliers to be able to fulfill demand with input from and implications from two or more degrees of separation in trade (see Figure 2.4).

This, therefore, required organizations to understand demand-supply "networks," as opposed to staying within the four walls, and multitudes of illustrated fluctuations caused by blindness to a network have been studied ("bullwhip effect").

Figure 2.3 Inputs to the Production Plan

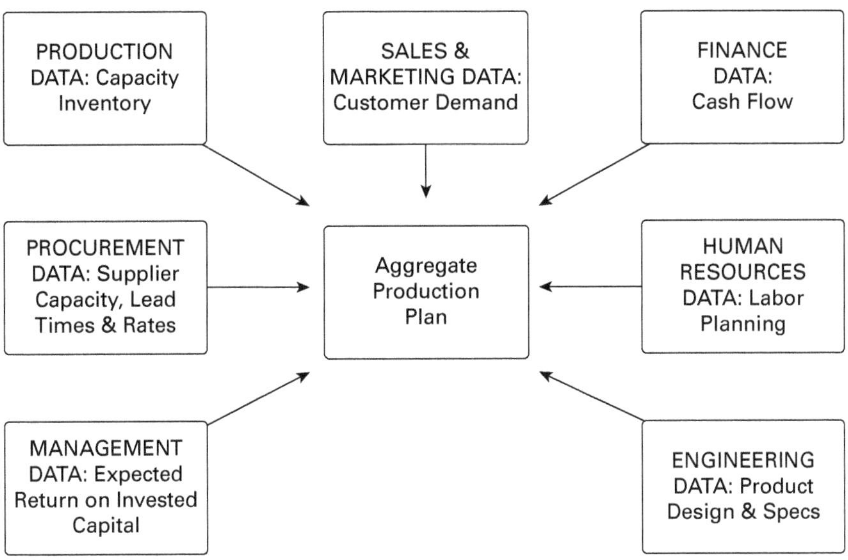

SOURCE USC Marshall-Randall R. Kendrick Global Supply Chain Institute

Figure 2.4 Two-Level SCOR Model

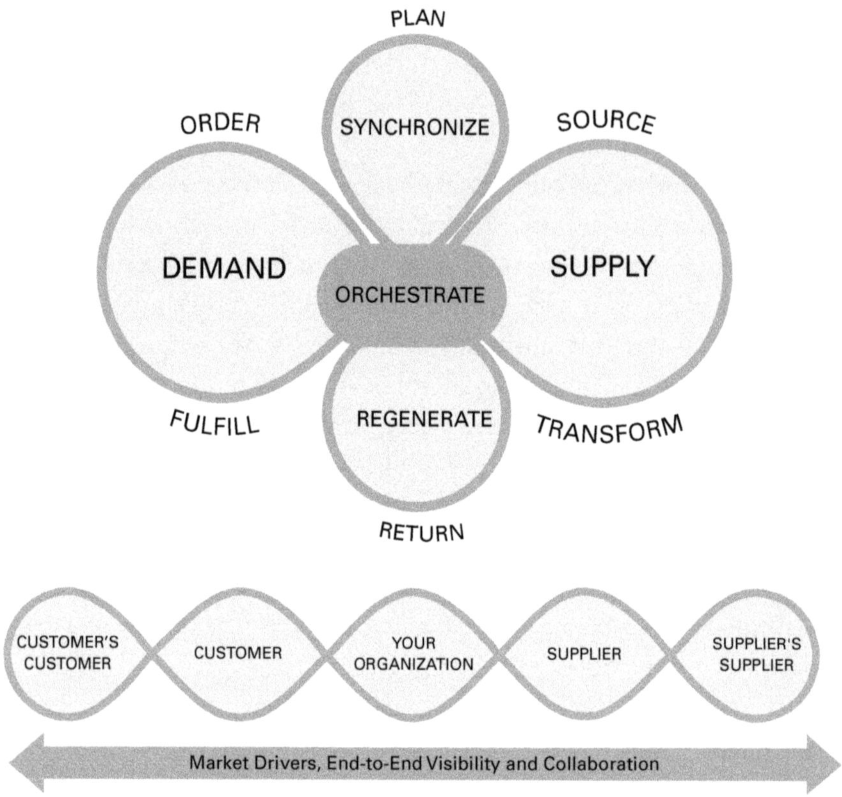

SOURCE ASCM

As the complexity of the network increased over time, walls of distrust were built between entities, resulting in a lack of "visibility" (a term that continues to drive challenges in the supply chain ecosystem), and therefore challenges in fulfilling demand at the total minimum "system cost," purportedly the objective of effective supply chain management. Figure 2.5 shows how this has evolved.

Between the 1990s and now, the optimization of this "network" of entities in a business ecosystem has been complicated by the variability and complexity of businesses. These have grown exponentially by several factors, primarily influenced by globalization, intensified competition, shorter product lifecycles, mass customization, and eliminating intermediaries by leveraging the internet and electronic commerce. Why is global network optimization hard? It is because the supply chain is complex, different entities have conflicting objectives, and the power structure, as well as the "system" in the supply chain, dynamically changes over time.

Figure 2.5 Traditional Business Environment—Vertically Integrated Companies

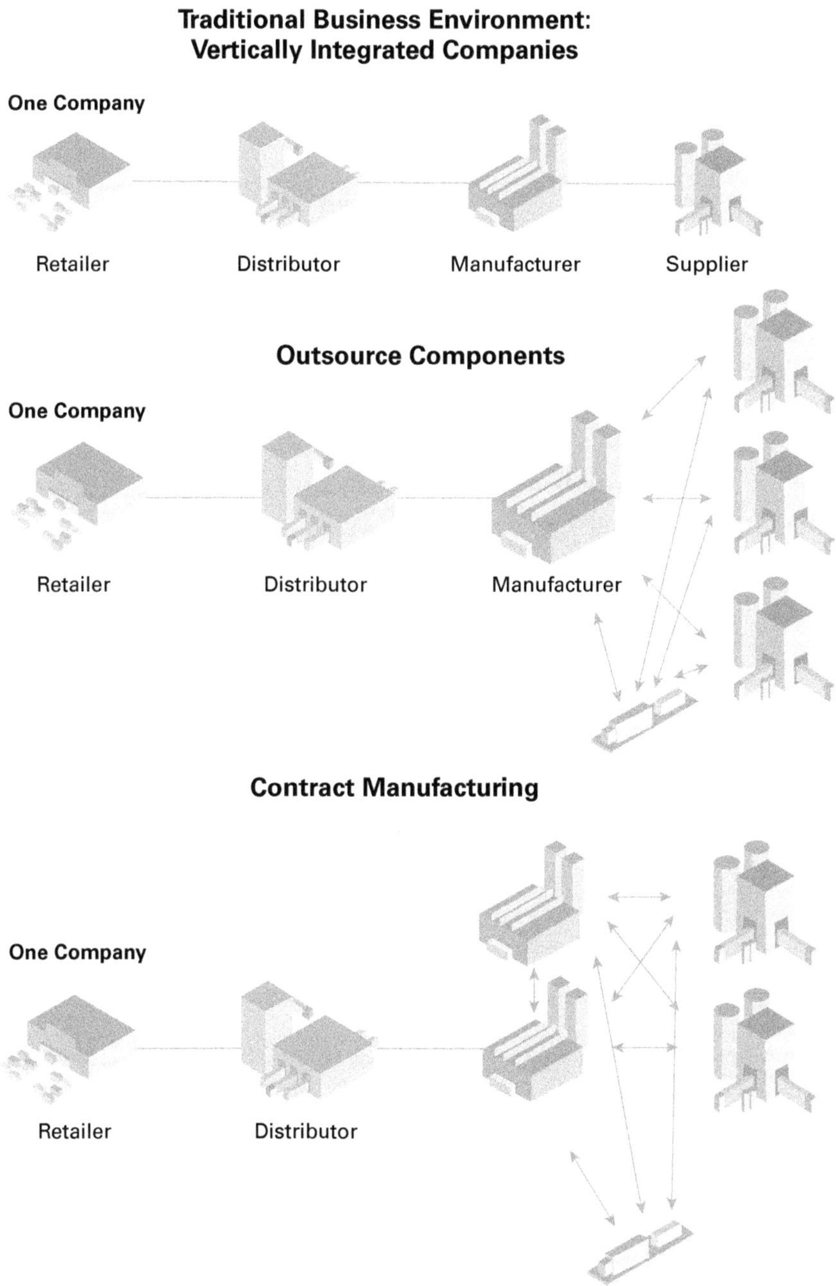

Complexity Increases, Communication Decreases

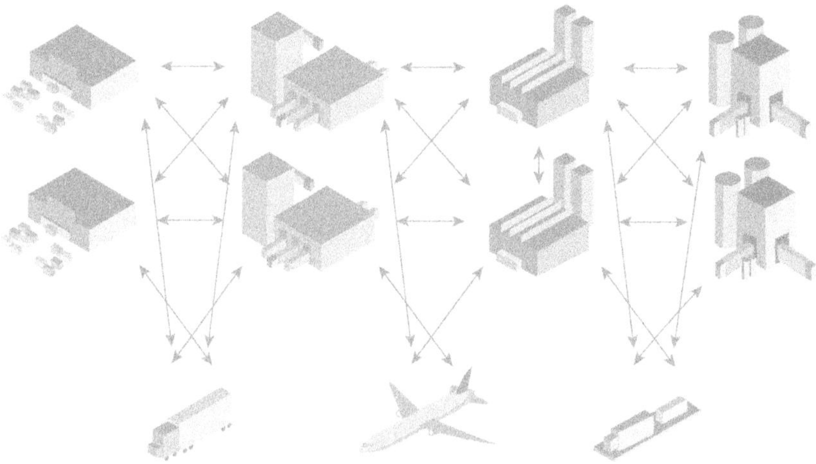

Build Walls Due to Poor Systems and Lack of Trust

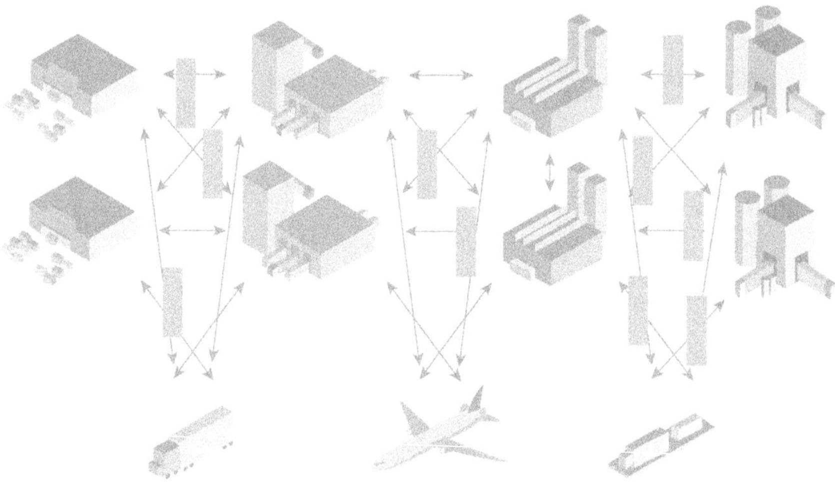

Examples of conflicting objectives can be illustrated with the following examples. Purchasing as a function is expected to work with volume requirements, flexible delivery time, very little variation in product mix, and securing bulk discounts with large quantities of product orders. At the same time, manufacturing is focused on long-run production with high-quality products, high productivity, and low production costs. Uncertainty in any area is hard to deal with. Matching supply with demand is difficult since forecasting does not "solve" the problem, inventory and back-order levels typically fluctuate widely across the supply chain, and demand is not the only source of uncertainty. There are uncertainties in lead times, yields, transportation times, natural disasters, and component availability.

Several processes and supporting technological tools have been developed to address these issues. "Pull systems," where demand is a signal that "pulls" products through the supply chain as an invisible string, with just about enough raw material and work-in-progress that is needed to make, ship, and deliver products to the end customers were popularized by the Kanban-card driven Just-in-Time manufacturing technology, as explained earlier in Chapter 1 of this book. A second approach is "risk-pooling," where multiple locations, products, and periods are aggregated to reduce the uncertainty and variability of demand. Centralization of procurement activities has contributed to volume savings while reducing inventory. Postponement, a strategy of configuring a final product at the very end of the process when demand is known with higher certainty, has been vital for HP, Dell, Benetton, and several other organizations that cater to consumer demand. Cross-industry collaboration, such as vendor-managed inventory (VMI) and Collaborative Planning, Forecasting, and Replenishment (CPFR), has been pioneered by the retail and consumer goods sectors. Organizations have developed internal "Sales and Operations Planning" (S&OP) processes to match planned demand and manufacturing, which later developed into "Integrated Business Planning" (IBP) to extend beyond these functions to include corporate strategy and finance.

The above strategies and processes have been enabled by technology with rapid speed, scalability, and accuracy. Electronic Data Interchange (EDI) protocols, XML, internet ordering, and point-of-sale (POS) data have helped share information, understand demand, and supply dynamics, and reduce the number of suppliers and customers, eliminating gaming from retailers on shortages and promotions.

Adopting advanced technologies such as AI, IoT, and blockchain can enhance supply chain visibility and enable real-time data-driven decision-making. By leveraging these technologies, businesses can identify potential risks, anticipate market trends, and respond swiftly to disruptions. We will dive deep into the technology levers in Chapter 5.

SCND: Current Practices and Applications

Supply Chain Network Design (SCND), a model that also prioritizes cost-efficiency and speed, has gained significance in response to the aforementioned disruptions. SCND is defined as a working model that delineates the overall framework of a supply chain to assess the time and costs required to bring goods to the market. This model helps a business spot inefficiencies and potential risks in the supply chain. It also increases visibility, identifies opportunities for cost savings, and reduces potential risks. SCND is so important because 80 per cent of supply chain costs are determined at the designing phase of the product and supply chain network. Failure to consider network design can cost the enterprise dearly and be counterproductive in the longer term. It forces organizations to have answers to questions such as "Why are the enterprise's only suppliers based overseas? Why are there so many warehouses? What are the best locations for the end customer? What type of inventory-holding model will best optimize my total cost of ownership, and why in those locations?"

There are organizations that will question whether the SCND model is essential to consider as a core process, but it will almost always be a resounding yes, due to its inherent value to organizations. Supply Chain Network Design is a dynamic process due to the ever-changing conditions of the environment, markets, customers, suppliers, and raw materials, and regularly updating the supply chain model with the current realities and parameters will provide accurate results over time. To ensure the successful integration of supply chain design as a core business process, organizations must ensure that a permanent network design center, operated by a cross-functional team with the necessary skill sets and experience, plans the frequency, understands vital issues that should flag the remodeling of the supply chain design, and has a dedicated consultant with in-depth knowledge and vast experience in SCND.

Unfortunately, many businesses have yet to regard supply chain design as a core process and instead treat it as a one-of-a-kind case, or tweak it on a project-to-person basis. However, if COVID-19 taught us anything, it was that we need to have more dynamic and flexible supply chain network designs and models to ensure that our organizations are agile, resilient, and sustainable during disruptions. The only thing we can be sure of is the amount of uncertainty that exists, and organizations must be prepared for anything as best as possible. This is why tech-savvy enterprises can thus leverage a dynamic supply chain model to ensure that their supply chains deliver and exceed business expectations long into the future.

The benefits of having a successful SCND include optimizing supply chains that reduce overall costs and enhance service and improve speed-to-market, flexibility, and risk management. Key benefits include discerning parts for streamlining and potential cost savings, working capital reduction, route optimization for reducing transit time and fuel costs, reduction in network fixed costs and variable costs, optimization of service levels and delivery dates for customer satisfaction, process, and cost visibility across the supply chain network.

Creating a successful SCND that is agile, resilient, and sustainable is not an overnight feat, but feasible when all the factors align. Factors to consider when designing a supply chain network model are as follows:

- Define the objectives as aligned with the enterprise's objectives and the supply chain design model parameters.
- Collate the required data.
- Use network optimization tools and necessary data for building a "living" model.
- Validate the model with historical "what if?" scenarios and compare the outcome with known results.
- Senior leadership must align with all processes.

Every product must go through a critical analysis to determine what and how to make a series of complex decisions and have the best possible scenarios to optimize and deliver results.

Organizations will find it advantageous to shift from a narrow focus on costs and profits to adopt the Triple Bottom Line (TBL) philosophy to determine the optimal network design across geographies. The TBL concept, introduced in the 1990s by John Elkington, sought to redefine the metrics for business success, expanding beyond mere profitability to encompass environmental and social impacts. It urges us to focus on three bottom lines: profit, people, and the planet, and in doing so, commit to making the organization more agile, resilient, and sustainable.

Types, features, and principles

Table 2.1 shows the types of SCND and their main features.

There are many schools of thought when discussing the different approaches and models. Traditional optimization approaches take a long time and do not necessarily accommodate end-to-end supply chain decision-making. Businesses often try to compress too much complexity into a single SCND model, which makes it too challenging in terms of computational complexity and prohibits expanding it to cover additional supply chain functions.

When we think about implementing a successful supply chain network design, we must consider factors such as infrastructure, government, and integrator roles. Infrastructure refers to the buildings, equipment, and IT required to run supply chain processes. Government plays a huge role in how supply chain processes are run because they typically control many trade regulations, affecting how organizations run their businesses. Lastly, integrators play a vital role in seamlessly implementing processes, so governments and corporations can work

Table 2.1 Major political forces that shaped global trade routes

Types of SCND	Main Features
Lean SCND	• JIT • Linear, long, single node • Lacks resilience • High-risk profile
Agile/Resilient SCND	• Responsive • Demand-sensitive
Sustainable SCND	• Ethical practices
Compliant SCND for international trade	• No human trafficking/child labor • No conflict in raw materials/ environmental compliance

together. This comes into play with any public–private partnerships. The Partnership of Central America (PCA) initiative (see the box below) is a good example of a cross-border government-business alliance formed to improve the functioning of supply chain networks, which, in turn, should stimulate economic growth.

All for PCA

When the government and private sectors come together, they can solve socioeconomic challenges in emerging economies such as Central America; for example in the case study of the Partnership of Central America (PCA). More than 100 private and public entities gathered $3.2 billion in investments with a 10-year goal to create 1 million jobs for those in Central America. Central America also has trade, geographic and human capital advantages as it only takes 2–5 days shipping time from ports, 50 of the labor force is below 39 years old, and existing free trade agreements allow for seamless trade conditions globally (Fantini-Porter and Blosser, 2023). The Partnership continues to engage with government authorities and business organizations to tackle important issues like rule of law, cross-border trade, customs, and competitiveness with an aim to advance prosperity and growth in the region.

Another use case is from the semiconductor industry. The National Science Foundation announces nearly $50 million partnership with Ericsson, IBM, Intel, and Samsung to support the future of semiconductor design and manufacturing.[10] The semiconductor manufacturing business is not one that will ever go away as the creation of them is essential to our daily lives. As a result, even though global tensions continue to rise with China, it opens the door for other countries to play a part in this industry, such as Vietnam, Thailand, and India.

While there are many schools of thought and approaches to how to optimize SCND successfully, some experts have proposed a "system-optimization perspective" because this model "enables the modelling of the economic activities associated with a firm as a network" (Nagurney, 2010). What sets this framework apart is its ability to be flexible with variables, so it can handle non-linear and non-separable costs and capture the reality of today's networks, especially with how interconnected everything is (Nagurney, 2010). Another study looked at optimizing freight transport network design, incorporating decentralized decisions made by multiple agents on the supply chain networks and their behavioral interaction (Yamada and Gebri, 2015). The study concluded that this approach has the potential to be used strategically for multi-modal freight transport planning and considers the efficiency of supply chain networks.

When we think about creating efficient supply chain networks, we must consider the environmental factors that play a role in them. A 2010 study looked at a multi-objective optimization for green SCND that captures the trade-off between the total cost of ownership and the environmental influence. It concluded that this model could indeed be used for both regional (decoupling) or global SCND with green consideration and found that improving the capacity of the network and increasing the supply to the facilities can decrease the carbon emission of the whole network and total cost (Wang et al., 2011). Other models, such as a stochastic model, explore supply chain network design from the perspective of being able to insert random variables to account for disruptions versus the single variable model that does not provide as much flexibility. We will dive into this more deeply in Chapter 3.

From Design to Delivery

Phrases in the relevant literature that say "design to delivery" and "farm-to-table" all speak to the end-to-end process from beginning to end of a product lifecycle. It all points to the integrated ways of looking at goods from point A to point Z. From design, every product starts as a raw material. From there, the raw materials are aggregated to be prepared for manufacturing. From there, coordination, resources, and planning are involved to strategize how to properly take the goods to their final destination of the end consumer. Other verticals such as finance and marketing are typically involved to ensure that the manufactured goods are cost-effective and aligned with Finance's budget. We can view this entire process as the front end and then head into middle-mile delivery, which focuses on transporting the goods from the ports to the warehouse or distribution center.

Once the goods are in the warehouse or distribution center, they are processed to go through last-mile delivery, where they are delivered to the end consumer. In the past, where the goods are created would also be directly delivered to the end customer, otherwise known as 1PL, but as supply chain processes have grown and processes have become more complex, even last-mile delivery has evolved to utilize 5PL. Figure 2.6 shows how we have evolved from a 1PL to 5PL.

Even though there is a rise in companies utilizing 5PL, most are using 3PL companies. The concept of a 3PL is to use multi-homing, otherwise known as a multi-modal dynamic fulfillment network. A 3PL's business model uses multiple fulfillment, shipping, and warehouse providers to help customers find the best supply chain network at the lowest cost. The growth in 3PLs has been tremendous in the last few years. The global third-party logistics (3PL) market size was valued at USD 962.1 billion in 2021. It is projected to reach USD 2018.22 billion by 2030, growing at a compound annual growth rate (CAGR) of 8.58% during the forecast period (2022–2030), which is indicative that multi-homing is becoming more common. The growth in fulfillment and warehousing providers means that 3PLs can now evaluate more options to find the most efficient delivery speed at lower costs and that sellers' demand has multi-homing and decentralized supply chain networks.

For illustrative purposes, let's look at the use of SCND for the iPhone.

Figure 2.6 Different Types of Logistics Service Providers (Source: Adapted from Warehouse Anywhere)

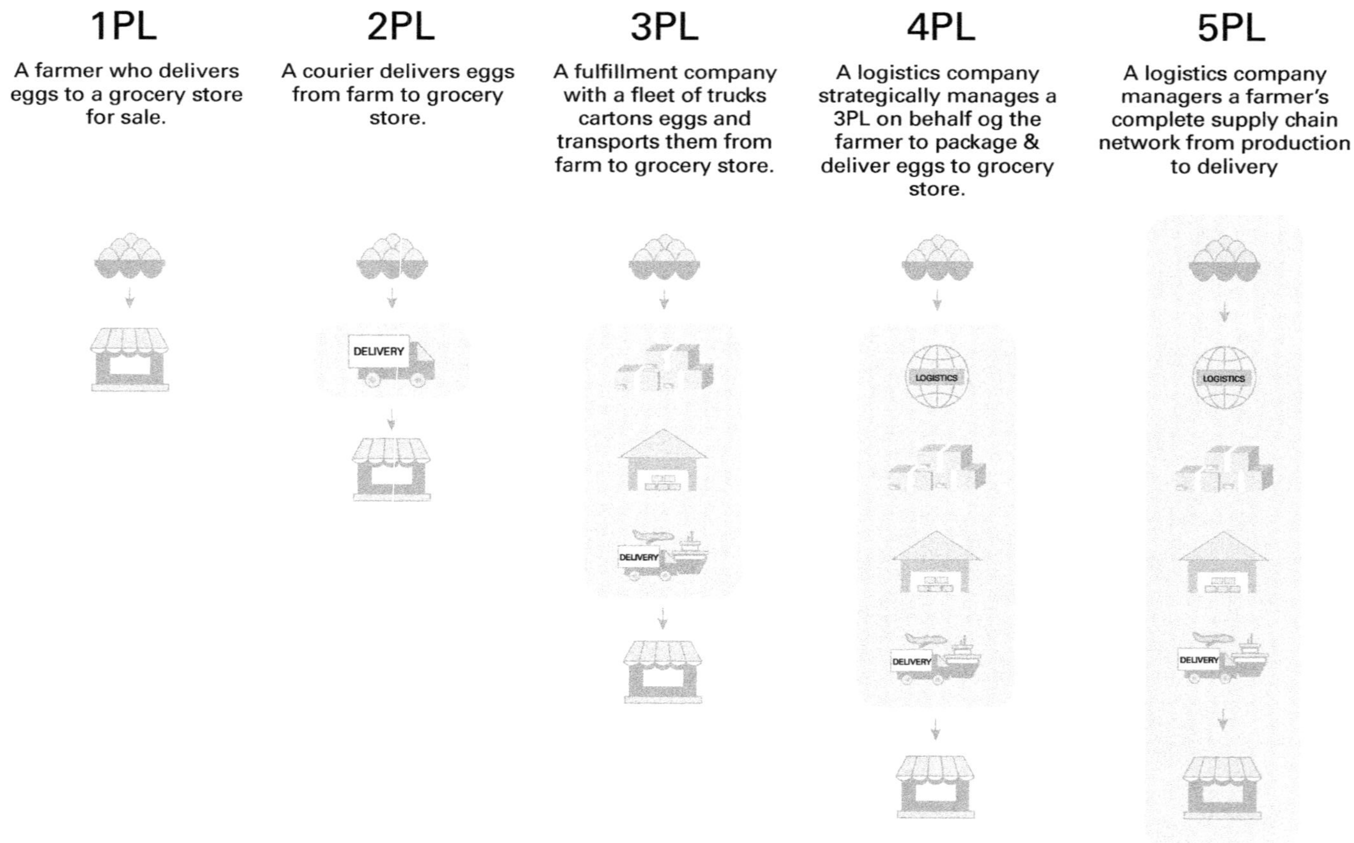

SCND for iPhone

Apple Inc., a global technology company, aimed to design an efficient and sustainable supply chain network for its flagship product, the iPhone. This endeavor required a synchronized framework that encompasses various aspects of network design.

Market analysis was conducted to understand global demand for iPhones and identify critical markets. This analysis considered regional preferences, growth prospects, and market dynamics. By evaluating customer demands, Apple strategically determined optimal locations for distribution centers and manufacturing locations, and ensured proximity to target markets.

Supplier selection played a crucial role in network design. Apple evaluated potential suppliers based on their capabilities, quality, reliability, and commitment to sustainability practices. Proximity to manufacturing facilities and a robust transportation infrastructure were considered to ensure efficient and timely delivery of components.

Transportation infrastructure formed the backbone of the supply chain network. Apple carefully assessed transportation modes and routes for importing raw materials and exporting finished products. Optimal transportation networks were designed to minimize transit times, costs, and environmental impact. Compliance with import and export regulations, customs requirements, and product safety standards were prioritized to ensure smooth operations across borders.

Moreover, regulatory compliance played a crucial role in Apple's network design. Adherence to data privacy laws, such as protecting customer information, was paramount. Apple ensured that its supply chain operations complied with local regulations, fostering transparency and accountability throughout the network.

This example highlights the importance of infrastructure considerations, focusing on hard and soft infrastructures. It would help if practitioners considered network nodes for SCND, both complex infrastructure such as power, road, rail, airports, ports, etc., as well as soft infrastructure such as governance, IP protections, legal framework, corruption, safety, education system and talent, and the stability of financial systems should be evaluated.

Apple continues to invest in robust IT systems and technologies to enable seamless information sharing, demand forecasting, and inventory management. Integrated IT systems across supply chain partners provide real-time visibility and enhance collaboration. This allows Apple to respond promptly to changing market demands and maintain agility within the network.

Human capital is another crucial element in Apple's supply chain network. The company recognizes the importance of a skilled and engaged workforce. Training programs are implemented to enhance employees' expertise in supply chain management, fostering a culture of continuous improvement. This human capital investment contributes to the network' efficiency, innovation, and resilience.

Alongside profitability, Apple prioritizes sustainability and resiliency in its network design. The company embraces environmentally friendly practices, such as energy-efficient manufacturing processes and eco-friendly packaging. Suppliers are evaluated based on their sustainability practices, encouraging responsible sourcing, and reducing the carbon footprint of transportation. By integrating all these factors, Apple creates a synchronized framework for its iPhone supply chain network. This framework enables the company to optimize its operations, achieve profitability, ensure regulatory compliance, leverage robust infrastructure, nurture human capital, and contribute to a sustainable future.

This outline provides a comprehensive overview of the integrated factors in network design for Apple's iPhone supply chain. However, it is essential to note that specific details and strategies may vary based on the company's strategic business plan and evolving market conditions.

As the iPhone's example shows, the evolution of modern SCND methods reflects a journey from early optimization techniques to sophisticated, data-driven, and resilient approaches. Academics and practitioners have pushed the boundaries of knowledge, incorporating advancements in technology, analytics, and sustainability considerations. As we move forward, integrating AI and ML promises to open new horizons, allowing supply chain networks to become more agile, responsive, and efficient than ever before.

SCND ensures products move more efficiently from suppliers to end customers. Different types of network design are utilized based on the requirements of the supply chain, customer demands, and the nature of the product. Here are several types of network design:

1. **Direct Shipment Network:** Products are shipped directly from the supplier to the customer or retail store, bypassing intermediary warehouses or distribution centers.
2. **Hub and Spoke Network (H&S Network):** All shipments are funneled through a central hub in this design. The H&S network is often used in the airline and parcel delivery industries, where regional spokes (like airports or local delivery centers) are connected via a central hub.
3. **Milk Run Network:** In a milk run system, instead of sending individual trucks to each supplier, a truck visits multiple suppliers on a single route (much like a person delivering milk having numerous stops), picking up partial loads from each. This system can lead to reduced transportation costs and improved truck utilization.
4. **Cross-docking Network:** In this model, products from the supplier or manufacturing plant are received at a warehouse or distribution center but are not stored for long periods. Instead, these products are quickly sorted, possibly consolidated with other products, and shipped to the final destination.
5. **Stock Keeping Unit (SKU) Proliferation:** Involves managing multiple versions of a product to cater to different market segments.
6. **Flexible Network Design:** This design is adaptable and can be reshaped as the demand or supply situation changes. It is helpful for industries with rapid shifts in demand or supply situations.
7. **Direct Store Delivery (DSD):** Manufacturers directly supply goods to retail stores, bypassing the retailer's distribution centers. This method can ensure product freshness, especially in sectors like bakeries or dairy.
8. **Closed-loop Network:** This system is designed to move products to the customer and return them for recycling or refurbishing. It

is used mainly in industries where products are returned, like beverage containers or electronics.

9 **Tiered Network:** Suppliers deliver products to central distribution centers, from where they are shipped to regional or local distribution centers and then to the end customer.

10 **Hybrid Models:** Combining two or more of the above network designs. Depending on the complexity of the supply chain, sometimes it is beneficial to use a mix of different models.

The ideal design for any company will depend on various factors, including product type, customer demand patterns, the geographical distribution of customers and suppliers, and the overall strategic goals of the business. Proper network design can reduce costs, improve service levels, and increase customer satisfaction.

Let us delve deeper into each network design concept, provide product examples, and discuss potential Key Performance Indicators (KPIs) to ensure traceability and regulatory compliance.

Direct Shipment Network (DSN)

- **Product example:** High-value electronics, like smartphones, shipped directly from a manufacturer to a flagship store or end consumer.
- **KPIs:**
  - Transit time
  - Order accuracy
  - On-time delivery rate

Hub and Spoke Network

- **Product example:** Airline cargo or parcel delivery by companies like FedEx.
- **KPIs:**
  - Hub throughput time
  - Spoke replenishment frequency
  - Cargo/parcel damage rate

Milk Run Network

- **Product example:** Automotive parts are collected from various suppliers for a car assembly plant.
- **KPIs:**
    - Route completion time
    - Loading and unloading times
    - Vehicle capacity utilization

Cross-docking Network

- **Product example:** Fresh produce moving quickly through a distribution center to reach multiple grocery stores.
- **KPIs:**
    - Dock turnaround time
    - Inventory dwell time
    - Cross-dock order accuracy

SKU Proliferation

- **Product example:** A soft drinks company offering multiple flavors and packaging sizes.
- **KPIs:**
    - SKU-level sales data
    - Inventory turnover by SKU
    - Stockout rate by SKU

Flexible Network Design

- **Product example:** The apparel industry reacting to fast-changing fashion trends.
- **KPIs:**
    - Lead time variability
    - Demand forecast accuracy
    - Supplier flexibility score

Direct Store Delivery (DSD)

- **Product example:** Bakery items or chips delivered directly to grocery stores.
- **KPIs:**
  - Store service frequency
  - Shelf stock rate
  - Product freshness index

Direct to Customer (D2C)

- **Product example:** Saatva Mattress (Click to Ship).
- **KPIs:**
  - Order to delivery cycle time
  - Broken promises
  - Delivery satisfaction

Closed-loop Network

- **Product example:** Refillable beverage containers or leased electronics.
- **KPIs:**
  - Return rate
  - Refurbishment/Recycling rate
  - Reverse logistics cost

Tiered Network

- **Product example:** Consumer electronics, first to a central DC, then regional DCs, and then to retail stores.
- **KPIs:**
  - Inventory levels at each tier
  - Transit times between tiers
  - Product availability rate

Hybrid Models

- **Product example:** A retail company using direct shipping for online orders but hub-and-spoke for store replenishments.

- **KPIs:**
  - Overall logistics cost
  - Service level agreement (SLA) compliance rate
  - Hybrid efficiency score

Along with designing the network for the above KPIs, we should also focus on traceability and regulatory compliance across all these designs. Some overarching KPIs could be as follows:

1. **Traceability rate:** The percentage of products traced back to their origin or batch.
2. **Regulatory compliance rate:** Percentage of shipments/operations adhering to regulations.
3. **Audit success rate:** Number of successful regulatory or internal audits versus total audits.
4. **Incident reporting time:** Time taken to report any breach of compliance or traceability issue.
5. **Recall response time:** Speed at which products can be recalled from the market in case of problems.

Remember, the exact KPIs and their relevance will vary depending on the specific industry, region, and nature of the product. It is crucial for businesses to continuously monitor, adjust, and align their KPIs with their strategic goals.

Let us delve deeper into these concepts and discuss how they might be integrated.

Circular Design

Circular design is a principle primarily associated with a circular economy. Traditional linear models often follow a "take, make, dispose" pattern where raw materials are extracted, manufactured into products, and discarded as waste. In contrast, the circular design focuses on ensuring that products can be reused, refurbished, or recycled at the end of their life, creating a closed-loop system. This can drastically reduce waste and make the most of resources.

Key elements:

- **Product life extension:** The approach focuses on designing products that last longer and can be easily repaired, refurbished, or upgraded.

- **Material recovery:** Ensuring that products can be recycled, or their materials repurposed at the end of their life.
- **Business model innovation:** Implementing strategies like leasing products or offering products as a service instead of one-time sales.

Farm-to-Table

Farm-to-table (or farm-to-fork) emphasizes a direct relationship between farmers and consumers. It focuses on producing food locally and delivering that food directly to consumers, thereby reducing middle steps, preserving the freshness of produce, and ensuring a clearer understanding of the source of one's food.

Key elements:

- **Local sourcing:** Prioritizing the purchase of locally produced food to reduce transportation emissions and ensure freshness.
- **Transparency:** Making it clear where food comes from and potentially how it is produced.
- **Sustainable farming practices:** Organic farming, non-GMO crops, and humane treatment of animals are often emphasized.

Cradle to Grave

Cradle to grave is a design concept that looks at a product's lifecycle from its creation (cradle) to its disposal (grave). It focuses on understanding the environmental impact at every stage of the product's life.

Key elements:

- **Lifecycle assessment:** Measuring a product's environmental footprint at each stage of its life, from raw material extraction to disposal.
- **Product stewardship:** Manufacturers take responsibility for their product's environmental impact.

Integration of Concepts

When integrating these concepts, one can envision a holistic, sustainable supply chain:

1. **Circularity in farming:** Use sustainable farming methods that prioritize soil health, water conservation, and reduced use of

chemical inputs. The crop waste could be composted and returned to the soil, and packaging could be designed for reuse or recycling.

2 **Farm-to-table in a circular economy:** Once the produce is ready, it gets transported using sustainable methods to the consumers. After consumption, any waste (like packaging) can be recycled or composted, ensuring a circular loop.

3 **Incorporating cradle to grave:** By understanding the complete lifecycle of each product, from the seeds used on a farm to the final dish served on a table, companies can make informed decisions about sourcing, production, transportation, and waste management to minimize environmental impact.

In essence, integrating these concepts would mean creating food systems that prioritize local, sustainable farming, transparent and direct delivery to consumers, and a complete understanding of the environmental impacts of every stage of the process. The goal is to have a system where resources are used efficiently, waste is minimized, and both people and the planet benefit.

Circular Design

- **Product example:** Smartphone
- **Network design:**
  - Resource extraction: Mining for metals like lithium, cobalt, etc.
  - Manufacture: Assembling the phone in factories
  - Distribution: Shipping to retailers or direct to consumers
  - Use: Customer uses the smartphone
  - End of life: Instead of discarding, the phone is returned to designated centers for refurbishment or recycling
- **Role of network design:** Efficiently linking refurbishment and recycling centers to production can ensure that materials from old phones are reused in newer models, reducing waste and the need for new raw material extraction.

Farm-to-Table

- **Product example:** Fresh organic vegetables

- **Network design:**
  - Farm: Vegetables are grown using sustainable practices
  - Local market/processing: Vegetables might be cleaned, sorted, or packaged
  - Table/consumer: Directly sold to consumers at local markets or delivered to homes
- **Role of network design:** Ensuring that transportation from farm to consumer is swift and direct, reduces food spoilage, ensures freshness, and reduces transportation costs and emissions.

Cradle to Grave

- **Product example:** Disposable plastic water bottle
- **Network design:**
  - Cradle (production): Producing plastic from petroleum sources and manufacturing bottles
  - Distribution: Shipping bottles to beverage companies, then to retailers
  - Use: Consumers purchase and drink the water
  - Grave (disposal): Most likely, the bottle ends up in landfill or is incinerated, although recycling is a more sustainable option
- **Role of network design:** Efficient distribution ensures these bottles quickly reach widespread markets. However, the environmental impact can be mitigated if the network incorporates return and recycling centers.

Integrated Concept

- **Product example:** A coffee cup from a brand promoting sustainability
- **Network design:**
  - Resource extraction: Sourcing sustainable materials, e.g., bamboo or bioplastics
  - Manufacturer: Production of the cup
  - Distribution: Getting it to cafes or consumers
  - Use: Consumers buy and use the cup for their daily coffee
  - End of life: Instead of discarding, the consumer can return the cup for a discount on a new one; the old cup is then recycled or composted

- Farm-to-table: If the brand also sells coffee, ensure the coffee beans are sourced sustainably and directly from farmers
- Cradle to grave: Assessing the environmental impact from sourcing the sustainable material to the decomposition of the cup

- **Role of network design:** A holistic network design ensures that sustainable materials are sourced, products are manufactured with minimal waste, efficient distribution, and end-of-life products are processed with minimal environmental impact. Additionally, direct relationships with coffee farmers ensure sustainable and fresh coffee for consumers. For all these concepts, network design plays a pivotal role in ensuring that products move through the supply chain efficiently, sustainably, and in line with the company's environmental and economic goals. Proper design can reduce costs, environmental impact and improve overall product quality.

Global Supply Chain Network Design (GSCND)

Network design is crucial, and it can also manifest itself as a Global Supply Chain Network Design (GSCND), which extends the concepts of traditional SCND by incorporating the complexities and challenges of operating in an international environment.

Here is how they differ and what makes GSCND unique.

Geographical Scope

- **Traditional SCND:** Focuses on domestic or regional networks.
- **GSCND:** Spans multiple countries or continents, involving a more comprehensive range of transportation modes, regulatory environments, and geopolitical considerations.

Complexity and Variability

- **Traditional SCND:** Has a relatively stable and predictable operating environment.
- **GSCND:** Encounters varied infrastructure quality, political climates, cultural differences, exchange rate fluctuations, and trade tariffs.

Lead Times

- **Traditional SCND:** Typically deals with shorter lead times.
- **GSCND:** Encounters longer and more variable lead times due to extended distances, customs processes, and potential transportation disruptions.

Regulations and Compliance

- **Traditional SCND:** Primarily needs to comply with local or regional regulations.
- **GSCND:** Must navigate multiple regulatory environments, import/export restrictions, and compliance standards.

Cost Structures

- **Traditional SCND:** Focuses on local costs like transportation, warehousing, and labor.
- **GSCND:** Considers additional costs like import/export duties, international freight charges, hedging against currency fluctuations, and potentially country-specific incentives or tax breaks.

Risk Factors

- **Traditional SCND:** Risks such as transportation disruptions or local market demand changes are relatively localized.
- **GSCND:** Faces broader risks like geopolitical tensions, global economic downturns, pandemics, and international trade wars.

Critical Aspects of GSCND

1. **Multi-echelon networks:** GSCND usually deals with multiple layers of suppliers, manufacturers, and distribution centers spread across the globe.
2. **Global sourcing:** Deciding where to source materials or products, weighing factors like cost, quality, lead time, and supplier reliability.
3. **Tax and tariff optimization:** Strategically placing assets and operations to leverage favorable tax treatments and minimize tariff impacts.

4 **Currency management:** Strategies for mitigating risks associated with currency fluctuations.
5 **Political and economic considerations:** Deciding how to configure the supply chain while considering the stability of political systems, potential economic sanctions, or trade agreements like USMCA or the EU common market.
6 **Environmental and sustainability considerations:** Adopting green supply chain practices can be challenging yet crucial globally.
7 **Cultural sensitivity:** Understanding and respecting cultural nuances when working with international partners.
8 **Technological integration:** Using integrated IT systems to ensure real-time communication and data sharing across time zones and regions.

KPIs for GSCND

Given the extended scope of GSCND, many traditional KPIs remain relevant, but they are complemented by new metrics tailored to the international context.

1 **Total landed cost:** This includes all costs from product inception to delivery at the destination.
2 **Duty and tariff efficiency:** Measures how effectively the company navigates and optimizes import/export duties.
3 **International on-time delivery rate:** Tracking on-time international deliveries becomes crucial given the longer lead times.
4 **Currency fluctuation impact:** Evaluating how currency changes affect the bottom line.
5 **Global supplier performance scorecards:** Evaluating suppliers globally based on cost, quality, reliability, and lead times.

In conclusion, while SCND fundamentals remain consistent, the global context introduces additional complexities. Successful GSCND requires a holistic understanding of international dynamics and the flexibility to adapt to rapidly changing global scenarios.

Some of the case study examples for each aspect of GSCND are worth considering.

Let us delve deeper into each case study.

Multi-echelon Networks

- **Product/Company:** Apple's iPhone
  - **Case study:**
    - Apple sources components from over 200 suppliers worldwide, including countries like China, the US, Japan, and South Korea. Once these components are gathered, a large portion of the assembly is done in China. The finished products are then shipped globally.
    - The multi echelon system spans tier-1 suppliers (direct component suppliers) to tier-2 or even tier-3 suppliers (raw material providers for components).
  - **Insights:**
    - Apple's supply chain involves a complex web of suppliers spanning various countries. For instance, the tiny A-series chip that powers the iPhone is designed in California, manufactured in Taiwan by TSMC, and tested in other parts of Asia before getting assembled in China.
    - Such a global spread allows Apple to tap into specialized capabilities (e.g., precision manufacturing in Japan) while diversifying risks. However, it brings challenges like managing longer lead times, ensuring quality consistency, and maintaining intellectual property rights.

Global Sourcing

- **Product/Company:** H&M
  - **Case study:**
    - H&M owns no factories; they source from independent suppliers, primarily in Asia and Europe. By maintaining a diverse supplier base, H&M can shift production based on costs, capabilities, and political stability.
  - **Insights:**
    - H&M's decentralized production strategy allows it to be nimble. They maintain close ties with over 800 suppliers, mainly in Asia

and Europe. This vast network lets them shift production based on evolving costs, risks, and capabilities.

- Their sourcing decisions are not solely cost-driven. H&M's sustainability commitment means they also evaluate suppliers on environmental and social criteria, ensuring ethical labor practices and reducing environmental impact.

Tax and Tariff Optimization

- **Product/Company:** Starbucks
  - **Case study:**
    - Starbucks opened a roasting facility in the Netherlands partly due to favorable tax treatments. This allowed them to efficiently distribute roasted beans throughout Europe while managing their global tax liability.
  - **Insights:**
    - With its strategic location and favorable tax regime, the Netherlands became an attractive hub for Starbucks' European operations.
    - By optimizing its supply chain structure, Starbucks could serve its European markets efficiently while benefiting from tax arrangements. However, such tax optimization strategies often face scrutiny from regulators and the public, which companies must navigate carefully.

Currency Management

- **Product/Company:** General Electric (GE)
  - **Case study:**
    - GE has vast global operations and faces significant currency fluctuation risks. To manage this, GE employs hedging strategies, using financial instruments to offset potential losses from unfavorable currency swings.
  - **Insights:**
    - With operations in over 180 countries, GE is exposed to significant currency risks. A sudden drop in a foreign currency against the dollar can erode GE's foreign earnings.

  - GE typically uses forward contracts and options to hedge against these fluctuations. They can stabilize their financial forecasts against unpredictable currency swings by locking in exchange rates for future transactions.

Political and Economic Considerations

- **Product/Company:** Ford Motor Company
  - **Case study:**
    - Ford canceled a planned $1.6 billion plant in Mexico after political pressure and potential tariff implications. Instead, they invested more in their US operations, showcasing how political and economic considerations can directly influence global supply chain decisions.
  - **Insights:**
    - Political pressures, especially surrounding trade and jobs, can directly affect supply chain decisions. Ford's Mexico plant decision was influenced by potential tariffs and broader US political sentiment favoring domestic manufacturing.
    - While the direct economic impact of not opening a Mexico plant was significant, Ford weighed it against potential tariff costs and benefits from strengthening its public image and relationship with domestic stakeholders.

Environmental and Sustainability Considerations

- **Product/Company:** Unilever
  - **Case study:**
    - Unilever's Sustainable Living Plan aims to halve the environmental footprint of its products by 2030. This impacts their supply chain by influencing where they source materials, how they manufacture, and the way they distribute products globally.
  - **Insights:**
    - Unilever's commitment to halve its environmental footprint by 2030 impacts its sourcing practices. For instance, they aim to source 100 per cent of their agricultural raw materials sustainably.
    - This strategy requires working closely with global suppliers, investing in sustainable farming practices, and often paying a premium for

sustainable raw materials. While this can increase costs, it builds brand value and future proofs against environmental risks.

Cultural Sensitivity

- **Product/Company:** McDonald's
  - **Case study:**
    - McDonald's menu varies globally, respecting cultural tastes and religious dietary requirements. For instance, in India, where a large population refrains from eating beef, the "Maharaja Mac" is made from chicken.
  - **Insights:**
    - Localizing the menu is just the tip of the iceberg for McDonald's. Behind the scenes, it means sourcing specific ingredients locally, adhering to local food safety standards, and even adjusting cooking methods.
    - In India, for example, McDonald's has separate kitchen areas for vegetarian and non-vegetarian food preparation, respecting the significant vegetarian population's sentiments.

Technological Integration

- **Product/Company:** Amazon
  - **Case study:**
    - Amazon's global supply chain relies heavily on sophisticated IT systems that track inventory, sales, and shipping in real time across various countries. This technological integration enables Amazon to move products across its global distribution network efficiently.
  - **Insights:**
    - Amazon's Fulfillment by Amazon (FBA) program allows third-party sellers to store their products in Amazon's fulfillment centers. This global network relies on an intricate IT system that tracks inventory across multiple countries, calculates customs duties, and optimizes shipping routes.
    - Technological prowess allows Amazon to promise features like Prime delivery in various countries, adjusting for local logistics capabilities. It also enables Amazon to rapidly integrate acquisitions (like Souq in the Middle East or Whole Foods in the US) into its global supply chain.

GSCND and the benefits of the TBL approach

For each case study, the global context introduces specific challenges and opportunities that companies need to address. The right GSCND strategy mitigates risks and leverages international opportunities for competitive advantage. Additionally, each of these case studies exemplifies how companies have tailored their global SCND strategies to navigate the complexities and leverage the opportunities of international operations. The designs are multifaceted, intertwining business objectives with geopolitical, economic, cultural, and technological factors.

Now the question is understanding how all these case studies tie into the TBL. Integrating the TBL mindset into GSCND means considering supply chain decisions' socioeconomic and environmental impacts alongside their financial implications. This concept is especially relevant for supply chain management, as supply chains are the backbone of many businesses and significantly affect society and the environment.

Supply chains are the networks of activities, resources, and organizations that transform raw materials into finished products and deliver them to customers. Supply chains involve various processes, such as sourcing, production, distribution, and consumption. Each process consumes resources, generates emissions, creates waste, and affects the stakeholders' well-being. Therefore, supply chains, directly and indirectly, influence the sustainability of the business and the world. However, many supply chains still operate under the traditional cost and speed optimization model, which focuses on minimizing expenses and maximizing efficiency. This model often neglects or externalizes the social and environmental costs of the supply chain operations, such as human rights violations, labor exploitation, pollution, deforestation, biodiversity loss, climate change, and resource depletion. These costs can have negative consequences for the business in the long run, such as reputational damage, regulatory fines, customer boycotts, operational disruptions, and competitive disadvantages. Sustainable supply chain practices play a crucial role in reducing environmental impacts. By implementing eco-friendly initiatives such as carbon footprint reduction, waste minimization, and renewable energy adoption, businesses can mitigate their environmental footprint and contribute to a greener future.

Therefore, supply chains must shift their focus toward TBL to build resilience and adaptability. By embracing the TBL approach, supply chains can balance their operations' economic, social, and environmental aspects and create a more sustainable and responsible business model.

Here are some of the benefits of adopting the TBL approach:

- **Improved customer satisfaction and loyalty:** Customers are becoming more aware and concerned about their purchases' social and environmental impacts. They are demanding more transparency and accountability from the businesses they buy from. By adopting the TBL approach, supply chains can demonstrate their commitment to sustainability and social responsibility, and meet or exceed customer expectations. This can enhance customer satisfaction and loyalty, and increase the market share and revenue of the business.
- **Enhanced employee engagement and retention:** Employees are also becoming more conscious and motivated by the purpose and values of their work. They want to work for businesses aligning with their beliefs and goals. By adopting the TBL approach, supply chains can create a positive work environment that respects and empowers employees and provides them with opportunities for learning and growth. This can improve employee engagement and retention, and reduce the turnover and recruitment costs of the business.
- **Reduced operational risks and costs:** The TBL approach can help supply chains identify and mitigate the potential risks and costs associated with their social and environmental impacts. For example, by implementing practices such as responsible sourcing, waste reduction, energy efficiency, renewable energy, circular economy, green logistics, etc., supply chains can reduce their dependence on scarce or volatile resources, lower their emissions and waste generation, avoid regulatory penalties or legal liabilities, enhance their operational efficiency and productivity, and save money in the long run.

- **Increased innovation and differentiation:** The TBL approach can also stimulate innovation and differentiation for supply chains. By considering their operations' social and environmental aspects, supply chains can discover new opportunities to improve their products or services, or create new ones that address their customers' or society's unmet needs or challenges. For example, by developing products or services that are more durable, reusable, recyclable, and biodegradable, consumer product companies can innovate at a lower cost while contributing to the Triple Bottom Line.
- **Environmental and social capital:** Supply chains must prioritize social impact by promoting fair labor practices, ensuring safe working conditions, and supporting ethical sourcing. Emphasizing human rights and ethical considerations in supplier selection fosters long-term partnerships and enhances brand reputation.
- **Collaboration among stakeholders along the supply chain:** this fosters transparency and trust. By working closely with suppliers, customers, and regulatory bodies, businesses can address shared challenges and collectively work toward a sustainable and secure supply chain.

Incorporating the TBL into GSCND post-COVID-19 has become more crucial due to the following.

- **Resilience and vulnerabilities:** COVID-19 exposed vulnerabilities in global supply chains, emphasizing the need for resilience. A TBL approach promotes diversification, local sourcing, and community engagement, which can enhance stability.
- **The shift in stakeholder expectations:** Post-pandemic, there has been increased public and stakeholder awareness about sustainability, ethical business practices, and corporate responsibility. Meeting these expectations can influence brand perception and customer loyalty.
- **Regulatory shift:** Governments focus more on sustainability, local job creation, and responsible business practices. Integrating TBL can ensure compliance and offer competitive advantages through tax breaks or other incentives.

- **Operational efficiency:** Sustainable practices, such as reducing waste or optimizing transportation, often lead to operational efficiencies and cost savings in the long run.

Integrating TBL into GSCND

People:

- **Case study:** Fair Trade certified products
- **Integration into GSCND:** Sourcing products from suppliers that follow fair trade practices ensures equitable wages and working conditions for workers.
- **Post-COVID importance:** The pandemic exacerbated inequalities and highlighted worker vulnerabilities. Fair sourcing can support vulnerable communities and enhance brand value.

Planet:

- **Case study:** IKEA's sustainable sourcing
- **Integration into GSCND:** IKEA commits to sourcing wood from sustainable sources and aims for a circular supply chain where products are designed to be reused, repaired, and recycled.
- **Post-COVID importance:** The pandemic reinforced the need for sustainable resource usage as supply chain disruptions highlighted resource scarcities. A focus on sustainability ensures a stable, long-term supply of resources.

Profit:

- **Case study:** Tesla's global supply chain for batteries
- **Integration into GSCND:** Tesla, while aiming for profitability, sources materials for its batteries, considering both cost and environmental impact, such as using nickel instead of cobalt.
- **Post-COVID importance:** Diversifying sourcing and considering long-term environmental implications can safeguard against supply chain disruptions and potential future regulations.

Integrating the TBL mindset into GSCND ensures that businesses are not just chasing short-term profits but are building sustainable, resilient, and ethical supply chains. Post-COVID-19, this approach becomes even more critical as businesses, consumers, and regulators increasingly know the interconnectedness of global systems and the need for holistic, responsible management.

Let us take a deeper dive into reviewing the TBL and geopolitical risks, and how corporations must change their mindset regarding GSCND.

Supply Chains must Plan with Geopolitical Awareness and National Security Concerns

Geopolitical Risks and Their Amplified Relevance

In the 21st-century era, supply chains sprawled across continents, aiming to leverage cost efficiencies, resource availabilities, and market access. However, this globalization of supply chains made them susceptible to geopolitical risks, ranging from trade wars and changing regulatory landscapes to national security concerns. The US–China trade disputes, Brexit, and regulatory changes in data privacy and environmental standards have been stark reminders of businesses' unpredictability.

The COVID-19 pandemic added another layer to this complexity, and it showcased the profound vulnerability and lack of resilience in many global supply chains.

We have seen how China and the 2022 Russian invasion of Ukraine have disrupted supply chains worldwide. The landscape of global supply chains is evolving rapidly, shaped by geopolitical dynamics and national security considerations. Traditional supply chain models, focusing solely on cost and efficiency, must be revised amid geopolitical uncertainties and security risks. Geopolitical tensions, trade disputes, and shifts in international relations have exposed supply chains to increased risks. As highlighted in a report by Deloitte ("Global Manufacturing Risk Index 2021"), 90 per cent of global manufacturing is vulnerable to geopolitical disruptions. The reliance on single-source suppliers or specific regions can make supply chains susceptible to sudden disruptions, highlighting the need to diversify sourcing strategies.

National security considerations also play a pivotal role in shaping supply chain models. The US Department of Defense's "Industrial Base Analysis and Sustainment (IBAS) Framework" emphasizes safeguarding critical industries to ensure domestic security. The supply of essential goods, technologies, and components may become compromised during geopolitical conflicts, necessitating the rethinking of supply chain networks to enhance national resilience.

Businesses are now exploring strategies such as nearshoring and reshoring to reduce dependence on distant and potentially unstable regions.

Collaboration between governments and businesses is crucial in addressing geopolitical and security challenges. Public–private partnerships creating policies that enhance supply chain resilience while ensuring national security interests is especially vital.

Businesses need to identify critical dependencies, vulnerabilities, and potential disruptions to design strategies that minimize risk exposure.

The transformation of supply chain models to incorporate geopolitical and national security awareness is no longer an option but a necessity. The disruptions caused by the COVID-19 pandemic have exposed vulnerabilities within supply chains, prompting a call for resilient and adaptive networks. By diversifying sourcing, leveraging technology, fostering collaboration, and considering national security implications, businesses can create supply chains capable of withstanding geopolitical uncertainties while contributing to economic growth and stability. As global dynamics evolve, supply chain models prioritizing security, resilience, and sustainability will undoubtedly become the cornerstone of successful business operations.

Trade policies can affect the cost, availability, quality, and competitiveness of supply chain inputs and outputs. For example, the US–China trade war-imposed tariffs on billions of dollars' worth of imports and exports, affecting various industries such as electronics, agriculture, steel, etc.

Regional integration is the degree of cooperation and coordination among countries and regions regarding economic, political, social, and cultural aspects. Regional integration can include free trade agreements, customs unions, common markets, etc. Regional integration can facilitate or hinder the movement of goods, services, capital, and labor across borders.

Security threats are the risks or dangers that can disrupt or damage the supply chain infrastructure, assets, operations, and information. Security threats can include wars, terrorism, cyberattacks, piracy, etc. Security threats can affect supply chain safety, reliability, and continuity. For example, the recent conflict between Ukraine and Russia has raised concerns over the security of key energy supply routes and pipelines in Europe.

Heightened geopolitical tensions and national security concerns underscore the need for supply chains to be resilient against potential disruptions in global trade and supply networks. Diversifying sourcing strategies and localization of production can enhance economic resilience and reduce dependency on single regions or countries.

These are just some of the geopolitical factors that can affect supply chains. Other factors may be specific to certain regions, industries, or situations. Therefore, supply chain managers and policymakers must monitor and assess the geopolitical environment and its implications for their supply chain models.

Integrating TBL into GSCND in a Geopolitically Volatile Landscape

People: The social component of TBL emphasizes ethical labor practices, community development, and stakeholder engagement. This demands a deep understanding of the socio-political landscapes in which corporations operate.

- **Geopolitical application:** When considering regions for sourcing or manufacturing, companies must weigh the stability and ethics of labor practices. This could mean preferring regions with stable labor relations, vital human rights records, and avoiding areas with conflict, political unrest, or histories of exploitation.

- **Post-COVID relevance:** The pandemic highlighted the plight of vulnerable workers—factory workers in congested urban areas, or migrant workers facing sudden unemployment. Ensuring supply chains prioritize and uplift people becomes an ethical imperative and a safeguard against disruptions.

Planet: With environmental crises looming, the planet component requires sustainable sourcing, waste management, and carbon footprint reduction.

- **Geopolitical application:** Environmental regulations vary widely across countries. Corporations might face stricter regulations in one region compared to another. Aligning supply chain design with areas prioritizing sustainable practices ensures long-term viability and reduced regulatory risks.
- **Post-COVID relevance:** The brief respite nature experienced during strict lockdowns showcased the impact of industrial activity on the environment. As industries restart, global momentum exists to "build back greener", making environmental considerations pivotal in GSCND.

Profit: While profit remains a primary driver, TBL insists on a longer-term and broader view of profitability.

- **Geopolitical application:** Short-term profit motives might suggest shifting production to the cheapest location, but considering geopolitical risks implies a deeper analysis. Investing in regions with stable political climates, transparent regulations, and fair-trade agreements might be more profitable in the long term.
- **Post-COVID relevance:** As the pandemic caused abrupt shutdowns, businesses with diversified sources and destinations fared better, reiterating that long-term profitability requires resilience and flexibility.

The changing face of geopolitics in a post-pandemic world demands that corporations revisit their GSCND strategies. Embracing a TBL approach, which values people and the planet alongside profit, offers a holistic roadmap. It is not merely a matter of ethical responsibility but a strategic imperative for resilience in an era of flux and uncertainty. The next generation of global supply chains will be those that are not just efficient but also ethical, sustainable, and resilient against the kaleidoscope of global geopolitical challenges. Now that we have covered network design principles, what they entail, and their impact, Chapter 3 will delve deeper into reworking supply chain models with an awareness of geopolitical, environmental, and national security concerns.

Endnotes

1 P S Goodman and N Chokshi. How the world ran out of everything. The New York Times, 1 June 2021, www.nytimes.com/2021/06/01/business/coronavirus-global-shortages.html (archived at https://perma.cc/XQQ6-ZPMZ)

2 R L Ackoff, W K Holstein, M Tanenbaum and S Eilon. Operations research. *Encyclopedia Britannica.* www.britannica.com/topic/operations-research (archived at https://perma.cc/PM9J-5LHS)

3 S Zuckerman. In the beginning – and later. Operational Research Quaterly, (1964) 15(4), 287–292. doi.org/10.2307/3007115 (archived at https://perma.cc/7PX2-TSQ4)

4 R L Ackoff, W K Holstein, M Tanenbaum and S Eilon. Operations research. *Encyclopedia Britannica.* www.britannica.com/topic/operations-research (archived at https://perma.cc/W5WR-YMS4)

5 World's first operational radar station to be restored. January 19, 2019. Heritage Fund. www.heritagefund.org.uk/news/worlds-first-operational-radar-station-be-restored (archived at https://perma.cc/R6C9-6JCG)

6 I Jawhar, N Mohamed and J Al-Jaroodi. Networking architectures and protocols for smart city systems. *Journal of Internet Services and Applications*, 2018, 9, 26. jisajournal.springeropen.com/articles/10.1186/s13174-018-0097-0 (archived at https://perma.cc/2MXQ-AD3F)

7 L Dablanc, S Ogilvie, A Goodchild. Logistics sprawl: differential warehousing development patterns in Los Angeles, California, and Seattle, Washington. *Transportation Research Record*, 2014, 2410 (1), 105–112

8 J Cidell. Concentration and decentralization: the new geography of freight distribution in U.S. metropolitan areas, *Journal of Transport Geography*. 2010, 18(3), 363–371

9 A Charles, M Lauras, L Van Wassenhove and L Dupont. Designing an efficient humanitarian supply network, *Journal of Operations Management,* 2016, 47 (1). doi.org/10.1016/j.jom.2016.05.012 (archived at https://perma.cc/E3J2-8BEC)

10 National Science Foundation. NSF announces nearly $50 million partnership with Ericsson, IBM, Intel, and Samsung to support the future of semiconductor design and manufacturing January 16, 2023. new.nsf.gov/tip/updates/nsf-announces-nearly-50-million-partnership (archived at https://perma.cc/DEN2-YYJM)

03 Intelligent Supply Chain Network Design: Integrating People, Environment, and Economy

Chapter 2 explained SCND principles and how operations research helped optimize them, primarily based on efficiency and cost minimization. We also saw how SCND was applied to improve resiliency, and emerging factors after COVID-19 include sustainability, AI and ML, and best practices and KPIs used to measure their impact.

This chapter expands on the concepts introduced in Chapter 2. Also, it explores the paradigm shift required in supply chain management, considering social, environmental, and economic impacts for a more holistic and responsible approach. A selected set of use cases presented at the end of Chapter 2 is expanded here with process description, benefits, challenges, and measures of success. These use cases of SCND are:

1. SKU Rationalization (Consumer Goods and Retail)
2. Cross-Docking (WalMart, Amazon)
3. Flexible Network Design (Sport Obermeyer)

4 Multi-echelon Networks (Boeing)
5 Technological Integration (Amazon FBA, and AFE)
6 Triple Bottom Line (Maria Yee Inc. – making “green” furniture in China)

SKU Rationalization for SCND

The retail industry is supplied with finished products by the consumer goods sector, and the relationship between these two industry players drives some 6 percent of the GDP. Consumer spending, which amounts to just under 70 percent of nominal GDP, grew by 1.6 percent in real annualized terms in Q2 of 2023 and has been a consistent source of growth in this expansion, boosted in part by the strong US labor market in 2023. The consumer goods sector is driven by market share and product assortment that is usually promoted with heavy spending on advertising, market research, consumer segmentation, and retail promotions. Since multiple generations, demographics, ethnicities, psychographics, and consumer needs and wants are prevalent and continually evolving, product assortments reflect this variety, resulting in a proliferation of SKU (stock-keeping units) (See Figure 3.1). Over time, some SKUs fall in demand with the changing consumer profiles, while demand for other SKUs increases. Some SKUs become gradually obsolete and excessive inventory buildups hurt profitability. SKU optimization is a technique used by analytical teams at consumer goods and retail companies.

Here are the ways that SKU optimization impacts SCND:

- **Increased complexity:** As the number of SKUs increases, so does the complexity of managing the supply chain. Forecasting demand, managing inventory, and determining replenishment policies for a more significant number of products, each with potentially different demand patterns, is necessary.
- **Warehousing challenges:** More SKUs typically mean more space requirements in a warehouse. It also complicates picking, packing, and inventory management processes. Warehouses may need to rethink layouts and storage solutions to accommodate the more comprehensive product range.

- **Inventory management:** SKU proliferation can lead to higher inventory levels. There's a potential for holding more safety stock for a wider variety of products. These increases carry costs and risks related to obsolescence.
- **Production and sourcing complexity:** A more comprehensive product range can complicate production scheduling or raw material sourcing for manufacturers or companies that source raw materials. This might lead to more frequent changeovers in production or sourcing from multiple suppliers.
- **Transportation costs:** Transportation planning becomes more intricate with more SKUs. There's potential for more partial shipments, increased handling, and the need for multi-stop routes.
- **Customer service levels:** With more SKUs, ensuring the right product availability in the right place at the right time becomes more challenging. This could impact service levels if not managed properly.
- **Demand forecasting:** Predicting demand for a broader range of products can be more challenging. Minor errors in demand forecasting for multiple SKUs can accumulate, leading to significant supply and demand mismatches.
- **Increased capital requirement:** More SKUs can mean a higher need for working capital to finance inventories, more facilities, or increased equipment.
- **Rethinking distribution center locations:** Companies might need to rethink their network design to handle SKU proliferation efficiently. For instance, introducing regional distribution centers or implementing postponement strategies, where specific product differentiation steps are delayed until a clearer demand signal is received.
- **Need for advanced technology:** To manage the complexity arising from SKU proliferation, companies might need to invest in advanced IT systems and tools for demand forecasting, warehouse management, inventory optimization, and transportation planning.
- **Risk management:** With more SKUs, there's also a diversification of risk. While this means that another might compensate for a

demand drop in one SKU, companies must be vigilant about not spreading themselves too thin and becoming vulnerable to external shocks.

- **Rationalization opportunities:** SKU proliferation often prompts companies to review their product portfolios periodically. Rationalization can help eliminate underperforming or redundant SKUs, helping streamline operations.

Companies often deploy advanced analytics, lean methodologies, and sophisticated supply chain software to address the challenges posed by SKU proliferation to maintain efficiency and customer satisfaction.

According to a recent report by Expak Logistics[1] (2023), Stanley Black & Decker, an American industrial tools supplier, is cutting nearly 50,000 SKUs as part of its supply chain transformation plan, fueled by COVID-19 and a push toward efficiency and resilience. Coca-Cola engaged in "ruthless" rationalization in 2020, eliminating the entire Odwalla juice brand. Note that an SKU optimization, despite pushback from sales and marketing, adds value to the TBL through less spending in logistics and transportation, reducing carbon footprint.

Figure 3.1 Six Steps of SKU Rationalization

1. Revisit your marketing strategy
2. Finetune your product catalog
3. Know your customers well
4. Forecast switching & cannibalization
5. Balance carrying costs vs. incrementality
6. Review and repeat

SOURCE USC Marshall-Randall R. Kendrick Global Supply Chain Institute

KPIs and Metrics

Key performance indicators (KPIs) and metrics employed to determine success include the cost per unit of products. The product cost includes the costs of designing, manufacturing, and packaging a product. Add to these costs associated with distribution, logistics, and returns.

A product portfolio optimization process offers deep insights and immediate, impactful actions that counteract the slow erosion of earnings before interest, taxes, depreciation, and amortization (EBITDA) that often results from the best day-to-day efforts of individuals in sales, product management, pricing, marketing, and other areas. Effective portfolio optimization is critical in maximizing margins and value. It targets a well-defined series of value-creation levers that routinely improve overall profit margin by 5–10 percentage points:[2]

- increasing revenues by targeting more profitable customers for both existing and new business
- increasing margin realization by increasing prices where appropriate and cutting unprofitable products
- decreasing product management costs by reducing complexity
- decreasing procurement cost by simplifying product set
- decreasing marketing spend by reducing offerings.

The critical steps of this approach to keep in mind when optimizing a product portfolio are:

- Align the organization on "true cost" to include discounts, customer support, product, logistics, distribution, and selling costs: product and customer profitability at SKU and account levels.
- Identify SKUs and product families for rationalization or pricing improvement.
- Get customer input, then align the organization on priorities and execution plan.
- Pilot and launch product optimization.
- Flow through product effects with product management, procurement, and marketing efficiencies.
- Initiate comprehensive tracking and continuous improvement program.

Figure 3.2 Product Portfolio Optimization Impact, Study by Beckway

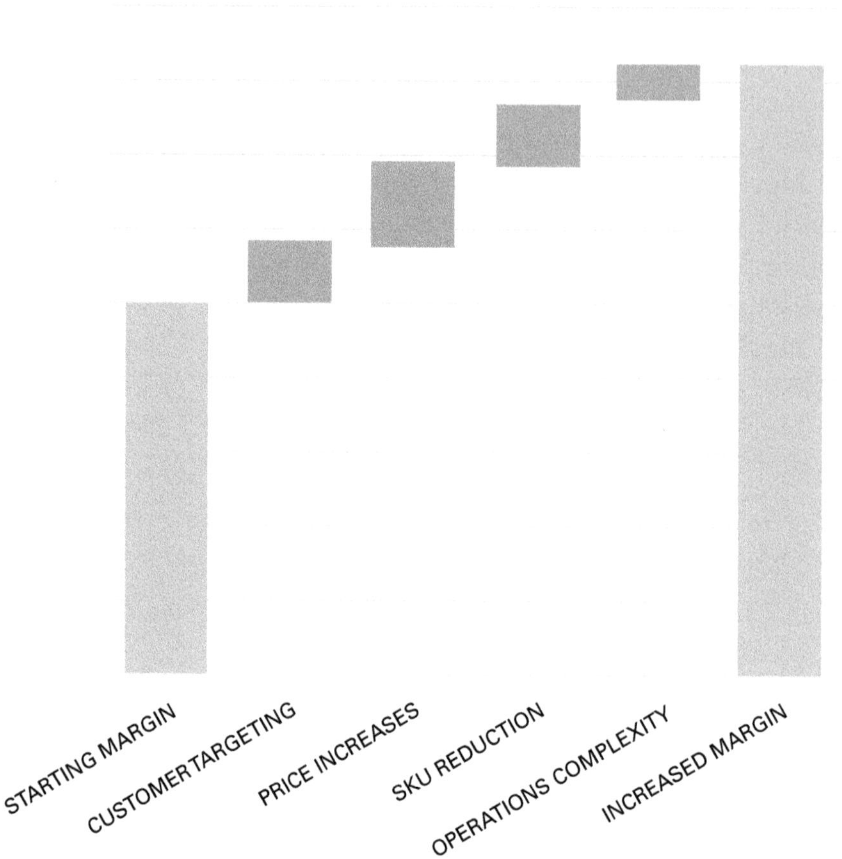

SOURCE Beckway Study

Challenges of SKU Rationalization

One major challenge is how intricate the process is. Managing SKU rationalization involves closely monitoring the performance of each SKU over time, and this can be quite a time-consuming and intricate task.[3] Businesses must keep an eye on various specific KPIs for each SKU, such as procurement costs, customer acquisition costs, storage costs, inventory turnover rate, fulfillment costs, and more.

Another challenge arises on the human side of things. Implementing SKU rationalization might lead to job cuts, affecting employee morale negatively. It's crucial for businesses to explain the reasons behind

SKU rationalization to their employees and offer support to those impacted.

Additionally, there's the potential for disruptions in the supply chain due to SKU rationalization. Businesses need a robust supply chain management system to minimize the impact on their operations.

Furthermore, reducing the number of SKUs, a common outcome of SKU rationalization, can lead to a drop in revenue. Striking the right balance between streamlining SKUs and maintaining a diverse product line that caters to customer needs is crucial for businesses.

Cross-Docking for SCND

Widely adopted by supply chain organizations, since WalMart pioneered cross-docking (see Figure 3.5) in the eighties,[4] cross-docking is a practice in the logistics and supply chain management where incoming shipments from suppliers or manufacturing plants are directly transferred to outbound trucks, trailers, or rail systems with little to no storage in between. Instead of receiving goods and storing them in a warehouse, products flow directly from the receiving dock to the shipping dock. There are several benefits to this SCND practice.

1. **Reduced storage needs:** Since products are not stored in the warehouse for extended periods, the need for storage space is reduced, leading to potential cost savings and more efficient use of warehouse space.
2. **Faster throughput:** Products move more quickly through the supply chain, enabling faster delivery times.
3. **Reduced handling:** With fewer touchpoints, there's a lower risk of product damage, and handling costs are minimized.
4. **Inventory reduction:** Cross-docking can help reduce the levels of inventory that companies need to hold, decreasing carrying costs and risks associated with holding stock.
5. **Streamlined processes:** The practice often simplifies the logistics process with fewer steps and reduced complexity.

6 **Freshness for perishables:** For perishable goods, cross-docking ensures that products spend minimal time in transit and reach the customer while still fresh.
7 **Consolidation:** Cross-docking facilities can consolidate smaller product loads into one method of transport to realize economies of scale in transportation.
8 **Reduced labor costs:** The need for labor associated with traditional warehousing activities, such as picking and putting away stock, is reduced.
9 **Increased customer satisfaction:** Faster delivery and turnaround times can increase customer satisfaction.
10 **Improved turnover rate:** Retailers can often realize faster product turnover rates, which is especially crucial for items with a short shelf-life or in high demand.
11 **Real-time product allocation:** Allows businesses to make real-time decisions on where a product is most in demand and then ship it directly to that location.

However, it's important to note that cross-docking is not suitable for all types of products or businesses. Successful implementation requires precise coordination, real-time data sharing, and timely transportation. The supply chain needs to be synchronized, and partners must be reliable for cross-docking to be effective. It's most beneficial for products that move quickly, are pre-tagged for sale (e.g., with barcodes or RFID tags), and don't require quality inspections upon warehouse arrival.

KPIs

Product traceability is a critical element of cross-docking. Since less perishability is a key benefit of cross-docking (which reduces the time between the inbound and outbound logistics), multiple organizations have collaborated on process improvements and technologies for developing best practices in cross-docking. For example, the Produce Traceability Initiative[5] Best Practices initiative of 2012 was heralded by the United Fresh Produce Association in collaboration with PMA, CPMA/ACDFL, and GS1/US to create and maintain efficient shipping

Figure 3.3 Organize a Cross-Dock in a Warehouse

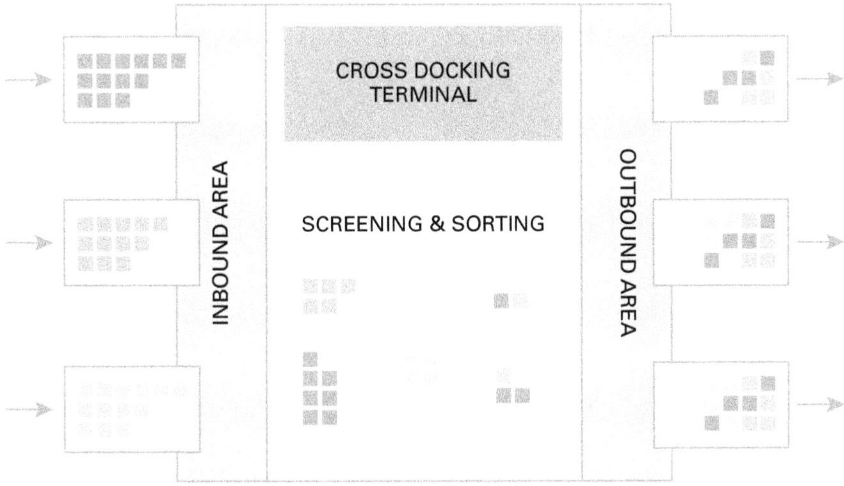

SOURCE USC Marshall- Randall R. Kendrick Global Supply Chain Institute

and receiving processes for cross-docking/load-only operations and maintain effective documentation reconciliation processes and formalize current industry practices.

Significant effort goes into inventory accuracy and defect identification for cross-docking. Some known areas that need to be managed well are Defects Per Million Orders (DPMO), and associated root causes such as wrong SKUs, wrong vendor labeling, wrong quantity, incorrect sorting, container inaccuracies, and internal mis-stickering.

Technologies in this area focus on Advanced Shipment Notifications (ASNs), logistical unit barcodes, and the Warehouse Management System (WMS), which must be integrated into the operations of the material handling system (MHS).[6]

Challenges of Cross-Docking

Smooth cross-docking hinges on a robust IT system. Yet, achieving this can pose a challenge amid market uncertainty since accurate customer demand forecasting is crucial for planning and executing product transfers. Also, the unpredictable nature of customer demand can lead to inventory mismatches, missed transfers, and logistical bottlenecks.

Another challenge involves the necessity for close coordination and real-time visibility among suppliers, manufacturers, retailers, and recipients. Failing to coordinate can result in conflicts, disruptions, and delays, impacting the flow of goods and leading to additional costs.[7]

For small companies lacking the right technology or sufficient staff, cross-docking poses additional challenges. Achieving close coordination and real-time visibility can be challenging without the proper tools and resources. Implementing cross-docking can potentially disrupt traditional supply chain operations, requiring businesses to make significant and potentially costly changes.

Flexible Network Design for SCND

Flexible network design in global supply chains refers to the design and configuration of a supply chain that can quickly adapt to various conditions, such as demand fluctuations, supply disruptions, geopolitical changes, etc. It emphasizes agility, scalability, and the ability to reconfigure the supply chain network in response to evolving circumstances.

Benefits of Flexible Network Design

1. **Adaptability to change:** It allows companies to rapidly adjust to unexpected changes, from demand spikes to supply shortages.
2. **Risk mitigation:** A flexible network design helps manage and mitigate risks by enabling swift changes in response to disruptions like natural disasters or political unrest.
3. **Competitive advantage:** Companies that adapt their supply chain swiftly can often meet customer demands more effectively, leading to higher customer satisfaction and potential market share gains.
4. **Cost savings:** By quickly shifting production or distribution tactics, companies can often realize cost savings or avoid potential cost increases.
5. **Efficient use of resources:** With flexibility, resources (like manufacturing capacity or transportation) can be allocated more effectively based on current conditions.

6 **Better response to market dynamics:** Enables companies to adapt to market trends, shifts in consumer preferences, or local market conditions.

7 **Opportunistic exploitation:** Flexible networks can exploit positive changes in the market, such as new sales channels or emerging markets.

Challenges of Flexible Network Design

1 **Higher initial costs:** Designing a flexible network may involve higher upfront investments in technology, infrastructure, and training.

2 **Complexity:** Managing a flexible supply chain can be more complex than managing a static one, requiring advanced management skills and tools.

3 **Coordination and collaboration:** Flexibility often requires tight coordination among various supply chain partners, which can be challenging, especially across global networks.

4 **Technology dependence:** Many tools that enable supply chain flexibility, such as real-time data analytics or advanced forecasting tools, rely heavily on IT systems. This dependence brings its risks and challenges.

5 **Potential for over-responsiveness:** A highly flexible system might react too quickly to perceived changes that might be short-lived, leading to inefficiencies.

6 **Training and skill development:** Employees and partners need to be trained to operate in a flexible environment, which can require time and investment.

7 **Trade-offs:** Sometimes flexibility in one area might compromise efficiency in another. For instance, holding excess capacity for potential demand surges might be seen as inefficient from a pure cost perspective.

8 **Cultural challenges:** Organizational cultures used to more static and predictable processes might resist the uncertainty and constant change associated with a flexible design.

Building a Flexible Network Design

Building a flexible network design in global supply chains involves strategic planning, coordination, and adopting advanced technologies. Here's a step-by-step approach with best practices on processes, technologies, and KPIs to measure its effectiveness:

1. **Strategic assessment:** Begin with thoroughly analyzing the current supply chain. Identify vulnerabilities, inefficiencies, and areas where flexibility is currently lacking.
2. **Define objectives:** Clearly define what flexibility means for your organization. Is it speed? Is it adaptability? Is it the ability to switch suppliers or production processes?
3. **Collaborative planning:** Engage with key stakeholders, suppliers, customers, and internal teams, to foster collaboration. Shared objectives and transparency will be foundational to flexibility.
4. **Redundancy and diversification:** Incorporate multiple suppliers for critical components, diversify transportation modes, and consider multiple manufacturing or distribution locations.
5. **Centralized data management:** Adopt a centralized system for data management to have a single source of truth, improving visibility and response times.
6. **Continuous monitoring and feedback:** Monitor the supply chain in real time and gather feedback constantly to make iterative improvements.

Best Practices on Processes and Technologies

Segmentation of products by demand, supply, and several other dimensions helps companies increase flexibility. Supply chain segmentation is critical to helping companies achieve the flexibility they need to meet the mantra of business agility. With segmentation, companies can strive to achieve flexibility across the entire spectrum, as defined in Figure 3.4.[8]

McKinsey proposes a "segment, stock, and plan" (SSP) approach for low-volume, high-mix companies.[9] This involves part segmentation, increasing the accuracy of stocking algorithms by segment, and then building flexibility into the planning process. The firm projects

Figure 3.4 Supply Chain Segmentation

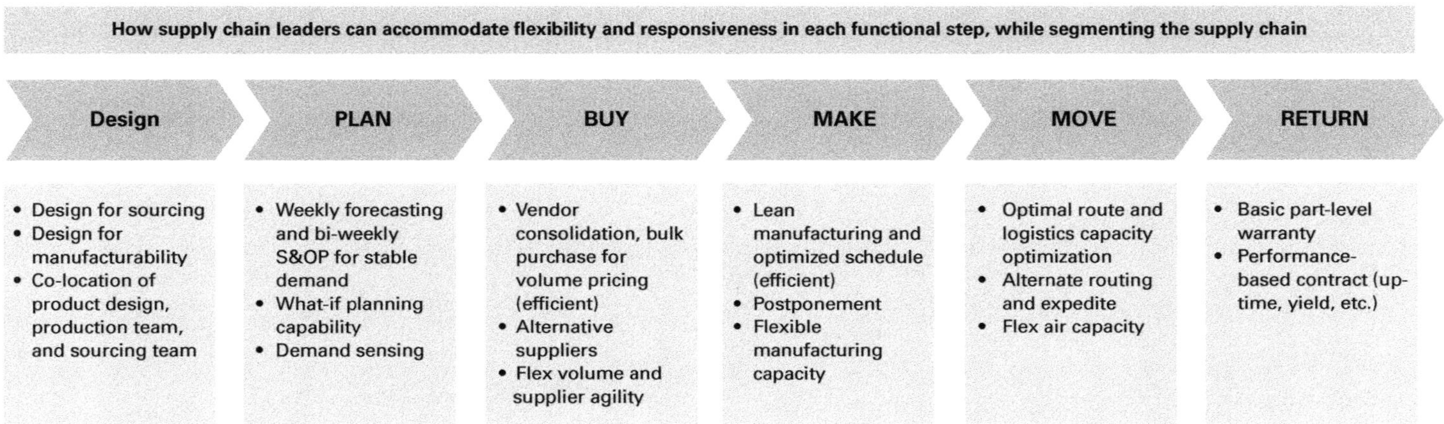

SOURCE USC Marshall- Randall R. Kendrick Global Supply Chain Institute

that by following this process, companies typically reduce part shortages by 50 to 90 percent while shrinking inventory by 15 to 25 percent below historical levels. These benefits translate into greater on-time delivery, lower inventory costs, and increased flexibility (see Figure 3.3).

1 **Invest in advanced technologies:**
   - **ERP systems:** Integrates all facets of an operation, including product planning, development, manufacturing, sales, and marketing.
   - **Supply chain management software:** Provides tools for logistics, warehousing, inventory management, and more.
   - **Advanced analytics & AI:** To predict potential disruptions, understand market dynamics, and recommend action points.

2 **Demand forecasting:** Use advanced analytics tools to predict demand better, allowing for a more agile response to market changes.

3 **Modular product design:** Create products that can be easily modified or customized, allowing for swifter changes in the production process.

4 **Regularly review supplier performance:** Maintain a supplier scorecard and hold regular reviews.

5 **Scenario planning:** Regularly simulate different supply chain scenarios to prepare for potential disruptions.

6 **Invest in training:** Ensure the workforce is trained to operate in a flexible and agile environment.

KPIs to Measure Effectiveness

1 **Lead time:** Measure the time from order placement to product delivery. Flexibility often aims to reduce this.

2 **Inventory turnover:** A higher turnover rate can indicate a more efficient, flexible supply chain.

Figure 3.5 SCND Case Study of Begpacker, Inc.

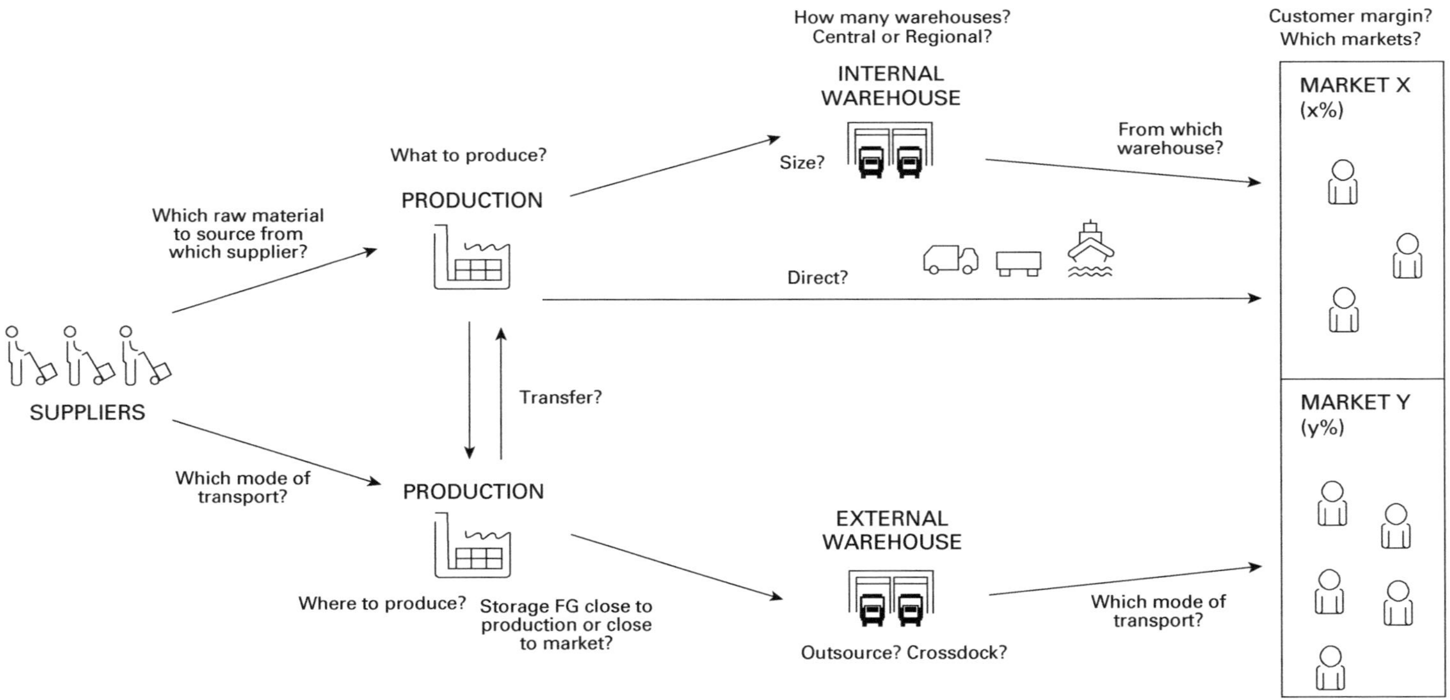

SOURCE Adapted for USC Marshall- Randall R. Kendrick Global Supply Chain Institute

3. **Order fill rate:** The percentage of customer orders that are fulfilled from stock on hand.
4. **Stockouts:** The number of times an item is out of stock. A flexible supply chain should reduce stockouts.
5. **Supplier performance scorecards:** Track on-time delivery, defect rates, and responsiveness metrics.
6. **Cost-efficiency metrics:** Measure transportation costs, warehousing costs, and other significant expenditure to ensure that flexibility doesn't come at an unsustainable cost.
7. **Customer satisfaction:** Track customer feedback, reviews, and complaints. A more flexible supply chain should lead to higher customer satisfaction levels.
8. **Return on Assets (ROA):** Evaluates how profitably a company is using its assets, providing insights into the efficiency of the supply chain.
9. **Capacity utilization:** Measures how effectively the available capacity is being used, indicating flexibility in adjusting to demand changes.
10. **Demand forecast accuracy:** Measures the difference between forecasted and actual demand. By integrating these steps, best practices, and KPIs, organizations can develop a more flexible network design that is resilient and responsive to the ever-evolving challenges of global supply chains.

Multi-echelon SCND

A multi-echelon SCND refers to a supply chain with multiple stages or "echelons" in the distribution network. Each echelon represents a level in the supply chain where inventory is held or transactions occur, such as factories, central warehouses, regional distribution centers, local warehouses, and retailers.

The business reasons for adopting a multi-echelon design are typically geographic spread, complex product assortments, customer service levels, risk management, and cost optimization. Companies operating across vast geographic areas might need multiple stages in their supply chain to efficiently serve all regions. Varied product lines or assortments might necessitate different handling and storage requirements, leading to distinct echelons. Different customer service levels are maintained to achieve desired service levels and ensure product availability. Spreading operations across multiple echelons can reduce the risk associated with disruptions at a single location. Also, having multiple echelons can lower transportation and inventory holding costs.

There are some benefits to this SCND type. It improves customer service due to better product availability and delivery times. Companies can minimize total inventory costs by considering the entire network's inventory. Efficiently planned routes and cargo consolidation can result from a well-designed multi-echelon network. Also, it allows for flexibility in the supply chain with better response to regional demand changes and disruptions.

However, there are challenges in this network. Managing multiple echelons can be complex, requiring sophisticated tools and expertise. Synchronized operations across all echelons are crucial to realize the benefits. More facilities might mean higher fixed overheads. Additionally, ensuring accurate and timely information across all echelons can be challenging.

A multi-echelon supply chain network design allows companies to optimize their supply chain operations on a larger and more intricate scale. While the benefits can be substantial, it requires precise management, advanced technological tools, and continuous monitoring to ensure efficiency and responsiveness across all echelons.

In service parts management, customer relationships are often established through service agreements that extend over months or years. These agreements typically apply to a product (or group of products) that the customer has purchased and specify the type of service that will be provided and the timing with which the service will take place. Service agreements may apply to several products for a customer operating in multiple locations.

For example, a major supplier's inventory problem is that it must maintain a competitive level of service on repair contracts for its parts. Typically, the company possesses a multi-echelon inventory system in which the lower-echelon warehouses provide customers directly with emergency repair parts while the upper-echelon warehouses repair parts returned from the lower-echelon and hold parts for replenishment of lower-echelon inventory. There are far fewer upper-echelon than lower-echelon warehouses.

Technologies Used in Multi-echelon SCND

Besides ERP, APS, WMS, TMS, and DP tools, some Multi-echelon Inventory Optimization (MEIO) tools are designed to optimize inventory across a multi-echelon network (see Figure 3.6). Also, with

Figure 3.6 Multi-echelon Inventory Optimization (MEIO)

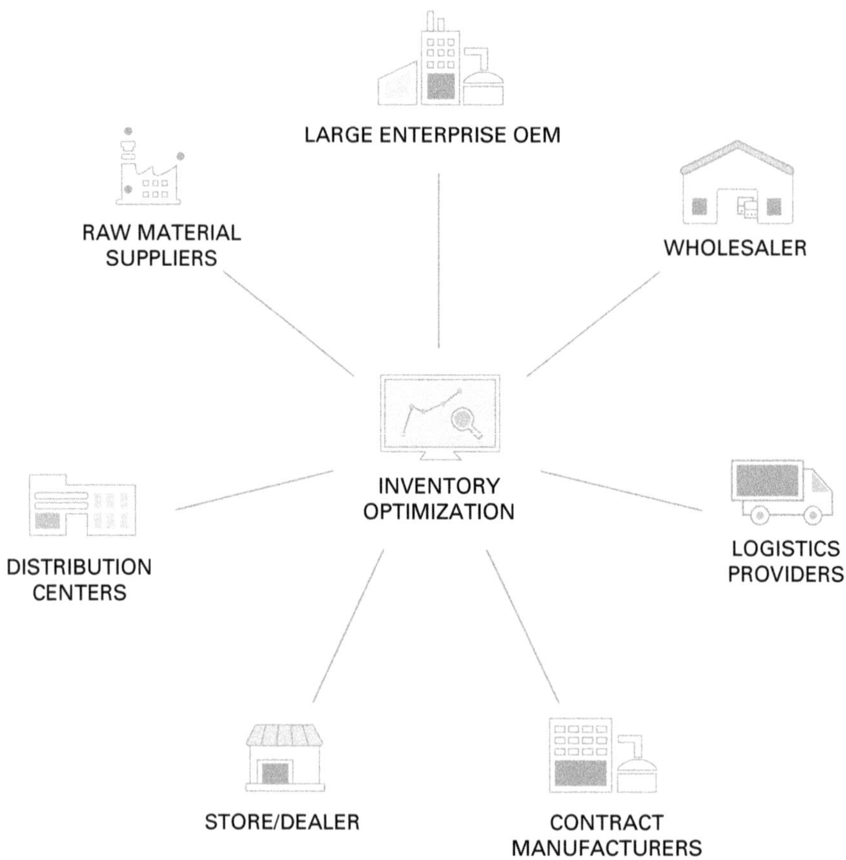

SOURCE Tools Group

increasing applications of the IoT and sensors, there are opportunities for real-time tracking and monitoring. AI/ML is increasingly used for advanced analytics, pattern recognition, and predictive modelling.

Academic studies have identified high-cost, low-demand parts that should be placed on a one-for-one, continuous review replacement policy and developed the Analytical Stocking Model to determine inventory levels for these parts. These models provide insights into relative quantities of parts that should be stored at both echelons, whether to store parts at some lower-echelon warehouses, and how to use risk pooling effectively. Reported cost reductions of 60 percent are possible while maintaining the current level of service, or alternatively, system backorder reductions of over 97 percent are possible while keeping total inventory costs constant at their current level.

KPIs and Metrics

1. **Inventory turnover:** How often inventory is sold and replaced over a period.
2. **Fill rate:** The percentage of customer orders that can be met with the current inventory.
3. **Order lead time:** The time taken from order placement to delivery.
4. **Total logistics costs:** Cumulative transportation, warehousing, and inventory holding costs.
5. **Demand forecast accuracy:** Measures the difference between forecasted and actual demand.
6. **Service levels:** Percentage of orders delivered on time and in full.
7. **Return on Investment (ROI):** Evaluate the profitability of the investment in the multi-echelon system.

Challenges of Multi-echelon SCND

One of the biggest challenges in multi-echelon network design is in creating a demand forecasting system that works and syncs seamlessly between the different tiers of the network. Not ensuring this can lead to inventory mismatches, missed transfers, and logistical bottlenecks.

Ensuring seamless coordination and real-time visibility among suppliers, manufacturers, retailers, and recipients is crucial. Lack of coordination can trigger conflicts, disruptions, and delays, impacting the smooth flow of goods and incurring extra costs.[10]

Additionally, performance monitoring and improvement in a multi-echelon supply chain network can prove to be a daunting task. Businesses must monitor various tier-specific KPIs, such as procurement costs, customer acquisition costs, storage costs, inventory turnover rate, and fulfillment costs. This process can be both time-consuming and complex.

Technological Integration (Amazon FBA and AFE)

Amazon's Fulfillment by Amazon (FBA) program allows sellers to store their products in Amazon's fulfillment centers. Amazon handles the products' storage, packaging, and shipping to the end customers. Here's a broad overview of how technology integration facilitates onboarding suppliers to the FBA program, as well as examples of companies that utilize the service:

Technology integration for onboarding suppliers:

1 **Seller central dashboard:** When a supplier decides to use FBA (see Figure 3.7), they set up an account on Amazon Seller Central, the primary interface for managing their FBA business.

Figure 3.7 Fulfillment by Amazon—Process Flow

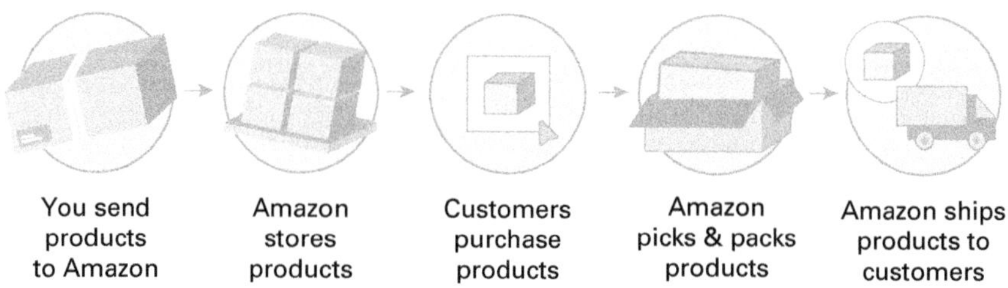

SOURCE Seller App

2 **Product listing:** Sellers can list their products one at a time, in bulk, or by integrating their inventory management systems with Amazon's API.

3 **Shipment creation:** Sellers create an FBA shipment in Seller Central once the products are listed. This process involves specifying the number of products and the destination Amazon fulfillment center.

4 **Product preparation:** Sellers must prepare their products according to Amazon's packaging and labeling guidelines. There are tools within Seller Central that help sellers understand these guidelines and generate necessary labels.

5 **Shipment tracking:** Suppliers can track their shipment status using the Seller Central dashboard once products are shipped to Amazon's fulfillment center.

6 **Integration with third-party tools:** Amazon offers a set of APIs that allow third-party tools and software to integrate with Seller Central. This enables sellers to automate many aspects of their FBA business, such as inventory tracking, price optimization, and customer reviews management.

Amazon Fulfillment Engine (AFE)

Another example of technology integration at Amazon is its internal fulfillment process for multiple items ordered by the same customer during a short period. Instead of sending separate packages from different fulfillment centers where the products may be located, this intelligent engine quickly analyzes to see if these items could be shipped in a single package to the customer, thereby creating a better customer experience while minimizing the total system cost of shipment. AFE is an acronym for Amazon Fulfillment Engine, a process and conveyance system that sorts individual items from hundreds of orders into completed shipments.

Without AFE, multi-item orders are grouped into batches. The size of these batches is constrained by the ability to sort the items and match them to complete shipments effectively. A picker can only pick an item that belongs to this relatively small set of orders. This means they frequently walk past items that must be picked simply because they are not in the current batch. With the AFE, the automation of the sortation process allows them to increase the number of units available to a picker from dozens to thousands. As a result, the pickers are much more effective.

In addition, the traditional "batchy" processes that Amazon followed required that all batch items complete processing in one area before the entire batch moves to the next area. All items must be picked before the batch can be sorted, then all items must be sorted before they can be packed. This means that the time it takes to process a shipment in the batch includes the picking and sorting time of all other units. With the AFE, as soon as all of the items for an order have been processed at each step, the shipment can progress to the following process. The reduced time required allows better execution for fulfilling orders departing soon.

Finally, the AFE processes are designed to be simple and repeatable. AFE Sort is typically an easier function, has a lower learning curve, and is less error-prone than batchy sortation. In general, AFE processes are simpler and more effective than batchy processes.

An AFE system typically contains induct workstations, rebin walls, chutes, pack stations and sorting trays.

Induct Workstations

Induct stations receive totes full of many items belonging to many customer orders. Associates at the station will singulate the items from pick into sorter trays to be routed to the correct destination to be combined with the other items from the order.

Rebin Walls

A rebin wall is a set of fixed chutes. These chutes will have fixed physical and virtual dimensions, as well as virtual properties that control the type of shipment they can hold. After items are singulated, they will be routed to a specific wall and the item will be placed into a specific chute which is assigned for the shipment. When all of the items for the shipment have arrived and are virtually in the chute, they are "pushed through" to be packed. Each virtual chute has two sides: a rebin side, which holds the shipment while it is incomplete, and a pack side, which holds the shipment after all items are present until it is packed.

The ability to process so many shipments in parallel allows AFE processes to be efficient and yield relatively short cycle times compared with other methods of processing multiple unit shipments.

Chutes

Chutes are the fundamental building block of the AFE system. Groups of chutes are set based on proximity to a given Rebin station to define a "Wall." AFE productivity is tied to workflow management through the chutes of a given Wall. In almost all cases, each AFE wall should be configured identically to the other AFE walls to avoid flow imbalances. For sortable sites, there are multiple sections of standups for each Wall. These sections are usually composed of a main section that is immediately behind the Rebin station, as well as side sections that are parallel to the Rebin conveyance.

Chute names are designed to tell you the physical location of the virtual chute.

Pack Stations

The AFE pack process is called "chuting" because shipments are packed out of the chutes in the Rebin walls. Because shipments of all sizes can be processed through AFE, the workstations typically contain all box types processed at the site. The stations are also equipped with wireless Bluetooth scanners to scan the source chute and complete the scan verification process for the shipment.

Pack workstations are aligned with specific Walls and are usually oriented parallel to the Walls to minimize travel distance for the packer (also commonly "chuter" in AFE). Each station will be responsible for a certain portion of the Wall. Each chute will have a light designating if it has a shipment available, and the color of the light will designate the relative priority of the shipment.

Sorter Trays

Sorter trays are the physical and virtual containers for singulated items routed to a specific destination. Physically, these are flat and wide plastic containers designed to hold any normal-sized product easily and to maintain orientation on fast-moving conveyance. They are containers that hold one virtual unit during transit between Induct and Rebin.

Trays are filled at Induct (in Pick for Non-Sort), routed to a specific wall, emptied at Rebin, and then returned to Induct to repeat the process. During the entire process, trays are never lifted from the conveyor. Normal travel time between Induct and Rebin is 2–4 minutes, depending on the fullness of the conveyor and to which Rebin Wall the tray is routed.

A defined number of trays in the sorter per wall should be open. When walls close, trays should be removed. When walls open, trays should be added. Most sortable sites run with 55–60 trays per wall.

Visual signals that the tray count may be too high:

1 Rebin consistently has >3 blue lights.
2 Sorter is in anti-gridlock (or gridlock) even though Rebin is keeping up.
3 The induct is frequently waiting for trays to advance on the merge.

Visual signals that the tray count may be too low:

1 Rebin is consistently waiting for work (too few trays).
2 Sorter consistently releases partial slugs (<16 trays—too few trays).

AFE Process

In the first step of the process, items are removed from their source location and placed into "trays." In Non-Sort AFEs, this is done when the item is initially picked. In Sortable buildings, multiple items are picked into totes, and each item may belong to a different shipment. The totes are routed to Induct stations, where individual items are removed from the totes and placed into AFE trays. Because there is only one item in the tray, it can be conveyed to a specific destination dedicated to the shipment.

The trays are assigned a destination to a specific Wall, with the item destined for a specific chute within the Wall. Within a given AFE system there may be between 8 and 44 Walls, each composed of dozens of chutes. Each shipment is given a specific chute assignment, and items will be collected in that chute until all items for the shipment are present, at which time the chute can be cleared, and the items packed.

AFE sortation processes are designed for simplicity. The Induct process for sortables involves only taking an item from a tote, scanning it, and placing it in a tray. There is a light curtain that confirms the physical placement and a conveyor that removes the full tray and replaces it with an empty tray. The associate will repeat until the tote is empty, then scans a new one and continues. The Rebin process is also quite simplified. Because the trays are brought directly to the Rebin station and the empty trays are taken from the station, the process for the associate is a quick four-step put-to-light process. Remove the item from the tray, press the button at the Rebin station, find the light on the wall, put the item into the chute, and press the light on the chute to acknowledge the move. When all the items for a shipment have been moved to the chute, the light at the chute will blink. This indicates that the shipment is ready to be pushed from the Rebin side to the Pack side of the chute. This causes the pack side light to turn on, indicating that the shipment is ready to be processed. For the packer, an area of each wall is assigned, and they work through the lights, prioritizing as needed based on a simple color scale.

Challenges of Technological Integration into SCND

The integration of technology into supply chain design usually faces its biggest hurdle at the level of organizational decision-making. CFOs and CEOs often hesitate to invest in technology for design, channeling budgets predominantly into operations and post-design optimization. This can impede the adoption of tech solutions that could enhance design efficiency.

Data security is a major concern as companies digitize operations, and rightfully so. Protecting sensitive information becomes crucial, creating a barrier to seamless tech integration in supply chain processes.

Ironically, the focus on technological advancements can overshadow human and environmental aspects, potentially leading to suboptimal integration strategies. Bridging this awareness gap is vital for a holistic and successful infusion of technology into SCND.

Triple Bottom Line for SCND

The Triple Bottom Line (TBL) is a sustainability framework that evaluates organizational performance based on three dimensions: people (social), planet (environmental), and profit (economic) (see Figure 3.8). When companies design their supply chain networks with the TBL in mind, they can create systems that balance economic objectives with social and environmental responsibilities.

The impact of SCND on the TBL (see Figure 3.8) as it pertains to people is improved labor conditions by opting for suppliers that offer fair wages, good working conditions, and respect workers' rights. Companies develop partnerships or programs that positively impact the local communities where the company operates. Also, diversity and inclusion can be achieved by prioritizing suppliers that maintain inclusive hiring practices.

When it comes to impacting the planet, companies can lower their carbon footprint by optimizing transportation routes, reducing transportation distances, and choosing eco-friendly transport modes. Waste reduction is possible by optimizing inventory, reducing overproduction, and focusing on circular economy principles. Resource efficiency is gained by sourcing sustainable raw materials, optimizing production processes, and reducing water usage.

All of these can be achieved without compromising profit. Profit comes from cost savings, where sustainable operations often lead to reduced waste, energy use, and resource consumption, which can translate to cost savings. A risk mitigation strategy also aids it by ensuring social and environmental compliance, so that companies can avoid regulatory fines and reputational damage. Finally, companies can get a substantial market differentiation since sustainable practices can be a strong selling point to environmentally conscious consumers.

Processes in SCND for TBL

- **Life Cycle Assessment (LCA):** Evaluating a product's or service's environmental impacts throughout its lifecycle, from raw material extraction to end-of-life.
- **Supplier audits:** Regularly evaluate suppliers for social and environmental compliance.

Figure 3.8 The Triple Bottom Line*

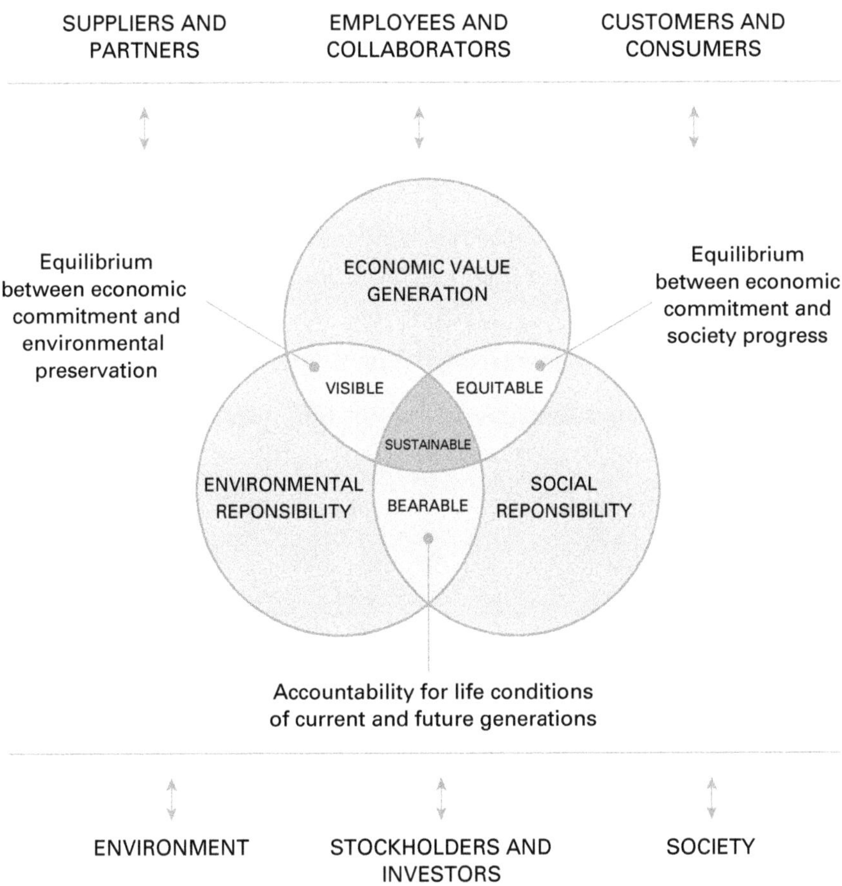

*Santos, R and Marins, F. 'Integrated model for Reverse Logistics Management of Electronic Products and Components'. *Procedia Computer Science*. 2015, 55, 575–585. 10.1016/j.procs.2015.07.047.

SOURCE Adapted from Santos and Marins, 2015

- **Demand forecasting:** Predicting demand accurately to avoid overproduction and waste.
- **Scenario planning:** Evaluating various scenarios to understand the TBL impact of different network designs.

Companies must be aware of the challenges in implementing TBL for SCND. For one, there are higher initial costs, since investing in sustainable technologies or processes might require significant upfront costs. Designing for TBL often adds layers of complexity to decision-making processes. Ensuring sustainability across every supply chain tier can be challenging due to a lack of transparency. Sometimes, there might be trade-offs between the three pillars of TBL, and finding the right balance can be challenging.

Measures of Impact

1. **Carbon footprint:** Measurement of greenhouse gas emissions from supply chain operations.
2. **Water usage:** Total water consumed in the production process.
3. **Waste generation:** Amount of waste produced and percentage recycled.
4. **Social compliance metrics:** Including fair wages, working conditions, and other labor-related metrics.
5. **Economic impact:** Job creation, local economic development, and profitability metrics.

Faculty & Research Case Study

Maria Yee Inc.: Making "Green" Furniture in China

By Glenn Carroll, Maria Shao

2009 | Case No. SI110

Organizational Behavior, Management

Case study: Maria Yee Inc.: Making Green Furniture in China[11]

In 2008, Maria Yee Inc. occupied a unique position as a premium "green" household furniture maker with two direct-owned factories in China and distribution through several large US retailers (see Figure 3.9).

Figure 3.9 Developing Sustainable Furniture

SOURCE USC Marshall-Randall R. Kendrick Global Supply Chain Institute

Yee, a Chinese-born entrepreneur in California, founded her business in 1988 with Asian-inspired designs and Chinese hand joinery techniques. Over the years, she pursued environmentally responsible principles such as using renewable bamboo and eco-certified wood. She believed in being green through thoughtful design and manufacturing, not just marketing.

The company was a leader in environmental initiatives within the furniture industry. But Yee wrestled with expanding and becoming a more mass market while staying true to her green values.

The biggest challenge was staying cost-competitive since environmental innovations such as using eco-certified timber or eco-friendly manufacturing processes tended to cost more. The company experienced problems developing a reliable green supply chain in China for wood, bamboo, and finishes.

It faced the challenge of getting consumers to value the environmental benefits of its products fully. It considered creating greater brand awareness and developing new market segments and distribution channels for its eco-furniture. This case addresses the unique challenges an entrepreneurial company faces in reaching its full potential while advancing its green strategy.

Challenges of TBL

Aligning SCND goals with TBL thinking necessitates a paradigm shift. Sustainable practices might incur higher upfront costs, impacting financial viability. Ensuring fair labor practices and community engagement adds a layer of complexity, as supply chains often span diverse socio-economic landscapes. Balancing the interests of stakeholders while maintaining operational efficiency becomes a delicate balancing act. TBL demands innovative solutions to minimize the ecological footprint, which may clash with traditional cost-centric approaches.

Endnotes

1 Camille. Supply Chain Trends 2023. Expak Logistics, December 8, 2022. expak.com/logistics/blog/supply-chain-trends-for-2023/ (archived at https://perma.cc/PZY8-SXEG)

2 Beckway. A winning strategy for your product portfolio, September 15, 2023. beckway.com/news/?category=beckway-insights&page=1 (archived at https://perma.cc/6PHA-HD58)

3 W Williams and F Mahmoodi. www.supplychainquarterly.com/articles/2109-sku-rationalization-finding-the-right-balance-between-too-many-and-too-few (archived at https://perma.cc/G5U4-J9X3)

4 Inbound Logistics. Cross docking: Definition, history, and process, 29 November 29, 2022. www.inboundlogistics.com/articles/cross-docking/#:~:text=And%20in%20the%201980s%2C%20one,costs%20as%20low%20as%20possible (archived at https://perma.cc/9B5J-3H9K)

5 www.producetraceability.org (archived at https://perma.cc/NE5Z-Z3WB)

6 Cognizant 20-20 insights on Improving Cross-Docking Efficiency in Four Key Areas, 2014. www.slideshare.net/cognizant/improving-crossdocking-efficiency-in-four-key-areas?sf23521873=1 (archived at https://perma.cc/9WPZ-HRJ8)

7 H Kotzab and M Bjerre.(2005) Retailing in a SCM-perspective, Copenhagen Business School Press, Denmark

8 T Dasgupta and D Bhattacharya (2012) Supply Chain Segmentation, EY publication.

9 R Fletcher et al. (2020) Building a flexible supply chain in low-volume, high-mix industrials, McKinsey & Company. www.mckinsey.com/industries/industrials-and-electronics/our-insights/building-a-flexible-supply-chain-in-low-volume-high-mix-industrials (archived athttps://perma.cc/2BA8-996Y)

10 K Petridis. (2017) Optimal design of multi-echelon supply chain networks under normally distributed demand. *Annals of Operations Research* (2017) 227, 63–91. doi.org/10.1007/s10479-013-1420-6 (archived at https://perma.cc/2K8S-FCQ5)

11 G Carroll and M Shao. (2009) Maria Yee Inc.: Making 'Green' Furniture in China, Stanford Graduate School of Business, Case No. SI110, 2009. www.gsb.stanford.edu/faculty-research/case-studies/maria-yee-inc-making-green-furniture-china (archived https://perma.cc/RC6L-BF52)

Intelligent Supply Chain Network Design Models (Multi-dimensional Models) 04

What is Intelligent Supply Chain Network Design?

At the end of 2015, many "returns" of large-screen televisions of a large e-commerce site's customers were marked "D/D," standing for "defective" and/or "damaged." This required a deep dive into consumer sentiment analysis using natural language processing technology, which helped the customer experience systems team identify several root causes. One such analysis showed that every time a large-screen television set traveled more than 500 miles, the probability of damage increased exponentially. One of the decisions to reduce such long-distance travel was to redesign the network throughout North America. How to do this? Should they build new warehouses and shut down others not within the desired distance? That would have cost them more than the benefit of having happy customers!

This was done intelligently. Large-screen TV inventory was relocated to fulfillment centers that covered areas with high demand within 500 miles of at least one fulfillment center. In this case, the network design team did not have to build a new fulfillment center but allocate products to the existing ones with additional capabilities of handling heavy and bulky products. A systemic change and several other countermeasures such as "over boxing" a TV set, photos of shipments where the sets were confirmed to be erect, and inbound shipment verification worked together to drastically reduce the defective and damaged sets.

Data-driven assessments comprising mining consumer sentiments, tracking evolving demand and supply locations, and adding insights from logistics and distribution practices work together in designing or re-designing an "intelligent" supply chain network. The term "intelligence" here refers to data-driven actionable insights starting with the customer and working backward, as one of the fundamental Amazon Leadership Principles prescribes.

If we expand the idea to a post-pandemic disrupted global supply chain, several ideas emerge:

- Smart supply chain network models are multi-dimensional.
- Demand is multi-dimensional.
- Describing a product is multi-dimensional. For example, a beverage company needs to view its products from all of its products (beverages), group (soft drinks, iced teas, and juices), subgroup (cola, ginger ale, root beer), and product (cola 16oz, light cola 16oz, cola 32oz, diet cola 32oz, etc.) lens, but also through its packaging type (glass or can), size (16, 32, or 48 ounces), and style (diet or regular). Each product type has different demands based on geographic location, demographics, ethnography, local culture, and purchase habits.
- Describing time is multi-dimensional. One may plan yearly, quarterly, monthly, and weekly. For each of these buckets, demand planning and forecasting have different levels of challenges. Additionally, the demand planning reality is that various people

work in various corporate and product dimensions, in various time increments, using different data, and creating different plans. These "people" need to collaborate, requiring a multi-dimensional environment.

- The marketing and sales teams need to view data with growth trends, promotions, new product introductions, competitive products in the market by category, retailer strategy, and consumer behavior patterns. The management team looks at demand at an aggregated level to make financial plan adjustments and invest in additional resources, while coming out of markets with a dead end.
- Supporting a demand planning collaboration is like solving a Rubik's cube on the fly. Figure 4.1 shows the dimensions from several angles.

Due to additional network complexities, this framework must be dynamically updated with continually changing trends. Based on several dimensions of demand characteristics by demographic, ethnographic, and psychographic profiles and the unmet and changing needs of customers or end-consumers, ongoing tracking is a crucial need of the hour. Similarly, supply is affected by many factors, such as changing economies, unprecedented events (such as the pandemic, tsunamis, and earthquakes), and geopolitical events, including wars and policy changes, which impact the availability of products, raw materials, and parts.

Intelligent Network Planning Needs Demand and Supply "Sensing"

Demand sensing is a forecasting approach that uses real-time data by amassing and harnessing volumes of data on consumer buying patterns. Sudden shifts in demand can be captured, and the forecasts and plans can be adjusted accordingly. The first step in implementing demand sensing is to use the most granular historical data available. Big retailers such as Walmart, Target, and others have captured store-by-SKU sales daily across thousands of stores and millions of SKUs,

Figure 4.1 Demand Collaboration is Multi-dimensional

SOURCE USC Marshall-Randall R. Kendrick Global Supply Chain Institute

generating huge volumes of records they share with their suppliers. A "Vendor-Managed inventory" (VMI) program that allows the suppliers to "sense" demand patterns across all of the stores in different regions and replenish stock to "chase the curve" has been in practice since the turn of the century when such computational scalability was possible. The retail-consumer goods ecosystem has been a step ahead in this practice.

The omnipresence of social media allows product manufacturers and retailers to sense the evolving pattern of demand for their products in real time. This is the exciting, fast-growing field of market analysis that almost every brand worth its salt is using not only to sense demand but also to devise product strategy.

Market Sentiment Analysis

When combined with advanced data analytics methodologies, market sentiment analysis empowers businesses to stay ahead of the competition by proactively sensing and responding to changing demand. Leveraging digital technologies like social media, web scraping, mobile apps, and data analytics tools enables us to gain valuable insights into customer sentiments, anticipate market trends, and make data-driven decisions to optimize product offerings and enhance customer satisfaction. It uses techniques like Sentiment Classification, where analysts employ machine learning algorithms such as Naive Bayes, Support Vector Machines, or deep learning models like LSTM for classifying sentiments as positive, negative, or neutral. Aspect-Based Sentiment Analysis, another popular technique, helps analyze sentiments at a granular level, focusing on specific aspects of our products, like features, functionalities, or customer service.

By conducting market sentiment analyses, companies can position themselves to be more agile, customer-centric, and successful in meeting market demand effectively. There are a few steps to do this right.

Data Collection

Businesses employ a multi-pronged approach to gather customer sentiments. For example, they use social media monitoring tools to collect real-time data from platforms like X (formerly Twitter), Facebook,

Instagram, and LinkedIn, keeping track of mentions, comments, hashtags, and user sentiments.

Companies also carry out web scraping to gather data from relevant websites, forums, and online communities where their products are discussed, extracting text data, user reviews, and ratings for sentiment analysis. In addition, they integrate analytics tools into their mobile apps to capture user interactions, feedback, and sentiments related to product usage. Most brands also conduct customer surveys by publishing feedback forms on their website and mobile apps to gather direct feedback on product experiences and sentiments.

Text Preprocessing

Text preprocessing, a crucial method in natural language processing (NLP), refines data for analysis. This involves techniques like tokenization, which breaks down text data into individual words or tokens; stop word removal, used to eliminate common words like "the," "and", "is" to focus on meaningful content; lemmatization and stemming to convert words to their base form, reducing inflections and improving analysis accuracy; and building a sentiment lexicon specific to the products that contains positive and negative words related to the offerings. These techniques, among others not mentioned here, help to clean, and prepare the data for effective analysis.

Data Visualization

Data visualization uses visual elements to represent data. It involves transforming large and small data sets into visuals that are easy to understand and process for humans. Using data visualization tools, one can quickly identify any outliers, patterns, or trends in the data. Word clouds and sentiment trends are two popular techniques used in data visualization. Word clouds are used to visualize frequent words and their sentiment polarities. On the other hand, sentiment trends create line charts or heatmaps to visualize sentiment trends over time, helping identify shifts in demand sentiment.

Demand Prediction

As the name suggests, demand prediction helps analysts estimate the future demand for a product or service. Further, it helps companies optimize their supply chain and inventory management. Time series analysis and machine learning models are two popular demand prediction methods. Time series analysis utilizes time series forecasting models like ARIMA (Autoregressive Integrated Moving Average) or Prophet to predict future demand trends based on sentiment insights. Machine learning models combine sentiment data, sales history, and external factors like seasonality and market trends to build demand prediction models.

Real-Time Monitoring

Real-term monitoring for market sentiment analysis involves using interactive dashboards and alerting systems to monitor real-time sentiment and demand patterns. Dashboards create interactive visualizations that allow stakeholders to monitor market sentiment and demand in real time. On the other hand, an alerting system is used to notify stakeholders of sudden changes in market sentiment or demand patterns.

Figure 4.2 shows the processes and technology architecture involved in managing marketing decision-making with Sentiment Analysis, with an evaluation of the main product features using text data mining.

Market sentiment analysis for consumer segmentation, targeting, and product positioning

For both B2B and B2C companies, data engineers wrangle the data obtained from multiple sources. Their job includes building data pipelines, cleaning the data, detecting outliers, transforming the data, categorizing it, and other techniques—an arduous process where data engineers usually spend most of their time. They deliver a "perfect rectangle," i.e., a table with thousands, and sometimes millions, of consumer "observations" in the rows, with several "feature variables" in columns.

Then comes the task of "feature engineering," a critical step in the machine learning pipeline that involves transforming raw data into informative features (or variables) that better represent the underlying patterns in the data, thus improving the performance of a machine learning model.

Figure 4.2 The Proposed Architecture using Sentiment Analysis (SA) and Text Data Mining to Identify the Main Positive/Negative Product Features

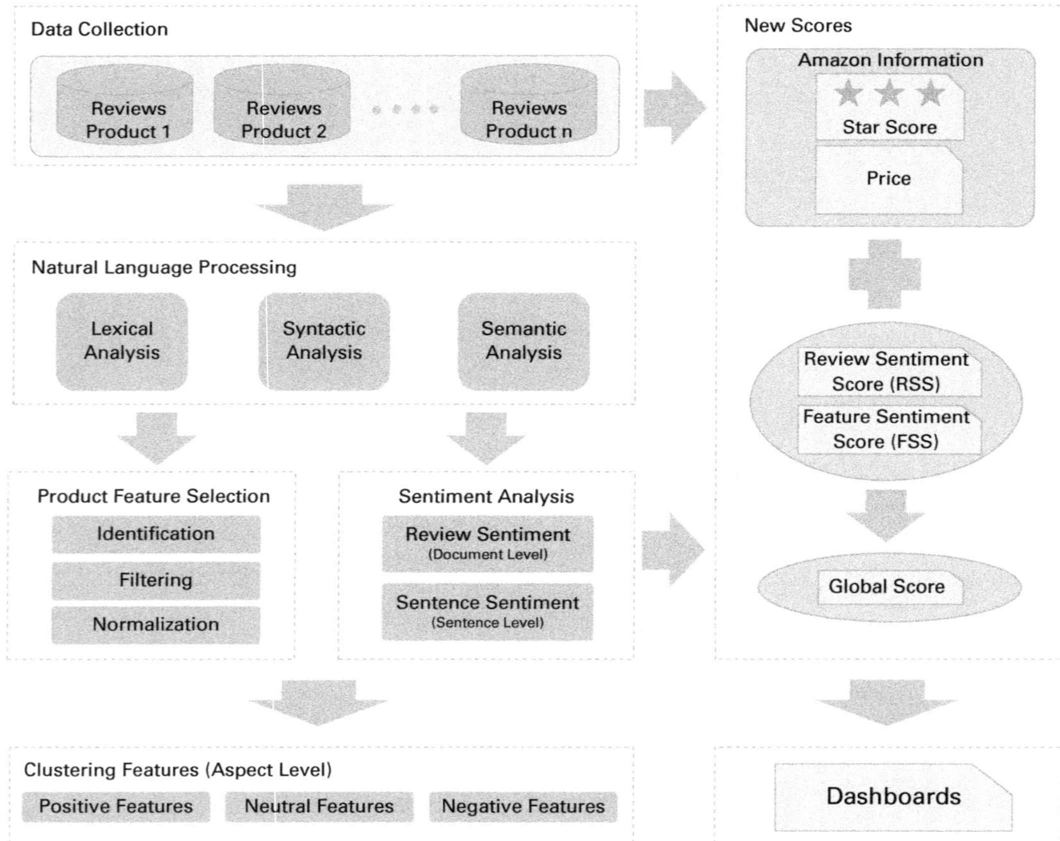

SOURCE Kauffman et al.

Effective feature engineering often requires domain knowledge. For example, if you're working with time series data, you might create features that capture seasonality, trends, or cycles which a standard model wouldn't inherently recognize. A step in studying the data would be the exercise of dimensionality reduction. Techniques like Principal Component Analysis (PCA) can reduce the number of features while retaining most information.

Typically, when the data set is ready for analysis, data scientists use one or more "clustering techniques" to form "segments" of consumers with similar needs and wants, who would now need to be targeted for building a media audience where digital marketing will reach them with the right message at the right time to generate demand.

Figure 4.3 is a diagrammatic representation of how segmentation, targeting, and positioning add value to a firm.

Intelligent Network Designs Track and Plan for Weather and Natural Disasters

Planning and designing a supply chain network to protect against disruptions caused by weather and natural disasters requires a comprehensive and resilient approach. Following are some critical steps and strategies to consider.

Risk Assessment and Mapping

Intelligent network design entails conducting a thorough risk assessment to identify potential weather-related and natural disaster risks in the regions where your supply chain operates. One needs to map out areas prone to hurricanes, earthquakes, floods, wildfires, and other potential hazards. Understanding the specific risks will help in developing targeted mitigation strategies.

Diversification of Suppliers and Facilities

An intelligent approach means avoiding heavy reliance on a single supplier or manufacturing facility. One must distribute production and sourcing across multiple locations to minimize the impact of

Figure 4.3 Market Segments may Require Different SCND to Address Different Customer Profiles

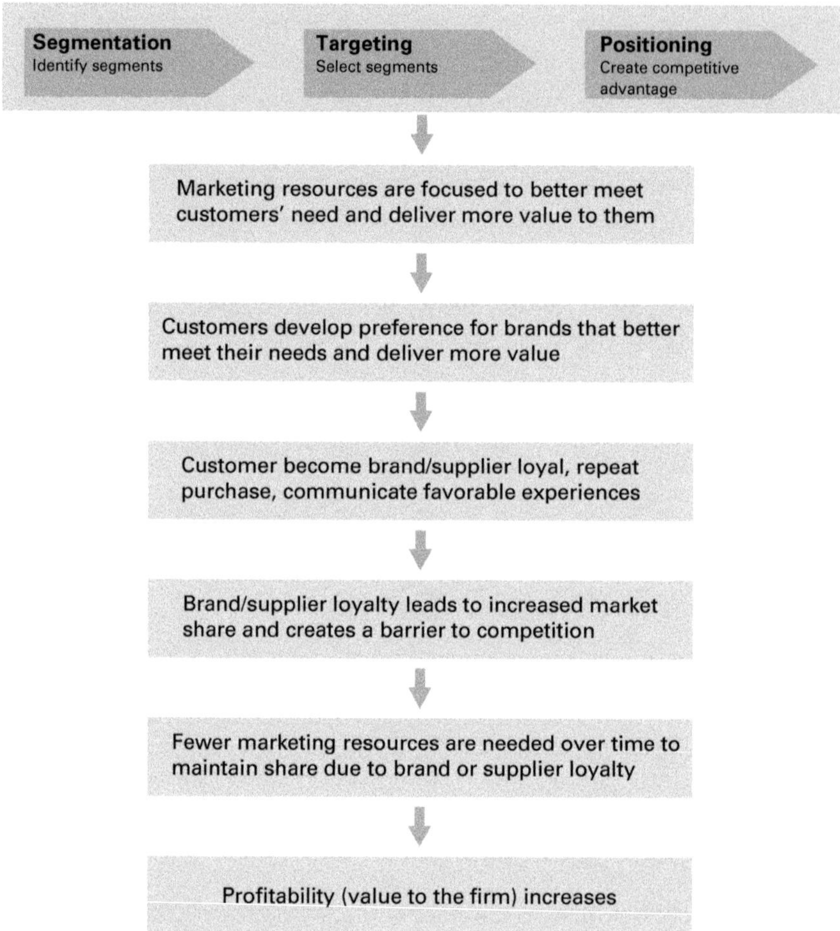

SOURCE Lilien & Rangaswamy, Marketing Engineering

disruptions in any single region. This diversification spreads risk and ensures continuity of supply.

Redundancy and Safety Stock

Maintaining safety stock levels for critical components and finished goods in different geographic locations is a critical part of intelligent network design. Redundancy in inventory can buffer against delays caused by weather-related disruptions, allowing for continued operations during recovery periods.

Transportation and Logistics Contingencies

An intelligent SCND builds in multiple transportation routes and carriers to provide flexibility during disasters. It provides sufficient scope for collaboration with logistics partners to create contingency plans for alternative transportation modes and rerouting options in case of road closures or transportation disruptions.

Communication and Collaboration

An intelligent SCND is communicative. It comprises a strong communication and collaboration network with suppliers, partners, and customers. Real-time information exchange during disasters can help coordinate responses and identify potential supply chain disruptions.

Resilient Infrastructure and Facilities

It contains the necessary tools for evaluating the resilience of supply chain facilities and distribution centers against potential natural disasters. Consider constructing facilities with reinforced structures and strategic locations to reduce susceptibility to damage.

Weather Monitoring and Predictive Analytics

Investments in advanced weather monitoring systems and predictive analytics is crucial. Early detection of weather-related events can provide valuable lead time to implement contingency plans and prepare for potential disruptions.

Disaster Recovery and Business Continuity Planning

The intelligent SCND learns from disruptions. It follows a comprehensive disaster recovery and business continuity plan. Identify critical processes, personnel, and resources needed to resume operations quickly after a disruption. Regularly test and update these plans to ensure effectiveness.

Insurance and Risk Transfer

Developers of intelligent SCND consider appropriate insurance coverage to protect against financial losses caused by weather-related disruptions and natural disasters. It pays to have options for risk transfer to minimize the financial impact on your supply chain.

Environmental Sustainability

A crucial component of intelligent SCND is adoption of environmentally sustainable practices to reduce carbon footprint and improve overall climate resilience.

Continuous Monitoring and Improvement

Regularly monitoring and evaluating the effectiveness of one's supply chain resilience strategies is a primary task. One must assess lessons learned from past disruptions and incorporate improvements into future planning.

By integrating these strategies, businesses can build a robust and adaptable supply chain network better equipped to withstand and recover from disruptions caused by weather and natural disasters. A resilient supply chain network enhances customer satisfaction, reduces costs, and fosters long-term sustainability.

Intelligent Network Designs Plan for Sensing Demand for Social Events

Social, commercial, and other events influence sales for the consumer product. These events could include holidays, festivals, trade shows, product launches, celebrity endorsements, social media campaigns, and more. Network designers must identify specific events of interest and determine their impact on consumer behavior and purchasing patterns. It begins with collecting historical sales data for the consumer product to identify trends and patterns, and analyzing sales data during and after events to measure the impact. Firms can also conduct surveys of customers to gather insights into their purchasing behavior during specific events to understand their motivations, preferences, and buying decisions.

A vast amount of data is available today to utilize social media listening tools to track conversations and mentions related to the consumer product during events. Planners can analyze sentiment and engagement levels to gauge the product's popularity. Marketing and sales could join the supply chain team to attend social and commercial events where the consumer product is promoted or exhibited, and observe customer reactions and interactions to assess the product's appeal.

Statistical techniques can be used to analyze sales data, correlate it with specific events, and measure the impact of events on sales volume, revenue, and customer acquisition. In parallel, planners can analyze survey responses and customer feedback to understand the emotional and psychological factors driving purchases during events.

Once actionable insights are available on the potential impact of these events, the marketing team can develop targeted marketing strategies to leverage the impact of events and align promotional campaigns with events to maximize exposure and engagement. This plan can now be shared with the supply chain team so that they can optimize inventory management based on event-driven demand patterns to ensure sufficient stock availability during peak sales periods.

Finally, continuous monitoring of sales performance and customer feedback during events can help planners assess the effectiveness of implemented strategies.

Global Economic Influences on Supply Chain Network Planning and Design

The ever-evolving global economy plays a significant role in shaping supply chain network planning and design. Factors such as commodity price shifts, consumer confidence, inflation, and other economic indicators can create business challenges and opportunities. This section of the book chapter delves into how these economic influences impact supply chain decision-making, emphasizing the importance of adaptability and resilience in modern supply chain networks.

Commodity Price Shifts

Commodity price fluctuations directly impact the cost of raw materials and resources throughout the supply chain. Sudden changes in commodity prices can disrupt sourcing strategies, affecting production costs and profitability. To mitigate these risks, supply chain planners must monitor commodity markets closely, engage in hedging strategies, and maintain alternative sourcing options to cushion the impact of price shifts.

Consumer Confidence

Consumer confidence is a key indicator of economic health and profoundly influences demand patterns. During periods of low consumer confidence, consumer spending may decrease, resulting in reduced product demand. This can lead to excess inventory and strained cash flow in the supply chain. Supply chain planners should prioritize demand forecasting accuracy, inventory optimization, and agile production capabilities to respond effectively to fluctuating consumer sentiment.

Inflation

Inflation affects the cost of goods and services, impacting the supply chain's input and output prices. Rising inflation can lead to higher production costs, squeezing business profit margins. Supply chain network planners must consider inflationary pressures while negotiating contracts, setting pricing strategies, and implementing cost-containment measures.

Exchange Rates and Currency Fluctuations

In a globalized economy, supply chain networks often span multiple countries with varying currencies. Exchange rate fluctuations can significantly impact import and export costs, affecting the competitiveness of products in international markets. Supply chain designers should consider currency risk management strategies, such as currency hedging and localized sourcing, to minimize the effects of exchange rate volatility.

Trade Policies and Tariffs

Changes in trade policies and tariffs can create uncertainties in supply chain networks, especially for businesses engaged in international trade. Supply chain planners need to closely monitor geopolitical developments, anticipate policy changes, and evaluate the impact of tariffs on sourcing decisions and transportation costs.

Economic Growth and Market Expansion

Economic growth in emerging markets presents opportunities for expanding supply chain networks. Supply chain designers should assess new infrastructure requirements, potential risks, and regulatory compliance as markets expand to ensure seamless operations in new regions.

In an interconnected global economy, supply chain network planning and design must consider various economic influences, such as commodity price shifts, consumer confidence, inflation, and trade policies. By proactively understanding and responding to these economic factors, businesses can build resilient and adaptable supply chains that can withstand economic fluctuations and capitalize on emerging opportunities. Supply chain planners should leverage data analytics, advanced forecasting techniques, and scenario planning to optimize network design and make informed decisions to maintain competitiveness in a dynamic global market.

Intelligent Network Designs are Aware of the Political Climate

The political climate in markets can significantly influence the demand for products. Political factors such as changes in government policies, regulations, trade agreements, and geopolitical tensions can directly impact consumer behavior, market dynamics, and supply chain operations. Here's how the political climate can influence product demand and how to plan for supply chain preparedness:

1. Regulatory Changes and Compliance

Political decisions regarding regulations and compliance requirements can impact product specifications, labeling, safety standards, and import/export procedures. Regulation changes may require product modifications or adjustments to meet new standards, affecting demand patterns. Supply chain planners should closely monitor regulatory developments, engage with relevant authorities, and have contingency plans to respond quickly to new requirements.

2. Trade Policies and Tariffs

Political decisions on trade policies, tariffs, and international trade agreements can affect the cost and availability of products in global markets. Imposition of tariffs or trade agreement changes can impact product competitiveness, leading to shifts in demand patterns. Supply chain preparedness involves diversifying sourcing strategies, identifying alternative suppliers, and considering localized production to mitigate risks associated with trade policy changes.

3. Geopolitical Tensions

International trade environments do not exist in isolation. When two or more economies exchange goods and services, they encounter each other's cultural values, ethical conduct, and political beliefs. The political climate and shifting patterns will strongly impact supply chain operations and distribution channels. Such uncertainties can lead to consumer apprehensions and alter demand for products in affected markets.

Geopolitical tensions between the US and China in recent years, for example, have significantly impacted global supply chains. The US has imposed tariffs on Chinese goods, which has led to a shift in the global supply chain, forcing many companies to consider reconfiguring their global supply chain to reduce their dependence on China. The Russia–Ukraine war has had a similar impact on global energy supply chain networks.

Therefore, building a resilient supply chain network means considering the impact of geopolitical climate on the network design and building redundancies into supply chain networks for businesses that should help supply chain actors reorient their activities to respond to sudden shifts in political climate. These strategies include diversifying their supplier base, mapping politically agnostic manufacturing locations, and creating room for investments in technology that can help them monitor and respond to political uncertainties, establish robust risk management protocols, and create contingency plans to ensure continuity of supply during challenging times.

4. Consumer Sentiment and Political Events

Political events like elections or policy debates can influence consumer sentiment and purchasing behavior. Uncertainty surrounding political developments may lead to cautious spending or changes in consumer preferences. Supply chain preparedness requires demand forecasting models that account for political events and sentiment, enabling agile responses to shifting consumer behavior.

5. Environmental Policies and Sustainability

Political actions addressing environmental concerns, such as emission regulations or sustainable practices, can influence the demand for eco-friendly products. Consumers increasingly prioritize sustainability, and supply chain planners should incorporate environmental considerations into product development and sourcing strategies.

6. Crisis and Emergency Preparedness

Political instability, protests, or natural disasters can disrupt supply chain operations and distribution networks. Preparedness planning involves identifying potential risks, establishing robust communication channels with suppliers and partners, and designing flexible supply chain networks that adapt to disruptions.

The market political climate can significantly influence product demand by impacting regulations, trade policies, consumer sentiment, and supply chain operations. Supply chain preparedness involves proactive monitoring of political developments, scenario planning, and risk assessment to navigate changing market dynamics effectively. Businesses should prioritize agility, flexibility, and data-driven decision-making to ensure their supply chains remain resilient and responsive to the evolving political landscape. By aligning supply chain strategies with political realities, companies can enhance their competitiveness and better serve the needs of their customers.

Building Resilient and Agile Supply Chains with Intelligent Network Designs

In a world characterized by volatility, uncertainty, complexity, and ambiguity, supply chain resilience and agility have become paramount for businesses aiming to thrive. The global COVID-19 pandemic highlighted the vulnerabilities in many supply chains, emphasizing the need for companies to rethink and reinvent their supply chain strategies. Building a resilient and agile supply chain involves robust processes, cutting-edge technology, skilled human capital, and conducive government policies. Let's delve into these areas.

Processes

To ensure the smooth functioning of the supply chain, companies need to take several key steps. Firstly, they should conduct regular risk assessments to identify any potential vulnerabilities in their supply chains. This involves evaluating supplier dependencies, geographic concentration, and transportation bottlenecks.

Secondly, companies should diversify their supplier base instead of relying on a single supplier or a particular geographic region. By sourcing from multiple suppliers, companies can ensure that a disruption in one area does not jeopardize the entire supply chain.

Thirdly, adopting a just-in-case inventory strategy instead of just-in-time can help provide a buffer against disruptions. Although this might increase holding costs, the trade-off for resilience can be worth it.

Fourth, companies should enhance collaboration with suppliers, customers, and logistics providers. Sharing data and insights across the supply chain increases visibility and helps quickly detect and respond to any disruptions.

Technology

To create strong supply chains, companies need to leverage advanced technologies. One such technology is the IoT, which uses sensors and devices to track products in real time and gather data on factors such as temperature, humidity, and the origin of components and raw materials. It is particularly useful for maintaining the quality of environmentally sensitive products, especially in industries like food and pharmaceuticals.

Blockchain is another technology that, along with IoT, is proving to be a game-changer for supply chain transparency, providing an unassailable record of transactions that prevents fraud and ensures product authenticity.

The powerful duo of AI and ML can help organizations sift through mountains of data to predict and prevent hiccups. Likewise, a technology like Digital Twin lets companies visualize potential pitfalls and strategize accordingly. Plus, it doubles as a testing ground for new products and processes before they hit the real deal.

We will dive deeper into the various emerging technologies to harness intelligent network design in Chapter 5.

Human Capital

Continuous training is essential in ensuring that employees are well-equipped to handle and respond to disruptions in the supply chain. Encouraging cross-functional teams is another effective way of addressing supply chain challenges. By involving members from different departments, such as logistics, procurement, sales, and finance, companies can benefit from diverse perspectives and a holistic approach to problem-solving.

Moreover, cultivating a leadership culture that values resilience and agility is crucial in ensuring that the importance of a flexible supply chain is understood and prioritized at the highest levels. This helps create an organizational environment that proactively seeks to identify potential supply chain disruptions and is prepared to respond to them quickly and effectively.

Government's Role and its Trade-related Policies

Governments have a crucial role to play in promoting international trade. One way they can do this is by investing in the development of robust transportation and communication infrastructures that ensure the smooth movement of goods. Another important step is to establish transparent and stable trade policies that help businesses plan their supply chains. Sudden tariff changes or trade bans can cause significant disruptions to established chains, which is why predictability is so important.

In addition, governments can act as facilitators, promoting public–private partnerships or collaboration between businesses from different countries. This can help to foster cross-border cooperation and create new business opportunities. Further, harmonizing regulations across different countries is crucial to making it easier for companies to navigate the complexities of international trade, especially in sectors like pharmaceuticals or food. By aligning regulations, businesses can more easily meet standards and comply with regulations, which can lead to more efficient and effective trade relationships.

In conclusion, while no supply chain can be entirely immune to disruptions, a blend of processes, technology, human capital investment, and supportive government policies can ensure they are both agile and resilient. By proactively addressing these areas, businesses can weather disruptions and gain a competitive advantage in the marketplace.

Harnessing Emerging Technologies in Supply Chain Network Design

05

With all the rapid advancements in artificial intelligence (AI), can we not sit back and let it design supply chain networks? Good question. Organizations have begun to use AI typically in combination with other emerging technologies such as blockchain, the Internet of Things (IoT), cloud computing, and data analytics to optimize operational efficiency and costs of supply chain networks.[1] A McKinsey report highlighting the uses of AI in supply chains found that early adopters of AI-enabled supply-chain management solutions saw improvements in logistics costs by 15% inventory levels by 35%, and service levels by 65%, compared with their slower-moving competitors. The report further noted that demand planning and inventory management areas have been transformed by integrating machine learning (an AI application), IoT, and data analytics.[2]

Still, a one-word answer to the question posed at the beginning of the chapter is no. The reason is that AI and other emerging technologies can help super-efficient design supply chain networks, but the task of supply chain network design (SCND) requires—and will do so going by the evidence—a strong component of human intelligence based on domain and field knowledge, experience, and imagination. This is for a simple reason: supply chain networks must be designed to operate and succeed in unconstrained ecosystems while navigating human-made errors, inefficiencies, uncertainties, and unpredictable changes in the socio-economic environments.

Analysts do have an approximation of the order of the respective roles that technology and humans need to play to design an effective SCDN. The example of Unilever's "perfect supply chain network" modelling has shown that about 80% of a supply chain network's value can be designed with the help of technological tools and available data, and the other 20% by factoring in the human and environmental constraints.[3] This is good news for tech-savvy firms. This means that with improved connectivity and, therefore, a greater availability of data, the role of technology in the design of effective, resilient, and agile networks will only increase.

Becoming Resilient and Agile in Supply Chain Network Planning and Design

In today's dynamic and unpredictable business landscape, supply chain resilience and agility have become imperative for organizations to thrive. To navigate disruptions, uncertainties, and rapidly changing market demands, supply chain planners and designers must embrace new processes, technology, and human capital while being mindful of domestic and international trade environments. This section explores the critical strategies for building a resilient and agile supply chain network.

1. Leveraging New Processes

a. Risk Management Adopt a proactive approach to identify and mitigate potential risks in the supply chain. Implement risk assessment tools, conduct scenario planning, and establish robust risk management protocols to effectively anticipate and respond to disruptions.

Supply chain risk management identifies, assesses, and mitigates potential threats and uncertainties that may affect the supply chain's performance, continuity, and resilience. These can arise from various sources, such as natural disasters, geopolitical conflicts, cyberattacks, supplier failures, demand fluctuations, regulatory changes, and operational disruptions. These risks can significantly impact the supply chain's efficiency, effectiveness, agility, sustainability, and the organization's reputation, profitability, and competitiveness.

Therefore, supply chain managers need to adopt a proactive approach to identify and mitigate potential risks in the supply chain rather than reacting to them after they occur. A proactive approach involves anticipating and preparing for various scenarios and contingencies, implementing risk assessment tools and protocols, and establishing robust risk management strategies and plans.

One of the key steps in adopting a proactive approach is to identify and prioritize the critical driving forces and uncertainties that may affect the supply chain in the future. These driving forces can be internal or external, positive, or negative, predictable, or unpredictable. They include customer preferences, market trends, technological innovations, environmental issues, social movements, political events, legal regulations, and ethical standards. Identifying these driving forces can help supply chain managers understand the current and future context of their operations and recognize the opportunities and threats that may arise from them.

To identify and prioritize the driving forces, supply chain managers can use various methods and tools, such as PESTEL analysis (political, economic, social, technological, environmental, and legal), SWOT analysis (strengths, weaknesses, opportunities, and threats), Porter's five forces analysis (industry rivalry, bargaining power of suppliers and buyers, threat of new entrants and substitutes), stakeholder analysis (identifying and assessing the interests and expectations of key stakeholders), and risk matrix (assessing the likelihood and impact of each risk). These methods and tools can help supply chain managers systematically scan their supply chain operations' external and internal environment and prioritize the most relevant and significant driving forces based on their potential impact on the supply chain objectives.

Another essential step in adopting a proactive approach is to conduct scenario planning for the supply chain. Scenario planning creates plausible stories or narratives about how the future may unfold based on different combinations of driving forces and uncertainties.

Scenario planning can help supply chain managers explore multiple possible futures for their operations and test the robustness and flexibility of their current strategies and plans under different conditions. Scenario planning can help supply chain managers identify early warning signs or indicators of emerging risks or opportunities and develop contingency plans or actions for each scenario.

To conduct scenario planning for the supply chain, supply chain managers can use various methods and tools, such as scenario matrix (creating a two-by-two matrix based on two key uncertainties or driving forces), scenario funnel (creating a hierarchy of scenarios based on different levels of uncertainty or detail), scenario cross-impact analysis (assessing the interrelationships and influences among different driving forces or scenarios), scenario simulation (using mathematical models or software to simulate the outcomes or impacts of different scenarios), and scenario storytelling (using narratives or visualizations to describe each scenario in detail). These methods and tools can help supply chain managers generate diverse and realistic scenarios for their supply chain operations and communicate them effectively to their stakeholders.

A third essential step in adopting a proactive approach is to establish robust risk management protocols for the supply chain. Risk management protocols (see Figure 5.1) are the policies, procedures, standards, guidelines, roles, and responsibilities. To establish robust risk management protocols for the supply chain, supply chain managers need to define and document the policies, procedures, standards, guidelines, roles, and responsibilities governing identifying, assessing, and mitigating supply chain risks. These elements should align with the organization's overall risk management framework and objectives and the relevant laws, regulations, and industry best practices.

Some critical steps to establish robust risk management protocols for the supply chain are:

- Develop a supply chain risk management **policy** that outlines the scope, purpose, objectives, principles, and roles of supply chain risk management within the organization. The policy should also specify the supply chain's risk appetite, tolerance, thresholds, and reporting and escalation mechanisms for supply chain risk issues.

- Establish a supply chain risk management **process** that describes the steps and activities involved in identifying, analyzing, evaluating, treating, monitoring, and reviewing supply chain risks. The process should also define the criteria and methods for prioritizing and categorizing supply chain risks and the tools and techniques for assessing and mitigating them.
- Define a supply chain risk management **standard** that sets the minimum requirements and expectations for managing supply chain risks across the organization. The standard should also provide guidance and best practices for implementing and maintaining effective supply chain risk management practices and controls.
- Create a supply chain risk management **guideline** that provides detailed instructions and examples for applying the supply chain risk management policy, process, and standards in different situations and scenarios. The guidelines should include templates and checklists for documenting and reporting supply chain risk information and actions.
- Assign a supply chain risk management **role** responsible for overseeing and coordinating the organization's supply chain risk management activities. The role should also have the authority and accountability for ensuring compliance with the supply chain risk management policy, process, standard, and guideline.
- Allocate a supply chain risk management **responsibility** assigned to each function, department, unit, or individual involved in the supply chain operations. The responsibility should also specify the tasks and duties each entity or person must perform concerning managing supply chain risks.

b. Demand Sensing Utilize advanced data analytics and market intelligence to sense real-time demand patterns. By understanding consumer behavior, businesses can optimize inventory, production, and distribution strategies to meet changing demands.

Demand sensing techniques include various approaches to effectively anticipate and respond to market needs. One method involves analyzing real-time point-of-sale (POS) data, extracting valuable

Figure 5.1 Supply Chain Risk Management Protocols

SOURCE USC Marshall- Randall R. Kendrick Global Supply Chain Institute

insights to adjust inventory levels promptly. Media monitoring is another avenue where one follows the news and social media activity and sentiment to discern emerging trends and shifts in consumer behavior that could influence demand. Additionally, incorporating weather data, including forecasts and historical information, aids in predicting the impact of weather events on demand patterns. Economic indicators, such as GDP growth, unemployment rates, and consumer confidence, are also used to forecast changes in demand. Employing machine learning algorithms further enhances the process by scrutinizing extensive datasets, and identifying pertinent patterns, trends, and relationships contributing to accurate demand predictions.

c. Lean and Agile Practices Combine lean principles with agile methodologies to optimize supply chain efficiency and flexibility. Streamlining processes and minimizing waste enables organizations to respond quickly to market fluctuations and customer demands.

Large organizations continually use a combination of lean and agile practices in supply chain management for efficiency improvements. Toyota, for example, is known for its lean manufacturing system, which focuses on reducing waste and increasing efficiency. The company uses agile practices to respond quickly to changes in demand and customer preferences. Consumer goods companies such as Proctor & Gamble and Unilever use lean practices to streamline their supply chain operations and reduce costs. The companies also use agile practices to respond quickly to changes in demand and customer preferences.[4]

2. Embracing New Technologies

Fast-advancing technology has made supply chain management highly competitive. Advanced analytics, machine learning algorithms, and the IoT have enabled companies to capture real-time data and generate short-term and mid-term forecasts based on the current realities of the supply chain. This has allowed companies to adjust their demand plans and inventory levels with more accurate demand forecasting, enhanced customer satisfaction, reduced inventory costs, and improved agility. Companies that adopt these technologies are more likely to gain a competitive edge over their peers. Slow technology adopters, on the other hand, are almost always sure to lose profitability and market share.[5]

a. Supply Chain Visibility Invest in advanced technologies such as IoT sensors, RFID, and blockchain to enhance supply chain visibility. Real-time tracking and traceability enable better decision-making, faster issue resolution, and increased transparency.

Consider how Amazon employs advanced analytics and machine learning algorithms to enhance its supply chain efficiency and visibility. The company leverages real-time data to monitor inventory levels, track demand patterns, and foresee future demand. Similarly, Walmart and Coca-Cola utilize IoT devices to monitor the location and condition of their products throughout the supply chain. This proactive approach enables these companies to pinpoint bottlenecks and inefficiencies and take corrective actions.[6]

b. Predictive Analytics Leverage predictive analytics and machine learning algorithms to forecast demand, optimize inventory, and anticipate potential disruptions. Data-driven insights empower organizations to address challenges and capitalize on opportunities proactively.

c. Automation and Robotics Integrate automation and robotics into warehousing and manufacturing processes to increase productivity, reduce lead times, and minimize reliance on manual labor.

Amazon uses robotics and automation in fulfillment, deploying over 750,000 robots worldwide, according to a June 2023 statement.[7] This makes Amazon one of the world's most significant users of industrial robots. The company utilizes advanced analytics, machine learning, and AR to optimize its supply chain, enhance visibility, and improve efficiency. Amazon's latest robots – including the autonomous mobile robot Proteus – handling systems Cardinal and Sparrow, and containerized storage for ergonomic product delivery operate seamlessly alongside its warehouse staff.[8] This integration of cutting-edge technology enables Amazon to minimize waste, boost efficiency, and enhance operational safety.

3. Developing Human Capital

The supply chain continues to be (and will likely be in the future) one of the few organizational functions primarily driven by people. The multitude of suppliers, services providers, and strategists help maintain the flow of goods through manmade and natural constraints and uncertainties, which is the reason the development of human capital is the most crucial aspect of supply chain network design.

a. Talent Development Nurture a culture of continuous learning and professional development within the supply chain team. Equip employees with the necessary skills and knowledge to adapt to emerging technologies and evolving market dynamics.

b. Cross-functional Collaboration Encourage cross-functional collaboration between different departments within the organization. Collaboration fosters knowledge sharing, accelerates decision-making, and promotes innovation.

c. Talent Retention and Recruitment Focus on attracting and retaining top talent in the supply chain domain. A skilled and motivated workforce is key to successfully implementing resilience and agility strategies.

4. Government's Role in Trade-Related Policies

The success of supply chain operations significantly hinges on local and international trade policies. Notably, the World Bank Group has pinpointed trade facilitation and logistics as pivotal areas for development policies.[9] Recognizing supply chain constraints as a significant hurdle to export-led growth, this emphasis underscores their critical role. Furthermore, the United Nations Conference on Trade and Development (UNCTAD) emphasizes[10] economic policies that enhance enterprise competitiveness while elevating reliability and efficiency. When designing supply chain networks, organizations must carefully consider the trade policies of the high-income economies of Europe and North America. These policies extend beyond their immediate reach, considering practices and norms, especially about human rights, and environmental sustainability, followed throughout the organizations' international supply networks.

a. Policy Advocacy Engage with government bodies and industry associations to advocate for trade policies that foster a stable and supportive business environment. Collaborating with policymakers allows supply chain stakeholders to voice concerns and influence trade-related decisions.

b. Compliance and Risk Mitigation: Stay informed about changes in trade policies, tariffs, and regulations. Ensure supply chain operations comply with government requirements and develop contingency plans to mitigate risks associated with trade-related uncertainties.

c. Trade Agreements and Alliances Capitalize on favorable trade agreements and alliances between countries to optimize sourcing and distribution strategies. Understanding trade dynamics and market access opportunities is vital for building a resilient and agile supply chain network.

Becoming resilient and agile in supply chain network planning and design is a multifaceted undertaking that requires organizations to embrace new processes, technology, and human capital. Businesses can create a responsive and flexible supply chain by leveraging advanced analytics, cutting-edge technologies, and cross-functional collaboration. Moreover, understanding and complying with government trade-related policies ensures supply chain operations remain compliant and adaptable in an ever-changing global business environment. By adopting a proactive approach and embracing innovation, organizations can build a resilient supply chain that enables them to thrive in the face of uncertainties and capitalize on emerging opportunities.

Evolution of Technology Solutions for Supply Chain Network Design

The enterprise application industry grew with two primary branches – enterprise resource planning (ERP) and supply chain management (SCM), with the latter being further divided into planning and execution (SCP and SCE). ERP companies marketed solutions for recording and accessing functional transactional data using a single relational database and user interface. SCP solutions were associated with demand, transportation, supply, and manufacturing planning. Major players were i2, Manugistics, Numetrix, Ilog, and Logility. SCE solutions were associated with execution tasks such as warehouse, transportation, and order management. Prominent players included IMI, McHugh software, and EXE technologies.

ERP and APS solutions such as SAP, Oracle, i2, all the way through JDA, and Blue Yonder have been written with the classical objective functions of historical demand forecasting accuracy improvement without intelligence on exogenous variables that truly influence demand. So, the focus has been on optimizing inventory levels and reducing lead times. Interestingly, the portfolio of solutions for managing the network in supply chains followed the same trajectory of evolution as the abovementioned processes. It all started within the four walls of a factory where the focus was to make the right products at the right time using minimal resources to ship to customers. As such, the computational task involved was to balance the factory's capacity with the demand and have adequate raw materials to manufacture the product.

As simple as it sounds, while MRP (and MRP-II) could develop material requirements and manufacturing capacity planning, customer demand would change, resource status would shift, and actual material availability would vary. This would require a complete re-planning, which would take a long time to complete, rendering the plan useless over the period. Several technology vendors, including i2 Technologies, came up with "Factory Planner," a tool that would enable companies to quickly synchronize factory production plans and schedules to meet changes in demand. It would assist planners and buyers in creating efficient material plans aligned with factory schedules, thus providing synchronized material flow through the factory. The result was a plan tailored to meet customer delivery requirements and other essential operational and financial objectives.

Among the capabilities for such factory planner solutions were quick identification of potential supply chain problems, feasible procurement and production plans against shop floor and supply chain constraints, accurate due-date quoting to improve customer service, modelling richness to represent a wide range of manufacturing environments and quick "what-if" scenario analysis for effective decision-making. In particular, a "constraint-anchored optimization" capability provided the planner with automated load-balancing algorithms to create an optimal finite-capacity-constrained plan based on various material flow and capacity utilization policies.

Since "demand" at the aggregate level may be accurate, it quickly loses mix-accuracy at a product (stock-keeping unit or SKU) level. A need for multi-party collaboration in the network has been an approach for many companies, and "collaborative demand planning" evolved as a tool that used a combination of historical demand data, causal variables such as planned promotions, and strategic plans to generate and consolidate demand forecasts from different departments and planning units within a manufacturer, as well as external input from customers. Even recently, as this book is being written, NVIDIA has begun engaging with its customers to understand actual demand from the ultimate source of truth, the end-customer, for its GPU chips. Therefore, demand planning (DP) tools were quickly needed to aid this process across the supply chain network.

Supply chain planner (SCP) grew as a tool that includes network players outside the four walls of a factory or organization and across a longer time horizon. A master planning module helped support decisions for an end-to-end supply chain at an aggregate level on when, where, and in what quantities to purchase, produce, store, and ship both intermediate and finished goods to meet customer demand and inventory targets.

The center of gravity (COG) method for creating network design

In SCND, facility location refers to choosing the locations for distribution centers, warehouses, and production facilities to facilitate logistical effectiveness and efficiency. There is strategic importance to facility location and a general process of determining an optimum number of facilities based on factors influencing facility location and specialized location characteristics. Simple grid systems have been used to determine these facility location decisions, further complicated by opening, closing, and relocation decisions. Typically, facilities include sourcing points such as plants, vendors, and ports; intermediate points such as warehouses, terminals, public facilities (such as fire, police, and ambulance stations), and service centers; and sink points such as retail outlets, as well as customers or users.

The key questions to answer are how many facilities there should be, where they should be located, and what size they should be. It is essential because it gives a structure to SCND, significantly affects inventory and transportation costs, and impacts the level of customer service to be achieved.

Known methods of solution are for single warehouse locations and multiple warehouse locations. Traditionally, a graphic or grid method (center of gravity (COG)) approach is taken for a single warehouse location. Companies have taken a simulation approach, optimization algorithms, and heuristics for multiple warehouses. When determining locations for manufacturing (plants and warehouses), the decisions are driven by *economics*. Relevant costs such as transportation, inventory carrying costs, labor, and taxes are traded against each other to find suitable locations. For retail locations, decisions are driven by *revenue*. Traffic flow and resulting revenue are primary location factors; cost is considered after revenue. For service locations, decisions are driven by *service factors*. Response time, accessibility, and availability are key dimensions for locating in the service industry.

SCND has three problem statements: picking the *optimal number, location, and size* of warehouses and/or plants; determining optimal *sourcing* strategy (which plant or vendor should produce which product); and determining best *distribution channels* (i.e. which warehouses should service which customers). The objective is to balance *service level* against production or purchasing costs, inventory carrying costs, facility costs (handling and fixed costs), and transportation costs. In other words, we would like to find a *minimal-annual-cost* distribution network configuration that satisfies product demands at specified *customer service levels*.

To answer how many locations need to be determined, we want to look at the impact of increasing the number of warehouses. For example, we could improve the service level due to a reduction in the average service time to customers. But then, we would increase inventory costs due to larger safety stock quantities. We would also increase overhead and setup costs. We may reduce transportation costs for outbound and increase inbound transportation costs for a specific range. The concept can be represented by Figure 5.2.

Based on industry benchmarks, the number of distribution centers may vary by the characteristics of the product, service, inventory costs, and transportation costs. Figure 5.3 shows a rough schematic based on pharma, food companies, and chemicals or biotech industries.

As shown in earlier chapters, mathematical optimization techniques for determining optimal "single" SCND locations have exact algorithms and heuristics, where we find "good" solutions that are not necessarily optimal. There are Simulation Models as well, which provide a mechanism to evaluate specified design alternatives created by the designer. Determining "multiple" locations is a more complex problem that most firms have. It involves trading off inbound and

Figure 5.2 Location Cost Trade-offs

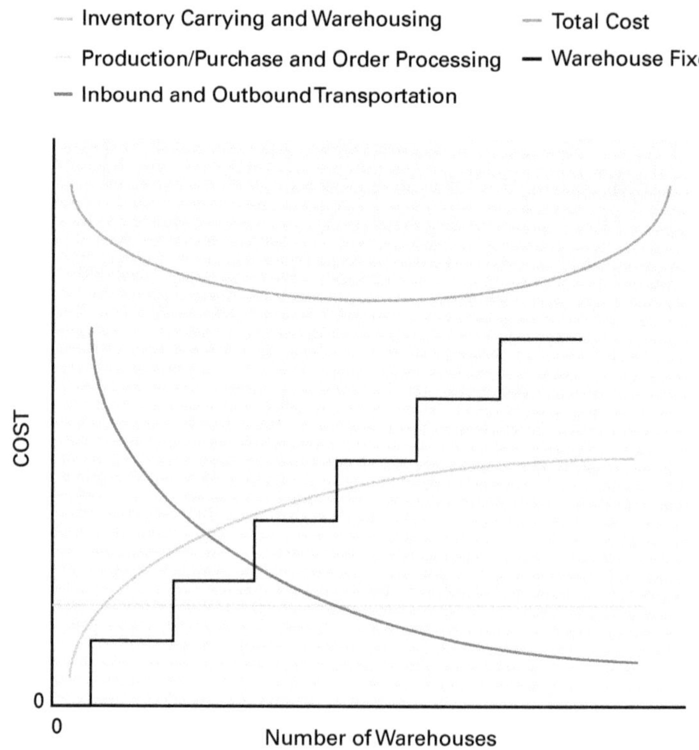

SOURCE USC Marshall-Randall R. Kendrick Global Supply Chain Institute

Figure 5.3 Industry Benchmarks – number of distribution centers

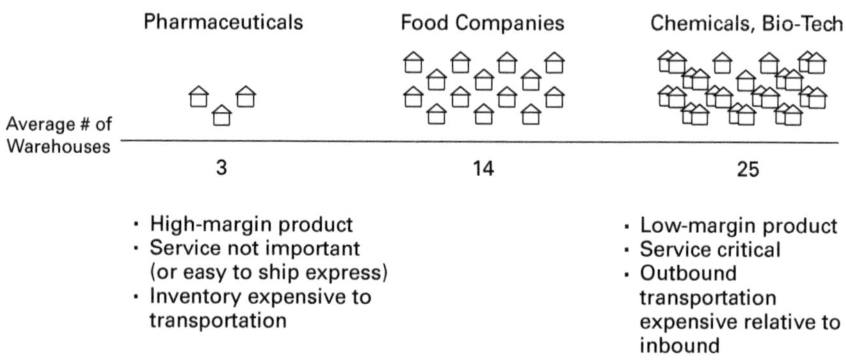

SOURCE CLM 1999, Herbert W. Davis & Co; LogicTools

outbound transportation costs, storage and handling, inventory carrying, production and purchase, and facility fixed costs. The objective function of cost minimization is subject to customer service and facility capacity constraints. Mathematical methods that search for the best combination of facilities to minimize costs and do so within a reasonable computational time and do not require enormous amounts of data for the analysis are popular for this type of problem.

The strategic importance of facility location includes customer or supply market locations, consumer demographics, and psychographics. Consumer demographics change over time, and facilities must chase the movements. Figure 5.4 shows how the five most populous states in the USA changed between the sixties and now:

Facilities are generally added when service levels become unacceptable. Software packages such as Llamasoft, now Coupa, exist to help determine the number and location of facilities. The critical issue is the time it takes from the facility to most of the USA (or target) population. A study by Chicago Consulting showed that moving from two to five facilities saves a day of lead time, while moving from five to 10 facilities saves half a day of lead time.

Natural resources have significant weightage on SCND. While pure material availability is always critical, nuances of product characteristics, such as weight-loss and weight-gaining products, may influence locating a facility. Suppose the materials lose considerable weight in processing, known as weight-losing products. In that case, the processing point should be near where they are mined or harvested, primarily to avoid paying unnecessary transportation charges. The processing point should be close to the market if the raw materi-

Figure 5.4 Changes in US Population Between the Sixties and Now

Rank	1960	1980	2005	2020	2023
1	New York	California	California	California (39.7M)	California (39.2M)
2	California	New York	Texas	Texas (29.0M)	Texas (29.5M)
3	Pennsylvania	Texas	New York	Florida (21.6M)	Florida (21.8M)
4	Illinois	Pennsylvania	Florida	New York (19.5M)	New York (19.8M)
5	Ohio	Illinois	Illinois	Pennsylvania (12.8M)	Pennsylvania (13.0M)

SOURCE USC Marshall-Randall R. Kendrick Global Supply Chain Institute

als, known as weight-gaining products, gain weight in processing. For example, sugar derived from sugar beets is an example of a weight-losing product, whereas bottled soft drinks are a weight-gaining product. Similarly, labor is based on population characteristics. Some companies use maquiladoras (factories) in Mexico, but export the goods to the companies' own countries Sweatshops, right-to-work laws, and expatriate workers are other considerations. The Rana Plaza disaster[11] in Bangladesh comes to mind when such location designs are poorly planned.

The Rana Plaza disaster was one of the worst industrial accidents in history and brought significant attention to the issues of building safety, worker rights, and global supply chains, especially in the garment industry.

On April 24, 2013, the Rana Plaza building in Savar, near Dhaka, Bangladesh, collapsed, killing over 1,100 people, and injuring over 2,500. Many of the victims were garment workers. The Rana Plaza building was initially designed for shops and offices but was converted into factories. Several stories were added without proper permits and consideration for the building's structural integrity. The day before the collapse, cracks appeared in the building, and police ordered an evacuation. Despite these warnings, the garment workers were forced to return to work the next day.

Workers in the building were among the lowest paid in the world. Many worked long hours in substandard conditions. The disaster highlighted the lack of rights and the Bangladesh garment workers' vulnerability. Due to the demands of fast fashion and tight delivery schedules, workers were often under intense pressure to meet production targets. This contributed to the decision to keep the factories open even after cracks in the building appeared. The disaster drew attention to the global garment supply chain, as many of the clothes produced in the Rana Plaza factories were destined for major Western brands. The incident sparked debates about international brands' responsibility to ensure workers' safety and well-being in their supply chains.

Over 200 apparel brands, trade unions, and NGOs signed Bangladesh's Accord on Fire and Building Safety in response to the tragedy. This legally binding agreement requires safety inspections, repairs, and the empowerment of workers. With support from international organizations, the Bangladeshi government increased oversight of the garment industry, inspecting and closing unsafe factories. The disaster raised global awareness about the conditions under which fast fashion is produced, leading to calls for more ethical and sustainable production practices.

The Rana Plaza tragedy brought the darker side of the global fashion industry into the spotlight. It catalyzed a broader conversation about corporate responsibility, consumer awareness, and the true cost of cheap clothing.

Other factors influencing SCND are taxes and incentives, where inventory taxes are involved, and incentive packages such as special economic zones (SEZs). Infrastructure for transportation, proximity to industry clusters, trade patterns, and quality-of-life considerations are essential considerations.

Specialized location characteristics involve current "zoning of the land," activity of local unions, title search processes, soil engineering issues for engineers to examine the site for proper drainage, brownfields with previous land use, weather, and free-trade zones. Depending on the global political milieu and government intervention, these characteristics could take a momentous scale. The Nandigram case is one of the most politically charged events in the recent history of West Bengal, India, and it brought to light the conflicts and complexities surrounding land acquisition for industrialization.

The West Bengal government, under the Communist Party of India (Marxist) or CPI(M), sought to industrialize and modernize the state. In the mid-2000s, they invited Tata Motors to set up their Nano car manufacturing plant in Singur. Also, they proposed the creation of an SEZ in Nandigram for a chemical hub in partnership with an Indonesian company. The government decided to acquire land from the farmers in Nandigram. However, a significant number of locals opposed this move. They were concerned about losing their agricultural land, livelihoods, and homes and potential environmental degradation due to the proposed chemical hub. The opposition turned violent with clashes between the protesters and the police. The Trinamool Congress led the opposition to the Nandigram SEZ, then in the opposition in West Bengal, and its leader Mamata Banerjee. The party leveraged the Nandigram and Singur issues to challenge the state's 34-year-old CPI(M) rule.

The Nandigram issue saw widespread violence, with allegations of police atrocities and clashes between CPI(M) cadres and protesters. Several deaths and injuries were reported, which caught national attention and led to a severe backlash against the state government. While Tata Motors initiated its plant construction in Singur, it eventually had to pull out due to sustained protests. It relocated its Nano car plant to Sanand in Gujarat. The Nandigram project, too, was shelved.

The Nandigram and Singur controversies significantly influenced the CPI(M) decline in West Bengal. In the 2011 state elections, the Trinamool Congress defeated the CPI(M), ending its 34-year rule under Mamata Banerjee's leadership. The Nandigram issue became emblematic of the challenges and conflicts in India between industrialization and agrarian rights, development and displacement, and political agendas and grassroots movements.

Facility closing occurs when a company discontinues operations at a current site because the operations may no longer be needed or can be absorbed by other facilities. Examples leading to facility closure include eliminating redundant capacity in mergers and acquisitions, improving supply chain efficiency, poor planning, and insufficient volume of business.

Center of gravity method – a mathematical approach

The center of gravity (COG) method is a continuous location method that locates a new facility based on transportation costs and volume. It involves determining the volumes by source and destination point (*V*), determining the transportation costs based on $/unit/mile (*R*), and overlaying a grid to determine the coordinates of the source and destination point, thereby finding the weighted center of gravity for the graph.

A simple COG equation to determine the coordinate points for the facility to be located is given as follows:

$$\underline{X} = \frac{\sum V_i R_i X_i}{\sum V_i R_i} \qquad \underline{Y} = \frac{\sum V_i R_i Y_i}{\sum V_i R_i}$$

where V_i = volume flowing from (or to) point i, R_i = transportation rate to ship V_i from (to) point i, X_i and Y_i are the coordinate points for point i, and and are the coordinates for the facility to be located. The total cost for this location is found by the equation as follows:

$$TC = \sum_i V_i R_i K \sqrt{(X_i - \overline{X})^2 + (Y_i - \overline{Y})^2}$$

Where K is the map scaling factor to convert coordinates into miles.

Note that the simple COG method for SCND does not necessarily give optimal answers but will give good answers if there are many points in the problem (typically more than 30) and the volume for any one point is a low proportion of the total volume. However, optimal locations can be found by the *exact COG method* as follows:

$$\underline{X}^n = \frac{\sum_i V_i R_i X_{i/} d_i}{\sum_i V_i R_{i/} d_i}, \text{ and } \underline{Y}^n = \frac{\sum_i V_i R_i Y_{i/} d_i}{\sum_i V_i R_{i/} d_i}$$

where

$$\underline{Y}^n = \frac{\sum_i V_i R_i Y_{i/} d_i}{\sum_i V_i R_{i/} d_i}$$

and n is the iteration number. This can be easily solved with a simple optimization engine solver.

Commercial models for locations include most relevant location costs, and they constrain specified capacity and customer service levels. They replicate the cost of specified designs, handle multiple locations over multiple echelons, and handle multiple product categories to come up with the best SCND.

The general long-range nature of the location problem in SCND is that network configurations take time to implement since fixed charges are associated with moving to a new SCND configuration. We seek to find a set of network configurations that minimizes the present value over the planning horizon. Retail locations differ from plant and warehouse locations since they are revenue-driven instead of cost. There are also other factors such as parking space availability, proximity to competitive outlets, and to important customers.

Figure 5.5 Commercial SCND solution methodology

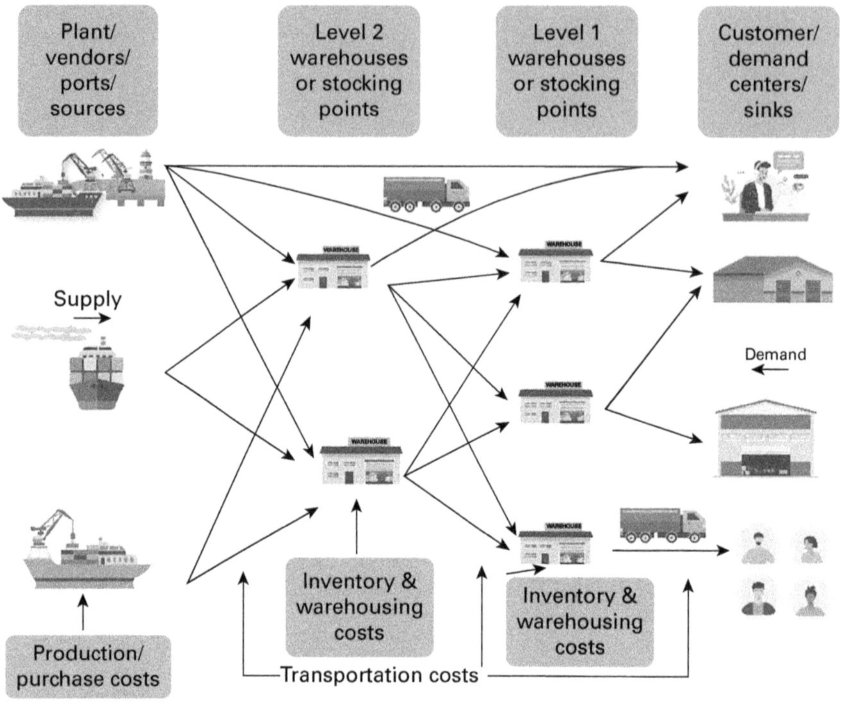

SOURCE USC Marshall-Randall R. Kendrick Global Supply Chain Institute

A collaborative method for determining the optimal location for retail SCND is a weighted checklist, also known as the "Pugh Matrix," which combines several "subjective" factors such as weights and quantifies the comparison among alternative locations. Table 5.1 is an example of a hypothetical Pugh Matrix for SCND for a retail location.

Once this matrix is completed for multiple SCND location candidates, we pick the location with the highest total index score. This process considers input from all stakeholders while quantifying the priorities and average scores on each factor. This is considered one of the most stakeholder friendly SCND decision-making processes.

Table 5.1 Hypothetical Pugh Matrix for SCND

Factor Weight (1 to 10)	Location Factors	Factor Score for location	= (1)*(2) Weighted Score
8	Proximity to competing stores	5	40
5	Space rent/lease considerations	3	15
8	Parking space	10	80
7	Proximity to complementary stores	8	56
6	Modernity of store space	9	54
9	Customer accessibility	8	72
3	Local Taxes	2	6
3	Community Service	4	12
8	Proximity to major transportation arteries	7	56
Total Index			391

Supply Chain Strategist and its Evolution to Technology supported SCND

In the 90s, i2 Technologies acquired a product called 'Supply Chain Strategist' (SCS), which was primarily focused on conducting simulation analysis of a supply chain network design based on demand, supply, network optimization, product availability, distribution, and logistics flows. This allowed planners to conduct what-if analysis visually, along with data-driven decision-making to determine the optimal network design. This tool was later acquired by Llamasoft and Coupa, where it is still available. Positioned as a "continuous supply chain design" tool, the recently updated version uses AI. In an HBS Analytic Services briefing paper (2022), the Vice President of Supply Chain Strategy Madhav Durbha provides the following sponsor perspective:

> ...Supply chain design that was done in an episodic, project-based manner and optimized for efficiency resulted in assumptions that did not keep pace with a rapidly evolving world, especially as resilience and sustainability emerged as high priorities.

> However, market leaders are forged during times of disruption. In these trying times, we have seen leading companies embrace the idea of continuous supply chain design—the practice of revisiting supply chain design in an ongoing manner to make rapid course corrections and adjust the supply chain structures, flow paths, and policies. Three things set these companies apart:
>
> They built connected digital models of their end-to-end supply chains, often called the "digital supply chain twins," which stress test their supply chains through advanced scenario planning that extends far beyond simple demand-supply balancing.
>
> They enabled and empowered supply chain centers of excellence with the skill sets to build and test these digital models and democratize the insights and recommendations to the broader organization by adopting best practices.
>
> They developed closer alignment and collaboration between supply chain, procurement, and finance-driven by executive solid sponsorship.

The challenge for achieving resilience is visibility, which does not let global supply chains determine the bottlenecks in the end-to-end network. This visibility required by continuous design involves scenario modelling, simulation analysis, artificial intelligence, data and analytics, and digital twins. The digital twin is set up with an ideal product flow from plant to warehouse and warehouse to customer. Once the nodes, plants, and linkages are in place, it can map out scenarios or options when the desired path is no longer optimal. Figure 5.6 shows what this might look like.

The technology footprint of supply chain network design grew with initial use cases of locating future warehouses and factories and building an optimal transportation network. As users adopted these solutions, new use cases came up on enabling fact-based decisions surrounding component and SKU rationalization, procurement optimization, optimizing order allocations, sustainability, and optimally supporting new product introductions. GM, Dell, and Dow Chemicals have used the tool to attain supply chain resilience, which has also helped with cost reduction from consolidation, carbon footprint reduction, and better demand fulfillment.

Figure 5.6 How Llamasoft software helps design supply chain networks

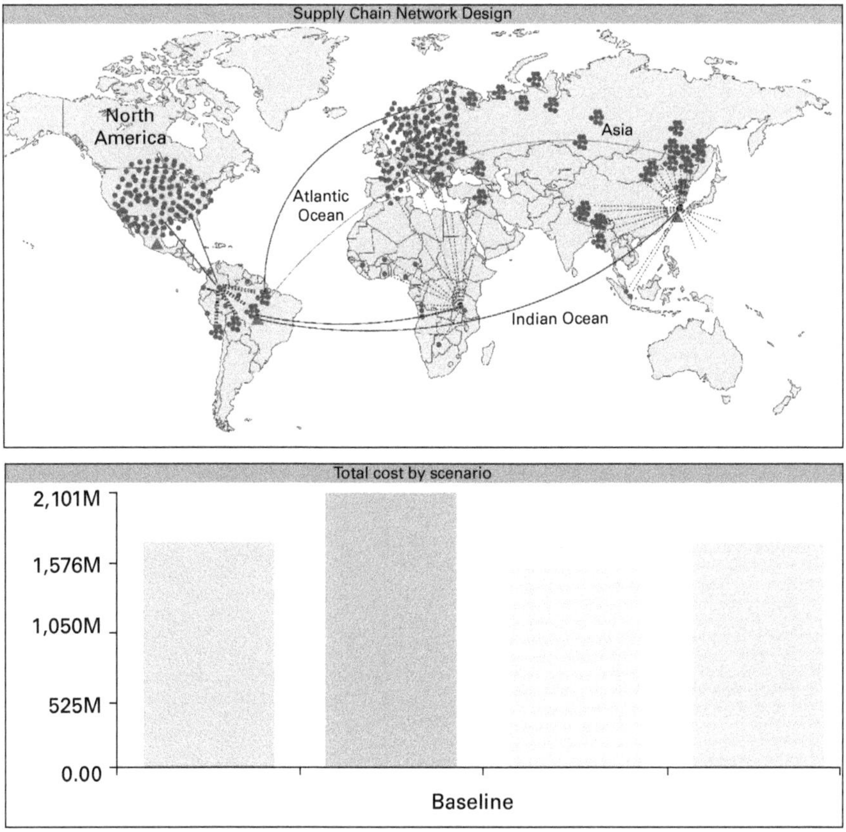

Cost breakdown by scenario

SCENARIO	TOTAL FIXED OPERATING COST	TOTAL PRODUCTION COST	TOTAL INV HOLDING COST	TOTAL
American Made Policy	4,111,000.00	1,500,822,526.30	34,505,768.57	185,854.5
Baseline	4,865,000.00	1,591,842,903.10	44,834,475.20	459,189,8
Tariff Policy Change Cr	8,115,000.00	1,354,817,462.80	31,923,881.59	145,324.4
Tax rate Increase	4,595,000.00	1,531,414,987.33	35,763,608.52	145,104.7

SOURCE: Llamasoft

The impact of SCND using these tools can only materialize when several organizational people-process-technology footprints work in unison. As MIT scholar David Simchi-Levi puts it, "When we talk about supply chain digitization, it extends beyond continuous supply

Figure 5.7 o9 Enterprise Knowledge Graph with AI/ML Intelligence Built-In

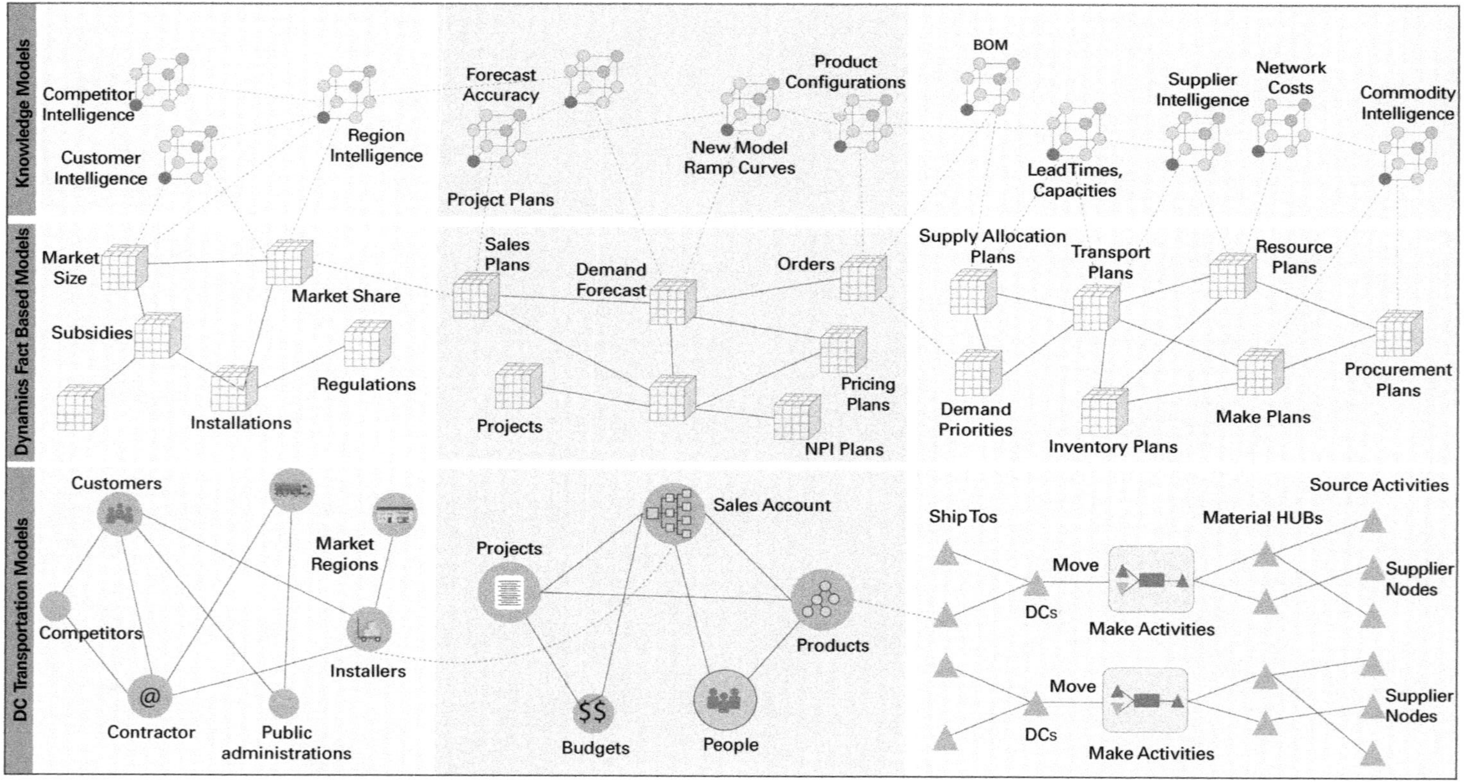

SOURCE USC Marshall-Randall R. Kendrick Global Supply Chain Institute

chain design. And cutting under it all is data and analytics. You must focus on multiple capabilities, a unified view of demand, supply chain segmentation, S&OP, and smart execution."

Enterprise Knowledge Graphs and AI/ML-driven SCND for planning

With the increasing adoption of AI in multiple areas of enterprises, technology solutions are being built in generative AI and large language models (LLMs) in the supply chain. A building block for SCND in this evolving ecosystem, as developed by o9 Solutions, for example, is an "enterprise knowledge graph" (EKG) based on a demand, market, and supply graph. This is a "digital brain" that exemplifies end-to-end operations knowledge for an enterprise. This graph has three components—market knowledge models, demand knowledge models, and supply chain knowledge models. The knowledge models have an underlying layer of dynamic fact-based models, and an organizational hierarchy and network graph model. This model's key features and capabilities are that it is a Big Data store that combines on-line analytical platform (OLAP) engines and supply chain network structures, and it evolves like "brain's model" with "knowledge", rather than just data models. The intelligence capabilities for this SCND are—Machine Learning Analytics, Demand-Supply matching algorithms, aggregation and disaggregation, bi-directional propagation of information, scenario planning, and post-game analysis. A diagrammatic representation of the model is below.

The architecture o9 has makes it easy to collect data from multiple sources and formats (structured and unstructured), and cleanse and process data into the enterprise knowledge graph. The interesting dynamic of the market EKG is that this data does not typically exist at enterprises; o9 accesses external data, which it connects to the demand and supply EKG. This can be used in multiple use cases. In demand, generally for forecasting, and in supply, it can be used to forecast raw material prices, detect logistics disruptions, and so on.

While the use of generative AI in management decision-making is in the early stages, o9's R&D initiatives demonstrate that generative AI, combined uniquely with its platform's industry-leading capabilities to model end-to-end supply chains and integrated planning processes, can dramatically impact productivity, knowledge, and transformation speed within companies.

Chakri Gottemukkala, Co-founder and CEO, o9 Solutions, Inc. says:

> Generative AI with Large Language Model (LLM) technology has captured the world's imagination with its power and potential. Of course, there are obvious use cases, like putting a natural language interface to your application to enable users to interact much more easily with your system, but fundamentally applying the technology to solve the complex challenges of enterprise planning and business decision-making needed a lot of innovation. And o9's architectural foundation built for enterprise-grade AI gave us a big advantage in leveraging Generative AI.

Endnotes

1 P Noble (2023) AI Speeds Manufacturing Supply Chains, Society of Manufacturing Engineers, February 9, 2023. www.sme.org/technologies/articles/2023/february/ai-speeds-manufacturing-supply-chains/ (archived at https://perma.cc/CZ2Y-Q3TJ)

2 K Alicke et al. (2021) Succeeding in the AI supply-chain revolution, McKinsey & Company, April 2021, www.mckinsey.com/industries/metals-and-mining/our-insights/succeeding-in-the-ai-supply-chain-revolution (archived at https://perma.cc/2GAC-TD5A)

3 D Gilmore. (2014) Insights from Unilever's perfect logistics network exercise, Supply Chain Digest, July 25, 2014. www.scdigest.com (archived at https://perma.cc/N6J4-TQ4F)

4 Agile supply chain: What it is, benefits, and applications, Inbound Logistics, January 2023. www.inboundlogistics.com (archived at https://perma.cc/9JJX-LHRF)

5 B Stackpole (2020) 5 supply chain technologies that deliver competitive advantage, February 14, 2020. mitsloan.mit.edu/ideas-made-to-matter/5-supply-chain-technologies-deliver-competitive-advantage (archived at https://perma.cc/Z7BH-PVG7)

6 M Law (2023) IoT tech streamlining supply chain in its hour of need, Supply Chain Digital, May 13, 2023. www.supplychaindigital.com (archived at https://perma.cc/Z5RB-M7JW)

7 J Quinlivan (2023) How Amazon deploys collaborative robots in its operations to benefit employees and customers, June 26, 2023. www.aboutamazon.com/news/operations/how-amazon-deploys-robots-in-its-operations-facilities (archived at https://perma.cc/QSA8-8ANU)

8 T Bishop (2023) A first-hand look at Amazon's new 'Sequoia' warehouse robotic system, Geek Wire, October 24, 2023. www.geekwire.com/2023/a-first-hand-look-at-amazons-new-sequoia-warehouse-robotic-system-in-action/ (archived at https://perma.cc/WR85-JETW)

9 Facilitating trade at the border, behind the border, and beyond, The World Bank, www.worldbank.org (archived at https://perma.cc/A3A6-NVPC)

10 Global Supply Chains: Trade and Economic Policies for Developing Countries, 2013 unctad.org/system/files/official-document/itcdtab56_en.pdf (archived at https://perma.cc/2PVQ-CMCS)

11 Rana Plaza, Clean Clothes Campaign, www.cleanclothes.org (archived at https://perma.cc/CC22-3HCY)

Integrating Sustainability in the Supply Chain DNA

06

In earlier chapters, we have discussed the importance of the triple bottom line in today's business environment. We will now provide an overview of the evolution from traditional to sustainable supply chains, emphasizing the integration of environmental, social, and governance (ESG) principles, and highlight diverse strategies employed by companies across various industries to address the complex challenges associated with sustainability. While the initial focus of sustainability initiatives was often on cost reduction, the motivations have shifted significantly in recent years, as we discuss later in this chapter.

We will then discuss the multifaceted challenges and opportunities posed by global events and legislative shifts, including the COVID-19 pandemic and Russian invasion of Ukraine. Such events emphasize the importance of resilience and local sourcing. They may also disrupt access to critical raw materials, prompting a reevaluation of supply chain strategies. We will conclude by emphasizing the value creation potential of sustainability efforts.

Sustainability-related challenges

In today's discourse, the term "sustainability" is often interpreted differently by various parties. Back in 1987, the United Nations Brundtland Commission defined sustainability as "meeting the needs of the present without compromising the ability of future generations to meet their own needs." The United States Environmental Protection Agency (EPA) offers the perspective that:

> Sustainability is based on a simple principle: Everything that we need for our survival and well-being depends, either directly or indirectly, on our natural environment. To pursue sustainability is to create and maintain the conditions under which humans and nature can exist in productive harmony to support present and future generations.

The term "The Tragedy of the Commons" was introduced in a 1968 *Nature* article by Garrett Hardin, illustrating situations in which people overuse common resources and bring ruin upon everyone involved. This phenomenon is increasingly relevant in the modern era, particularly with the rise of affluence and consumerism in developed nations, coupled with the challenges posed by climate change. A Business Week article by Peter Coy (2015) discussed the plight of California's drought, concluding that the water table keeps receding and the land is subsiding, damaging bridges and canals, in yet another example of a tragedy of the commons.

Tragedy of the commons issues extend beyond resource depletion and also encompass pollution. A Stanford brief by Andrew J. Hoffman (2015) points out, "… Climate change represents a deep shift in the way we view ourselves, the environment, and our place within it. It is the ultimate 'commons problem' where every individual has an incentive to emit greenhouse gases to improve their standard of living, while the costs of this activity are diffused among many…"

Climate change, partly exacerbated by the tragedy of the commons, wields a significant influence over business operations and their intricate supply chains. A case in point is Nike, which, as of April 2023, operates in 482 factories across 36 nations for manufacturing finished goods and sources materials from 147 facilities in 14 countries.[1] Consequently, natural disasters occurring anywhere in the world can reverberate through Nike's supply chain, triggering production delays, necessitating product redesigns, and prompting adjustments to the materials in use. This, in turn, compels Nike to revise its sourcing strategies.

To illustrate, the floods that ravaged Thailand in 2008 led to the temporary closure of four Nike factories, disrupting the flow of their supply chain. A comparable scenario unfolded in 2011 when a substantial portion of Thailand was inundated, again impacting Nike's operations.[2] Another climate-induced concern arises from the escalating droughts in cotton-producing regions – a critical material in Nike's athletic apparel. The diminishing water supply curbs cotton yields, giving rise to supply shortages and elevated prices. In this intricate landscape, the influence of climate change underscores the imperative for businesses to anticipate, adapt, and reimagine their supply chains to navigate the challenges imposed by a changing environment.

In the realm of operations management and supply chain courses, Zara has often served as a prime example due to its pioneering strides in supply chain management, which catalyzed the arrival of "fast fashion." Central to fast fashion's identity are its fleeting trends, ushering in frequent product turnovers. However, this hallmark comes intertwined with intensive water and cotton usage, exerting strain on limited resources. Furthermore, the brisk pace of product cycles creates waste accumulation when consumers refresh their wardrobes, worsening pollution concerns.

In a world increasingly attuned to sustainability, these characteristics inherent to fast fashion could instigate adverse publicity, potentially tarnishing a company's image. The repercussions could ripple outward, eroding sales and profitability. This confluence of factors underscores the pressing necessity for fast fashion industry players to recalibrate their strategies, embracing more eco-friendly practices and aligning with sustainability principles to navigate the evolving landscape and safeguard their reputation in an environmentally conscious era.

Confronted with the imperative of sustainability, supply chains must embark on a transformative journey to reduce their environmental footprint. Companies like Nike and Zara are employing multifaceted strategies to address sustainability-related challenges.

In their response to the 2022 Climate Disclosure Project questionnaire[3], Nike has shown a proactive approach. Aware of the escalating threat posed by extreme weather events to their operations and supply chain, Nike initiated a comprehensive water risk assessment for their suppliers. This endeavor, compelling suppliers to evaluate and counteract water-related vulnerabilities like flooding and drought, has yielded fruit. All 13 high-risk facilities have now implemented water risk mitigation plans.

Recognizing that 91 percent of their freshwater consumption is tied to material sourcing and manufacturing, Nike champions judicious water use. Their activities span various fronts, including augmenting the successful organic cotton blending program and expanding the integration of recycled cotton into apparel. The latter innovation circumvents the resource-intensive growth phase, thus alleviating water and energy burdens.

Embracing synthetic materials as a buffer against weather-driven uncertainties, Nike has spurred innovative breakthroughs. Examples like Flyknit, a lightweight fabric derived from recycled plastic bottles, epitomize this spirit of innovation. This groundbreaking material, with a 6 percent reduction in waste compared to traditional footwear upper manufacturing, underscores Nike's commitment to sustainability. Furthermore, Nike's Flyleather, artfully blending recycled leather fibers with synthetics via a water-powered process, has emerged as a prime alternative to traditional leather. This not only mitigates waste but also curbs climate impact, a vital stride toward a greener future.

Nike's Re-Creation initiative represents a paradigm shift, channeling vintage, and dead-stock pieces into new, locally crafted products. This embodies a circular ethos, steering the company closer to their aspiration of a zero-carbon, zero-waste future (Nike, 2022).

Similarly, Inditex, the parent company of Zara, has embarked on a journey toward heightened sustainability, demonstrated by the unveiling of new sustainability objectives on its official platform. This paradigm shift is reinforced by a commitment to embrace organic and recycled cotton, sustainable man-made fibers, eco-friendly linen, and recycled polyester. Inditex's pioneering spirit is further illustrated by the development of Infinna, a novel recycled fiber, and strategic investments in startups like CIRC. The latter is dedicated to pioneering technology that enables the large-scale recycling of textile products composed of polyester and cotton blends.

In the world of evolving supply chains, Zara and Nike align their practices with sustainability imperatives. As they pioneer novel solutions, these companies reiterate the transformative potential of industry-wide activities to foster a more sustainable future. Both examples center on the apparel sector and underscore a broader trend within the industry—namely, the integration of circularity into business frameworks. This shift is encouraging, highlighting a collective consciousness among apparel companies to embrace sustainability principles. Nevertheless, this growing drive for circularity is contrasted with a noteworthy concern: a visible underemphasis on prolonging product lifecycles. A recent report (Makower et al., 2023) substantiates this observation, shedding light on the dynamics at play within the textile, apparel, and luxury goods sector. The study reports that 85 percent of companies within this domain have embraced circular fashion as a foundational aspect of their operational model. Impressively, 76.5 percent of these entities allocate dedicated resources to research and development within the realm of circular fashion, even spanning cross-industry collaborations. However, a more sobering statistic emerges when considering the extension of product longevity: a mere 29.4 percent of these companies are formulating strategies to extend the fashionable appeal of their products over time. This disconnect signifies an area where the industry could deepen its commitment to circularity, bridging the gap between sustainability and longevity (see Figure 6.1).

In sum, while there is palpable progress toward circularity in the apparel sector, the sector must synergize its sustainability pursuits with endeavors to extend the lifespan of its products, embracing a holistic transformation that aligns environmental stewardship with enduring style.

In the rest of this chapter, we will explore the challenges that various industries encounter within their supply chains as they strive to embrace sustainability objectives.

Sustainable supply chains practices

Expanding traditional supply chain functions to incorporate sustainability entails a comprehensive approach that goes beyond the conventional scope of activities. While there are diverse interpretations of sustainability in the context of supply chains, ranging from environmental considerations to encompassing social and governance aspects (ESG), the aim is to integrate responsible practices into every aspect of operations. Embracing ESG principles within supply chain management often involves some of the following measures, tailored to the specific industry.

Figure 6.1 Percentage of companies in the Textile, Apparel and Luxury Goods industry that report using different programs for circular fashion

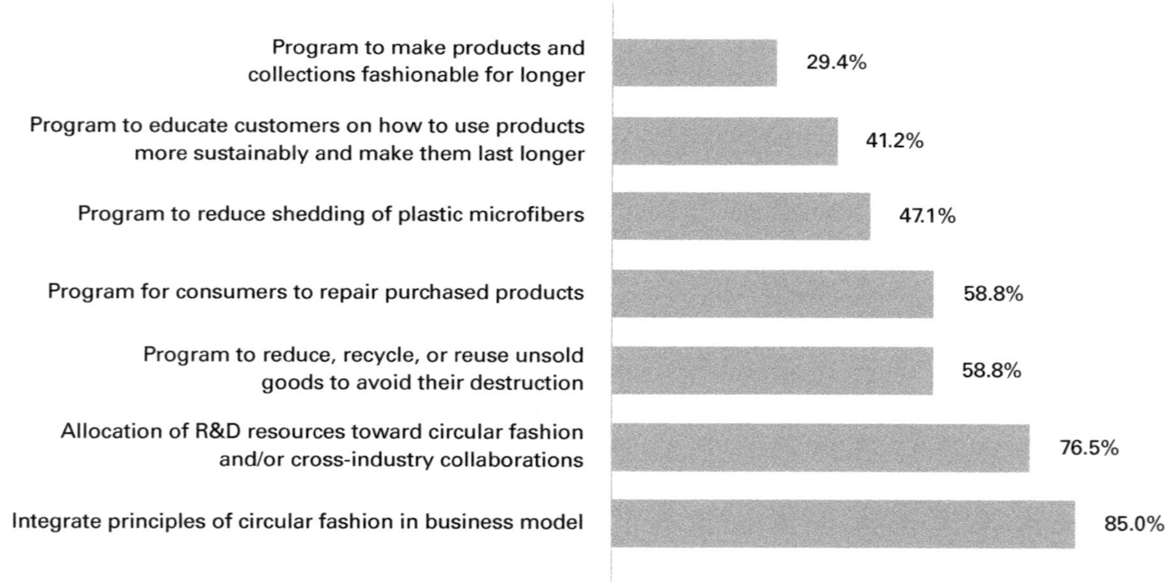

(**DATE SOURCE** Makower et al., 2023)
SOURCE USC Marshall- Randall R. Kendrick Global Supply Chain Institute

Reducing water consumption and cleaning water used in manufacturing processes

As the tragedy of the commons and climate change worsens water scarcity and high-water stress in various regions, businesses are realizing the imperative to address their water usage and environmental impact. Industries like the beverage sector, where water is a primary ingredient, face challenges. The Coca-Cola Company, for instance, has encountered protests and criticisms due to its substantial water consumption and potential water pollution associated with its manufacturing processes. The production of beverages like Coca-Cola involves not only the direct use of water in manufacturing but also the water required to cultivate raw materials like sugarcane. This comprehensive water footprint demonstrates the broader impact of production.

Coca-Cola's self-reported water usage statistics have attracted attention and concern. While the direct manufacturing process uses around 3 liters of water per liter of beverage, the complete supply chain, encompassing ingredient cultivation, packaging, and other operations, contributes to a much higher water requirement. The Coca-Cola Company estimates that approximately 70 liters of water are utilized to produce a single liter of Coca-Cola, accounting for all these factors.

The real-world consequences of this water consumption have manifested in various instances, such as the Plachimada struggle in India in the early 2000s. Here, the establishment of a Coca-Cola factory resulted in protests and legal disputes after local villagers experienced drying wells and contaminated water. These events highlight the interconnectedness of industrial activities, water resources, and community livelihoods.

Recognizing the importance of sustainable water management, The Coca-Cola Company has shifted its focus towards water stewardship. By proactively addressing water stress, safeguarding local water sources, and enhancing communities' capacity to adapt to evolving conditions, the company aims to mitigate its impact on water resources. This approach is essential not only to maintain the sustainability of the business but also to foster positive relationships with the communities in which it operates.

The case of Coca-Cola illustrates the necessity for businesses to assess their water consumption throughout the supply chain and develop strategies to reduce water usage and enhance water quality. By doing so, companies can contribute to addressing water scarcity challenges, promote environmental sustainability, and cultivate responsible corporate practices that benefit both the business and the communities it serves.

Using sustainable/recycled materials

In addition to water conservation, manufacturers must scrutinize all ingredients incorporated into their products and evaluate their environmental impact. This process may involve reevaluating materials and redesigning products to integrate more sustainable alternatives. As the specter of the tragedy of the commons looms over an expanding array of finite resources, companies are increasingly turning to eco-friendly and recycled materials. This shift serves not only to contribute to environmental preservation but also to ensure a viable future supply for their products.

Various organizations, such as the Forest Stewardship Council (FSC), the Marine Stewardship Council (MSC), and the Global Organic Textile Standards (GOTS), offer certification for companies that adhere to environmentally sustainable practices. These certifications aid companies in making informed decisions about their supply chain partners. The Sustainable Apparel Coalition (SAC), comprising over 280 brands, retailers, manufacturers, NGOs, academics, and industry organizations, aims to establish sustainability standards for the apparel industry. Their creation of the Higg Index in 2011 encompasses five distinct tools that gather and quantify data related to textile and footwear manufacturing and supply chains.[4]

Seafood, a vital resource for a significant portion of the global population, faces the challenge of overfishing, with over one-third of fish being harvested at unsustainable levels. The MSC addresses this issue through its certification and labeling program, which encourages sustainable seafood production and consumption. The organization has introduced the MSC Ocean Champion Awards to recognize partners that surpass their MSC commitments, displaying dedication to both a healthier ocean and a more transparent supply chain. Recipients of this award include Walmart, Whole Foods, US Foods, and Sam's Club.[5] Wood plays a pivotal role for IKEA, the world's largest furniture manufacturer, which initiated its sustainability strategy in 2012. By 2022, 15 percent of the wood used in IKEA products was sourced from recycled wood, while 99.9 percent of total wood utilized was either FSC-certified or recycled (IKEA, 2023).

Companies like Unifi, Inc., a textile manufacturer established in 1971, have ventured into innovative recycling solutions. In 2007, they introduced Repreve, a recycled performance fiber derived from plastic bottles. Unifi had recycled over 38 billion bottles by July 2023, and its Repreve fibers are incorporated into products by prominent brands including Nike, Patagonia, The North Face, J. Crew, and Levi Strauss & Co.[6] A similar example is Thermore, an Italian firm established in 1972 specializing in thermal insulation. Thermore has integrated recycled PET bottles into insulation for apparel since the 1980s, culminating in the introduction of Ecodown in 2016—a 100 percent–recycled down alternative. Their customer roster includes renowned names like Eddie Bauer, Patagonia, Levi Strauss & Co, Fila, and Nordica.[7] These initiatives underscore the growing commitment across industries to embrace sustainable materials and practices as a means to address environmental concerns and promote circularity in supply chains.

Recycling materials and products

The responsible recycling of materials and products plays a crucial role in mitigating the effects of the tragedy of the commons. By reducing waste and minimizing the depletion of natural resources, companies are taking proactive steps toward a more sustainable future. Various industries are embracing these practices, building on the examples we discussed earlier, including Tesla's approach to recycling EV batteries. Here are additional instances of companies adopting such measures.

The concept of extended producer responsibility (EPR) is gaining traction as an approach that holds producers accountable for the end-of-life management of their products. EPR can encompass both financial and operational responsibilities. While only four US states had passed EPR legislation concerning packaging by the end of 2022, 11 states introduced similar measures in 2023.[8] Electronic waste (e-waste) is a notable area where EPR has been implemented due to its rapid growth as a waste stream. As consumers upgrade to newer electronic products, older devices are often discarded, resulting in a global reported average collection rate of only about 17 percent for e-waste. In contrast, Europe's Waste from Electrical and Electronic Equipment (WEEE) legislation introduced in 2003 has led to a collection rate of approximately 55 percent.[9] In the US, Maine was the pioneer in enacting e-waste legislation in 2004. Currently, 25 US. states and the District of Columbia have electronics recycling laws, of which 23 fall under EPR (mandatory schemes).[10] It's worth noting that the progress of e-waste EPR legislation in the US appears to have slowed down, with 19 of these programs being implemented between 2009 and 2011.[11]

In 2018, Burberry's annual report revealed that the company had burned 28.6 million pounds worth of clothing and cosmetics. This wasteful practice was not unique to Burberry and has been employed by other luxury brands to prevent unsold items from being sold at significant discounts, which could potentially impact regular pricing. However, such practices have faced criticism, particularly as consumers become more environmentally conscious. In response to backlash, Burberry announced its decision to cease the destruction of unsold merchandise. The company disclosed that they were already taking steps to reuse, repair, donate, or recycle unsold products. They further pledged to collaborate with Make Fashion Circular, an initiative of the Ellen MacArthur Foundation dedicated to waste reduction in the fashion industry (Paton, 2018). This move reflects the industry's growing awareness of the importance of circular practices and sustainable consumption.

Reducing packaging

Packaging reduction is a strategy that holds the potential to simultaneously decrease a company's environmental footprint and enhance its financial performance. This win-win approach is evident across a wide spectrum of companies, spanning both manufacturing and retail sectors.

In manufacturing, Puma stands out as an example of innovative packaging design. The company received the Industrie Forum (iF) Design Gold Award in 2011 for introducing the Clever Little Bag. This inventive solution combines a bag and a box. A single sheet of cardboard is folded into a box that securely holds the shoes. This box is then nestled within a cloth bag, maintaining the box's shape without requiring tissue paper. By employing this system, Puma manages to utilize 65 percent less cardboard compared to a traditional shoe box.[12]

Detergent manufacturers, including Method and Seventh Generation, are selling concentrated detergents that eliminate excess water from their products. This reduction in water content translates to smaller packaging containers. For instance, the original Tide laundry detergent, packaged in a 92 oz container, offers 64 loads.[13] In contrast, Method's 4x concentrated version, housed in a 53.5 oz container, provides 66 loads,[14] while Seventh Generation's 40 oz container offers 53 loads.[15] Both companies have continued their efforts by transitioning to ultra-concentrated formulations, such as Seventh Generation's 66 loads from a 23.1 oz package.[16] This size reduction not only results in less waste but also facilitates efficient pallet loading, leading to reduced transportation and storage costs, which subsequently decreases emissions from transportation.

On the retail front, Amazon has employed machine learning to determine the suitability of flexible packaging, like padded mailers and bags, for various products. These alternatives are notably lighter, weighing up to 75 percent less than equivalently sized boxes. Amazon's adoption of this approach has led to a substantial reduction in the use of corrugated boxes by more than 35 percent across North America and Europe between 2017 and 2023. Furthermore, the implementation of algorithms specifically designed to minimize packaging for shipments involving multiple items has resulted in packaging size reduction for 7 percent of shipments in North America from 2018 to 2023. This approach not only aligns with sustainability goals but also leads to significant cost savings and waste reduction.[17]

Optimizing transportation routes

When a delivery vehicle is tasked with multiple stops along its route, the choice of routes can lead to substantial variations in mileage, fuel consumption, and carbon emissions. Fortunately, modern IT tools enable companies to optimize their routes, enhancing their environmental performance while concurrently reducing costs.

A prime example of a company that recognizes the significance of route optimization is UPS. In the year 2022 alone, UPS successfully delivered an average of 24.3 million packages per day, spanning across more than 220 countries.[18] Back in 2012, the company introduced its proprietary on-road integrated optimization and navigation (ORION) platform. This advanced technology leverages sophisticated algorithms, artificial intelligence, and machine learning to provide drivers with the most efficient routes for their deliveries.

Building on this foundation, UPS continued to innovate. In 2019, they integrated UPSNav into ORION, a feature that offers detailed turn-by-turn directions. These directions guide local delivery drivers not only to addresses but also to specific package drop-off and pickup points, even those concealed from the street view. To further enhance efficiency, in 2021, UPS introduced dynamic routing to ORION. This update ensures that the routes dispatched to drivers' handheld devices are automatically adjusted throughout the day, in response to changing conditions. This dynamic adaptation significantly reduces mileage and consequently the associated emissions.

Since implementing ORION, UPS estimates that it has conserved around 100 million miles and 10 million gallons of fuel on a yearly basis.[19] To put this achievement in perspective, the EPA approximates that one gallon of gasoline consumed emits about 8,887 grams of CO_2, while one gallon of diesel emits about 10,180 grams of CO_2. Assuming an equal distribution of fuel consumption between gasoline and diesel, these figures equate to an annual reduction of 95,335 tons of CO_2 emissions. This impact corresponds to removing over 21,000 gasoline-powered passenger vehicles from the roads. (The EPA estimates annual passenger vehicle emissions at 4.49 metric tons CO_2e.)

UPS's commitment to route optimization illustrates how innovative technological solutions can not only boost efficiency and cost-effectiveness but also substantially contribute to environmental sustainability by significantly reducing carbon emissions.

Using environmentally friendly transportation modes

In the early 21st century, several companies took the initiative to adopt hybrid vehicles, marking a significant step towards environmental responsibility. In 2003, FedEx emerged as a pioneer in this regard by becoming the first delivery company to employ hybrid vehicles for pickup and delivery services. At the time, commercially available hybrid vehicles were scarce, prompting FedEx to collaborate with Eaton Corporation to develop hybrid electric powertrains.[20] FedEx has consistently advocated for improved fuel efficiency standards and policies that foster the commercial deployment of alternative-fuel vehicles. In 2022, they achieved another milestone by receiving their initial batch of 150 electric delivery vehicles from BrightDrop, a technology startup by General Motors (GM), aimed at decarbonizing last-mile delivery.[21]

Globally, more and more countries are enacting legislations designed to bolster the adoption of zero-emission vehicles, both in passenger and freight transportation. While medium- and heavy-duty vehicles constituted only 6 percent of registered vehicles in 2018, they accounted for over 26 percent of fuel consumption and 23 percent of greenhouse gas (GHG) emissions within the US transportation sector.

Some companies are proactively embracing these changes and committing to early adoption strategies. For instance, IKEA has set its sights on electrifying all home delivery vehicles by 2025. Amazon, on the other hand, has placed an order for 100,000 electric delivery vans from Rivian and aims to deploy them by 2030. PepsiCo/Frito-Lay is taking a similar path, making the shift from diesel-powered to electric-powered freight equipment at manufacturing and distribution sites across the US, as reported by the Electrification Coalition in 2023.

However, despite the efforts of these trailblazing companies, certain obstacles still impede wider adoption of these sustainability-focused strategies. Challenges such as elevated upfront vehicle costs, limited model selections, uncertain delivery timelines, prolonged charging durations, and a nascent charging station infrastructure stand as primary factors that are slowing the momentum of this trend. Nonetheless, the trajectory is promising, as companies increasingly recognize the importance of transitioning to electric and alternative-fuel vehicles as a key step towards reducing their environmental footprint and fostering long-term sustainability.

Reducing energy use

According to the EPA, electric power accounted for 25 percent of the country's GHG emissions, ranking just behind the transportation sector at 28 percent.[22] On a global scale, energy is responsible for a significant 41.7 percent of total GHG emissions.[23] As more jurisdictions around the world are adopting carbon penalty mechanisms like carbon taxes or cap-and-trade systems, companies can enhance their sustainability efforts and realize cost savings by reducing their electricity consumption.

A noticeable example of energy efficiency measures can be observed in Target stores. In certain low-traffic areas, lighting is activated only when someone enters the space, reducing the need to keep lights continuously on. Additionally, Target is actively implementing hydrofluorocarbon (HFC)-free refrigerants in their food distribution centers and refrigerated display cases within stores. HFCs are potent GHGs frequently used in various applications such as refrigeration and air-conditioning, and they possess high global warming potential (GWP), indicating their capacity to trap heat in the atmosphere relative to CO_2. For instance, the GWP of HFC-134a is 1,430, signifying that it has a warming impact 1,430 times greater than CO_2.

Another effective approach involves enhancing the energy efficiency of buildings. Despite incurring initial investment costs, such initiatives can yield substantial savings in energy consumption within a relatively short span. An illustrative case is the Empire State Building's renovation completed in 2010. Originally budgeted at $550 million, an additional $13 million investment (for improved windows, upgraded heating and cooling systems) resulted in an annual energy cost reduction of $4.4 million (Nunez, 2011). Consequently, the supplementary investment paid for itself in less than three years, exemplifying the practical gains of energy-efficient strategies.

Using renewable energy sources

Switching to renewable energy sources is a critical strategy for companies aiming to enhance their sustainability. Different companies approach this transition in various ways, such as by installing solar panels on their facilities or investing in wind farms.

Nike has established an ambitious objective to power all its owned and operated facilities with 100 percent renewable energy by 2025.[24] The company has taken significant strides toward achieving this goal. Through a collaboration with Avangrid Renewables, LLC, Nike has been able to utilize the power generated by the 307 MW Karankawa Wind Farm in Texas, which was completed in 2019. Consequently, as of 2020, Nike's owned and operated facilities in North America are powered by 100 percent renewable energy. Furthermore, Nike initiated an on-site rooftop Solar PV program at various participating facilities, focusing primarily on locations in Vietnam, Greater China, and Thailand. Over the span of 2019 to 2022, Nike has contracted 190 MW of rooftop solar across 64 facilities, a capacity sufficient to power more than 30,000 households in the United States[25] (Nike, 2023).

Likewise, Levi Strauss & Co. has established a commitment to achieve 100 percent renewable electricity for all its company-operated facilities by 2025. As a step toward realizing this objective, the company proactively purchased a portion of the renewable energy output that the Sunflower Wind Farm in Kansas is projected to generate over a 12-year period. This substantial investment equates to around 250,000 MWh of wind power annually and shows Levi Strauss & Co.'s dedication to transitioning to renewable energy sources.[26]

Reducing waste

Reducing waste presents a straightforward approach to simultaneously decreasing resource consumption, pollution, and costs. There are diverse methods to achieve waste reduction, ranging from adopting new technologies within the same materials and product design to selecting alternative materials and rethinking product design entirely.

Apparel manufacturers like Zara frequently utilize computer-assisted design (CAD) systems that optimize cutting patterns to minimize material waste. Alternatively, Nike introduced the Flyknit technology, as discussed earlier in this chapter, which involves knitting the shoe body instead of cutting and assembling distinct components. A comparison between Nike's Pegasus 25 shoe design from 2008 and their Flyknit Lunar2 shoe from 2014 demonstrates an estimated waste reduction of 35 percent (Nike, 2014).

Interface, a commercial flooring company, embarked on a journey to reduce their environmental impact in 1994. Their environmentally friendly product offerings include i2 modular carpet tiles, designed to be simpler to install and maintain compared to traditional carpets. These tiles emulate the random patterns of a forest floor, allowing seamless blending of tiles purchased or installed at different times. Instead of replacing the entire carpet, worn-out sections in high-traffic areas can be swapped out, resulting in less waste.[27]

Cattle farming contributes substantially to methane emissions through the digestion process of animals and the decomposition of animal manure. Although methane remains in the atmosphere for a shorter period than CO_2 (about 12 years), its GWP over a 20-year span is 84, signifying that it has a warming impact 84 times greater than CO_2. On a positive note, methane can be harnessed to generate energy. Many cattle farmers are turning to anaerobic digesters to convert cow manure into electricity, simultaneously reducing methane emissions and producing energy. Vanguard Renewables, for instance, has contracts with 130 farms in the US and ongoing projects worth $800 million as of 2023. The company aims to establish 100 digesters by 2026; a single digester can generate over 6,000 MWh annually, equivalent to powering 550 homes. The American Biogas Council estimates that numerous similar systems could be established throughout the country, potentially exceeding 15,000 installations.[28]

Eliminating child labor

A recent report (Save the Children, 2023) examined data from 20 Supply Chain Child Rights Risk Assessments involving both public and private partners across Asia, the Middle East, Africa, and South America. The study revealed that child labor was evident in 10 out of 20 assessments, with a very high risk of child labor in 8 out of the remaining 10 assessments.

The intricate nature of global supply chains poses challenges for companies headquartered in regions like Europe or North America to identify child labor issues within their smaller suppliers, particularly those located overseas. The report's findings indicate that in sectors like toy manufacturing in India, while there are no indications of child labor in tier 1 and tier 2 factories, there is a notable child labor risk in lower tiers. Similarly, within India's garment industry, child labor tends to be pushed from tier 1 suppliers to the more informal sector higher up in the supply chain. Another trend identified is the use of child workers for home-based artisanal work in many Asian countries.

The agriculture sector also experiences significant child labor. Various crops across the globe, such as tea in Sri Lanka, cocoa and rattan in Indonesia, hazelnut and rose in Turkey, coffee in Vietnam, or cassava in Brazil, involve children in different stages of cultivation. Artisanal or small-scale mining (ASM) is another industry prone to hazardous child labor. The report found that 10 percent of children aged 12–14 and 19 percent of children aged 15–17 in ASM communities are engaged in cobalt mining in the Democratic Republic of Congo.

While many companies claim to adopt a zero-tolerance stance toward child labor, the reality often involves the displacement of child labor from first-tier suppliers to less monitored and controlled sectors further upstream, putting children at even greater risk. However, there are steps that companies are taking to improve the living conditions of families and reduce the need for child labor:

- *Providing access to childcare for manufacturing workers:* Initiatives like The Centre for Child Rights and Business's Child Friendly Space (CFS) program work with suppliers to establish safe and secure childcare facilities in factories and farms. For example, in China, nearly one hundred factories had opened child-friendly spaces by 2021, supporting over 10,000 parent workers and their children. The CFS program has expanded to 24 countries.[29]
- *Paying living wages and fair prices*: Companies like Tony's Chocolonely have committed to paying fair prices for crops and partnered with organizations like Fairtrade to establish Living Income Reference Prices. These efforts aim to ensure that workers receive fair compensation for their labor, such as the premium of 68 percent over the farmgate price that Tony's Chocolonely paid in Côte d'Ivoire.[30]

- *Improving access to education*: Initiatives like IKEA's Youth Development Support Program provide technical and life skills training and mentoring for young workers in their supply chain, contributing to creating safer workplaces and providing educational opportunities.[31]

These efforts collectively contribute to addressing the root causes of child labor and improving the overall well-being of children and families involved in global supply chains.

Supply chain transparency

Increasing supply chain transparency is crucial for ensuring that companies' supply chains are free from forced labor and human rights violations. Many industries face these challenges, and various jurisdictions have enacted legislation to address these issues on a global scale.

Conflict minerals, including tantalum, tin, tungsten, and gold, have been linked to funding armed conflicts and sometimes involve forced labor in their extraction. Despite their critical role in manufacturing products like cellphones and cars, the goal is to ensure that their sourcing does not contribute to human rights abuses. Legislation such as section 1502 of the Dodd-Frank Wall Street Reform and Consumer Protection Act of 2010 in the US and the Due Diligence Guidance for Responsible Supply Chains from Conflict-Affected and High-Risk Areas in the EU seek to hold importers accountable for meeting responsible sourcing standards and promoting local development while preventing abuse of local communities.

However, tracing minerals and metals from their origin to manufacturing locations can be a complex task. Technologies like the ones offered by companies such as bext360[32] use blockchain-powered SaaS platforms to provide traceability along the supply chain. This technology not only applies to conflict minerals but also has broader applications in industries like agriculture, where knowing the origin of crops and ensuring fair treatment of farmers is essential. bext360's approach involves working with various commodities and producers across different countries to enhance transparency and ethical practices throughout the supply chain. With over 30,000 producers across more than 40 countries, these efforts contribute to responsible sourcing and fair treatment of workers across industries.

Governance accountability

ESG principles emphasize a broader responsibility of businesses beyond just maximizing profits for shareholders. This includes considering the impact on workers, customers, suppliers, communities, and the environment. Many companies have started creating ESG reports to showcase their efforts in these areas, but challenges like standardization and objectivity persist.

B Lab, a non-profit organization, has been instrumental in setting standards and tools for measuring and improving companies' social and environmental impact.[33] The B Impact Assessment, used by many businesses, covers categories like Governance, Workers, Community, Environment, and Customers. This assessment helps companies evaluate and manage their positive impact on these dimensions. B Lab's certification process has led to the creation of B Corporations, which are companies that meet rigorous standards of performance, accountability, and transparency across these categories.

Becoming a certified B Corporation requires achieving a high score on the B Impact Assessment, making a legal commitment to consider all stakeholders, and exhibiting transparency by sharing performance information publicly on B Lab's website. This certification process ensures that companies align with ESG principles and continuously work towards improving their social and environmental impact. As of now, thousands of companies across various industries and countries have become certified B Corporations, demonstrating a growing commitment to sustainability and accountability beyond traditional profit measures.

Sustainability drivers

While some strategies like reducing energy consumption, minimizing waste, and optimizing transportation routes can yield cost savings, others such as adopting eco-friendly transportation modes or sustainable materials may indeed increase operational expenses. This prompts a fundamental question: Why would businesses opt to invest in greening their supply chains and embracing sustainability, especially when it may entail higher costs?

For instance, Walmart embarked on its sustainability journey in 2005, achieving significant fuel efficiency improvements resulting in substantial financial savings and reduced carbon emissions. However, they now face the challenge of transitioning to electrified fleets and achieving zero emissions by 2040. This transition demands collaboration with multiple stakeholders and entails higher upfront costs.[34] So, what motivates businesses to commit to these environmentally conscious efforts?

A survey conducted in 2019 with sustainable business leaders from 125 companies shed light on key drivers behind sustainability initiatives (GlobeScan and BSR, 2019). Notably, reputational risks/benefits, customer/consumer demand, and investor interest emerged as the top three motivators for pursuing sustainability, while budget/cost reduction was the last. Intriguingly, while reputational risks/benefits and budget/cost reduction remained constant over time, other drivers fluctuated: market growth opportunities experienced a decline in importance, moving from third place in 2015–2016 to seventh in 2018–2019. Conversely, customer/consumer demand and investor interest surged in significance, shifting from seventh and eighth places in 2015 to second and third in 2019 (Table 6.1).

This dynamic landscape signifies that motivations for integrating sustainability into decision-making are evolving. While reputational risk consistently drives efforts, the changing preferences of consumers and investors play an increasingly critical role in shaping companies' sustainability policies. Simultaneously, factors such as operational risks and market growth prospects, once prominent, are diminishing as primary drivers. Interestingly, cost reduction appears less influential as a motivating factor in the surveyed companies.

In conclusion, businesses recognize the need to align with shifting consumer and investor attitudes towards sustainability, even if it entails initial costs. As sustainability gains prominence as a business imperative, the reasons behind embracing greener supply chains are multifaceted and extend beyond immediate financial gains.

Table 6.1 Drivers of companies' sustainability efforts

Driver	2019	2018	2016	2015
Reputational risks/benefits	1	1	1	1
Customer/consumer demand	2	2	2	2
Investor interest	3	3	3	3
Operational risks/benefits	4	4	4	4
Talent recruitment/employee engagement/retention	5	5	5	5
Regulatory requirements	6	6	6	6
Market growth opportunities	7	7	7	7
Product and process innovation	8	8	8	8
CEO interest	9	9	9	9
Budget/cost reduction	10	10	10	10

SOURCE GlobeScan and BSR, 2015; GlobeScan and BSR, 2016; GlobeScan and BSR, 2018; GlobeScan and BSR, 2019

Global challenges in 2020s and sustainability

Since GlobeScan and BSR's last survey in 2019, the business landscape has undergone significant changes due to various events and legislative shifts, shaping supply chain operations. Some notable events include:

- *COVID-19 Pandemic*: The pandemic increased online sales, exposed supply chain vulnerabilities, and emphasized the importance of securing local supplies.
- *Russian Invasion of Ukraine*: This geopolitical event limited access to crucial raw materials and supplies from Russia and Ukraine.
- *President Biden's Executive Order 14057*: This order mandates that all new light-duty vehicles sold in the US must be 100 percent electric by 2035, impacting the automotive industry.
- *Inflation Reduction Act 2022*: This act requires a baseline for critical minerals in electric vehicle batteries to be extracted, processed, or recycled within specific regions, influencing sustainability considerations.

- *Uyghur Forced Labor Prevention Act (UFLPA):* This law prohibits US importation of goods produced with forced labor from Xinjiang, highlighting human rights and ethical concerns.

Despite the seeming negative impact of these events on prioritizing sustainability, it is essential to understand that sustainability has multifaceted implications, including the resilience of operations. Supply chain disruptions and new legislation can influence companies to incorporate sustainable practices to ensure operational continuity. Several examples from diverse industries and locations illustrate this point.

COVID-19 and Nike's Supply Chain Transformation

Nike responded to changing consumer patterns during the pandemic by building a digital-first supply chain for faster and more sustainable consumer service (Rowsell, 2022). Their transformation involved:

- *Greater Regional Diversity*: Moving from centralized distribution to regional centers.
- *Inventory Optimization*: Enhanced demand prediction and planning.
- *Automation and AI*: Utilizing AI and robots for sorting and packing.
- *Sustainable Freight and Packaging*: Emphasis on ground shipping, refurbishing damaged shoes, and eco-friendly packaging.

These changes, although not solely focused on sustainability, indirectly contribute to it. Decentralized distribution reduces shipping distances and emissions, optimized inventory minimizes unsold inventory and resource waste, and automation enhances resource efficiency and reduces errors.

This example underscores that sustainability intertwines with operational efficiency and resilience. The events mentioned have compelled businesses to incorporate sustainable practices not only for ethical reasons but also to ensure their viability in a changing world. As the business landscape evolves, sustainability continues to play a central role in decision-making, reflecting evolving consumer attitudes, investor demands, and operational imperatives.

Ukraine Invasion and Renewable power in Europe

In 2020, Russia supplied 24.4 percent of the EU's gross available energy, while domestic production satisfied only 41.7 percent of its needs. Notably, the natural gas sector experienced a significant shift. In 2021, the EU imported 83 percent of its natural gas, with nearly half of those imports originating from Russia, constituting almost 50 percent of the total imports (Yanatma, 2023). However, this scenario underwent a substantial change, with Russia's contribution dropping to 12 percent in October 2022. To mitigate the reduced Russian contribution, the EU sought to increase imports from alternative sources, including the United States.

In response to Russia's decision to curtail oil and gas supplies to EU countries, the EU launched the REPowerEU campaign. This initiative is aimed at bolstering the adoption of renewable energy sources, decreasing overall energy consumption, and diversifying the energy mix. Consequently, as of 2022, the EU generated 22 percent of its electricity from wind and solar energy, whereas only 20 percent was derived from fossil gas. Looking forward to 2030, RePowerEU envisions achieving more than 40 percent of the EU's total power generation from renewable sources (U.S. Mission Russia, 2023).

The integration of renewable energy into the power generation mix can have a substantial impact on reducing a company's carbon footprint. This is particularly crucial in regions that have implemented carbon penalties such as carbon taxes or cap-and-trade systems, as seen in the European Union. Transitioning to renewable power sources not only aligns with sustainability goals but also aligns with regulatory frameworks designed to mitigate environmental impact and promote cleaner energy alternatives.

Executive Order 14057, Inflation Reduction Act, COVID-19, and Car Manufacturing

Executive Order 14057 and the Inflation Reduction Act have significantly impacted the automotive industry's trajectory, particularly in the realm of electric vehicles (EVs). These mandates require American car manufacturers to focus on the development of EVs as part of efforts to reduce carbon emissions and promote cleaner transportation alternatives. The majority of current EVs rely on lithium-ion batteries, a technology that has rapidly gained prominence. However, this increased demand has brought about a shift in the dynamics of the lithium market.

As of 2022, three countries dominated the world's lithium production, with Australia accounting for 52 percent, Chile for 25 percent, and China for 13 percent (Bhutada, 2022). Notably, lithium use for batteries has grown substantially, rising from less than 30 percent in 2015 to 80 percent in 2022. Consequently, the global production of lithium (excluding the US) stood at 130,000 tons in 2022, with expectations that demand for EV batteries could increase from about 340 GWh to over 3500 GWh by 2030 (IEA, 2022).

Addressing the need for a reliable and localized supply of lithium has become pivotal for nations worldwide. Initiatives such as the EU's Critical Raw Materials Act aim to achieve a substantial extraction capacity by 2030. Several countries, including India and Iran, have identified significant lithium reserves, underlining the importance of domestic sources in securing the required raw materials for lithium-ion batteries.

The Federal Consortium for Advanced Batteries (FCAB, 2021) has emphasized the critical importance of building a strong and secure domestic industrial foundation for lithium-based batteries. This entails ensuring reliable access to various stages of material inputs, including raw materials, refined resources, and processed materials. Additionally, the FCAB advocates for the parallel development of sustainable substitutes and diversification of supply sources from unconventional and secondary channels.

The US government recognizes that establishing a domestic supply of raw materials for lithium-ion batteries is not only a strategic move for economic and technological advancement but also a critical step in achieving clean energy goals and addressing the impacts of climate change. By reducing reliance on external sources and fostering domestic capability, the US aims to enhance its energy security, reduce carbon emissions, and contribute to global efforts to transition to cleaner and more sustainable energy sources.

In the United States, Southern California's Imperial Valley has emerged as "Lithium Valley," capitalizing on geothermal energy projects that yield lithium-rich brine. This region has the potential to produce vast amounts of lithium carbonate, aiding the U.S. in establishing a local lithium supply chain (Stringfellow and Dobson, 2021).

However, merely relying on Lithium Valley and traditional mining practices might not ensure a sustainable lithium supply over the long term. Recycling is crucial to ensure a consistent lithium supply while minimizing environmental impact. United States Geological Services note that domestic recycling facilities have been expanding rapidly, with numerous companies in North America, Europe, and Canada engaging in lithium battery recycling. As of November 2022, 44 companies in Canada and the US and 47 companies in Europe recycled lithium batteries or planned to do so, up from about 25 companies in North America and Europe combined in 2020.

The changing landscape emphasizes the significance of securing local sources of raw materials for lithium-ion batteries, both to promote clean energy goals and to address potential supply shortages in the future. Initiatives that combine mining, localized production, and recycling play a pivotal role in ensuring a sustainable and resilient lithium supply chain.

The UFLPA and the apparel industry

The apparel industry faces a multitude of challenges in its sustainability efforts, ranging from fast fashion's impact on consumerism to resource-intensive processes and supply chain complexities. Addressing these challenges requires collaborative efforts from all supply chain partners, given the industry's global reach and intricate network of suppliers.

A recent survey conducted by EY in 2023 among Fortune 1000 C-suite executives reveals a growing emphasis on integrating sustainability into business models. While previous years focused on strategy and program development, the current trend centers on tangible and diverse sustainability initiatives. A significant portion of executives, over 40 percent, are prioritizing sustainability and ESG initiatives related to social equity.

The apparel industry's commitment to sustainability gained momentum following incidents like the Rana Plaza collapse in Bangladesh in 2013, prompting a focus on worker safety. However, more recent attention has shifted to the issue of Uyghur forced labor in China.

Over the past decade, a large portion of China's cotton production has relocated to the Xinjiang Uyghur Autonomous Region, raising concerns about forced labor practices. Customs and Borders Patrol enforces the Uyghur Forced Labor Prevention Act (UFLPA) by presuming goods from Xinjiang involve forced labor and restricting their entry into the US market unless proven otherwise (Burstein, 2023).

In response to evolving legislation and growing awareness, businesses are adapting their practices. Walmart, for instance, introduced its Supplier Requirements for Supply Chain Traceability (Walmart, 2022), mandating that suppliers uphold environmental and social standards across their supply chains and provide detailed documentation of each step in the chain of custody.

As the industry navigates these challenges, the importance of sustainability and ESG principles remains a central theme, with a growing focus on social equity and supply chain transparency. Collaborative efforts are crucial for driving positive change across the entire apparel supply chain and fostering a more sustainable and responsible industry.

Creating value by adopting sustainability

In the face of evolving challenges and shifting priorities, the third decade of the 21st century has brought a new perspective to sustainability efforts within companies and their supply chains. When confronted with disruptions in supply chains or increased operational costs, companies might be tempted to relegate sustainability initiatives to a lower priority. A recent survey (McKinsey & Co., 2021) highlighted a prevailing sentiment among respondents. Around 22 percent of participants reported experiencing modest or significant value from sustainability efforts in the past five years, while a similar percentage noted that such programs led to moderate or significant cost increases. Approximately one-third of respondents indicated that their sustainability initiatives had minimal or no financial impact, implying that a considerable portion of those surveyed do not perceive sustainability efforts as value-creating activities.

Interestingly, the survey also revealed that companies deriving value from sustainability investment often have CEOs who prioritize sustainability as a strategic imperative. These companies align their sustainability activities with their mission, values, and goals, aiming to make a tangible impact on relevant issues. Conversely, companies that do not find value in sustainability efforts tend to engage in such activities due to industry norms, regulatory requirements, and reputation-building.

Several dimensions contribute to capturing value from sustainability efforts:

- *CEO involvement*: Active engagement of the CEO is critical. CEOs must define a clear vision for sustainability implementation, set priorities and objectives, and establish metrics and performance indicators. Companies like IKEA[35], Interface[36], Levi Strauss & Co.[37], Nike[38], and Walmart[39], among others, have CEOs who consistently emphasize sustainability's importance.
- *Corporate culture*: Sustainability should be ingrained in the corporate culture, gaining buy-in from all employees. This involves educating employees about how sustainability aligns with the company's strategy and integrating sustainable practices into their roles. Clearly defined responsibilities for implementing sustainability initiatives are essential. Since 2018, Patagonia has given nearly $14 million to groups working to slow climate change. The company is encouraging individuals to get involved in community activism, they are pushing the industry to adopt higher standards, and they are demanding progressive regulations and significant investment from government.[40]
- *Customer engagement*: Addressing customer demand for sustainability is a significant driver for adopting sustainable practices. Companies should actively engage with customers, gather insights about their expectations, enhance supply chain transparency, share product information, and modify products when necessary.

McKinsey & Co. (2023) cite a study by NielsenIQ, which revealed that 78 percent of US consumers consider a sustainable lifestyle important. Companies adopting ESG-related claims experienced higher growth than those that didn't, regardless of their size. Products with ESG-related claims achieved an average cumulative growth of 28 percent, compared to 20 percent for products without such claims.

- *Supplier sustainability*: Given that each company represents a fraction of its broader supply chain, collaboration with suppliers is crucial to achieving sustainability goals. Incorporating sustainability performance into supplier selection and evaluation processes is vital. Companies should support their suppliers in enhancing sustainability performance through training, financial assistance, and other means.

For instance, Levi Strauss & Co., which sources products from over 500 suppliers in various countries, maintains a comprehensive supplier assessment process. Violations are categorized by severity, ranging from zero tolerance violations through immediate action items to continuous improvement items. Such approaches emphasize partnership and continuous development.[41]

Each company operates within a unique business landscape, and different industries face distinct challenges and opportunities. The size and location of a company can also influence whether sustainability efforts result in value creation or added costs. Nevertheless, regardless of these factors, every company must chart a course to embrace ESG principles to not only survive but also thrive in the current and future business environment.

Final takeaways

Today's companies are engaged in multifaceted efforts in their transition towards sustainable supply chains. The surroundings in which they operate are characterized by interconnectedness of environmental and social issues that create ongoing challenges that have to be addressed through innovative solutions in the pursuit of a more responsible and sustainable global business landscape. The imperative to transition to renewable energy and address human rights concerns has become integral to sustainable business practices. The examples provided illustrate the growing commitment to environmentally responsible practices, and the interconnectedness of sustainability, operational efficiency, and resilience.

Sustainability is no longer just a corporate responsibility but a strategic necessity. Companies that actively embrace ESG principles are better positioned to navigate challenges, build resilience, and create long-term value in an ever-changing business environment.

Endnotes

1 Nike. Nike Sustainability - Interactive Map, Nikeinc.com. 2021, manufacturingmap.nikeinc.com/ (archived at https://perma.cc/376B-HHED)

2 BBC News. Thailand floods disrupt production and supply chains, BBC News, October 13, 2011, www.bbc.com/news/business-15285149 (archived at https://perma.cc/5RBM-KEBB)

3 CDP. www.cdp.net (archived at https://perma.cc/33CS-VS2R).

4 Sustainable Apparel Coalition. Apparel Coalition, 2019, wwwapparelcoalition.org (archived at https://perma.cc/D58W-ZF8N)

5 MSC. Certified Sustainable Seafood, MSC, 2023, www.msc.org/en-us (archived at https://perma.cc/M944-24W4)

6 REPREVE® | Sustainable. Certifiable. Recycled. High-quality performance fiber, REPREVE®, 2018, www.repreve.com (archived at https://perma.cc/8U3M-LVGH)

7 Thermore. www.thermore.com (archived at https://perma.cc/9SM7-HU5M)

8 Coalition (SPC), S. P. (n.d.). Extended Producer Responsibility - SPC's Guide. Epr.sustainablepackaging.org. epr.sustainablepackaging.org/ (archived at https://perma.cc/CYX2-Z8FS)

9 Circular Online. 20 years of e-waste legislation in Europe: what's the way forward? (n.d.). Circular Online, 2024, www.circularonline.co.uk/insight/20-years-of-e-waste-legislation-in-europe-whats-the-way-forward/ (archived at https://perma.cc/8HK2-T3ZK)

10 US EPA. (2015, September 4). Regulations, Initiatives and Research on Electronics Stewardship. US EPA. www.epa.gov/smm-electronics/regulations-initiatives-and-research-electronics-stewardship (archived at https://perma.cc/9X7F-PZH3)

11 Electronics EPR in the United States | READ online. (n.d.). Oecd-Ilibrary.org. www.oecd-ilibrary.org/search?value1=extended+producer+responsibility&option1=quicksearch&facetOptions=51&facetNames=pub_igoId_facet&operator51=AND&option51=pub_igoId_facet&value51=%27igo%2Foecd%27&publisherId=%2Fcontent%2Figo%2Foecd&searchType=quick (archived at https://perma.cc/7EBY-WJZR)

12 iF Design - Clever Little Bag. (n.d.). Ifdesign.com, 2024, ifdesign.com/en/winner-ranking/project/clever-little-bag/68777 (archived at https://perma.cc/XX96-WGDU)

13 Amazon. Tide Laundry Detergent, 2024,www.amazon.com/Tide-Laundry-Detergent-Liquid-Original/dp/B085V5PPP8/ref=asc_df_B085V5PPP8/?tag=hyprod-20&linkCode=df0&hvadid=459481700288&hvpos=&hvnetw=g&hvrand=16594166766713744506&hvpone=&hvptwo=&hvqmt=&hvdev=c&hvdvcmdl=&hvlocint=&hvlocphy=9031079&hvtargid=pla-944166378153&th=1-- (archived at https://perma.cc/L9B2-DU9X)

14 Method products. www.methodproducts.com/home-care/laundry/laundry-detergent-66-loads-coconut-cactus-water-53-5-fl-oz (archived at https://perma.cc/CG3S-3XNU)

15 Seventh generation. www.seventhgeneration.com/concentrated-laundry-detergent-fresh-lavender (archived at https://perma.cc/EL5G-6LFE)

16 Seventh Generation. www.seventhgeneration.com/easydose-ultra-concentrated-laundry-detergent-lavender (archived at https://perma.cc/9FB5-9VLJ)

17 Amazon. How Amazon is reducing packaging. US about Amazon. December 13, 2020, www.aboutamazon.com/news/sustainability/how-amazon-is-reducing-packaging (archived at https://perma.cc/J5AS-PZJ6)

18 UPS. Company Profile, United Parcel Service, Inc. 2023, www.investors.ups.com/company-profile#:~:text=We%20deliver%20packages%20each%20business (archived at https://perma.cc/58PG-3A2G)

19 UPS. UPS To Enhance ORION With Continuous Delivery Route Optimization | About UPS. January 29, 2020, about.ups.com/us/en/newsroom/press-releases/innovation-driven/ups-to-enhance-orion-with-continuous-delivery-route-optimization.html (archived at https://perma.cc/3CC2-QKEZ)

20 FedEx Express Introduces Hybrid Electric Truck. FedEx Newsroom, May 20, 2003, newsroom.fedex.com/newsroom/united-states-english/fedex-express-introduces-hybrid-electric-truck (archived at https://perma.cc/R97M-P8GK)

21 FedEx Continues Advancing Fleet Electrification Goals with Latest 150 Electric Vehicle Delivery from BrightDr. FedEx Newsroom, June 21, 2022, newsroom.fedex.com/newsroom/global/fedex-continues-advancing-fleet-electrification-goals-with-latest-150-electric-vehicle-delivery-from-brightdrop (archived at https://perma.cc/XVK4-54HY)

22 Environmental Protection Agency. (2023, October 5). Sources of Greenhouse Gas Emissions. United States Environmental Protection Agency, October 5, 2023, www.epa.gov/ghgemissions/sources-greenhouse-gas-emissions (archived at https://perma.cc/5WLX-VQLF)

23 H Ritchie and M Roser, M. Emissions by Sector, Our World in Data, 2020, ourworldindata.org/emissions-by-sector#energy-electricity-heat-and-transport-73-2 (archived at https://perma.cc/8QW6-ZNQJ)

24 Nike. What to Know About Nike's Stance on Tackling Climate Change. Nike, September 19, 2019, about.nike.com/en/newsroom/releases/nike-move-to-zero-climate-change-initiative (archived at https://perma.cc/9FVZ-B37C)

25 What's in a Megawatt? (n.d.). SEIA. www.seia.org/initiatives/whats-megawatt (archived at https://perma.cc/ME3X-7CDC)

26 U Staff. LS&Co. Invests in Renewable Wind Energy. Levi Strauss & Co. October 19, 2022, www.levistrauss.com/2022/10/19/lsco-invests-in-renewable-wind-energy/ (archived at https://perma.cc/BNC4-DWNS)

27 i2. Commercial Carpet Tile & Resilient Flooring, Interface, www.interface.com/US/en-US/carpet-tile/i2.html (archived at https://perma.cc/SNG5-KNX8)

28 S Magazine and R. M Gorman (n.d.). How Dairy Farmers Are Turning Manure Into Money. Smithsonian Magazine, www.smithsonianmag.com/innovation/dairy-farmers-turning-manure-into-money-180981809/#:~:text=Micro%2Dorganisms%20break%20down%20the all%20the%20farm%27s%20heating%20needs. (archived at https://perma.cc/YJ2G-L7E3)

29 The Centre for Child Rights and Business. (n.d.). Childrights-Business.org. www.childrights-business.org (archived at https://perma.cc/YZL7-GTWL)

30 Tony's Chocolonely. The living income model for cocoa. (n.d.). Tony's Chocolonely. www.tonyschocolonely.com/us/en/our-mission/serious-cocoa-info/living-income-model (archived at https://perma.cc/EUN2-NXYR)

31 Inclusion of Young Workers in the IKEA Supply Chain in Indonesia - Our Impact - The Centre for Child Rights and Business. (n.d.). Www.childrights-Business.org. Retrieved February 26, 2024, from https://www.childrights-business.org/impact/inclusion-of-young-workers-in-the-ikea-supply-chain-in-indonesia.html (archived at https://perma.cc/6RW8-NB6U)

32 Bext360. (n.d.). www.bext360.com/#/home (archived at https://perma.cc/59JN-9AEX)

33 B Lab. B Lab Global Site, 2023, www.bcorporation.net/en-us/ (archived at https://perma.cc/7P9Y-F7V9)

34 Transportation. Walmart Sustainability Hub, April 5, 2022, www.walmartsustainabilityhub.com/climate/project-gigaton/transportation (archived at https://perma.cc/C5SS-N7E2)

35 J Brodin. How Ikea Is Prioritizing Sustainability. (2023, June 4). Time, June 4, 2023, www.time.com/6284013/ikea-ceo-jesper-brodin-interview-leadership/#:~:text=Under%20Jesper%20Brodin%2C%20the%20CEO (archived at https://perma.cc/6HSM-YY8P)

36 Interface @ 50: A conversation with CEO Laurel Hurd, GreenBiz. (n.d.). www.greenbiz.com/article/interface-50-conversation-ceo-laurel-hurd (archived at https://perma.cc/AY3J-YTY7)

37 C Bergh. Sustainable fashion at Levi Strauss, July 27, 2022, ceo-na.com/executive-interviews/levi-strauss-sustainable-fashion/ (archived at https://perma.cc/ECA7-BL4C)

38 L Thomas. Nike CEO John Donahoe: Shoppers care about sustainability. CNBC, February 5, 2020, www.cnbc.com/2020/02/05/nike-ceo-john-donahoe-shoppers-care-about-sustainabilty.html (archived at https://perma.cc/7LMT-22QD)

39 S Naussauer. Walmart CEO Says Companies Should Make Sustainable Products More Affordable. WSJ, January 18, 2023, www.wsj.com/livecoverage/davos2023/card/walmart-ceo-says-companies-should-make-climate-friendly-products-more-affordable-STltkIWF9pXscb5hIV0z# (archived at https://perma.cc/F9YL-3SFN)

40 Climate Goals - Patagonia. (n.d.). www.patagonia.com/climate-goals/#asset-modal-our-activism-toolkit (archived at https://perma.cc/F4K6-473L)

41 Levi Strauss & Co. Supply Chain: Going Beyond Compliance. Levi Strauss & Co, 2021, www.levistrauss.com/sustainability-report/community/supply-chain/ (archived at https://perma.cc/7N39-N2QS)

Circular Economy and its Influence on Supply Chain Network Design

07

After discussing sustainability in the previous chapter, we now focus on the concept of the circular economy, highlighting its contrast with the traditional linear model and its potential for sustainable resource management. We will discuss several strategies for achieving circularity and various facets of transitioning from a linear to a circular supply chain network design (SCND). The circular SCND paradigm shift offers both challenges and opportunities, requiring companies to rethink their operations, collaborate across the supply chain, and leverage technology for informed decision-making.

What is circular economy?

Industrial development has frequently been associated with the proliferation of a linear economy model (Figure 7.1), often characterized as the "take-make-waste" paradigm.

A classic illustration of this model is the utilization of fossil fuels, a finite resource, for energy production. Fossil fuels are extracted from the Earth ("take"), subjected to processing and conversion into energy ("make"), a procedure that concurrently generates a variety of pollutants and greenhouse gases ("waste"). Consequently, the

Figure 7.1 Linear Economy

SOURCE USC Marshall-Randall R. Kendrick Global Supply Chain Institute

linear economy perpetuates the depletion of resources and can ultimately lead to issues of resource scarcity and overconsumption. In stark contrast, renewable energy sources, such as hydroelectric power stations, wind turbines, and solar panels, tap into resources that are naturally replenished. This approach generates a continuous cycle, "closing the loop," wherein resources are not discarded at the end of their productive lifespan. Instead, they are reintegrated into the economy, possibly being repurposed for diverse uses. This cyclic pattern fundamentally contrasts with the linear model, contributing to sustainability and minimizing the impact on finite resources.

The "Dust Bowl" crisis of the 1930s caused ecological devastation in the parts of the United States. While extensive droughts were a primary catalyst behind this phenomenon, human activities, particularly the destruction of natural topsoil, emerged as another crucial contributing factor. Farmers, through practices like deep plowing, destroyed native deep-rooted grasses that played a vital role in conserving moisture and preventing soil erosion. Additionally, cotton farmers left their fields barren during winter months and employed controlled burns to manage weeds before planting, actions that further removed stabilizing vegetation (Borowski, 2012).

Contrastingly, Indigenous farming practices, established in the territories that constitute the present-day US, have spanned centuries, and centered on land management and farming approaches that safeguarded local ecosystems and biodiversity. These practices encompassed techniques such as intercropping, polycultures, water management, and permaculture (Heim, 2020). Numerous elements of Indigenous American agricultural practices persist today and have been integrated into the regenerative agricultural movement, which champions sustainable farming and land stewardship, guided by the principles of circularity. This approach not only respects Indigenous knowledge but also aligns with circular economy principles, striving to ensure agricultural sustainability and ecological preservation.

The aforementioned instances provide just two examples that underscore the disparities between a linear and circular economy. It becomes evident from these cases that the circular economy model aligns more harmoniously with the inherent natural cycles that unfold without human intervention. This alignment ultimately fosters greater sustainability by conserving resources and diminishing waste.

In the realm of nature, resources are consumed only when necessary. Waste generated by one process is seamlessly integrated as input for another, thereby fostering a continual and harmonious flow. The coexistence of animals and plants creates an equilibrium that drives mutual development. This harmony is observed through several mechanisms:

- *Predator–prey balance*: Predators pursue herbivores, effectively controlling their numbers and preventing overgrazing that could otherwise detrimentally affect the ecosystem.
- *Nutrient cycling*: Herbivores generate waste that nourishes the soil, nurturing plant growth. This cyclical nutrient flow sustains the balance of the ecosystem.
- *Ecosystem evolution*: The movement of animals from one area to another allows for uninterrupted plant growth. This sequential pattern perpetuates a recurring cycle that ensures ecological equilibrium.

In essence, nature's self-sustaining processes follow circular patterns where waste is minimized, resources are efficiently utilized, and balance is created. This harmony in nature serves as a compelling testament to the potential and efficacy of circular economy principles.

While terms "sustainability" and "circularity" are often used interchangeably due to their alignment, they represent distinct concepts. Sustainability is a broader notion encompassing practices that ensure the longevity and well-being of the environment, society, and the economy. Circular economy, on the other hand, constitutes a specific approach that contributes to sustainability by addressing resource consumption, waste reduction, and environmental impact in a systematic manner.

The Ellen MacArthur Foundation's definition of a circular economy aptly captures its essence. A circular economy is "a system where materials never become waste and nature is regenerated. In a circular economy, products and materials are kept in circulation through processes like maintenance, reuse, refurbishment, remanufacture, recycling, and composting. The circular economy tackles climate change and other global challenges, like biodiversity loss, waste, and pollution, by decoupling economic activity from the consumption of finite resources."[1]

The concept of circularity can extend beyond individual products or companies to encompass larger-scale projects, industries, or even entire cities. One such remarkable illustration is the Händelö Eco Industrial Park situated in Norrköping, Sweden, where a compre-

Figure 7.2 Transforming linear to circular economy

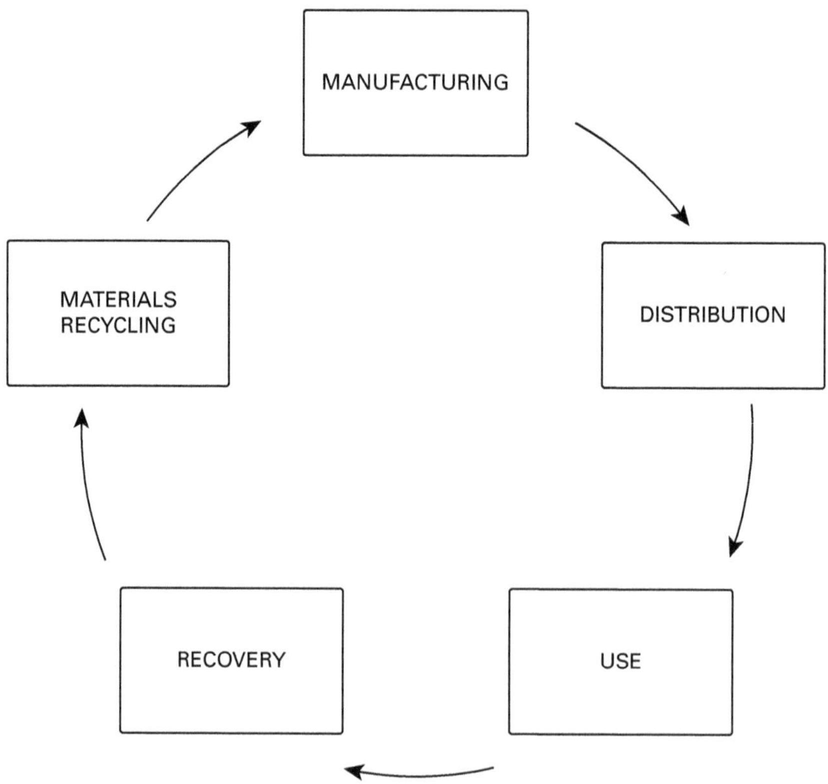

SOURCE USC Marshall-Randall R. Kendrick Global Supply Chain Institute

hensive circular economy approach is adopted to foster synergy and sustainability among various stakeholders. An exemplar is E.ON's waste incineration facility located in Händelö. This facility receives combustible waste from the city and reciprocally generates electricity and district heating for Norrköping. The excess steam produced as a byproduct at the incineration plant is redirected to fuel the operations of Lantmännen Agroetanol, a nearby grain-based ethanol production plant. The production of bioethanol by Lantmännen Agroetanol generates valuable by-products—protein-rich animal feed and carbon dioxide. These by-products are reused in adjacent farms and a carbonic acid factory, respectively. This system operates as a closed loop, where one entity's waste is another entity's resource, thereby exemplifying a circular economy in action.[2]

The Händelö Eco Industrial Park serves as a testament to the potential of collaborative efforts, symbiotic relationships, and circular economy principles applied on a broader scale. These initiatives not only foster economic growth but also showcase how multiple stakeholders can collectively address resource utilization, waste reduction, and sustainable development at a community level.

Before exploring various strategies for achieving circularity and examining their implications, we will provide a brief history of the circular economy.

History of circular economy

Although it is challenging to pinpoint the precise moment or author responsible for originating the concept of the circular economy, it is closely associated with the paper titled *The Economics of the Coming Spaceship Earth* by Kenneth E. Boulding, published in 1966. In this influential paper, Boulding introduced the idea of a new economic paradigm that was necessary to address the shifting environmental and resource constraints of our planet. He contrasted this emerging paradigm with the prevailing economic model of the time, which he referred to as the "cowboy economy."

Boulding proposed the concept of the "spaceman" economy as a way to describe the economic principles needed for a closed and interconnected Earth, where resources are finite, and pollution cannot be indefinitely absorbed. He envisioned Earth as a closed system resembling a spaceship, highlighting the necessity for a cyclical and sustainable approach to resource management. Although the term "circular economy" was not explicitly used in the paper, Boulding's ideas foreshadowed the core principles of circularity, emphasizing the importance of continuous material reproduction within ecological limits and the need to move away from the linear "take-make-waste" model. The paper laid the groundwork for discussions and developments that eventually contributed to the formation and popularization of the circular economy concept.

In his 1981 paper "The Product-Life Factor", Walter Stahel introduced the term "spiral-loop system" as a foundational concept for an alternative economic approach. Stahel's spiral-loop system consists of four interconnected loops: reuse, repair, reconditioning, and recycle. Each loop corresponds to one of the key principles of circular economy, aligning with the 4R framework that emphasizes reducing, reusing, repairing, and recycling materials to minimize waste and resource consumption. Stahel is also credited with coining the term "cradle-to-cradle," which contrasts with the linear "cradle-to-grave" concept of resource use and disposal. The notion of a circular relationship within the economy was introduced in the book *Economics of Natural Resources and the Environment* by Pearce and Turner (1989). The authors advocated for a transformation from the prevailing approach that treats the environment as a waste repository to a circular model where waste serves as a source of new resources.

While the practical movement toward circularity gained traction in the late 20th century, widespread adoption and recognition surged in the 21st century. Various international organizations, including the United Nations[3] and the World Circular Economy Forum[4], have taken steps to provide resources and guidance for businesses, governments, and individuals interested in integrating circular economy principles into their practices. These initiatives aim to facilitate the transition towards more sustainable and circular economic systems. Below, we explore some of these initiatives in more detail.

European countries

The Council of the European Communities took a significant step towards promoting circular economy principles when it adopted the initial Waste Framework Directive in July 1975. This directive emphasized the importance of waste recovery and the utilization of reclaimed materials to conserve natural resources (Council of the EU, 1975). Over the years, the directive underwent multiple amendments, including revisions in 1991 and 2006. The most recent proposal for amendment was introduced in July 2023 (European Commission, 2023). This latest iteration of the directive emphasizes the need for stronger and swifter action at both the EU and Member State levels. It particularly highlights the environmental sustainability of sectors with high resource intensity, such as textiles and food, which have been identified as significant contributors to negative environmental impacts. These sectors have encountered obstacles related to financing and technology, hindering their progress towards circular economy transition and decarbonization. Notably, food and textiles rank as the first and fourth most resource-intensive sectors respectively. The directive also underscores the importance of adhering to the fundamental principles of the EU waste management hierarchy, which places priority on waste prevention, followed by preparation for re-use and recycling.

It's worth noting that the first formal Circular Economy Action Plan was adopted by the European Commission in December 2015. This plan marked a crucial milestone in the EU's efforts to transition towards a circular economy. The action plan was subsequently revised in March 2020, with a focus on various aspects of circular economy implementation. This revised plan aimed to address areas such as product design, promotion of circular processes, encouragement of sustainable consumption practices, and the establishment of waste prevention measures. The overarching goal was to ensure the efficient utilization of resources, prolong the retention of resources within the economy, and minimize waste generation.

The United States

The systematic advancement of circular economy principles in the United States has progressed at a somewhat slower pace compared to

Europe. In November 2021, the EPA took a significant step by publishing the National Recycling Strategy (EPA, 2021). This strategy outlined a comprehensive approach to enhancing recycling practices within the country. Building upon this effort, in April 2023, the EPA released the Draft National Strategy to Prevent Plastic Pollution (EPA, 2023) for public review and commentary. This draft strategy aimed to address the pressing issue of plastic pollution by proposing measures to prevent its occurrence.

Additionally, collaborative efforts have been undertaken by organizations to facilitate the integration of circular economy principles into business operations. The US Chamber of Commerce Foundation Corporate Citizenship Center, in partnership with The Sustainability Consortium and The Retail Industry Leaders Association, developed a web-based Circular Economy Toolbox. This toolbox serves as a practical resource to assist companies in incorporating circularity into their business practices. It offers guidance, tools, and insights to help businesses navigate the challenges and opportunities associated with adopting circular economy strategies.[5] While the US approach may have taken time to gain momentum, initiatives such as these demonstrate a growing commitment to advancing circular economy principles within the country.

The Ellen MacArthur Foundation

Following her remarkable accomplishment of becoming the fastest solo sailor to complete a circumnavigation of the globe in 2005, Ellen MacArthur founded the Ellen MacArthur Foundation in 2010, driven by the vision of establishing a circular economy characterized by the elimination of waste and pollution, the continuous circulation of products and materials at their highest value, and the regeneration of nature.

Since its inception, the Ellen MacArthur Foundation has been a prominent advocate and thought leader in the field of circular economy. The foundation has published numerous reports addressing various aspects of circular economy and its global potential. These reports cover topics such as circular economy opportunities, policy frameworks, plastic usage and initiatives, textiles and fashion, global trade, and supply chains, among others. The foundation's research is accompanied by practical efforts to drive change.

The Ellen MacArthur Foundation actively engages with diverse stakeholders to promote circular economy principles. It organizes summits and events to facilitate collaboration among companies, governments, and innovators. Additionally, the foundation develops educational resources for teachers and academics to raise awareness and understanding of circular economy concepts.[6] By fostering connections, sharing insights, and offering practical solutions, the Ellen MacArthur Foundation has played a significant role in advancing the adoption of circular economy practices worldwide. We can now explore the various strategies that companies can embrace when transitioning to a circular economy model.

Steps for achieving circularity

Traditionally, circularity was encapsulated by the 3 R's ("Reduce-reuse-recycle")[7] as a counterpoint to the "take-make-waste" principle that characterizes the linear economy. However, in recent times, this framework has expanded to encompass additional R's, evolving from 4 R's, 5 R's, and 6 R's to as many as 10 R's ("Refuse-rethink-reduce-reuse-repair-refurbish-remanufacture-repurpose-recycle-recover") (Potting et al., 2016). This growing diversity in descriptions occasionally leads to confusion, as different strategies exist within models featuring varying numbers of R's. For instance, a 6 R or 10 R model can include different strategies depending on the perspective of different authors.

In Table 7.1, we present a description of the 10R strategies, as outlined by PBL Netherlands Environmental Assessment Agency. These strategies are ordered by priority, ranging from those that exhibit the highest level of circularity to those of lower priority. For instance, the redesign of a product often enables more efficient resource utilization compared to repairing an existing product. In contrast, incineration is allocated the lowest priority due to its removal of materials from the regenerative cycle.

Table 7.1 Circularity strategies within the production chain, in order of priority

Smarter product use and manufacture	Refuse	Make product redundant by abandoning its function or by offering the same function with a radically different product
	Rethink	Make product use more intensive
	Reduce	Increases efficiency in product manufacturing or use by consuming fewer natural resources and materials
Extend lifespan of products andtheir parts	Reuse	Reuse by another customer of discarded product which still fulfil its original function
	Repair	Repair and maintenance of defective product so it can be used with its original function
	Refurbish	Restore and update an old product
	Remanufacture	Use parts of discarded roduct in a new product with the same function
	Repurpose	Use parts of discard product in a new product with a different function
Useful application of materials	Recycle	Process materials to obtain the same or lower quality
	Recover	Incinerating of material with energy recovery

SOURCE Adapted from Potting et al., 2016

Next, we explore more comprehensively each of the ten strategies. A higher level of circularity implies higher environmental benefits, often arising from the prolonged retention of materials within supply chains — potentially as parts of different products — while simultaneously maintaining their quality. This subsequently translates to a reduced necessity for virgin resources.

Refuse

"Refusing" a product either due to not requiring its function or offering a comparable function through a radically different product is regarded as the strategy yielding the highest degree of circularity. This approach typically leads to a substantial reduction in the consumption of virgin materials and/or the generation of waste and pollution. Simultaneously, it represents the most challenging strategy to enact due to its potential requirement for pioneering technologies, substantial shifts in product design, alterations in manufacturing processes, and/or changes in customer behavior.

A recent exemplar of such a transformation, wherein an older product is superseded by a novel product delivering the same functionality, is the increasing market penetration of electric vehicles (EVs) at the expense of conventional gasoline- and diesel-powered internal combustion engine (ICE) vehicles. Another instance is the displacement of fax machines by the electronic exchange of PDF files. These instances underscore the transformative potential of the "refusing" strategy in reshaping industries and achieving enhanced circularity.

Rethink

The "rethinking" strategy encourages us to fundamentally redesign a product or alter the way we utilize it. This endeavor typically demands a considerable degree of creativity, involving the reimagining of established processes. It frequently necessitates the introduction of novel technologies into the production process, although exceptions exist, as illustrated by our second example.

Not too long ago, individuals had to purchase a dedicated calculator to perform tasks more complicated than basic arithmetic. They also needed to acquire vinyl records and a turntable to enjoy their favorite tunes. Additionally, they had to procure paper maps for various locations they planned to traverse, invest in telephones, and phone books to stay connected with friends, buy cameras and films for capturing cherished memories, and purchase floppy disks and hard drives to store and safeguard data. This list could extend endlessly. These pursuits often entailed acquiring distinct devices for performing specific tasks and different means for conserving data, sound, or imagery. Today, all these functions are streamlined through a single device—the smartphone. This versatile product has evolved into an indispensable aspect of daily existence, yet it was non-existent until the early 21st century. The smartphone exemplifies the convergence of various activities and functions into a singular, multi-functional entity that has revolutionized how we can increase intensity of product use.

On the spectrum of low-tech solutions, we can consider the paradigm of hotel bathrooms. In the past, a night in a hotel often entailed encountering tiny bottles of shampoo, conditioner, and body lotion in the bathroom. This practice not only entailed substantial consumption of plastics for making the containers but also resulted in the wastage of leftover product within the bottles. To counterbalance their adverse environmental impact, numerous hotels have undertaken a shift and now opt for a more environmentally conscious approach, providing larger, wall-mounted bottles containing personal care products. These bottles are shared among room occupants and can be replenished when necessary. This seemingly uncomplicated alteration has yielded a marked reduction in the volume of waste generated by the hotel industry. This illustrative change underscores the significance of relatively simple shifts in practice that can significantly contribute to a more sustainable approach.

Reduce

The concept of "reducing" the quantity of materials and/or virgin resources used in production was explored in a previous chapter, through examples such as the integration of CAD systems for inputting patterns into cutting machines or the adoption of concentrated detergents to minimize container.

Another notable instance involves the innovation of waterless textile dyeing machines by DyeCoo Textile Systems, a Netherlands-based company collaborating with renowned brands like Nike, Adidas, and IKEA. DyeCoo's technology replaces water with CO_2 in the textile dyeing process. Given that a conventional textile dyeing process consumes approximately 100–150 liters of water per kilogram of textile material, DyeCoo's solution significantly conserves water — a resource that is increasingly scarce.[8] This advancement not only underscores the potential of resource-efficient practices but also aligns with the imperative of sustainable resource management.

Reuse

"Reusing" is the strategy harboring the highest circularity within the second tier of strategies, all of which are aimed at prolonging the lifespan of products. Reuse practices have long been employed in various industries, even predating the widespread discussion of circularity. A few illustrations encompass:

- *Automotive industry*: Numerous car dealerships sell both new and pre-owned vehicles, offering customers the opportunity to trade in their existing automobiles to offset the cost of acquiring new ones.
- *Education sector*: Many students opt to purchase secondhand textbooks rather than new ones. Given the temporary nature of textbook usage and students' financial constraints, acquiring used books supplies essential resources while economizing.
- *Retail*: Stores like Goodwill retail clothing items no longer desired by their original purchasers. These gently used items, still in good condition, can enrich another person's wardrobe.

In addition to the above instances, there exists a myriad of similar cases. The rise of e-commerce has further amplified the popularity of the reuse strategy. Platforms like Amazon, eBay, and analogous websites facilitate customers in reselling products they no longer require, providing value to both them and future buyers. This concurrently diminishes environmental impact.

Several apparel companies, such as Patagonia[9] and Levi's[10], actively encourage customers to return worn yet well-maintained items for store credit. These companies then market such secondhand items on their platforms, exemplifying how the reuse strategy can be seamlessly integrated into contemporary business models.

Repair

"Repairing" was a common practice for a diverse array of products before the advent of globalization. During this era, new products often carried substantial costs, making repairing an existing item an economically smart choice that simultaneously benefited household budgets and had a positive impact on the environment. With the evolution of global supply chains and companies capitalizing on cheap manufacturing options, the paradigm shifted. Replacing malfunctioning or non-operational products with new ones was frequently perceived as a faster and more cost-effective alternative. Unfortunately, this approach contributed to the proliferation of waste generation, aggravating the tragedy of the commons.

However, the concept of repair has remained steadfast in the context of pricier items like automobiles, high-end electronics, jewelry, and analogous products. These sectors recognize the value of preserving items of substantial worth through repair, illustrating a more sustainable and conscious approach that counteracts the disposable culture propagated by rapid consumption.

With the surge in the relevance of sustainability across an increasing segment of the population, both consumers and companies have renewed their focus on repair as a fundamental practice. Diverse companies are stepping forward to assist their customers by providing repair services, be it free of charge or for a nominal fee. For example:

- *Patagonia*: This company actively warns its customers about the perils of excessive consumerism and empowers them with tutorials on mending their own products. Additionally, Patagonia offers complimentary repair services within their stores or through a convenient mail-in program.[11]
- *Levi's Tailor Shops*: Renowned for their denim, Levi's provides a suite of repair services that encompass tasks such as patching rips, hem mending, and button replacement, reinforcing their commitment to product longevity.[12]
- *Osprey*: This outdoor backpack manufacturer offers to rectify any damage or defect in their products, free of charge, throughout the product's lifetime.[13]
- *JanSport*: Offering a dual approach, JanSport provides complimentary repairs for manufacturing defects and charges a nominal fee for damages resulting from accidents, inadequate care, or typical wear and tear.[14]

- *Zippo*: Zippo's dedication to their products is epitomized by their willingness to repair their lighters, regardless of the date of purchase or the cause of malfunction.[15]

These instances underscore the transition toward more sustainable practices, as companies actively facilitate the repair of their products, prolonging their utility and diminishing the prevalence of disposable culture.

Refurbish

"Refurbishing" represents a strategy closely linked to reuse, wherein a used product undergoes a process of updating or "rejuvenation" before being sold to a new customer. This practice spans various industries and is gaining traction as the number of sustainability-conscious consumers grows.

While the automotive sector has long offered certified pre-owned vehicles, the electronics industry has witnessed substantial growth in the adoption of refurbishing. Notably, original manufacturers like Apple[16], Samsung[17], and Dell[18] have embraced this approach. Furthermore, major retailers such as Amazon[19] and eBay[20] have entered the arena, extending certified refurbished products to an expansive range of offerings beyond electronics. These encompass household appliances, power tools, bathroom fixtures, kitchen faucets, and an array of other product categories.

The healthcare industry also demonstrates the application of refurbishing through programs like GE Healthcare's GoldSeal initiative, which provides refurbished imaging and ultrasound systems[21]. This expansion of the refurbishing strategy across diverse industries highlights its alignment with sustainability goals and the evolving preferences of discerning consumers.

Remanufacture

While "refurbishing" relates to the sale of the original but upgraded product to customers, "remanufacturing" encompasses a process in which components of the original product are used to create a new product with identical functionality.

Numerous instances of remanufacturing are observed in consumable products or products featuring consumable parts. In the era preceding digital cameras and smartphones, companies like Fuji and Kodak sold many single-use cameras. Both companies retrieved a significant portion of these cameras post-film development, replaced the film, and resold the cameras to customers. Comparable practices extend to ink and toner printer cartridges.

Within the durable product category, Xerox stands out as a trailblazer in remanufacturing. According to their official website, "Beginning with our first commercial product, the Xerox 914, Xerox introduced electronics remanufacturing long before the term 'circular economy' was coined".[22] In the present day, numerous companies have adopted this approach. For example, Caterpillar's Cat Reman program collects used products that might be unusable, disassembles them into components, examines the parts for salvageable elements, and repurposes them as components for new Caterpillar machines[23]. Similarly, John Deere's Powertrain ReLife Plus program refreshes a machine that is either failed or approaching the end of its life with a new powertrain and other remanufactured components.[24] Cisco follows suit by offering certified remanufactured products spanning diverse categories like collaboration devices, routers, and switches.[25] These instances illustrate the evolving landscape of remanufacturing, manifesting its alignment with circular economy principles and sustainable practices.

Repurpose

"Repurposing" differs from remanufacturing in that components of used products are integrated into new products with distinct functionalities. In a preceding chapter, we cited instances like Unifi and Thermore, firms employing plastic bottles to create materials for the apparel industry. Notably, Levi's facilitates their customers in transforming deteriorated jeans into shorts, shorts into wallets, and wallets into patches through tutorials and videos.[26]

Additional instances from various industries include:

- *Plastic road construction (India):* Dr. Rajagopalan Vasudevan devised a patented method that amalgamates plastic waste like bags, cups, and packaging chips with bitumen, employing the blend for road construction. India has successfully built over 2,500 km of plastic roads between 2006 and 2023, illustrating this inventive repurposing approach (Patil et al., 2023).

- *Recycled bottles and jars*: Crushed recycled bottles and jars offer multifaceted applications, including utilization in water treatment, organic pesticides, beach replenishment, and integration into glass wool insulation for residential spaces.[27]
- *Reclaimed lumber market*: In 2020, the reclaimed lumber market attained a valuation of $49.27 billion. Lumber sourced from bridges, pallets, or construction projects finds new life in an array of applications, ranging from furniture and paneling to flooring, boxes, and toys (Grand View Research, 2021).

These examples underscore the dynamic landscape of repurposing, showcasing how creative adaptation can yield valuable solutions across diverse industries while mitigating waste generation.

Recycle

"Recycling" is the strategy with the highest circularity in the final tier of strategies, concentrating on the useful application of materials. This phase transitions from product components to materials, a process that may yield materials of either the same or diminished quality. As recycling discarded products usually implies that pollutants and other materials are combined with inputs, maintaining the original quality can pose challenges. Nevertheless, certain instances do exist where quality retention is attainable. Examples include:

- *Municipal solid waste (MSW) recycling*: Within the recycling of materials from the MSW stream, aluminum cans stand out, displaying potential for a 100 percent yield rate. Glass containers closely follow, achieving an 85 percent yield rate.
- *Levi's Circular 501 Jeans*: Levi's introduces the concept of repeatedly recyclable products with their Circular 501 jeans. These jeans incorporate certified organic cotton blended with Circulose fiber, an environmentally sourced viscose composed partially of

post-consumer recycled denim and textiles. By eliminating pollutants that could disrupt the cotton recovery process, elements like pocketing details, labels, and threads—typically woven from synthetic fibers—feature 100 percent cotton composition in this product.[28]

These illustrations highlight how recycling, despite its complexities, can offer sustainable solutions by providing materials with new applications, often enhancing the lifespan and minimizing environmental impact.

There are many more instances that demonstrate quality degradation after recycling, including:

- *Paper recycling*: Paper and paper products constitute a significant portion of the US MSW stream and maintain the highest recycling rate compared to other materials in MSW.[29] This practice carries numerous environmental advantages; for instance, producing 1,000 kg of paper conserves around 7,000 gallons of water, 17–31 trees, and 4,000 kWh of electricity.[30] However, paper recycling results in the diminishing quality of fibers with each recycling cycle. After undergoing recycling 5–7 times, fibers become too short to effectively bond into new paper, necessitating their amalgamation with fresh fibers during manufacturing.[31]
- *Recycled plastics for food storage*: Specific types of plastics, including PET, HDPE, LDPE, PP, and PC, hold FDA approval for food storage applications. However, not all of them maintain their safety for food contact following the recycling process. While recycled PET remains FDA-approved for food contact, recycled LDPE is excluded from such categorization, and the safety of recycled HDPE is assessed by the FDA on a case-by-case basis.[32]

These examples underscore the nuanced intricacies of recycling, where material quality degradation is an inherent challenge that necessitates careful consideration for optimal environmental and health outcomes.

Recover

The strategy of energy "recovery" from incineration occupies the least preferable position in the circularity spectrum. According to the

EPA, this approach does not constitute waste minimization. Instead, energy recovery should be considered as a course of action only after all other avenues for waste minimization have been exhaustively explored. Energy harnessed from waste incineration can be transformed into heat, electricity, or fuel.

Waste incineration in the United States originated in the late 19th century, primarily focused on disposal rather than energy generation. Unfortunately, this practice also contributed to substantial air pollution. The introduction of the Clean Air Act in 1970 triggered the shutdown of numerous incinerators that had not adopted emission-limiting technologies. However, by the 1980s, waste combustion witnessed a resurgence, with many new facilities incorporating energy recovery practices. Presently, the EPA reports the presence of 75 energy recovery facilities spread across 25 US states, primarily concentrated in the Northeast. In 2017, these facilities collectively combusted over 34 million tons of MSW for energy recovery purposes.[33]

Circularity and supply chain network design

Transitioning from a linear to a circular economy has a profound impact on the design of supply chain networks. To understand this shift, it's essential to examine the fundamental changes in designing a traditional linear supply chain versus a circular one.

In a linear supply chain, the focus is on optimizing the flow of goods from raw material acquisition to processing, manufacturing, distribution, and finally, consumption. This linear model ends with disposal, typically in landfills once products have reached the end of their useful lives. The design is optimized for one-way movement of materials and products, often resulting in resource depletion, waste generation, and environmental degradation. In contrast, a circular economy demands a complete overhaul of this linear approach. The circular supply chain model requires the optimization of flows in the opposite direction, prioritizing the reuse, refurbishment, and recycling of products and materials. This requires a dynamic and flexible network that can handle the complexities of returning products from end consumers back into the system.

The shift to a circular supply chain network design introduces several challenges:

- *Reverse logistics optimization*: The circular model necessitates efficient reverse logistics systems to retrieve used products from consumers. This involves establishing collection points, transportation, inspection, sorting, and decisions on whether to repair, refurbish, remanufacture, or recycle products.
- *Demand forecasting*: Predicting the demand for new products becomes more challenging due to the uncertain volume and timing of product returns. Traditional demand forecasting methods may need to be adapted to account for these uncertainties.
- *Product lifecycle extension*: Extending the life of products through repair, refurbishment, and remanufacturing introduces new processes that require specialized skills and resources.
- *Multi-channel distribution*: Circular supply chains may involve multiple channels for returning products, such as in-store returns, online returns, or collection centers. These channels need to be coordinated and integrated.
- *Collaboration and partnerships*: Circular supply chains often require collaboration between manufacturers, retailers, refurbishers, recyclers, and consumers. Building strong partnerships is essential for effective material flows.
- *Economic and environmental metrics*: Traditional supply chain metrics like cost and efficiency must be supplemented with metrics that assess environmental impact, resource utilization, and circularity performance.
- *Technology and data management*: Advanced technologies like IoT, RFID, and data analytics play a crucial role in tracking returned products, assessing their condition, and making informed decisions on the appropriate circular strategy.

Overall, the transition to a circular SCND involves a paradigm shift from linear resource consumption to a regenerative and sustainable approach. This transformation not only challenges traditional supply chain practices but also opens opportunities for innovation, increased resource efficiency, reduced waste, and positive environmental impact.

Smarter product use and manufacture—Refuse, Rethink, Reduce

The first and most desirable set of strategies for achieving circularity in SCND from Table 1 requires companies to reevaluate their operational approaches. This often entails revisiting the drawing board to explore diverse material options and design possibilities. Naturally, the adoption of alternative materials may entail engaging a different set of suppliers, potentially located in alternate parts of the world.

As mentioned earlier, the strategies within this first set typically necessitate modifications in product design, the utilization of different materials, and/or adjustments in how customers use the products. Companies committed to the principles of a circular economy should approach these strategies with a focus on minimizing adverse environmental effects while facilitating the extension of product lifespans and the longevity of their components. In essence, this approach should facilitate the seamless application of strategies from the second set to novel products. Such an approach encompasses steering clear of toxic materials, simplifying product structures by reducing the number of parts and diverse materials employed in construction, and designing for easy disassembly and recycling.

Car manufacturing

One industry that exemplifies the "refuse" strategy is car manufacturing. EV powertrains feature approximately 60 percent fewer moving parts compared to those in conventional vehicles. As car manufacturers transition from ICE vehicles to EVs, they must consider a broader range of factors, such as lithium suppliers, lithium processors, cell component manufacturers, battery production, and more, which were not needed in ICE manufacturing.

- *Lithium suppliers*: In 2022, lithium production was distributed as follows: Australia accounted for 52 percent, Chile for 25 percent, and China for 13 percent.[34]
- *Processing and cell component manufacturing*: China is a significant player in processing and cell component manufacturing, producing nearly 60 percent of lithium chemicals and around

61 percent of the world's cathodes.[35] Efforts to diversify supply are underway, including ongoing projects for lithium hydroxide production in Australia, the US, the EU, and other locations.[36] The US Department of Energy (DOE) announced a $2.8 billion investment in bolstering domestic EV supply chains through the Bipartisan Infrastructure Law in October 2022.[37] Approximately $1.6 billion is designated to support domestic processing of lithium and other battery materials among 11 companies. The EU's Critical Raw Materials Act aims to achieve processing capacity for 40 percent of the EU's annual needs by 2030.[38]

- *EV battery production*: In 2021, global EV battery production capacity was led by China at 77 percent, followed by the EU and the US at 7 percent each, Korea at 5 percent, and Japan at 4 percent.[39] The US Inflation Reduction Act, enacted in August 2022, prioritized strengthening domestic supply chains for EVs, prompting a $52 billion investment in North American EV supply chains by major EV and battery manufacturers.[40] The DOE's Vehicle Technologies Office forecasts a nearly 20-fold increase in total battery manufacturing capacity in the US between 2021 and 2030.[41] According to estimates from Argonne National Laboratory, EV battery production capacity in the US is projected to reach 750 GWh by 2025, further expanding to 900 GWh by 2030.[42] If other figures from S&P Global forecasts remain constant, this shift would reduce China's share to 45 percent, adjust Europe's share to 17 percent, and allocate 36 percent to the US.

As a notable example, in the realm of EVs, General Motors (GM) is strategically forming partnerships with semiconductor manufacturers and making substantial investments in battery production. They are also collaborating with companies to ensure a stable supply of cathodes, enhancing processing capabilities, and establishing domestic lithium mines in the United States. It is acknowledged, however, that achieving the desired production volume through these partnerships will require several years. In the interim, GM remains significantly reliant on sources based in China.

Simultaneously, GM recognizes the necessity of sustaining its ICE supply chain, as conventional and hybrid vehicles are not expected to vanish suddenly. The development of new ICE vehicles necessitates adherence to stricter standards, and the manufacturing of components for existing ICE vehicles remains imperative. As a result, GM needs to maintain collaboration with ICE suppliers and invest in innovation, recognizing that the workload in this domain is gradually diminishing.

Anticipating a notable shift towards EV adoption, certain suppliers are divesting and consolidating aspects of their ICE-related business. This transformative trend is reshaping the existing supplier landscape, as discussed in Ludwig (2023).

Servicizing

An effective approach to enhancing the intensity of product utilization ("rethink") involves embracing "servicizing." This entails a shift in investment focus from traditional product purchasing models to service-based purchasing models. Numerous business models have successfully employed servicizing, and a few illustrative examples include:

- *Third Party Logistics (3PL):* In this model, third-party logistics providers offer comprehensive services related to logistics, encompassing storage, delivery, customer service, customs clearance, supplier hubs, and more. Businesses that engage 3PL providers can forgo the necessity of procuring or expanding their own transportation fleet and warehouse space.
- *IT "Lifecycle Solutions":* Providers offering IT lifecycle solutions present companies with configuration, maintenance, repair, and upgrades for their leased IT equipment. This obviates the need for businesses to invest in the outright purchase of their IT resources.
- *Car Sharing:* Car-sharing services provide access to vehicles located in designated parking areas for short-term usage. Companies that embrace car sharing eliminate the need to acquire and maintain their own fleet of vehicles.

The concept of servicizing entails a transition of expenses that were traditionally categorized under Capital Expenses (CAPEX)—typically representing long-term investments—into Operational Expenses

(OPEX), which are associated with shorter-term operational costs. This shift not only assists companies in conserving their capital but also enhances their flexibility. Additionally, it brings forth distinct tax implications.

Manufacturers can derive notable advantages from adopting servicizing strategies as well. For instance, Xerox has effectively implemented a model wherein they lease their printers and photocopiers to corporate clients. This approach allows Xerox to maintain ownership of its products while capitalizing on modular design principles that facilitate reuse, refurbishment, and recycling. Consequently, Xerox can curb costs and generate a favorable environmental impact by minimizing the consumption of virgin materials.

Extending lifespan of products and their parts—reuse, repair, refurbish, remanufacture, repurpose

Companies that embrace strategies from the second set from Table 7.1 (Extending lifespan of products and their parts) must incorporate a pivotal step: the collection of used or discarded products, regardless of the specific strategy chosen. Consequently, the initial phase of adopting any of these strategies involves establishing a "reverse" supply chain, designed to facilitate the return of products from customers back to the company. This endeavor is notably distinct from the typical "forward" supply chain, which optimizes the flow of resources from suppliers to end consumers. Enhancing efficiencies in the reverse direction presents a complex challenge.

Forecasting the locations, timing, and volume of product returns can be significantly more intricate than predicting new product demand, distribution locations, and timing. This inherent uncertainty further complicates the task. Once the returned products are received by the company, a meticulous inspection process is required. This assessment aims to determine the condition of the products and whether they are suitable for any of the strategies under consideration by the company. Alternatively, the products might necessitate recycling or, regrettably, disposal in a landfill.

Extending the lifecycle of a product often involves repairing or replacing specific components. This implies a demand for new parts, albeit with a different and less foreseeable volume compared to the production of new devices, as not every component requires replacement. Simultaneously, the reintegration of previously owned products into a company's product offering will influence the demand for new products. Consequently, even the segments of the process that mirror the "traditional" flow of the supply chain—moving from manufacturer to customer—are confronted with challenges stemming from higher uncertainty.

Furthermore, the implementation of such strategies mandates a workforce composed of specialized and highly skilled individuals. These professionals are essential for performing tasks such as inspections, repairs, and various other activities, which contribute to the successful execution of the reverse supply chain and the broader circular economy approach.

Levi's SecondHand

As an exemplification of the "reuse" strategy, Levi's SecondHand website gives customers the opportunity to purchase pre-owned Levi's clothing. Customers are encouraged to return their used items to Levi's, a process currently limited to participating US stores. This approach requires careful planning due to its specific requirements, such as appointments and the acceptance of only jeans, denim shorts, and Trucker Jackets in satisfactory condition.

Levi's undertakes the task of optimizing the reverse logistics process only for a designated subset of their stores. The trade-in process requires prior appointments and consultations with a stylist responsible for inspecting the items. Acceptance is granted solely to jeans, denim shorts, and Trucker Jackets that are in wearable condition. Items deemed unwearable include those featuring significant rips, holes, stains, missing buttons, nonfunctioning zippers, and similar issues. Each individual item requires a thorough inspection, and if it passes the evaluation, the customer receives a gift card in return.

The subsequent stages include professional cleaning, categorization, and listing on the SecondHand.levi.com website. In cases where an item is deemed unwearable, Levi's either donates the product or follows proper disposal policy. Although this process does not involve repairs or manufacturing, it entails on-site inspections, the "reversed" transportation of items from stores to the processing center, as well as the coordination of cleaning, sorting, and responsible disposal.

Levi's SecondHand initiative implies a complex operational model that leverages careful assessment, transportation logistics, cleaning protocols, and organization to successfully integrate pre-owned items into their product offerings.

Apple trade-in

As an illustration of the "refurbish" strategy, Apple extends its customers the opportunity to trade in their Apple devices, as well as third-party devices, in exchange for a trade-in credit or an Apple gift card. To ensure the safeguarding of customers' data, Apple provides step-by-step guidelines for device preparation prior to the trade-in process. This trade-in service can be accessed online or through an Apple store. In scenarios where a device is ineligible for trade-in value, Apple offers to recycle it at no cost.[43]

To facilitate this process, Apple establishes both an online reverse logistics channel, responsible for transporting products from individual customers to Apple facilities, and a reverse logistics channel for transporting products from Apple stores to refurbishing facilities. Devices that meet the criteria for refurbishment undergo comprehensive cleaning and inspection. If necessary, genuine Apple replacement parts are used. The company replaces batteries and outer shells across all devices, in addition to providing accessories, cables, operating systems, and repackaging items within a new box. In this context, elements of "forward" logistics come into play, including components with varying degrees of predictability. These include elements such as batteries, outer shells, accessories, and boxes—parts that are universally replaced during the refurbishment process. However, certain parts introduce an element of higher uncertainty due to the unpredictable nature of damaged or malfunctioning components.

Apple's refurbishment initiative showcases the thorough organization of both reverse and forward logistics, exemplifying how a circular economy approach can integrate customer convenience, data protection, component refurbishment, and sustainable disposal practices.

Useful application of materials—Recycle, recover

The strategies of recycling and energy recovery, the third set from Table 7.1, introduce specific challenges and considerations to supply chains, depending on the context and approach taken by companies and industries.

Recycling Considerations

When it comes to recycling, the impact on supply chains can vary based on whether a company is legally required to recycle its products under Extended Producer Responsibility (EPR) legislation or whether it chooses to incorporate recycled content voluntarily.

- *EPR legislation*: In cases where EPR regulations are in place, companies are legally obligated to manage the end-of-life disposal of their products. This often involves outsourcing recycling activities to specialized third-party firms. In this scenario, a company's primary supply chain for manufacturing and distribution might remain relatively unchanged.
- *Incorporating recycled content*: If a company decides to incorporate recycled content into its products, it might need to seek new suppliers and adapt manufacturing processes to accommodate recycled materials. The sourcing and processing of recycled materials can differ significantly from virgin materials, requiring adjustments in production techniques and quality control.

For example, the paper industry usually combines both recycling paper and paper made from trees, which have different supply chains and follow different processes.[44]

Recycling Paper

1. *Collection and Sorting*: Used paper is collected from various sources, such as homes, offices, and recycling centers. This collected paper is then sorted to separate different types of paper and remove contaminants like staples, ink, and other non-paper materials.
2. *Pulping*: The sorted paper is mixed with water and chemicals to create a pulp. The pulp is agitated to break down the paper fibers into a slurry-like mixture.

3. *Cleaning and Screening*: The pulp is then subjected to cleaning processes to remove inks, coatings, and other contaminants. Screens and filters are used to further refine the mixture.
4. *Deinking*: In cases where the recycled paper contains ink, deinking processes are employed to remove the ink particles from the pulp.
5. *Papermaking*: The cleaned and refined pulp is used to produce new paper products through the same papermaking process used for virgin wood pulp. The pulp is spread onto a moving wire mesh to drain water, and the fibers are then pressed and dried to form sheets of paper.

As the recycled paper fibers are shorter than those from virgin wood pulp, the number of recycling cycles is limited, and paper manufacturing necessitates a blend of recycled and virgin pulp.

Energy Recovery Considerations

Energy recovery involves using waste materials at the end of their useful life to generate energy. This strategy doesn't directly impact the supply chains of product manufacturing companies. However, it can have implications for energy companies and waste management systems. For instance, in Sweden, where waste-to-energy is a prominent strategy, only a small percentage of waste is sent to landfills, while the majority is turned into energy or recycled. Sweden's efficient waste management system has led to importing waste from other countries, which pay Sweden to accept their waste for energy generation. This practice can potentially impact energy companies' supply chains by requiring efficient management of waste streams and maintaining a steady supply of waste material for energy production.[45]

In summary, the strategies of recycling and energy recovery introduce specific dynamics to supply chains, ranging from adapting recycled materials for product manufacturing to optimizing waste management processes for energy generation. The choice of strategy will depend on various factors, including regulatory requirements, industry practices, environmental goals, and economic considerations.

Which strategy should a company use?

Choosing the right strategy for a company involves evaluation of different aspects of the company's products and its supply chain:

1 Does a product retain its value?

If a product retains its value well, it might be suitable for strategies that involve reusing, refurbishing, remanufacturing, or repurposing, as these strategies focus on maintaining or even enhancing the value of the product.

2 How easy is it to collect products and bring them back to the company? Is it easy to establish a reverse supply chain for products? Is it expensive to bring products back?

If products are easy to collect and bring back to the company, it opens up possibilities for strategies related to extending the lifespan of products and their parts. Products that can be easily retrieved for repair, refurbishment, or remanufacturing can benefit from these strategies.

3 How easy/expensive is it to perform required operations on products to bring them to a usable condition?

If it's relatively easy and cost-effective to perform operations that bring products to a usable condition, strategies like repair, refurbishing, and remanufacturing become more viable.

Choosing the Strategy Sets:

- *Smarter product use and manufacture*: This set of strategies is applicable when products do not maintain their value or when the return and necessary operations on products are impractical or cost prohibitive. Emphasizing intelligent product design and manufacturing can lead to reduced waste and improved resource efficiency. This approach spans diverse industries and methods, ranging from Levi's and Interface's minimizing materials and components, and altering designs for easier end-of-life recycling; the creation of smartphones that integrate various functionalities to decrease the need for multiple devices; transitioning from fossil-fuel energy generation to renewable sources, and more.

- *Extend lifespan of products and their parts*: When products retain value and their return for further use is feasible, companies can explore reuse, refurbishment, remanufacturing, or repurposing of products or their components. Numerous companies across various sectors, including Apple, Samsung, Xerox, Caterpillar, Nike, Levi's, and Patagonia, align with this category.
- *Useful application of materials*: In cases where products do not retain value and the collection or restoration of products poses challenges, strategies that center on recycling and retrieving materials from products at the conclusion of their lifecycle should be pursued. For example, while electronic products can be refurbished in their initial stages, the technology eventually becomes outdated, diminishing its value. Recycling valuable materials emerges as the most viable method to sustain it within the circular economy.

Final takeaways

As seen from above, the circular economy presents a compelling alternative to linear models, aligning with nature's cyclical patterns and offering solutions to environmental challenges. The historical evolution of circular economy concepts, coupled with global initiatives and organizational strategies, underscores a growing commitment to sustainability. Through collaborative efforts, innovative thinking, and a focus on responsible business practices, the transition to a circular economy becomes not only an environmental necessity but also a pathway to long-term economic viability. As companies adopt and integrate these strategies into their SCND, they play a crucial role in shaping a more sustainable and regenerative future. The circular economy, with its emphasis on minimizing waste, efficient resource utilization, and holistic collaboration, emerges as a promising framework for addressing the interconnected challenges of climate change, resource depletion, and environmental degradation.

Circular practices should be integrated into the entire product lifecycle, from design and manufacturing to consumption and disposal.

Regular assessment and adaptation of strategies based on technological advancements and changing consumer behaviors are crucial for achieving a truly circular economy. The examples provided illustrate how different industries are adapting to circular principles. Ultimately, the transition to a circular economy holds the promise of increased resource efficiency, reduced waste, and positive environmental impact.

Endnotes

1 Ellen MacArthur Foundation. What is a circular economy? Ellen MacArthur Foundation, 2023, www.ellenmacarthurfoundation.org/topics/circular-economy-introduction/overview (archived at https://perma.cc/SK6Z-LRNF)

2 Industrial Symbiosis at Händelö Eco Industrial Park. News. (n.d.). Smart City Sweden smartcitysweden.com/best-practice/186/industrial-symbiosis-at-handelo-eco-industrial-park/ (archived at https://perma.cc/5VJF-B9VB)

3 UNEP circularity platform. (n.d.). www.buildingcircularity.org (archived at https://perma.cc/BT9P-XAX5)

4 The World Circular Economy Forum WCEF. (n.d.). Sitra. www.sitra.fi/en/projects/wcef/ (archived at https://perma.cc/K296-2P4S)

5 US Chamber Foundation www.uschamberfoundation.org/search?query=circular%20economy (archived at https://perma.cc/JHC9-KVVP)

6 Ellen MacArthur Foundation. About us - What we do, 2023, www.ellenmacarthurfoundation.org/about-us/what-we-do (archived at https://perma.cc/H5JJ-WS7S)

7 United States Environmental Protection Agency. (2018, November 16). Reduce, Reuse, Recycle, US EPA, November 6, 2018, www.epa.gov/recycle (archived at https://perma.cc/2GFZ-6LFZ)

8 Home. (n.d.-c). Dyecoo. www.dyecoo.com/ (archived at https://perma.cc/X3BL-S4BN)

9 Used Patagonia® Clothing & Gear | Worn Wear. (n.d.). Patagonia Worn Wear, February 26, 2024, wornwear.patagonia.com/ (archived at https://perma.cc/SSN9-92LD)

10 Levi. help.levi.com/hc/en-us/articles/360050121872-What-is-Levi-s-SecondHand-#:~:text=Levi%27s®%20SecondHand%20includes%20jeans, they%27re%20exclusively%20sold%20online (archived at https://perma.cc/3LP9-7PAM).
11 Patagonia Customer Service & Help Center. (2023). Patagonia.com, 2023, http://www.patagonia.com/stories/repair-is-a-radical-act/story-17637.html (archived at https://perma.cc/SS5G-YHMX)
12 Levi. www.levi.com/ (archived at https://perma.cc/XU2C-R8S8)
13 Osprey. Osprey.com, 2023, www.osprey.com/us/en/customer-support/all-mighty-guarantee (archived at https://perma.cc/WR4V-5AS8)
14 Lifetime Warranty for Backpacks and Bags | JanSport. (n.d.). Www.jansport.com. Retrieved February 26, 2024, from https://www.jansport.com/customer-service/warranty.html (archived at https://perma.cc/XT8B-U3WA)
15 Repairs: Windproof Lighter. (n.d.). http://www.zippo.com. https://www.zippo.com/pages/repairs-windproof-lighter (archived at https://perma.cc/WFB9-KNAU)
16 Apple. www.apple.com/shop/refurbished?afid=p238%7CsjFItAiXM-dc_mtid_1870765e38482_pcrid_644453066844_pgrid_13945964647_pntwk_g_pchan__pexid__&cid=aos-us-kwgo-brand--slid---product- (archived at https://perma.cc/RP2T-QCQV)
17 Samsung. www.samsung.com/us/app/smartphones/certified-re-newed-phones/ (archived at https://perma.cc/2ETZ-4QJA)
18 Dell. www.dellrefurbished.com (archived at https://perma.cc/SGM4-NBE8)
19 Amazon. www.amazon.com/Certified-Refurbished/b?node=12653393011&tag=googhydr-20&hvadid=229153382584&hvpos=&hvexid=&hvnetw=g&hvrand=11906310091187003648&hvpone=&hvptwo=&hvqmt=b&hvdev=c&hvdvcmdl=&hvlocint=&hvlocphy=9031079&hvtargid=kwd-319733665605&ref=pd_sl_61c74cd80i_b (archived at https://perma.cc/53TR-GGJA)
20 Ebay. www.ebay.com/b/eBay-Refurbished/bn_7040708936 (archived at https://perma.cc/M8FS-6FLR)
21 GE Healthcare. www.gehealthcare.com/products/goldseal---refurbished-systems (archived at https://perma.cc/57GC-MZAN)
22 The Circular Economy in Our Manufacturing 2018 - Xerox. (n.d.). Xerox Corporate Social Responsibility Report. www.xerox.com/corporate-social-responsibility/2018/environment/circular-economy.html (archived at https://perma.cc/7QVM-MER4)

23 Caterpillar. Cat Reman Process, 2020, www.caterpillar.com/en/company/sustainability/remanufacturing/process.html (archived at https://perma.cc/6S8P-W57S)

24 Sustainability. Remanufacture. John Deere US. (n.d.). Www.deere.com. www.deere.com/en/our-company/sustainability/remanufacture/ (archived at https://perma.cc/72P5-VHJK)

25 Cisco Refresh. Certified Remanufactured Equipment. (n.d.). Cisco. www.cisco.com/c/en/us/products/remanufactured.html#~benefits (archived at https://perma.cc/Y3LF-8WVX)

26 Levi. 2023, www.levi.com/US/en_US/features/sustainability

27 Applications. (n.d.). Sioneer. www.sioneer.com/applications/ (archived at https://perma.cc/6SKD-QAAL)

28 Levi. 2023, www.levi.com/US/en_US/blog/article/501-renewcell (archived at https://perma.cc/KM4G-NA5P)

29 US EPA. Paper and Paperboard: Material-Specific Data, US EPA, December 3, 2022, www.epa.gov/facts-and-figures-about-materials-waste-and-recycling/paper-and-paperboard-material-specific-data (archived at https://perma.cc/9EYR-YU3P).

30 Departmental Recycling Program.Pw.lacounty.gov, pw.lacounty.gov/epd/drp/Paper.aspx (archived at https://perma.cc/C8ZM-8EN9).

31 US EPA, OSWER, Office of Resource Conservation and Recovery. Frequent Questions | Paper Recycling | US EPA. Epa.gov, 2013, archive.epa.gov/wastes/conserve/materials/paper/web/html/faqs.html (archived at https://perma.cc/Y98G-8WY7).

32 FDA Approved Plastics for Food Contact — Which Plastics Make the Cut? | A&c Plastics, www.acplasticsinc.com/informationcenter/r/fda-approved-plastics-for-food-contact#:~:text=While%20many%20plastics%20are%20only (archived at https://perma.cc/Y23K-RKCT).

33 US EPA, OLEM. Energy Recovery from the Combustion of Municipal Solid Waste (MSW). US EPA, March 24, 2016, www.epa.gov/smm/energy-recovery-combustion-municipal-solid-waste-msw#:~:text=Energy%20recovery%20from%20waste%20is (archived at https://perma.cc/3S3D-7B85).

34 B Govind. Visualizing 25 Years of Lithium Production, by Country, Elements by Visual Capitalist, December 23, 2022, elements.visualcapitalist.com/25-years-of-lithium-production-by-country/ (archived at https://perma.cc/R32B-SZJB).

35 The Commanding Heights of Global Transportation, SAFE, chrome-extension://efaidnbmnnnibpcajpcglclefindmkaj/https://secureenergy.org/wp-content/uploads/2020/09/The-Commanding-Heights-of-Global-Transportation.pdf

36 The Role of Critical Minerals in Clean Energy Transitions, International Energy Agency, March 2022, www.iea.org/search?q=global%20supply%20chain (archived at https://perma.cc/ZWG2-9NL3)

37 Bipartisan Infrastructure Law: Battery Materials Processing and Battery Manufacturing Recycling Selections, Office of Manufacturing and Energy Supply Chains, www.energy.gov/mesc/bipartisan-infrastructure-law-battery-materials-processing-and-battery-manufacturing-recycling (archived at https://perma.cc/VR9C-3T4F)

38 International Energy Agency, Global EV Outlook, 2023, www.iea.org/search?q=global%20supply%20chain (archived at https://perma.cc/ZWG2-9NL3)

39 International Energy Agency, Global Supply Chains of EV Batteries, International Energy Agency, www.iea.org/search?q=global%20supply%20chain (archived at https://perma.cc/ZWG2-9NL3)

40 IEA. Demand for Electric Cars Is Booming, with Sales Expected to Leap 35% This Year after a Record-Breaking 2022 - News. IEA, April 26, 2023, www.iea.org/news/demand-for-electric-cars-is-booming-with-sales-expected-to-leap-35-this-year-after-a-record-breaking-2022 (archived at https://perma.cc/VC2S-JS2J).

41 FOTW #1271, January 2, 2023: Electric Vehicle Battery Manufacturing Capacity in North America in 2030 Is Projected to Be Nearly 20 Times Greater than in 2021. Energy.gov, 2023, www.energy.gov/eere/vehicles/articles/fotw-1271-january-2-2023-electric-vehicle-battery-manufacturing-capacity (archived at https://perma.cc/RF8L-A58M).

42 D Gohlke, Y Zhou, X Wu and C Courtney, Assessment of Light-Duty Plug-in Electric Vehicles in the United States, 2010 – 2021, November 2022, www.anl.gov/argonne-scientific-publications (archived at https://perma.cc/6F6P-VHU6)

43 Apple. Apple Trade In. Apple, 2023, www.apple.com/shop/trade-in (archived at https://perma.cc/JA2E-59ZW).

44 Paper Products | AF&PA. Www.afandpa.org, www.afandpa.org/paper-wood-products/paper (archived at https://perma.cc/988G-YN5B).

45 Mauborgne, K Chan and Renée. Turning Waste to Energy: Sweden's Recycling Revolution. Blue Ocean Strategy, August 27, 2021, www.blueoceanstrategy.com/blog/turning-waste-energy-sweden-recycling-revolution/#:~:text=Rather%20than%20sending%20trash%20to (archived at https://perma.cc/37EX-ZUN5).

Smart Cities, Smart Infrastructure, Smart Nations (New Perspective on Infrastructure) 08

The emergence of smart cities demands a recalibration of traditional SCND models. Smart cities have evolved a response to the accelerated pace of urbanization and technological advancements, leveraging the latter to address the challenges posed by the former. Supply chain practitioners can benefit from understanding the phenomenon and the ways in which technology is being harnessed to optimize various infrastructural components, including transportation networks, roads, buildings, and public utilities.

But, what is a smart city?

Smart is What Smart Does

Large metropolitan cities such as Barcelona and Kigali are using digital technologies like intelligent sensors, Big Data, and automation to optimize infrastructure, efficiently deliver public utilities and integrate sustainability into their operational framework. This, in essence, is what smart cities are about. Limited, at the start of the millennium, to a handful of global financial hubs such as New York and London, the concept of smart cities has witnessed a significant expansion over the last two decades because of a rapid pace of urbanization (see Table 8.1).

The increased pace of demographic shift from rural areas to urban centers over the past 50 years has led to a concentration of people and economic activities in and around select urban areas around the world. The World Bank estimates that between 1970 to 2020, over three billion people moved from rural to urban areas, with the sharpest increase seen in the developing economies.[1] It expects the share of urban population at the global level to reach 68 percent by 2050.

Table 8.1 Some smart cities and initiatives

Smart Cities	Population	Smart Initiatives
Singapore	5.92 million	A global leader in smart city development, its smart initiatives include intelligent transportation systems, smart grids, and digital citizen services.
Greater Copenhagen, Denmark	1.3 million	One of the most sustainable cities in the world. Implemented several initiatives to reduce its carbon footprint and improve its livability, including a district heating system that runs on renewable energy, a network of electric buses, and a bike-sharing program.
Amsterdam, Netherlands	918,100	A city committed to sustainability and livability. Smart initiatives include a network of sensors that monitor traffic and air quality, a smart lighting system that reduces energy consumption, and a digital platform that allows residents to access city services.
Oslo, Norway	1.1 million	A leader in the use of smart technology to improve its public transportation system. Smar initiatives, including a real-time travel information system and a network of autonomous vehicles.
Zurich, Switzerland	**1.83 million**	**Smart initiatives include a smart parking system, a smart waste management system, and a smart energy grid.**

SOURCE: Media sources, government publications, 2023

Urbanization poses significant challenges for sustainable development, such as environmental degradation, social inequality, public health, and governance. Many cities are adopting digital technologies and data-driven solutions to address these challenges to enhance their efficiency, resilience, and livability, and are joining the growing list of smart cities.

Smart cities are a means to achieve a broader vision of a smart nation. A smart nation is a country that leverages digital technologies and data to improve the well-being of its citizens, foster social innovation, and enhance its competitiveness in the global economy. A smart nation is more than a collection of smart cities; it is an integrated system that connects urban and rural areas, its public and private sectors, and human and natural resources. Supply Chain Network Design can be implemented optimally when the entire infrastructure of a smart nation is built into the logistics ecosystem of the supply chain network.

Smart Infrastructure Development

Developing smart infrastructure that supports delivering smart services and applications is essential to build a smart nation. Smart infrastructure is the physical and digital infrastructure that enables data collection, transmission, processing, and analysis from various sources, such as sensors, devices, networks, platforms, and applications. Smart infrastructure can improve the performance, reliability, safety, and sustainability of various sectors, such as energy, water, transport, health, education, and governance.

Further to some examples of smart cities shared earlier, the following are detailed examples of initiatives that smart cities have adopted to effectuate smart infrastructure and supply chains, from different regions of the world.

Singapore's Life's Moments

The city-state of Singapore has developed a comprehensive vision called Smart Nation Singapore, which aims to harness digital technologies and data to create a better home, environment, and

Figure 8.1 Smart Cities. Smart Infrastructure

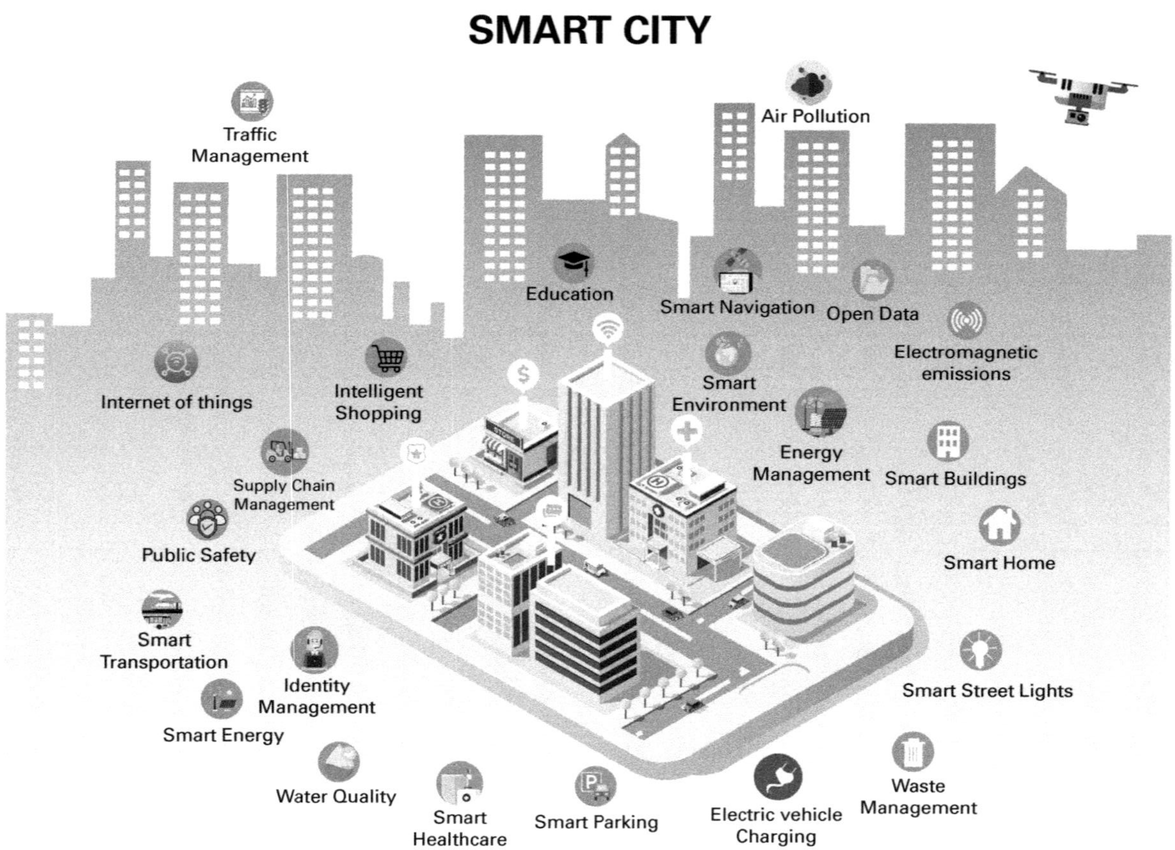

opportunities for its people. Some of the initiatives that have contributed to making it a smart city include:

- **Smart Nation Sensor Platform:** This is a nationwide sensor network that collects real-time data on various aspects of urban life, such as traffic, parking, waste management, air quality, and public safety. The data is then used to optimize urban operations, improve public services, and enhance situational awareness.
- **National Digital Identity:** This is a secure and convenient way for citizens and residents to access online services from both public and private sectors using their smartphones. The National Digital Identity also enables digital verification, authentication, authorization, and consent.
- **Moments of Life:** This mobile app provides personalized and integrated services for citizens at different stages of their lives. For example, it helps parents with newborns register their births, apply for baby bonuses, find childcare options, and access health records.

Barcelona's Decisions by Digital

Barcelona is one of the pioneers of smart cities in Europe It developed a strategic plan called Barcelona Digital City 2017–2020, which aims to transform the city into an open, inclusive, and innovative platform that empowers its citizens. Some of its key projects include:

- **Sentilo:** This is an open-source sensor platform that collects data from more than 10,000 sensors deployed across the city, such as noise, air pollution, energy consumption, and irrigation. The data is then used to improve urban management, environmental quality, and citizen participation.
- **Decidim:** This digital platform enables citizens to propose, debate, and vote on policies and projects that affect the city. Decidim also allows citizens to monitor the implementation and evaluation of the decisions made by the city council.
- **Fab Lab Barcelona:** This network of fabrication laboratories provides access to digital fabrication tools and technologies for

citizens to create, learn, and innovate. Fab Lab Barcelona also supports the development of local and global solutions for social and environmental challenges.

Kigali's Innovation City

Kigali is the capital and largest city of Rwanda. It has been recognized as one of Africa's most livable and cleanest cities. It has also embarked on a journey to become a smart city that leverages digital technologies and data to enhance its economic growth, social development, and environmental sustainability. Some of its notable initiatives include:

- **Kigali Innovation City**: This is a planned hub for innovation and entrepreneurship that will host universities, research centers, startups, and multinational companies. Kigali Innovation City will also provide state-of-the-art infrastructure and services for its residents and visitors.
- **Irembo**: This online platform provides access to more than 100 public services for citizens and businesses. Irembo also enables digital payments, notifications, and feedback.
- **Smart waste management**: This system uses smart bins equipped with sensors and GPS to monitor the level and location of waste in the city. The system then optimizes the collection routes and schedules for waste management trucks.

Applications of Intelligent SCND

Smart cities, infrastructure, and nations leverage advanced technologies such as IoT (Internet of Things), Big Data analytics, AI, and blockchain to transform traditional operations and management. One significant transformation in supply chain management is ensuring an intelligent, efficient, and responsive system.

The Top 10 Smart City use cases, cited by IoT Analytics, are presented below.

Smart Traffic and Route Optimization

Smart cities use real-time traffic monitoring and predictive analytics. For a supply chain, this means trucks and delivery vehicles can be routed in real-time to avoid congestion, reducing delivery times. In Singapore, the government has implemented a smart urban freight system (SUFS) that uses IoT sensors, GPS trackers, and cloud-based software to monitor and optimize the delivery of goods in the city. The system collects data on traffic conditions, vehicle locations, and delivery schedules. It provides real-time recommendations to drivers and dispatchers on the best routes, parking spots, and loading/unloading zones. The system also enables dynamic pricing of parking fees based on demand and availability. The SUFS aims to reduce traffic congestion, emissions, and delivery costs while improving customer satisfaction and service quality.

In Barcelona, Spain, the city has deployed a smart traffic management system that uses cameras, sensors, and Big Data analytics to monitor and control the flow of vehicles in the city. The system adjusts traffic lights, speed limits, and lane directions according to real-time traffic conditions and provides information and guidance to drivers through variable message signs and mobile apps. The system also integrates with public transport and emergency services to prioritize their movements. The system has reduced travel times by 21 percent, emissions by 20 percent, and accidents by 30 percent.[2]

In Los Angeles, United States, the city has partnered with NoTraffic to install a smart traffic signal network that uses AI and edge computing to optimize real-time traffic flows. The network uses cameras and sensors to detect vehicles, pedestrians, cyclists, and scooters and adjusts traffic signals accordingly. The network communicates with connected vehicles and delivery platforms to provide optimal routes and arrival times. The network has reduced travel times by 25 percent &, emissions by 15 percent, and collisions by 10 percent.

Amsterdam has implemented a smart traffic management system that uses a network of sensors, cameras, and cellular routers to monitor and automatically direct traffic, reducing congestion. The system[3] can be scaled to any size and upgraded at any time, preparing Amsterdam for future technology evolutions, including Connected

Figure 8.2 Smart and Connected Supply Chain Management Scenario

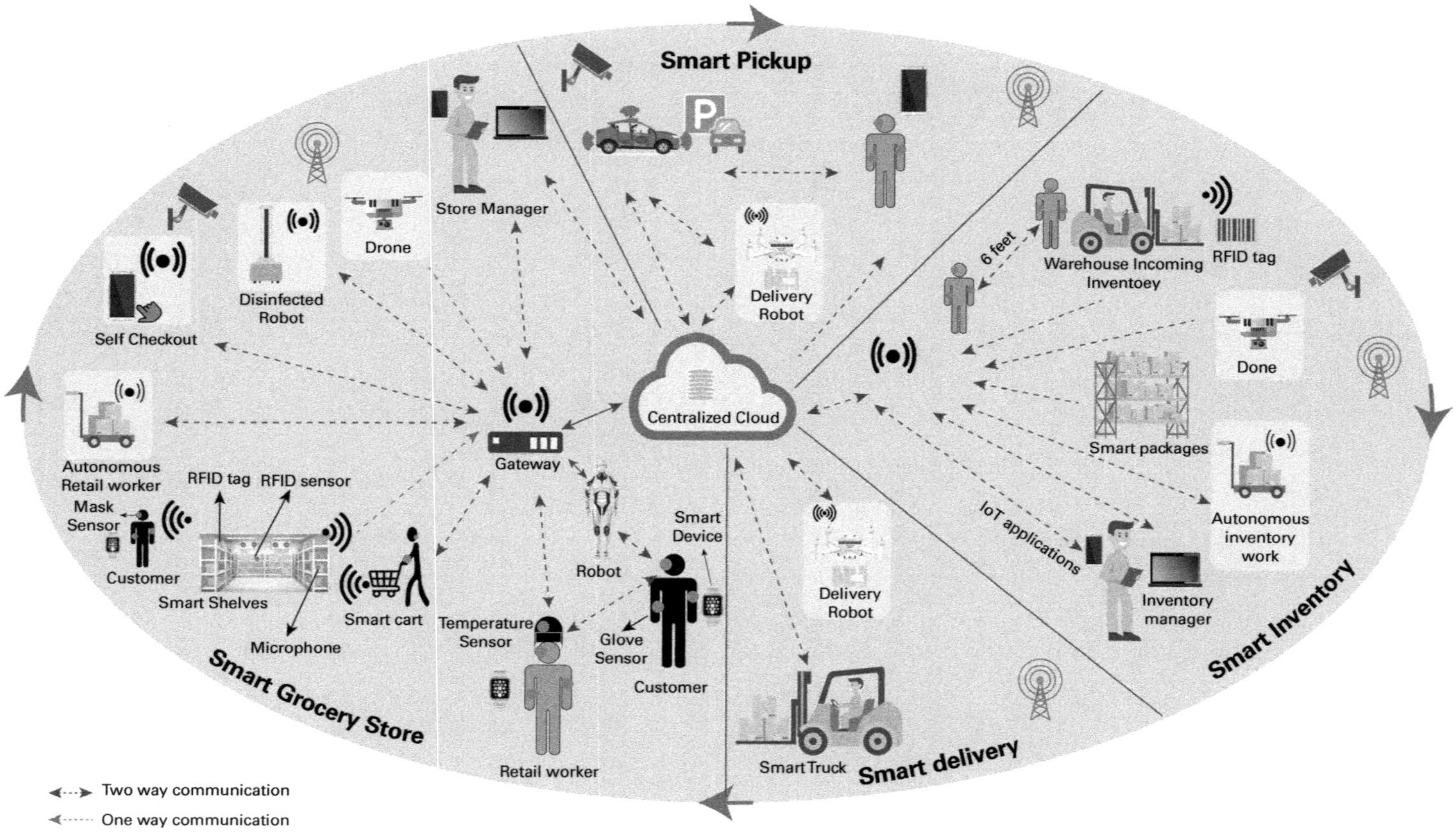

SOURCE USC Marshall-Randall R. Kendrick Global Supply Chain Institute

Figure 8.3 The Top 10 Smart City Use Cases

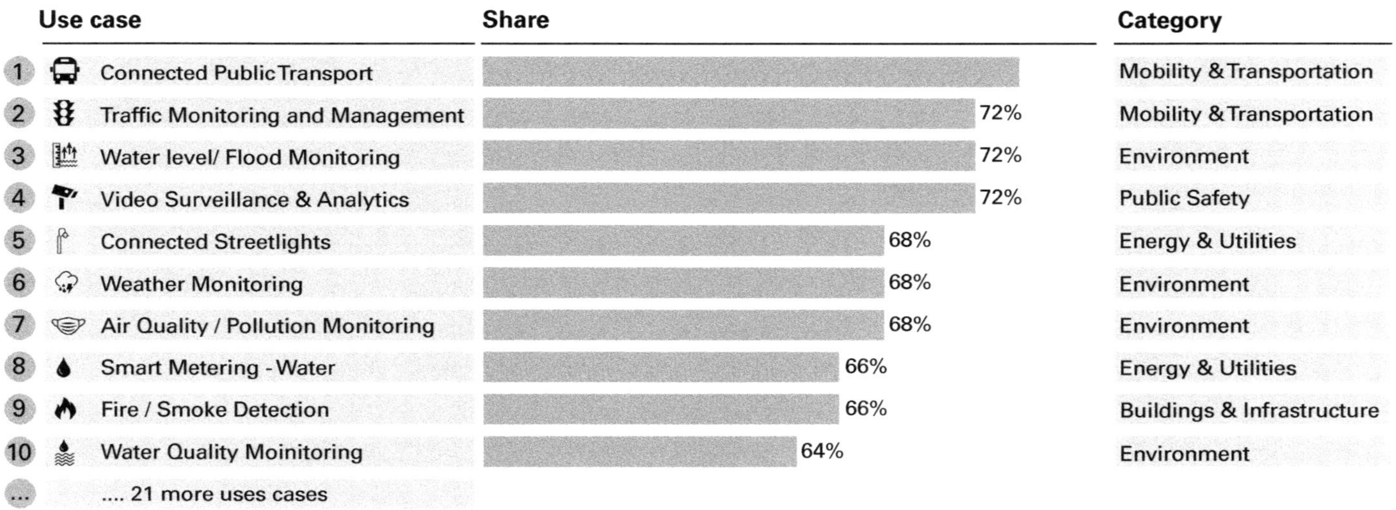

SOURCE IoT Analytics Research

Vehicle and the full deployment of 5G networks.[4] Similarly, San Francisco's transitioning into smart city is noteworthy. The city has implemented of several mobility-as-a-service initiatives which include intelligent traffic flow routing and the optimization of logistics.[5]

A prime example of a company that recognizes the significance of route optimization is UPS. In the year 2022 alone, UPS successfully delivered an average of 24.3 million packages per day, spanning across more than 220 countries. Back in 2012, the company introduced its proprietary on-road integrated optimization and navigation (ORION) platform. This advanced technology leverages sophisticated algorithms, artificial intelligence, and machine learning to provide drivers with the most efficient routes for their deliveries.

Building on this foundation, UPS continued to innovate. In 2019, they integrated UPSNav into ORION, a feature that offers detailed turn-by-turn directions. These directions guide local delivery drivers not only to addresses but also to specific package drop-off and pickup points, even those concealed from the street view. To further enhance efficiency, in 2021, UPS introduced dynamic routing to ORION. This update ensures that the routes dispatched to drivers' handheld devices are automatically adjusted throughout the day, in response to changing conditions. This dynamic adaptation significantly reduces mileage and consequently the associated emissions.

Since implementing ORION, UPS estimates that it has conserved around 100 million miles and 10 million gallons of fuel on a yearly basis[ii]. To put this achievement in perspective, the EPA approximates that one gallon of gasoline consumed emits about 8,887 grams of CO_2, while one gallon of diesel emits about 10,180 grams of CO_2. Assuming an equal distribution of fuel consumption between gasoline and diesel, these figures equate to an annual reduction of 95,335 tons of CO_2 emissions. This impact corresponds to removing over 21,000 gasoline-powered passenger vehicles from the roads. (The EPA estimates annual passenger vehicle emissions at 4.49 metric tons CO_2e.)

Smart Warehousing

In Barcelona, smart logistics solutions provide real-time visibility into warehouse inventory, helping in just-in-time inventory management. Barcelona is a major logistics hub in Europe, and the city is home to several innovative smart logistics solutions. These solutions are helping businesses to improve their inventory management and to achieve just-in-time (JIT) inventory.[6]

One example of a smart logistics solution in Barcelona is using RFID tags to track warehouse inventory. RFID tags are small electronic tags that can be attached to products or product packaging. RFID readers can read these tags, which can be used to track the movement of products throughout the warehouse.

RFID tags can provide businesses with real-time visibility into their inventory levels. This information can be used to improve inventory management and to ensure that businesses have the right products in the right place at the right time.

Another example of a smart logistics solution in Barcelona is automated storage and retrieval systems (AS/RS). AS/RS systems are computer-controlled systems that automatically store and retrieve products. This can help businesses to improve the efficiency of their inventory management and to reduce labor costs.

AS/RS systems can also be used to implement JIT inventory management. JIT inventory management is a system in which businesses only order inventory when needed. This can help businesses to reduce inventory costs and to improve cash flow.

The use of smart logistics solutions in Barcelona is helping businesses to improve their efficiency and profitability. Some of the specific benefits that businesses have achieved by using smart logistics solutions include reduced inventory costs, improved inventory management, reduced labor costs and improved customer service. Similarly, examples of smart logistics solutions that are being used in Barcelona include the use of RFID and AS/RS systems for enhancement of the quality of the city's logistics services.

Top trends in the use of IoT in warehouses in 2023

- **Predictive maintenance:** IoT sensors can be used to monitor the condition of equipment and predict when maintenance is needed. This can help to prevent equipment failures and reduce downtime.
- **Digital twins**: Digital twins are virtual representations of physical assets. IoT sensors can be used to collect data from physical assets and feed it into digital twins. This data can be used to simulate different scenarios and optimize operations.
- **Artificial intelligence (AI):** AI analyzes data from IoT sensors and identifies patterns and trends. This information can be used to improve decision-making and automate tasks.

Energy-Efficient Smart Warehouses

Warehouses embedded with IoT for lighting, temperature control, and equipment management reduce operational costs and enhance sustainability. Walmart has deployed IoT sensors to monitor temperature and humidity levels in its warehouses. This data helps Walmart to ensure that its products are stored in optimal conditions, which reduces spoilage and saves money. Amazon is another company that is using IoT in its warehouses. Amazon uses IoT sensors to track the location of inventory, optimize picking and packing operations, and predict maintenance needs. This has helped Amazon to improve efficiency and reduce costs.

FedEx is using IoT to improve the efficiency of its shipping operations. FedEx uses IoT sensors to track the location of packages, monitor the condition of packages in transit, and predict delivery times. This has helped FedEx to improve customer service and reduce costs.

The benefits of using IoT in warehouses include reduced operational costs, where IoT can help to reduce spoilage, improve efficiency, and reduce maintenance costs. It can also help enhance warehouse sustainability by reducing energy consumption, waste, and air quality. Finally, IoT can help improve safety and security in warehouses by monitoring for hazards, detecting unauthorized access, and tracking the location of assets.

Smart Waste Management

In Seoul, South Korea, smart waste management systems ensure timely collection and disposal of waste, a critical part of the reverse logistics in the supply chain. Seoul is one of the most densely populated cities in the world. With over 10 million people, the city produces significant waste each day. Seoul has implemented several smart waste management systems to manage this waste effectively.

One of the key components of Seoul's smart waste management system is a network of smart bins. Smart bins are equipped with sensors that can monitor the level of waste in the bin and transmit this information to a central waste management system. The waste management system then uses this information to optimize collection routes and schedules.

Smart bins can also help to reduce the number of times that waste collection trucks need to empty bins. This can help to reduce fuel consumption and emissions.

A public education campaign is another important component of Seoul's smart waste management system. The campaign encourages residents to recycle and to compost waste. The campaign also provides residents with information about the location of smart bins and the waste collection schedule.

Implementing smart waste management systems has helped Seoul improve its waste collection and disposal rates. The city now recycles over 60 percent of its waste—one of the world's highest rates.[7]

The following are some of the technical details of the smart waste management systems that are being used in Seoul:

- *Smart bins*: Smart bins are typically equipped with a variety of sensors, including weight sensors, ultrasonic sensors, and infrared sensors. These sensors can monitor the level of waste in the bin and transmit this information to a central waste management system. Smart bins can also be equipped with solar panels to power their sensors and other components.
- *Waste management system*: The waste management system is a software system that collects data from smart bins and other sources. This data is then used to optimize waste collection routes and schedules. The waste management system can also be used to generate reports on waste collection and disposal rates.

Smart Ports and Terminals

The inefficiency of operations at the world's ports and transshipment hubs is a significant issue. Despite the expansion of container trade, many ports struggle with handling efficiency. The slow adoption of technologies and excessive paperwork often lead to delays and congestion. These factors cause supply-side constraints which lead to increased costs, poor service reliability, and an overall underutilization of global value chains. Therefore, smart cities are adopting digital technologies at their ports to improve efficiency and resilience.

For example, the Port of Rotterdam employs IoT sensors and AI to monitor real-time ship movements, predict estimated departure times, and optimize cargo handling, thereby improving the efficiency of the

Table 8.2 Smart Ports and Terminals

Smart Ports and Terminals: The Building Blocks
IoT Sensors: The port deployed thousands of IoT sensors across its entire expanse. These sensors collect real-time data on various parameters like water and weather conditions, temperature, ship movements, and berth availability.
AI and Data Analytics: By harnessing AI, the port processes the vast amounts of data the IoT sensors generate. Machine learning algorithms are utilized to predict ship arrival and departure times, cargo handling metrics, and even to forecast potential maintenance needs.
Digital Twin: The Port of Rotterdam has created a "digital twin" of the port, a real-time digital replica. This model is continuously updated with sensor data and provides stakeholders with a comprehensive overview of all operations. Decision-makers can simulate various scenarios to drive operational efficiency.
Integration with Shipping Companies: The digital platforms at the port are integrated with the systems of shipping companies, enabling seamless communication. This helps synchronize logistics, reduce waiting times, and optimize cargo handling.
Benefits associated with such technologies include enhanced efficiency, where real-time monitoring and predictive analytics reduce waiting times and ensure optimal utilization of berths. Cost savings come from predicting maintenance needs and optimizing operations so the port can significantly cut operational costs. Environmental benefits include efficient cargo handling and reduced ship idling times, contributing to decreased emissions, and supporting sustainability goals.

supply chain. The Port of Rotterdam spans over 42 kilometers and handles hundreds of ships and millions of containers annually. Rotterdam embarked on its digital transformation journey with an ever-increasing demand for efficiency and a vision to become the "smartest port" in the world.

Smart Roads and Railways

Technologically augmented surface transport infrastructure improves efficiency, safety, and sustainability. Smart roads and railways can optimize traffic flow, reduce congestion, and minimize environmental impact. With applications like predictive maintenance, smart transport solutions improve reliability and reduce operational costs, significantly improving the transportation experience for users.

In an increasing number of cities around the world, smart roads are being equipped with sensors to monitor road conditions. Supply chain systems can use this data to decide on transportation modes, reducing wear and tear on vehicles and ensuring goods safety. One example of how smart roads can help supply chain systems is the project of the Wyoming Department of Transportation (WYDOT) and the U.S. Department of Transportation (USDOT) to deploy connected vehicle technology along the Interstate 80 corridor. This project aims to improve safety and mobility for freight and passenger vehicles, especially during adverse weather conditions. The project uses roadside units (RSUs) to communicate with onboard units (OBUs) installed in trucks and other vehicles, providing real-time information on road conditions, traffic, and hazards. The project also uses a data management system to collect, store, and analyze the data from the RSUs and OBUs. This system can help supply chain managers monitor the location and status of their trucks, optimize routes and schedules, and reduce fuel consumption and emissions.[8]

Another example is the SmartWay Transport Partnership, a collaboration between the U.S. Environmental Protection Agency (EPA) and the freight industry to improve environmental performance and efficiency. The partnership provides tools and resources for freight carriers and shippers to measure, benchmark, and improve their operations. One of these tools is the SmartWay Drayage Program, which helps drayage trucking companies to reduce emissions and fuel use by adopting cleaner technologies and practices. The program also helps port authorities and terminal operators to implement smart road technologies such as intelligent transportation systems (ITS), traffic management systems, automated gate systems, and truck reservation systems. These technologies can improve traffic flow, reduce congestion and idling, and enhance security and safety.[9]

A third example is the European Union's C-Roads Platform, a joint initiative of road operators and authorities to harmonize the deployment of cooperative intelligent transport systems (C-ITS) across Europe. The platform supports developing and testing C-ITS services that use wireless communication between vehicles and infrastructure to provide information on traffic, weather, road works, accidents, and other relevant events. The platform also facilitates cross-border interoperability and compatibility of C-ITS services among different countries. The platform can benefit supply chain systems by improving road safety, efficiency, and sustainability for freight transport.[10]

Smart Nations

A smart nation is a country that uses technology and data to improve the lives of its citizens and businesses. Smart nations use various technologies, including the IoT, AI, and Big Data, to collect and analyze data from various sources, including sensors, social media, and government databases. This data is then used to improve the efficiency and effectiveness of government services, infrastructure, and businesses.

Smart nations strategically focus on various key functional areas to enhance overall efficiency and quality of life. To improve transportation, for example, they leverage IoT sensors to gather data on traffic patterns and road conditions, subsequently utilizing this information to optimize traffic flow, alleviate congestion, and enhance public transportation systems. For energy efficiency, smart nations employ IoT sensors to monitor energy consumption, pinpointing areas for improvement of distribution and consumption efficiency.

Environmental sustainability is a priority as well, with smart nations utilizing IoT sensors to monitor air and water quality, along with other environmental factors. This data-driven approach aids in the identification and resolution of environmental issues. In the educational sphere, smart nations harness technology to improve the quality and accessibility of education. This involves the integration of online learning platforms, interactive whiteboards, and various educational tools.

For an efficient delivery of healthcare, telemedicine, electronic health records, and other healthcare, IT solutions play a crucial role in ensuring that citizens have efficient and effective access to healthcare services.

Smart nations rely on a variety of technologies to collect and analyze data. Some of the most common technologies include:

- *IoT sensors*: IoT sensors are small, low-cost devices that can be used to collect data from a variety of sources, such as the environment, equipment, and people.
- *Big Data analytics*: Big data analytics is a process of analyzing large amounts of data to identify patterns and trends. This information can then be used to improve decision-making and operations.
- *Artificial intelligence*: AI is a computer science field that deals with the creation of intelligent agents, which are systems that can reason, learn, and act autonomously. AI is being used in a variety of ways to improve the efficiency and effectiveness of smart nations, such as by automating tasks, optimizing operations, and predicting future events.

Several countries around the world are developing smart nation initiatives. Some of the leading examples include:

1 **Cross-border trade facilitation:** Singapore is one of the most advanced smart nations in the world. The country has implemented a wide range of smart initiatives, including a smart transportation system, a smart energy grid, and a smart healthcare system. Singapore's National Trade Platform is a one-stop digital portal for businesses to submit customs clearance documentation, improving cross-border supply chain efficiency.

2 **National data platforms:** Estonia is a small country but a leader in e-government and digital services. The country has implemented several innovative smart initiatives, such as an electronic residency program, an online voting system, and a blockchain-based land registry. Estonia's X-Road is a decentralized data exchange platform facilitating secure data transfer. This means faster verification processes for supply chains, be it for product origins or regulatory compliance.

3 **Integrated multi-modal transport systems:** South Korea is another leader in smart nation development. The country has implemented several smart initiatives, including a nationwide smart grid, a smart city pilot project in Sejong, and a smart agriculture initiative.

Methodology and approach for building smart cities, smart infrastructure, and smart nations

The methodology and approach for building smart cities, smart infrastructure, and smart nations are based on a set of guiding principles.

The first principle is the need to adopt a people-centric philosophy, aiming to enhance the quality of life for individuals. This involves designing and implementing smart solutions based on the needs, preferences, and feedback of citizens and stakeholders, ensuring an equitable distribution of benefits and risks across diverse societal groups.

Secondly, it needs to have a data-driven approach. Systematic, transparent, and ethical practices govern data collection, management, analysis, and sharing. The use of data is guided by evidence-based decision-making and policymaking.

To add, a commitment to constant innovation is integral to the development and deployment of smart solutions. Flexibility, agility, and collaboration are key in adapting to changing circumstances and emerging opportunities. The innovation ecosystem is fostered through support for research and development (R&D), entrepreneurship, and education.

- As importantly, smart cities, infrastructure, and nations must contribute to environmental, social, and economic sustainability. Minimizing environmental impact involves the use of renewable energy sources, reducing greenhouse gas emissions, and promoting a circular economy. Social impact is maximized through efforts to enhance social inclusion, participation, and cohesion. Moreover, economic impact is optimized by creating new jobs, skills, and markets.

Steps to Building Smart Cities

Building smart cities, smart infrastructure, and smart nations is a complex and challenging task, but it is also essential for creating a more sustainable and equitable future.

1. Assessment and planning:
    a. **Current infrastructure audit:** Evaluate the existing infrastructure and services.
    b. **Stakeholder workshops:** Engage community members, local businesses, and civic organizations.
    c. **Identify key challenges:** Address city-specific issues (e.g., traffic congestion, waste management).
2. **Develop a vision and strategy.** The first step is to develop a clear vision and strategy for the smart city, smart infrastructure, or smart nation being built. This vision should be based on the needs and aspirations of the community, and it should be aligned with the broader goals of sustainable development.
3. **Identify key stakeholders and partners.** Smart cities, smart infrastructure, and smart nation development are complex and multifaceted undertakings, so it is important to identify and engage with all key stakeholders and partners early on. This includes government agencies, businesses, civil society organizations, and community members.
4. **Collect and analyze data.** Smart cities, smart infrastructure, and smart nation development are data-driven endeavors. Collecting and analyzing data on various factors, such as population demographics, transportation patterns, energy consumption, and

environmental conditions, is essential. This data can be used to identify problems and opportunities and to develop and evaluate solutions. There should also be a 'control tower' with a data analytics center, which would act as a centralized data processing and analysis hub. This would help smart cities anticipate issues before they become critical.

5 **Design and implement smart solutions.** Once the key problems and opportunities have been identified, smart solutions can be designed and implemented. These solutions can involve various technologies, such as sensors, data analytics, artificial intelligence, and the Internet of Things (IoT). Smart infrastructure development includes building smart grids for efficient energy distribution and consumption; intelligent traffic management to minimize congestion and improve road safety; smart buildings or energy-efficient buildings that self-regulate electricity and water consumption; and digital twins, which are virtual replicas of physical entities to simulate and predict real-world scenarios.

   Integration and interoperability between systems through a unified platform will help combine all smart services into a user-friendly platform. This would include API-based Interactions to ensure seamless integration of various services.

6 **Monitor and evaluate progress.** It is important to monitor and evaluate the progress of smart cities, smart infrastructure, and smart nation development on an ongoing basis. This will help to ensure that the solutions are working as intended and that they are meeting the needs of the community.

Examples of SCND Solutions for Smart Cities

The following are some examples of smart solutions that can be implemented in cities, infrastructure, and nations so that effective supply chain network design can be enabled:

- **Smart transportation:** Smart transportation systems can help to reduce congestion, improve safety, and reduce emissions. Examples of smart transportation solutions include traffic signal synchronization, real-time public transportation information, and intelligent transportation systems.

- **Smart energy:** Smart energy systems can help to reduce energy consumption, improve efficiency, and integrate renewable energy sources. Examples of smart energy solutions include smart meters, smart grids, and energy storage systems.
- **Smart water:** Smart water systems can help to conserve water, improve water quality, and reduce water pollution. Examples of smart water solutions include water leak detection systems, smart irrigation systems, and water recycling systems.
- **Smart waste management:** Smart waste management systems can help to reduce waste production, improve waste collection and disposal, and increase recycling rates. Examples of smart waste management solutions include smart bins, waste tracking systems, and waste-to-energy systems.
- **Smart buildings:** Smart buildings can help to reduce energy consumption, improve comfort and safety, and increase productivity. Smart building solutions include building energy management systems, smart lighting, and smart HVAC systems.
- **Smart healthcare:** Smart healthcare systems can help to improve the quality and efficiency of healthcare delivery. Examples of smart healthcare solutions include telemedicine, electronic health records, and wearable devices.

Smart Infrastructure Solution: Socio-Economic Considerations and Benefits

In addition to the technical aspects of building smart cities, smart infrastructure, and smart nations, it is also essential to consider the social and economic dimensions. Smart cities, smart infrastructure, and smart nation development should be inclusive and equitable and benefit all community members. It is also important to ensure that smart solutions are secure and privacy-preserving.

Benefits

1 **Urban efficiency:** Smart cities, smart infrastructure, and smart nations represent the pinnacle of integrated urban design, leveraging advanced technologies to optimize operations and enhance services. By incorporating IoT sensors, AI, and data analytics, urban areas can monitor and analyze various real-time metrics, such as traffic flow, energy consumption, and public service utilization. For instance, smart cities employ adaptive traffic management systems that adjust signal timings based on current traffic conditions, reducing congestion, and improving commuter experiences. Smart infrastructure, like energy-efficient buildings and connected public utilities, can dynamically adjust resource usage based on demand, leading to cost savings, and reduced environmental impact. On a broader scale, smart nations integrate data across cities and regions, streamlining public services, from healthcare to public transportation, ensuring seamless, efficient, and responsive service delivery for all citizens. Through such interconnected and intelligent systems, urban operations and services are significantly optimized, enhancing residents' quality of life and sustainability.

   Some examples of urban efficiency from smart cities, smart infrastructure, and smart nations include traffic management. For example, Barcelona implemented a smart traffic light system prioritizing emergency vehicles. This system detects ambulances, police cars, or fire trucks approaching and changes the light to green, ensuring swift and unhindered passage.

2 **Waste management:** Smart solutions in waste management involve the use of sensors and IoT devices to monitor waste levels in real-time, optimizing collection routes and schedules.

   Example: **Seoul** uses sensors in waste bins to notify collection trucks when they are full. This optimizes collection routes, saving fuel and reducing unnecessary pickups.

3 **Energy management:** Smart energy management systems use advanced metering infrastructure to monitor energy consumption, enabling more efficient use of resources and reducing costs.

   Example: In **Amsterdam**, smart grids adjust energy distribution based on demand, ensuring efficient electricity usage. Homes equipped with solar panels can sell back excess energy to the grid, optimizing overall energy management.

4 **Water conservation:** Smart water systems use sensors to detect leaks and monitor water usage, helping to conserve water and reduce waste.

Example: In **Singapore**, the PUB (Public Utilities Board) has set up smart meters that provide real-time water usage data to households. This makes consumers aware of their consumption patterns and helps detect early leaks.

5 **Public transport:** Smart public transport systems use real-time data to optimize routes and schedules, improving efficiency and reducing congestion.

Example: **Copenhagen** has implemented a real-time traffic monitoring and management system for its public buses and trains. This allows for dynamic route planning and ensures timely arrivals and departures.

6 **Healthcare services:** Smart healthcare solutions use telemedicine and remote monitoring technologies to improve access to care and patient outcomes.

Example: In **Estonia**, e-health solutions are deployed nationwide, providing digital health records accessible by any healthcare provider with the patient's permission. This optimizes the provision of medical services and ensures continuity of care.

7 **Public safety:** Smart public safety solutions use video analytics and predictive policing technologies to enhance security and emergency response.

Example: In **New York City**, the Domain Awareness System integrates data from various sources like surveillance cameras, license plate readers, and environmental sensors. It helps law enforcement agencies to respond to threats and maintain public safety quickly.

8 **Infrastructure Maintenance:** Smart infrastructure systems use sensors and predictive analytics to monitor the condition of infrastructure and schedule preventative maintenance.

Example: In **Melbourne**, sensors are embedded in public infrastructure like bridges and roads. These sensors monitor wear and tear in real time, allowing timely maintenance before any major issues arise.

These examples show how intelligent systems in smart cities, infrastructure, and nations are pivotal in refining and optimizing urban operations and services.

Endnotes

1 World Bank. Urbanization and commodity demand, World Bank, October 2021, openknowledge. openknowledge.worldbank.org/server/api/core/bitstreams/90c7f8d1-7d60-56f6-8475-59ed8b34a5f7/content (archived at https://perma.cc/SX9T-85UW).

2 V Prasad, Driving Towards a Smarter Future: How IoT & AI Can Ease Traffic Congestion in Smart Cities? LinkedIn , May 19, 2023, www.linkedin.com/pulse/driving-towards-smarter-future-how-iot-ai-can-ease-traffic-prasad/ (archived at https://perma.cc/D43W-B9RL).

3 IIOT World. Smart traffic systems throughout Amsterdam: three use cases, IIOT World, August 29, 2019, www.iiot-world.com/smart-cities-buildings-infrastructure/smart-cities/smart-traffic-systems-throughout-amsterdam-three-use-cases/ (archived at https://perma.cc/7FQ2-MAMQ).

4 Connect, Smart Cities. Los Angeles Installs Intelligent Traffic Signal Controllers at 1,500 Intersections. Smart Cities Connect, August 23, 2018, smartcitiesconnect.org/los-angeles-installs-intelligent-traffic-signal-controllers-at-1500-intersections/ (archived at https://perma.cc/G6DH-LN86).

5 O Wyman et al. San Francisco Pursues Mobility Vision through Fog of Disruption. Oliver Wyman Forum, January 22, 2022, www.oliverwymanforum.com/mobility/2022/jan/san-francisco-pursues-mobility-vision-through-fog-of-disruption.html.html (archived at https://perma.cc/5MS6-JU7Y).

6 R Soriano-Gonzalez et al. Smart logistics in Barcelona: A case study of the use of RFID tags and AS/RS systems. Journal of Supply Chain Management 56, no. 1 (2020): 12–25.

7 J. H Kim. Smart waste management system in Seoul, South Korea: A case study. Journal of Environmental Management, 280 (2021): 111701.

8 E Smith. The Future of Intelligent Transportation Systems (ITS): Applying Lessons Learned from 30 Years of Innovation | FHWA. Highways.dot.gov, 2022, highways.dot.gov/public-roads/spring-2022/03 (archived at https://perma.cc/B7C4-79UT).

9 E Smith. The Future of Intelligent Transportation Systems (ITS): Applying Lessons Learned from 30 Years of Innovation | FHWA. Highways.dot.gov, 2022, highways.dot.gov/public-roads/spring-2022/03 (archived at https://perma.cc/FE46-C5A2).

10 V Kuprenko. Artificial Intelligence in the Logistics Industry - the Network Effect. The Network Effect, September 23, 2019, supplychainbeyond.com/artificial-intelligence-in-the-logistics-industry/ (archived at https://perma.cc/9X6H-DP35).

09 Implementing Effective Network Design Change within your Organization

The Role of Leadership

Navigating the New Normal: Innovative Strategies for Triple Bottom Line in Global Supply Chain Network Design

The pandemic has irrevocably altered the landscape of global supply chain management. The leaders who will thrive in this new era understand that the strength of a supply chain lies not just in its efficiency or cost-effectiveness but in its ability to serve the broader interests of society and the environment while still generating profit. The Triple Bottom Line is not just a framework for measuring success; it's a call to action for leaders to reshape the world, one decision at a time.

This chapter will weave together modern leadership principles with tangible examples from various industries, illustrating how the Triple Bottom Line is a comprehensive guide for resilient and sustainable supply chain management in a post-pandemic era. It would serve as both a reflection on recent history and a roadmap for future leadership strategies. The onset of the COVID-19 pandemic marked a pivotal shift in organizational priorities. Leaders found themselves at the helm of navigating unprecedented challenges within their enterprises and the intricate global supply chains they depended upon. The disruption highlighted the fragility of existing systems and the need for a leadership approach that transcends traditional financial metrics. The Triple Bottom Line—people, planet, and profit—emerged as the beacon for this new leadership paradigm. In essence, post-COVID leaders must be visionaries capable of seeing beyond the horizon to prepare for and mitigate future crises. They need to be champions of change, embodying the Triple Bottom Line principles in their strategies and operations to ensure that the global supply chain is efficient, profitable, resilient, and responsible. The imperative is to address the Triple Bottom Line: people, planet, and profit. This holistic approach has become a cornerstone of strategic leadership, as it recognizes the interdependence of social responsibility, environmental stewardship, and financial viability.

The Circle of Influence

The concept of a "circle of influence" is pivotal in understanding the dynamics of successful leadership, and this can be further explored through the theme of a "circle of confluence." This circle of confluence represents the merging of various elements—knowledge, wisdom, leadership. Along with these, ethics, empathy, and visionary thinking—collectively shaping a leader's ability to influence effectively.

Successful leaders expand their circle of influence by integrating knowledge and wisdom, just as rivers converge in a circle of confluence. In this context, knowledge is akin to the streams of information and understanding that leaders continuously gather. It's not static but ever evolving, reflecting a deep curiosity and an unending pursuit of learning. Wisdom is the process of filtering and applying this knowledge judiciously, much like a riverbed directs and shapes the course of the water. It involves ethical considerations, moral insights, and

Figure 9.1 Circle of Influence

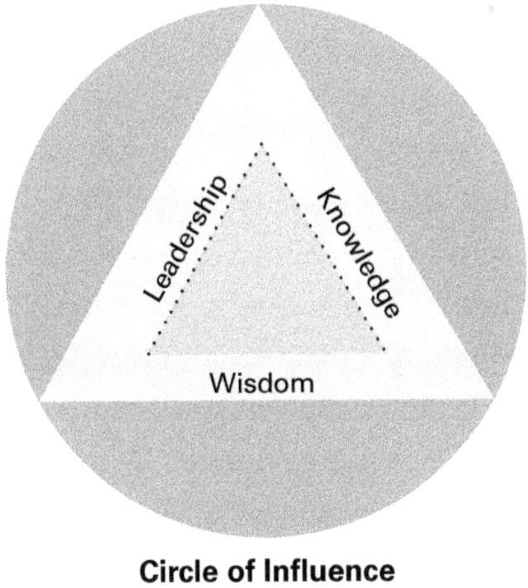

SOURCE USC Marshall-Randall R. Kendrick Global Supply Chain Institute

the ability to foresee consequences, resonating with the Aristotelian concept of practical wisdom.

The leadership aspect within the circle of confluence (see Figure 9.1) is akin to the powerful current that drives the river forward. Philosophically, it's an existential commitment to influence the world positively. Leaders embody their values and convictions, inspiring others through their actions and integrity. This aspect of leadership is not just about directing or managing but about incorporating the change one wishes to see, reflecting the existentialist idea of authentic existence.

Ethical and moral leadership are the banks that contain and direct the flow of this river. Leaders guided by ethics and morality ensure their influence is far-reaching and positively impactful. Drawing from Kantian ethics, their actions are those they wish to become universal laws, emphasizing justice, fairness, and respect.

Visionary thinking in leadership is the horizon where the river meets the sea—the broader vision leaders have for their organizations or societies. It's about dreaming big and possessing the practical skills to make these dreams a reality. This future-oriented thinking, akin to the Platonic ideal, is about striving towards a better and more ideal state.

Empathy and compassion are the life-giving waters in this river. Just as water sustains life, empathy and compassion sustain the human connections essential for effective leadership. This element echoes the Buddhist concept of compassionate living, where understanding and caring for others is central to a leader's influence.

Finally, community and collaboration are the ecosystems supported by the river. Successful leaders recognize that leadership is not a solitary endeavor but a collective journey. By fostering collaboration and building a sense of community, leaders create a confluence where ideas, talents, and visions merge, much like rivers coming together. This aspect aligns with the communitarian philosophy, emphasizing the value of collective good and community.

In summary, the circle of confluence in leadership beautifully encapsulates how successful leaders expand their circle of influence. It's a dynamic, interconnected system where knowledge, wisdom, ethical leadership, visionary thinking, empathy, and collaboration flow together, creating a powerful force that can profoundly shape organizations and societies.

Leadership Models

Modern leadership theories have evolved to emphasize various styles and aspects critical for today's dynamic and diverse work environment. Among these, emotional intelligence stands out as a crucial element of the "art" of leadership. It involves the ability to understand and manage one's emotions and empathize with others. This skill is essential for effective stakeholder engagement, allowing leaders to connect with their teams and clients more deeply.

Agile leadership is another critical aspect in today's fast-paced environment. Leaders must be adaptable and flexible, facilitating collaboration, promoting teamwork, and driving innovation. This style is characterized by openness to change and a commitment to continuous improvement, ensuring that organizations can swiftly respond to evolving market demands and internal challenges.

Servant leadership takes a different approach, focusing on the leader serving the team. Here, the leader puts the needs of team members first, aiding their performance and emphasizing their development and well-being. This approach creates a supportive and nurturing environment, boosting team morale and effectiveness.

Transformational leadership is about inspiring teams to achieve exceptional results. Transformational leaders align individual goals with the organization's vision and are known for their ability to initiate and sustain significant change. They are motivators and visionaries who encourage their teams to reach beyond their current capabilities.

Inclusive leadership is increasingly important in a diverse and globalized workplace. It involves recognizing and valuing different perspectives and ideas. Inclusive leaders know their biases and strive to create an environment where all team members feel they belong and can contribute their best work. With the increasing importance of digital technologies, digital leadership has become a vital skill. Leaders in this domain must be competent in navigating digital transformations, understanding the impact of digital tools, and leveraging data analytics for informed decision-making.

Integrating these ideas with the Circle of Influence, leaders should focus on:

- **Expanding their circle:** Includes influencing those within their immediate team, stakeholders, and other departments that the LSS initiative might impact.
- **Adapting their style:** Using different leadership styles depending on the situation and the team members they are trying to influence.
- **Developing people:** Investing in developing team members' skills and knowledge to equip them better to handle the changes the LSS initiative will bring.
- **Fostering innovation:** Encouraging a culture where team members can propose ideas and improvements without fear of failure.

As we discussed, the importance of post-COVID leadership has underscored the importance of the Triple Bottom Line—people, planet, and profit—in creating resilient and sustainable global supply chain networks. Here's how leadership can align with these principles and view the new generation of Circle of Influence (see Figure 9.2).

Figure 9.2 Circle of Influence

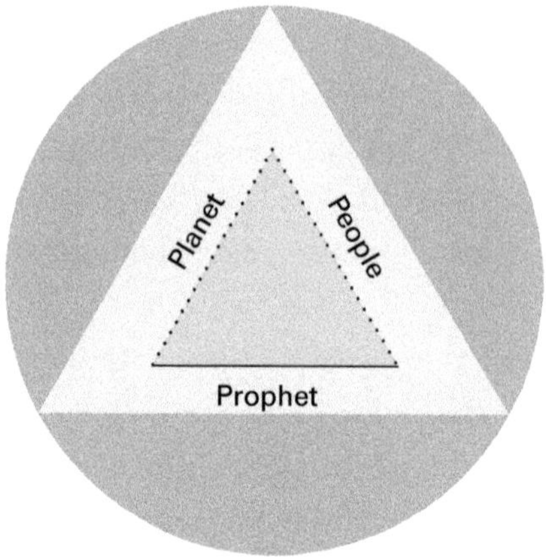

Circle of Influence

SOURCE USC Marshall-Randall R. Kendrick Global Supply Chain Institute

1. **People-centric leadership:** The pandemic has highlighted the critical role of employee well-being and safety. Leaders must prioritize the health and development of their workforce, ensuring safe working conditions and fostering a culture of care and support. This includes offering flexibility, mental health resources, and continuous learning opportunities to adapt to new working methods.
2. **Planetary responsibility:** Leaders must integrate environmental considerations into every aspect of the supply chain. This involves reducing carbon footprints, minimizing waste, and ensuring ethical sourcing. Investing in green technologies and sustainable practices is no longer optional but necessary for long-term viability.
3. **Profit through sustainability:** Profitability remains essential, but the approach has shifted. Sustainable practices are increasingly linked to cost savings and long-term financial performance. Leaders must balance short-term gains with the company's long-term health, which includes investing in sustainable practices that drive profitability.

To achieve these objectives, leaders need to (see Table 9.1 and 9.2):

- **Adopt agile methodologies:** Being agile allows organizations to respond quickly to disruptions. Agile leadership in supply chain management means having the flexibility to adapt to changes, whether a sudden demand surge or a supplier outage.
- **Build resilience:** Resilient supply chains can withstand and recover quickly from disruptions. This requires diversification of suppliers, investment in risk management, and the development of contingency plans.
- **Innovate continuously:** Post-COVID leadership must encourage innovation to improve supply chain processes. This could involve adopting advanced analytics, artificial intelligence, and machine learning to enhance forecasting, inventory management, and customer service.
- **Collaborate widely:** Partnerships with suppliers, customers, and competitors can lead to a more robust supply chain. Shared learning and risk can create a more resilient network.
- **Focus on digital transformation:** Embracing digital tools can lead to more transparent, efficient, and responsive supply chains. Digital leadership involves understanding the potential of these technologies and guiding their implementation.

Table 9.1 Deeper Dive into 3 P's of Leadership

Principle	Case Example	Leadership Insight
People-Centric Leadership	**Case Example: Flexible Work Solutions:** When the pandemic forced lockdowns, SCND, a multinational with a vast supply chain, pivoted to remote work arrangements. They invested in mental health programs and upskilling their workforce for digital proficiency. The result was a more satisfied workforce, increased productivity, and a robust supply chain that could operate effectively despite lockdowns.	**Leadership Insight:** This shift required leaders who could empathize with the workforce's challenges and swiftly implement support systems. It demonstrated that prioritizing people could also lead to strengthened operational resilience.

(continued)

Table 9.1 (Continued)

Principle	Case Example	Leadership Insight
Planetary Responsibility: Sustainable Supply Chain Practices	**Case Example**: SCND Logistics, a key player in global distribution, implemented a fleet of electric vehicles and optimized route planning for reduced emissions. They also partnered with suppliers to minimize packaging waste. Their efforts decreased their carbon footprint and operational costs, proving that environmental sustainability can coexist with fiscal responsibility.	**Leadership Insight**: Leaders at ABC Logistics had to balance immediate investment costs against long-term benefits, showing that a commitment to the planet could drive innovation and cost savings.
Profit Through Sustainability: The Financial Viability of Ethical Practices	**Case Example: Ethical Sourcing and Customer Loyalty** A fashion retail giant, SCND Apparel, overhauled its sourcing policies to ensure fair labor practices and environmental protection. Although initially more costly, this move bolstered its brand image and attracted a loyal customer base willing to pay a premium for ethically produced goods.	**Leadership Insight:** The leaders of DEF Apparel recognized that modern consumers value corporate ethics, and by aligning their business model with these values, they could drive profitability through customer loyalty.
Agile Methodologies: Building Adaptive Supply Chains	**Case Example: Modular Manufacturing** SCND Electronics adopted a modular approach to its manufacturing processes, allowing it to swap out parts and adapt its product line as demand shifted during the pandemic. This agility enabled them to minimize losses and capture new market opportunities as consumer needs evolved rapidly.	**Leadership Insight:** The agility of SCND Electronics was a direct result of foresighted leadership that invested in flexible production systems, showcasing the importance of adaptability in supply chain design.

(continued)

Table 9.1 (Continued)

Principle	Case Example	Leadership Insight
Resilience in Supply Chain: Risk Management and Diversification	**Case Example: Diversified Sourcing** SCND Pharma, faced with the risk of supply shortages for essential medicines, diversified its supplier base geographically. By not relying on a single source, they ensured a continuous supply of pharmaceuticals during border closures and trade restrictions.	**Leadership Insight:** SCND Pharma's leadership had to engage in risk assessment and proactive planning, demonstrating how strategic diversification is critical to resilience.
Continuous Innovation: The Role of Technology in Future-Proofing Supply Chains	**Case Example: Digital Integration** SCND Industries implemented blockchain technology to track the provenance of raw materials: this increased transparency, reduced instances of fraud, and improved compliance with regulatory requirements.	**Leadership Insight:** SCND's leaders had to champion technological adoption and foster a culture that was receptive to innovation, illustrating how technology can be a catalyst for transformation.
Collaborative Networks: Enhancing Supply Chain Robustness	**Case Example: Cross-Industry Collaboration** A consortium of food producers, distributors, and retailers created a shared logistics platform to pool resources, reduce costs, and ensure food security during the pandemic.	**Leadership Insight:** This collaborative effort was driven by leaders who recognized the value of shared goals and mutual benefits, underlining the power of partnership in overcoming complex challenges.

Essential Leadership Transformation system to successfully integrate and reprogram cultural DNA

Designing and executing a leadership transformation system to integrate and reprogram a company's cultural DNA in the context of a Supply Chain Network Design Change involves the following steps.

Table 9.2 Deeper Dive into 3 P's of Leadership

Principle	Insight
Emotional Intelligence	Modern leadership theories emphasize the importance of emotional intelligence as a part of the "art" of leadership. This includes understanding and managing one's emotions and empathizing with others, which is essential for effective stakeholder engagement.
Agile Leadership	Leaders must be adaptable and flexible in today's fast-paced environment. Agile leadership involves facilitating collaboration, promoting teamwork, and driving innovation by being open to change and encouraging a culture of continuous improvement.
Servant Leadership	This approach focuses on the leader serving the team, putting the needs of the team members first, and helping them to perform as effectively as possible. It emphasizes the development and well-being of others.
Transformational Leadership	Transformational leaders inspire their teams to achieve exceptional results by aligning the individual's goals with the organization's vision. They are characterized by their ability to initiate and sustain significant change.
Inclusive Leadership	Recognizing and valuing diverse perspectives and ideas. Inclusive leaders know their biases and seek to create an environment where all team members feel they belong and can contribute.
Digital Leadership	With the increasing importance of digital technologies, leaders must be competent in navigating digital transformations, understanding the impact of digital tools, and leveraging data analytics for decision-making.
Sustainable Leadership	Leaders are now expected to look beyond short-term gains and consider the long-term impact of their actions on the environment, society, and the economy.

Assessment and Alignment

Before launching a transformative project such as (re-)designing a supply chain network, a crucial first step is to comprehensively assess current supply chain processes and leadership behaviors. This assessment aims to align leadership transformation objectives with the desired supply chain network design outcomes and ensure that the leadership team understands and is committed to the change initiative. A

360-degree assessment of an entire supply chain framework covers all supply chain elements such as strategy, operating system, management infrastructure, mindsets, and capabilities.

Under strategy, we consider supply chain strategy, service level management, product portfolio complexity management, supply chain segmentation, network design, and supply chain risk management areas. The operating system to support this strategy comprises a sales and operations planning (S&OP) process re-design, order and demand management system, forecasting, inventory management, production management, supply management, and operational logistics. The management infrastructure elements include the supply chain organization model, incentives, performance management, and information technology management. Finally, the mindsets and capabilities needed to implement the design successfully focus on the mindsets and behaviors of staff capabilities, resulting in a comprehensive training and development program.

Figure 9.3 shows a "spider chart" where we can plot the assessment results across all elements rated between 1–5 for each factor and overlayed against industry benchmarks. McKinsey & Co. uses this methodology to assess and build a strategy based on the top areas of improvement.

Leadership Development Program

Once an assessment is done, companies should create a leadership development program tailored to supply chain excellence, focusing on strategic thinking, change management, and cross-functional knowledge. Typically, such programs include workshops, seminars, and training modules on leading transformational change. Following this, implement a mentorship and coaching system where senior leaders can guide emerging leaders through the transformation process.

One of the authors of this book had the opportunity to develop several such programs by means of cross-functional and cross-hierarchical workshops in multiple organizations in the CPG/Retail and Media/Entertainment space, spanning more than a decade as a consultant. Learning from these workshops is summarized at the end of this chapter.

Figure 9.3 Target Performance Levels

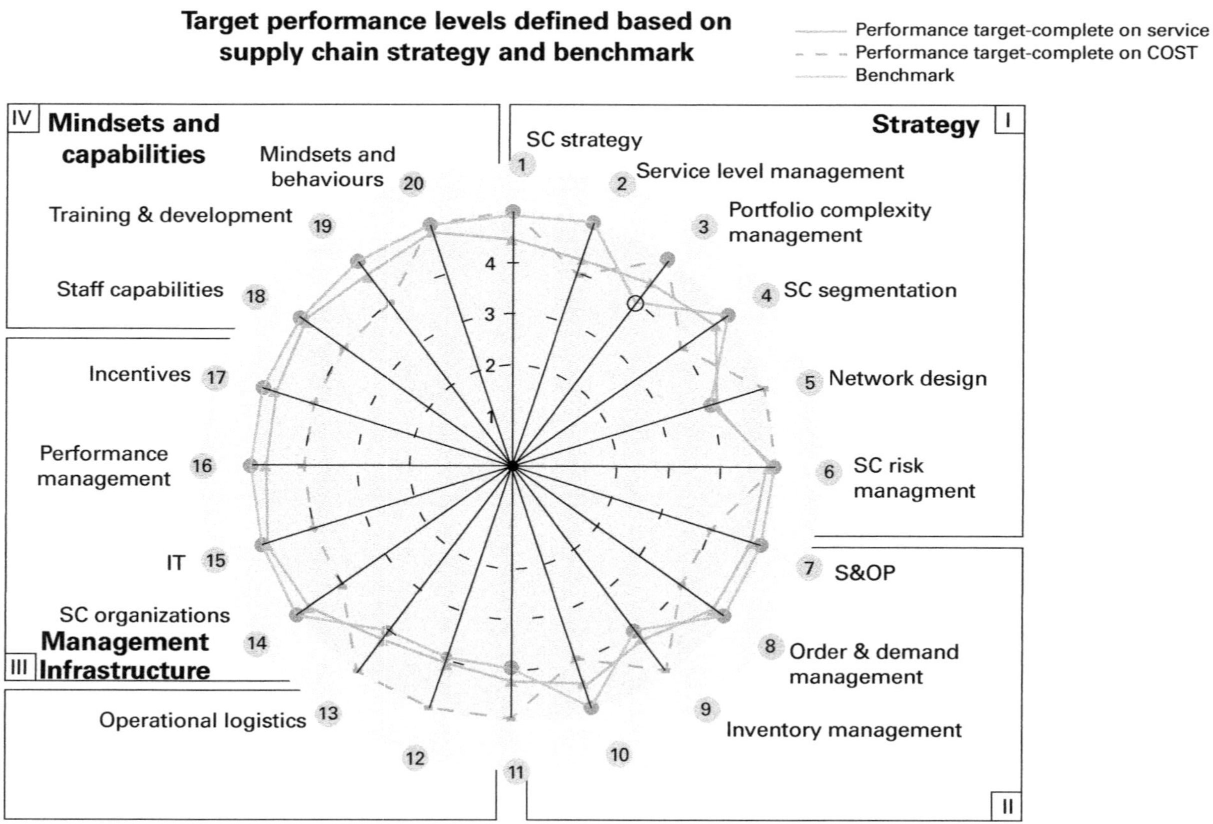

SOURCE USC Marshall-Randall R. Kendrick Global Supply Chain Institute

Communication Strategy

To kick off the leadership transformation initiative with workshops, we recommend companies develop a clear communication strategy to convey the changes and their benefits to all organizational levels. Use a mix of communication channels to reach different audiences within the organization effectively. A sample agenda is to include the purpose and background of the initiative, business objectives, scope, draft timeline of deliverables, resources with RACI charts (with clearly named leaders who are Responsible, Accountable, Consulted, and Informed on the transformation), metrics, project participants, and a program management office announcement.

The top question on the participants' minds is, "What's in it for me?" To effectively communicate a Supply Chain Network Design initiative, the communication needs to show how each participant and leader would benefit from the initiative and how their cooperation would positively impact the organization.

Cultural Reinforcement

Identify and promote cultural values that support the new supply chain network design, such as agility, innovation, and collaboration. Recognize and reward behaviors that exemplify the desired cultural change. A fundamental question to ask on the cultural mindset is whether the supply chain management function is recognized in the organization as a leading role of integrated coordinator of all functions involved in the supply chain to achieve the required service level at minimum costs. If not, what should be a determined program to create that mindset?

Change Management Framework

Companies should adopt a structured change management framework to manage the transition. They should include change agents in different departments to facilitate and advocate for the change.

Change Management Programs in Organizational Transformations

Organizational transformations are complex endeavors that require careful planning and execution, especially when managing the human aspects of change. Change management programs are crucial in these transformations, ensuring that changes are implemented smoothly and effectively. These programs are designed to help organizations transition from their current state to a desired future state while minimizing employee disruptions and resistance.

Widely adopted change management programs typically include several key elements:

1. **Leadership engagement and support:** Successful change management begins at the top. Leadership must endorse the change and actively participate in and support the change process. This includes clear communication about the change's purpose, benefits, and expected impact on the organization and its employees.
2. **Stakeholder analysis and communication:** Identifying and understanding all stakeholders' needs, fears, and expectations is vital. Tailored communication strategies are developed to address these concerns and keep everyone informed.
3. **Training and development:** Employees may need to acquire new skills or knowledge as organizations transform. Change management programs often include comprehensive training and development plans to prepare employees for new processes, technologies, or roles.
4. **Change agents and advocacy networks:** Change agents or champions within the organization can facilitate the change process. These individuals are typically influential and can help promote and legitimize the change within their teams or departments.
5. **Resistance management:** Resistance to change is natural. Effective change management programs include strategies for identifying and addressing resistance through direct communication, additional training, or involvement in the change process.

6 **Feedback mechanisms:** Regular feedback loops are essential to understand how the change is being received and to make necessary adjustments. This could be through surveys, focus groups, or an open-door policy for feedback.
7 **Sustainability and reinforcement:** Ensuring the change is sustainable over the long term is a crucial objective. This involves reinforcing the change through ongoing support, monitoring, and integration into the organizational culture.

Programs like ADKAR (Awareness, Desire, Knowledge, Ability, Reinforcement) by Prosci, Kotter's 8-Step Change Model, and Lewin's Change Management Model are among organizational transformations' most adopted frameworks. Each offers a structured approach to managing change, focusing on the organizational and human aspects of transformation.

Integration of Technology and People

Companies must utilize technology to support the change process, including data analytics and collaborative tools. Ensure that people are trained and comfortable with new technology and processes. An integral part of this cultural (re-)orientation is information technology. Ensuring that information technology supports supply chain processes, provides complete, real-time visibility, and automates processes where applicable is critical. Since IT is increasingly viewed as an "application maintenance" team, re-examining a cultural identity for IT is essential.

Performance Management

Supply Chain performance target setting and monitoring process drives continuous improvement. These targets should be aligned across the organization (SCM, business units, and senior leadership) and derived from a fact-based understanding of what can be achieved.

Redefine performance metrics to support the new supply chain strategy, regularly review progress against these metrics, and adjust strategies as needed. The supply chain performance measurement should cover all dimensions for service cost and capital; a relevant level of detail should provide a robust platform for the decision-making process. For example, a segment-level detail for service level and production-line level detail for adherence to the production schedule should be visible to all stakeholders. Data availability in a short time (or near-real time) is often an issue that stands in the way of enabling escalation and decision-making. Finally, the metrics should have standard definitions and be aligned across the business units, functions, and senior management. The industry standards put forth by the Supply Chain Operational Reference (SCOR) model are a great place to start putting together a performance management framework for SCND.

Feedback Loops and Continuous Improvement

Companies should establish feedback mechanisms to capture lessons learned and integrate them into ongoing operations. There is a need to promote a culture of continuous improvement, encouraging feedback and innovation from all levels of the organization. Standardized and regular review processes across the organization must be implemented, complete with performance dialogs. There should be internal comparison or benchmarking conducted used to drive improvement levels.

Sustainability and Ethical Considerations

Companies must ensure the transformation plan includes sustainable practices and ethical considerations in supply chain operations. A detailed discussion on this topic is covered in Chapter 6.

Execution and Monitoring

We recommend that companies roll out the transformation in phases, each followed by a monitoring and review period. They should adjust the plan based on performance data and feedback to ensure continuous alignment with strategic goals.

Considering its unique challenges and opportunities, this plan should be detailed and adapted to the organization's specific context. It is essential to have top management's full support and involve key stakeholders throughout the process to ensure the successful integration of the new supply chain network design and the reprogramming of the organization's cultural DNA.

Leadership Transformation Workshops – learnings from several engagements in Consulting

A decade ago, the music industry was decimated by digitization, piracy, and ubiquity, while the physical media groups of the home video industry are going through a similar creative destruction process. While it was anticipated that the compact disc (CD) would be entirely out of use in the music industry, it still constitutes a large part of music sales. It is interesting to observe the product lifecycle of CDs as music media and make predictions on the DVD media for movies, and the lessons learned from both throw significant light on industry demise and what companies have done to maximize the life of these products and continue to transform to protect profits.

The home video business units of film studios in the United States supply their films (intellectual property) on DVD and Blu-Ray discs, package them, and ship them to retail customers. These units of the larger studios, which brought close to 50 percent of the total revenue stream for the studios, generally operate as if they are fast-moving consumer goods (FMCG) companies that serve the retail chain stores market through vendor managed inventory (VMI) arrangements and some order-based distribution strategy for non-VMI customers. The studios prefer this arrangement since it allows them to "see" how products are "selling through" the shelves of the stores of their retail customers continually, and based on trends, they can decide to replenish additional units of the title so that the risk of stockouts or shortages do not outweigh the risk of excess and hence obsolete titles. On the supply side, almost every studio uses a manufacturing vendor (often called a "replicator", and some major ones are Technicolor, Cinram, Delux Media, and Sony DADC) who also pick, pack and ship products on behalf of the studios, who maintain a staff in-house for planning, forecasting, and making decisions on manufacturing, storing, and distribution.

Big retailers such as Walmart and Best Buy rule the market, and their arrangement with vendors on VMI contracts is that if sell-through is lower than expected, the studios are responsible for accepting all unsold items as "returns." Therefore, the risk of high shipment, holding inventory, transportation, shrink, and obsolescence costs must be balanced against very high stockout costs incurred within a concise time span (generally, a new release high-earner movie title enjoys top revenue for one to two weeks).

The author of this article was a management consultant to leaders of a major studio who led this transformation for over seven years between 2005 and 2011.

In the grand scheme of things spanning the seven years, the initiatives could be outlined as follows:

- i **Develop organizational competency and change readiness through global supply chain management workshops:** To design and roll out a global supply chain strategy, process, people alignment, and technology needs for added efficiency and accurate reporting of costs, beginning with headquarters, and subsequently rolled out to Europe, Middle East, and Asia (EMEA), Asia Pacific (APAC), and Latin America (LATAM) (two years);
- ii **Gain consensus among multiple functional groups in the organization by designing and rolling out a global sales & operations planning (S&OP) process:** To design and roll out global sales and operations planning (S&OP) process to have companywide alignment on manufacturing the exact number of units per SKU- first in headquarters, and then worldwide (one year);
- iii **Identify key management levers to improve through Root Cause Analysis:** To map the studio's upstream and downstream supply chains, uncover key business challenges and pain points to through Root Cause Analysis (RCA) (six months);
- iv **Measure the key performance criteria for improvement using SCOR Metrics:** To recommend the right metrics and then implement the SCOR model (Supply Chain Operational Reference)

along with the following metrics tailored to meet the above unique business conditions: perfect order fulfillment, order fulfillment cycle time, demand management accuracy, supply chain flexibility and total supply chain costs (six months);

- v **Accrue savings and previously unrealized revenue through initiatives called "commercial benefits realization (CBR)":** To develop cross-functional and cross hierarchical teams encompassing Sales, Marketing, Operations, HR, and Finance across all Business units who would discover key opportunities for meaningful enterprise cost reduction (ECR) without sacrificing processes and people who actually enable revenue generation; this was called "commercial benefit realization" initiative (CBR) (2 years);
- vi **Capture sustainable savings by optimization tools (Lean Six Sigma):** To empower the teams with optimization toolsets derived from the proven body of knowledge in lean continuous improvement so that they could apply these along with the right problem-solving approach (1 year);
- vii To date, the above initiatives have accrued savings that have passed $100 Million, which has paid for the enterprise-wide license fees and implementation costs of ERP software (SAP) purchased by the studio.

The Process, mindset, and approach of Studio leadership

By 2005, the home video industry was slowing down from its double-digit growth days due to rising digital media growth, slowing economy, and internet-based subscription models for home entertainment. Costs were already high due to heavy investments in enhanced feature development of titles, marketing and format wars, and SG&A expenses. The costs of the business were not easily manageable since they were spread across scores of homegrown custom-designed software tools, and these tools did not "talk to each other", thereby ruling out the possibility of a centralized management reporting ability.

To have a central visibility to enterprise-wide costs, and to bring costs down so that profit margins could be maintained, the studio engaged in a due diligence on ERP software and kicked off a series of Global Business Transformation (GBT) workshops with the mediation of a consulting firm. Following these workshops, one of the key organizational realignments was to accept the fact that home video is essentially a supply chain management unit, and their focus should be to be able to meet fleeting consumer demand on the retailer's shelves without producing excess product that would eventually incur holding costs in outsourced warehouses. This required the organizations to remain flexible to changing market demand while introducing efficiencies on a large scale at the same time.

Like all other studios, this studio also outsources their manufacturing and distribution functions to an outside vendor, called Replicator. They used to receive manufacturing orders, replicate DVDs, pack them using studio-developed creative art, and store them. When an order was generated by the order management system at the studio that would transmit the order to the replicator, they would ship the order to the specific retail store where it would be needed.

The outcome of GBT was a decision to integrate the global organization by implementing all the relevant modules of an ERP system (SAP) such as general ledger, accounts payable, accounts receivable, human resources, inventory, sales and distribution, supply network planning, advanced planning optimization, demand planning, and supply chain planning under one central umbrella, with instances running in certain offshore territories such as Europe and Asia. This would replace all existing "legacy" systems such as video distributed order entry (VDOE), video cost accounting system (VCAS), and about a dozen others, except one module that gave the studio a competitive differentiator in the industry called retail inventory management (RIM), written to optimize replenishment policies by SKU and Stores. RIM would stay on, with SAP systems interfacing with it, and the expectation was that the overall system would generate key insights that would help management have real time visibility to costs and make appropriate management decisions.

Typically, in the case of every expensive ERP implementation such as SAP or Oracle, people are expected to conduct business in a new way without which the intended benefits would never be realized. This would require a thorough organizational transformation which must be endorsed by and participated by the C-level executives and their middle-level management to make sure that a blueprint is developed to change the company from "as-is" processes to a "to-be" vision.

Approach

> Tell them what to do, and they will forget it. Show them, and maybe they will remember. Involve them, and they will learn. —Ancient Chinese proverb.

The studio's senior management team engaged a consulting team (headed by the author) to design and roll out a cross-functional and cross-hierarchical workshop-based approach, since most transformational projects fail due to misalignment between people of different stakeholder groups, lack of clear ownership, ineffective division of responsibilities, failure to involve middle management, and lack of jointly agreed metrics to measure success. Failed transformations result in finger-pointing battles across functions, groups, teams, divisions, and people, resulting in more hurt egos, burnt self-esteem, and an overall death spiral. To make organization-wide projects successful, people from the impacted business divisions need to be aligned with a common understanding and appreciation of the project strategy and solution *prior* to implementation. Employees need to *own* their projects. The workshop-based methodology was designed to facilitate total **employee ownership** of projects.

Exhibit 2 shows how the workshop participants were chosen with a balance of the following levels of employees at the studio:

1. L3 – Executors (frontline transaction level folks) – 30 percent
2. L2 – Middle management (supervisors and tactical decision makers) – 60 percent

3 L1 – Director level folks (strategic decision makers and negotiators)– 10 percent
4 Input from selected vendors
5 Input from selected customers

Several observations on this selection of workshop participants are noteworthy. Level 1 senior management folks often do not have visibility to the frontline challenges and issues. This cross-hierarchical teaming allowed them to be aware of key frontline challenges that gave them data to design a fact-based approach to the transformation. Similarly, level 3 frontline employees who rarely have the opportunity to understand the 'big picture' vision of the organization were able to directly listen to their leaders and understand the pieces of the puzzle, along with where they fit it. When explained the big picture, they were able to put the pieces of the puzzle together, reflect, and come up with innovative ideas that they took ownership of.

Customers, who were interviewed by the consulting team offline, were intrigued and appreciated the fact that their vendor had initiated improvement projects, and candidly shared their ideas and opinions on how they could improve. Additionally, they understood that cooperation from the customer's side was also necessary, and the independence of the third-party consultant was key in generating commitment from the customer's side on helping the studio through their process redesign and transformation.

Finally, the vendors were key in providing insights on how and where the studio could save costs, including cutting down redundant activities, non-key operations, and old processes and policies that were never repealed, causing bottlenecks in operations.

Thus, with a wealth of ideas from several stakeholders, both from inside and outside the organization, a "360°" view of benefit realization opportunities was possible, thereby allowing the studio to collect 100+ ideas on improvement and cost reduction. It was now time to filter through the ideas and recommendations generated, and narrow down to the key opportunities. To do this through fact-based analysis, a comprehensive quantitative benefit analysis was conducted that included root cause analysis.

Benefit Analysis

Once facilitated cross-functional team workshops had agreement and alignment on opportunities, several white-boarding sessions were conducted to determine the opportunities, root causes, enablers, and benefits to be collaboratively realized.

Opportunity

The opportunities identified by the studio at a high level were explored further to try and quantify an approximate cost-savings or revenue-enhancing or customer-service level enhancing opportunity. A dollar value for each opportunity was developed with the help of the finance function or controller, or accounting teams. Typically, this would be obtained by asking questions like "How much is our annual trade spend", or "How much costs do we incur in Returns Management", and so on. These are "big pockets" of opportunities that require further analysis to determine if it was possible at all to put a dent in to the costs.

Root-Cause Analysis

To each of the opportunity areas, the teams asked themselves a series of "why?" questions (like five whys analysis in the six sigma body of knowledge), one leading to the other, to determine the root causes that are challenges to attain and achieve these opportunities. The teams often used Ishikawa's Fishbone analysis method to arrive at unique, indivisible root causes. They then mapped these root causes to solutions.

Enablers

The teams were then coached, and brainstorming sessions were facilitated to come up with innovative and collaborative suggestions on solutions, while the consulting team conducted research on best practices, known solutions, market benchmarks, or helped design solutions around **people, policies, processes, and technologies**.

People enablers

The people solutions are essentially organizational structure recommendations with perhaps new responsibilities assigned to a group of people who have been doing things differently. In these workshops, everyone participates equally, making it easier for people to accept changes in their work pattern since they are "involved" in it, not just observers. We play interactive games, simulations, and problem-solving exercises where everyone feels that they are a part of the solution, and their fingerprint is captured in the final solution. This gives a sense of ownership that is not possible in instructive recommendations that outsiders are typically known to provide.

Policy enablers

Many times, the team found that some policies had been in place for a long time since no one took the initiative to change it or re-examine it. Sometimes these remained hidden since there was no facilitated process of uncovering them, and the people who knew about them were not senior enough to effect changes to these policies. The cross-hierarchical workshop-driven methodology brought senior people and matched them with junior folks who were aware of these challenges. Through these workshops, change proposals for obsolete and meaningless old policies that hurt performance were re-visited and the senior members of the team took it to top management for their decisions on changing or dropping them. Additionally, recommendations of new or altered or alternative policies were brought up by the team for the consideration of the senior management team.

Process enablers

An end-to-end process flow was also mapped and developed by the workshop teams to come up with a to-be process with substantiated logic behind each step, mapping it to people following RACI charts (who is/are Responsible for a new process, who is Accountable, who needs to be Consulted, and who needs to stay Informed). Examples of such processes involved a step-by-step guide on building deep supplier relationships, negotiating best rates with vendors based on volume, performance, quality, location, and total landed cost.

Technology Enablers

In the final step, where opportunities for automated efficiencies and optimized planning surfaced, relevant technology solutions were mapped to the transformation initiative to capture real benefits. For each root cause, the teams tried to map an enabler, whether or not it was supported by the software/technology implementation. This ensured that a holistic solution was designed rather than a spot solution. The technical recommendations were passed on to the team of solution engineers who would treat these as requirements and develop or tailor/configure the solution accordingly.

Dollar Savings/Benefits

Once the teams completed the analyses of the first three areas of opportunity, root causes, and solution enablers, they had the information necessary to determine a realistic assessment of the benefits associated with implementation. This calculation helps prioritize initiatives by providing details on ROI. Often, this calculation could be a rule of thumb, such as "what percent of the root causes would be gone if the appropriate people, process, and technology changes were made?". This could be generated by consensus, by participation of relevant accounting and finance teams, or by experience. At other times, the finance team would be asked for benchmarks on similar savings from other initiatives. At any rate, the most conservative dollar savings would be reported, with a most likely and optimistic estimate, along with a time and resource plan for the management team.

Business Plans were developed by Business Users

At the end of the workshops, each team took ownership of an initiative and developed a "business plan" with the aid of consultants. A business plan would typically have a set of integrated changes that result in a specific business improvement that focused on business results, provided expected completion date and responsibility, as well as short-term, well-defined goals to give quick results throughout the duration of the project. The teams also pointed out to the management team that the business plan may result in changes to one or more of the following areas: people and their roles, technology functions, data changes, process changes, policy changes, metrics, key performance indicators, and governance, with performance management criteria.

How The Workshops Were Conducted

A functional session plan was designed and tailored to each session. For example, ten or twelve sessions were planned at the beginning of a quarter, each lasting three or four hours depending on how deep and wide the transformation was expected to be. In those sessions the top leadership members were often invited to conduct a part of it. This showed true commitment and got alignment quicker. Each session also had team presentations on a chosen topic as it related to business. The teams were formed cross-functionally. They are also cross-hierarchical. Each team was put together with a balance of people from the frontline, some from the middle management, and whenever needed, some even from top management. The teams were presented with problems that they needed to take up and that needed to be addressed. They identified the low-hanging fruits and a design on how this will be done through a set of business releases, using some of the proven process changes or solutions that were shared with the team. The discussions and brainstorming were led by the consulting team. The consultants often facilitated a root-cause analysis session. Finally, the workshop teams presented their findings and plans back to the senior management.

The questions that run these workshops were not "how could we make sweeping cost reductions in SG&A or Supply Chain and Distribution?". Rather, they challenged long-existing functional silos and asked, "Which decisions could sales take an ownership on, that could result in significant reduction of inventory and freight costs?" or "What advertising and promotional planning activity should be communicated to the operations team so that they do not run a shortage of products?" and so on. In essence, these workshops were fundamentally cross-functional in nature.

The action was in the hands of the level-two folks who had a desire to grow, to be promoted, and who had a desire to see the company be successful. There was a lot at stake if they did not do those things. Therefore, once they took ownership, the company really benefited from all sides. This is why these authors believe that the workshop approach provided the business teams with a platform to be able to prove themselves, come with a plan, and get a lot of visibility and support. Most importantly, it got the top management vision socialized across all functions and levels in the organization.

Workshop Results

Results reported by the studio as of Q3 2011 have exceeded a hundred million dollars of actualized savings over a period of four years based on these transformations, paying for the SAP implementation. This had been counted after the implementation was over. A year or two passed by to prove that this kind of approach works. It was tangible in dollars and cents, along with a lot more employee retention, empowerment, and a lot less frustration in the frontline. Senior leadership also felt that they were heard, and their vision was embraced; middle management felt that they were ready and that they had essentially earned their right to be promoted to the next levels. Overall, according to the feedback received from senior management, the company's health from an employee satisfaction perspective significantly improved.

The consultant team brought core competencies in supply chain management that are both detailed and rigorous as well as process driven. The detailed and rigorous aspects include mathematical quantitative elements of supply chain management, such as inventory management or forecasting algorithms, demand management and demand management processes. The process-driven approach included setting up, designing, and rolling out a sales-and-operations-planning process, lean continuous improvement using six sigma tools, vendor-managed inventory, CPFR (collaborative planning, forecasting, and replenishment processes) and leveraging best practices from other consumer-packaged goods, retail, high-tech life sciences sectors, as well as manufacturing sectors.

Supply Chain Management Workshops

The first step for the studio was to design an end-to-end supply chain transformation. In executing these services, best practices from industry standards such as supply chain operational reference (SCOR) model, lean management principles and six sigma methodology were applied. Exhibit 3 shows the activities in a SCOR model that were mapped to the studio operations. As the program was designed, the key alignment points that were determined by management were as follows:

i Since a big part of customer demand driven fulfillment for home video takes place through an arrangement known as vendor management inventory (VMI), much of the focus, attention, energy, spend, and investment in the studio is around the people, processes, and technology around supporting its VMI contract with major retailers such as Wal-Mart, Best Buy, and club accounts such as Costco, Sam's Club, and others. Many of these accounts are experienced participants of the VMI process, and they measure the vendors (including the studio) with such key performance indicators such as in-stock rates, on-time delivery, and proactive replenishment processes. To accommodate such a massive scale of decision-making points at the store/SKU level, effective technology support is instrumental. The author (consultant) was engaged prior to these initiatives to help design and build an advanced version of an existing software program called "retail inventory management" (RIM), and its replenishment policies, based on speed of sales of a particular title in a specific store were well known to the author.

ii Additionally, forecasting at these levels of minuscule movements of stock in widely dispersed selling points is extremely difficult and could be influenced by myriad factors, yet studios keep working hard to get better store/SKU forecast accuracies.

iii Much of the final product assortment from a studio that would be displayed on store shelves of high volume and fast-moving retail chains, along with titles from other studios, were decided by a "category captain," often a competing studio that won the contract from the retailer based on their ability to predict product movement on the shelf level and show superior profits for the retailer based on chosen assortment. Since this studio has been a category captain off and on with Wal-Mart and in some other accounts there was organizational learning on this process that needed to be dispersed within the ranks.

iv A vast majority of the events experienced by the operations management teams were effects of upstream decision-making activity that was oblivious of downstream impact. For example, advanced notification of special promotions would always need to be communicated to operations so that enough safety stock planning could be done. This, among several other challenges such as inability to get a digital image (formerly digital linear tape or DLT) on time prohibited operations to send their final product to the "replicator" (CINRAM at the time of these events, currently Technicolor) on time, thereby imposing severe capacity issues. An awareness of such cause-effect relationships was crucial for the organization to be agile, aligned, and adaptable to the continually changing market.

v Since flexibility is expensive in such a fast-moving environment, organizational coordination in the face of uncertainty was deemed to be a critical factor to be successful.

The supply chain workshops were designed to train such central challenges of home video supply chain in seven to ten sessions—again, with representation from sales, marketing, retail operations, planning, distribution, IT, finance, and several other related functions unique to the studio. They were given material to read and consider using insights from as they developed their hypotheses on the key topics of sales forecasting, category management, vendor managed inventory, sales and operations planning, collaborative planning, forecasting, and replenishment, IT landscape and enablers of the supply chain, and related areas. Cross-functional teams were asked on each session to present on a known challenge and leverage the workshop material to show how it could be approached for solution. Additionally, one or two top leaders from the leadership team were invited to present in the workshops each day on how things work at their levels—this gave them tremendous visibility and socialization of their wisdom among the ranks and created an organizational alignment. At the end of the workshop, each team presented their business case on a set of improvement initiatives along with potential dollar benefits, risks, timeline, resource needs, and budget in front of the senior management team.

The results of this workshop exceeded expectations. More than anything else, there was this organizational alignment and readiness that evolved through the workshops among the chosen participants. These attendees were primarily chosen by their roles as "influencers and connectors" who would communicate the vision to their peers. Additionally, when they saw potential to succeed and be recognized and promoted, they embraced the vision and the associated "changes" that come with it—such as newer roles, responsibilities, openness to process changes, and an overall readiness to technology related novelty that the upcoming ERP implementation would impose of them. An associated identification of $49 million of potential savings and unquantifiable revenue to be captured was also motivating.

S&OP Process Design and Roll Out

The supply chain management workshops identified that the singular problem that plagues the home video industry is an accurate estimate of demand, in a SKU level, by retail store level. With each major account (such as Wal-Mart, Best Buy, and others) having several thousand stores and each movie title with 3 to 40 SKU's, the potential number of combinations could easily lead to several million "forecasting decision points," a phenomenon unique to CPG companies who supply to their retail customers. Forecasting, therefore, was key both at a national level, account level, and store level for titles that were not only released recently, but also those that have been released in the past (catalog titles). However, this was not limited to historical time-series based statistical forecasting alone, there were several other elements that needed to be taken in to consideration—such as marketing plans on promoting a title, retailers' plans on offering special deals to consumers on seasonal events, sales teams offering deals to retail customers for discounts, rebates, and temporary price reductions, management team strategizing on capturing market share in newer and evolving channels, finance announcing a budget that needed some products to be pushed more than others, and so on. These are decisions that come from multiple functions that needed to be captured in the final "number of units" of a movie title, and therefore, a collaborative decision-making process was felt to be essential.

At this juncture, the leadership at the studio engaged in to designing a "sales and operations planning process" (S&OP), an industry-standard methodology to get all hands from marketing, finance, sales, operations, and management to decide collaboratively what the final number of a title should be, that must be manufactured, so as to meet demand at each demand point, without excess inventory that would be returned and devalued eventually. A studio-specific design was put in place as a straw man, when representatives from marketing, sales, business unit leadership, planning (forecasting), market research, operations planning, distribution planning, sales communication, credit and customer operations, retail planning, and finance would come up with their "cards on the table", a metaphor that represents the "magic number" of units of a title that they expect to sell through for the movie under consideration. In home video parlance, the release date for a home video unit is called "street date," and the act is often referred to as "streeting." On poker day, when all business functions meet, they come up with their calculated projection, including the effect of such factors event plans, promotional plans, advertisements, retail customer specials, and others. The business unit head, who owns the profit and loss of the title is expected to take all these numbers into consideration and stamp a final number for approval.

A consultant (one of the authors) and his team was engaged by the EVP of Worldwide Supply Chain Management (the co-author) to collect pockets of practices across the three business units to standardize the processes, socialize them for alignment across the organization, and then roll out the final strawman to the global territories. The consulting team flew out to London, Stockholm, and Hamburg three times each in a year, and helped a series of workshops where a global supply chain process design was accompanied by S&OP process design. These cities were primarily chosen as hubs in three territories—UK, Nordic, and Benelux (Belgium-Netherlands-Luxembourg) where leaders and managers from local nations flew in to attend these workshops and help co-design the S&OP process.

Commercial Benefits Realization (CBR)

Once the metrics for supply chain operational reference were established and begun to collect data, there was enough information that accumulated within the first two quarters to conduct analysis. This led to a substantiated set of hypotheses that operations cannot perform in a vacuum—they need collaboration and assistance from sales, marketing, and finance. Since the emphasis of these functions are predominantly on the commercial side, a new initiative was designed by the leadership of the studio—related to realization of commercial benefits. The purpose of this initiative was to identify key areas of cost containment where upstream activities added to downstream costs, with the help of cross-functional examination of potential opportunities. Leadership included the general managers of the three major business units—theatrical new release, catalog, and franchise, whose direct reports included marketing and sales. From an organizational psychology, this was an appropriate time to introduce CBR, since the operations teams were now acknowledged by everyone to have "done their job in fixing delivery issues", and now it was the turn of the commercial side to help. A significant set of hypotheses were selected by the three levels of employees through a series of cross-functional workshops, that were subsequently filtered and ratified by the president and leadership team of the studio.

A sample of some CBR initiative activity summaries are given in Tables 9.3, 9.4, 9.5, 9.6 and 9.7 below. Names of individuals have been erased due to confidentiality reasons:

A second part to this initiative that was combined with it is "reduction of excess inventory." The scope of that project is shown in Table 9.8.

Lean Continuous Improvement

With CBR initiatives identifying, executing, and accruing more than $50MM in realized savings, despite the sense of enterprise-wide achievement, senior management did not want complacency to set in.

Table 9.3 Optimize Freight Costs

Team Members	Approach	Milestones		
		Short Term	**Medium Term**	**Long Term**
Field Sales Order Management Marketing Distribution Management Transportation Operations Creative ExecutiveSponsor	1. Identify freight costs by top 10 accounts 2. Compare % of revenue vs. % of freight costs against respective totals 3. Determine root causes of high cost areas by account 4. Highlight reasons Identify whether conscious choice or reactionary 5. Quantify $ opportunity by cause Determine enabler 6. Review current rules in place Evaluate potential changes vs. cost of service 7. Determine short-, medium- and long-term initiatives	1. Identify all business rules around expedited freight. They should be coupled with enforcing reason codes to ensure governance of business rules 2. Identify consistent and reliable processes to consolidate Messenger Services	3. Review, evaluate, and streamline rules and governance mechanism for customer requested order expedition 4. Streamline rules, guidelines, and governance mechanism on customer chargeback 5. Explore ERP functionality to provide visibility to expedited cost by customer	1. Review compliance policies and governance mechanism around customer order due date to ensure that customers send complete orders by order due date

Table 9.4 Optimize Initial Shipment and Replenishment

Team Members	Approach	Milestones		
		Short Term	**Medium Term**	**Long Term**
Sales Communications Demand Planning Order Management Business Decision Support Project – Sponsor- General Manager	Improve accuracy at the store level using optimal initial distribution methodology 1. Implement the initial distribution method for all VMI accounts across all BUs 2. Incorporate competitive data into the new model wherever possible 3. Extend the method to key non-VMI accounts for major titles and promotions 4. Use the bottom-up viewpoint to validate the overall account forecasts	5. Develop and roll out a genre classification matrix for all VMI accounts 6. Use an optimal distribution method for all new release titles and roll out to the rest 7. Educate VMI customers about optimal initial distribution method 8. Work with accounts to obtain competitive data and incorporate into genre-classification matrix	3. Roll out optimal initial distribution method to all product families 4. Continue to incorporate competitive data 5. Link accuracy metric into the S&OP meeting to measure improvements 6. Bring bottoms-up validation into the formal goal-setting process	2. Develop process to extend new method to non-VMI accounts for key titles and promotions
Sales Communications Demand Planning Order Management Business Decision Support Project - Sponsor- General Manager	Incorporate the demand management accuracy metric into the S&OP process to drive improved accuracy at the national and account levels 1. Incorporate new release metric reports into the S&OP process 2. Design and develop a replenishment methodology for base catalog and promotional demand metric reports 3. Incorporate these reports into the S&OP process to drive improvements 4. Share summary metrics with senior management	1. Complete development of new release metric reports 2. Share with BU's and develop timing for incorporation into the S&OP process	1. Design and develop replenishment method, base catalog, and promotional demand metric reports 2. Share with BU's and develop timing for incorporation into the S&OP process	1. Work with Accuracy Improvement Teams to drive increased accuracy for all demand streams

Sales Communications Demand Planning Order Management Business Decision Support Project - Sponsor-General Manager	1. Ensure replenishment accuracy to further optimize store-level performance for VMI customers 2. Evaluate current rules, practices, and parameters governing replenishment orders 3. Establish rules for new release replenishment reaction based on performance criteria 4. Formulate policy for promotional replenishment Compare the RIM forecasts to actual POS	1. Establish VMI replenishment rules, parameters for new release business 2. Expand replenishment rules to catalog and franchise titles	1. Expand replenishment rules to promoted titles	1. Evaluate non-VMI reorders, analyze, and "right-size" response (e.g., EDI 855)

Table 9.5 Collaboratively Plan Sales Deals

Team Members	Approach	Milestones		
		Short Term	**Medium Term**	**Long Term**
Sales-Communication Credit & Collections Field Sales Sales Administration Sales Finance Sales Service Marketing Order Management Sales Force Automation MIS Master Data Mgmt Legal	1. Put in place longer term promotional planning. Customers should also be involved on quarterly basis to get their buy-in ahead of time 2. Educate customer on process, timelines, and consequences of late requests 3. Revisit business rules for accepting late requests and late changes 4. Improve communication of relevant information across all affected departments 5. Evaluate creating incentives for Field Sales and/or accounts to follow process and key dates 6. Evaluate system improvements to reduce manual labor 7. Visibility to the end-to end Sales Deals process should be made available to all parties	1. Reduce delays in communicating Sales Deal announcements 2. Develop business rules to ensure that customers detail discount codes on PO 3. Update distribution lists of Field Sales, Sales Communication, and Sales Administration to ensure that OM and CCO are given timely visibility to Sales Deals pipeline 4. Identify POS discrepancies with all accounts 5. Field Sales should ask each account to provide contact that Sales Finance can work with when calculating rebates	1. CRM should enable visibility, monitoring, and tracking of sales deals 2. Improve Business User friendliness of Interfaces between ERP and other systems 3. Bring customers up to speed on the sales deals process and educate them that last minute changes hurt both sides 4. Introduce business policy requesting accounts to reference Sales Deal Number on claim	1. Develop business rules to ensure effective "Exception Handling" (MIS solution) in the Sales Deals internal processing 2. Introduce "Finger printing: of customer orders to reduce the processing delays 3. Establish a business process to reconcile POS rebates with accounts before credit is processed

Table 9.6 Optimize and Rationalize SKU's

Team Members	Approach	Milestones		
		Short Term	**Medium Term**	**Long Term**
Marketing Sales Communication Operations Field Sales Demand Planning Creative Retail Marketing Accounts Payable Legal Business Decision Support (BDS)	**PRE-STREET to STREET DATE** 1. Proactively determine Optimal number of New Releases 2. Proactively manage the number of new SKU's created for a new release/new-to-format initiative 3. Ensure new releases meet minimum margin contribution 4. Develop consistent approach to evaluating account exclusives and line-look / o-sleeve requests (profitability and desired retail support); leverage pre- and post-learning 5. Initiate discussion with retailers about benefits of accepting non-expiring and non-competitive inserts	1. Work with BDS team to develop metrics appropriate for each BU to determine a "green-lighting threshold" for additional SKU's	1. BDS to develop guidelines on profitability of additional SKU's using metrics developed in short term milestone	1. Utilize business rules to drive down initial SKU count 2. BDS should generate quarterly report to summarize additional SKU profitability by each BU 3. Incorporate regular findings into S&OP meeting or other appropriate venue

Table 9.7 Commercial Benefits Realization

Team Members	Approach	Milestones		
		Short Term	**Medium Term**	**Long Term**
Marketing Sales Communication Operations Field Sales Demand Planning Creative Retail Marketing Accounts Payable Legal Business Decision Support (BDS)	**STREET DATE to 6 months POST STREET DATE** 1. Manage down initial SKU count and inventory to one generic SKU for catalog 2. Limit initial ship on account exclusives 3. Replenish exclusives only with what is available on hand/base SKU 4. Cut-out account exclusives after set period of time 5. Rework returned account exclusives by 2-packs to generic SKU 6. Eliminate dual format inventory where possible 7. Explore one-way policy on exclusives	1. Team to create detailed "SKU optimization" process map including business rules	1. Work with IT to understand system issues that will be impacted (cut-out process, returns handling of cut-out SKU's, reporting limitations), and groups that will be impacted (MIS, Sales Admin, Accounting, Ops) 2. Obtain Senior Management approval of process map/business rules	3. Implement SKU optimization process map across all BU's 4. Develop quarterly reports on SKU counts and "zero-net" inventory of non-generic SKU's

Marketing Sales Communication Operations Field Sales Demand Planning Creative Retail Marketing Accounts Payable Legal Business Decision Support (BDS)	**6 months POST-STREET DATE to END of LIFECYLCE** 1. Create a consistent approach to determine when an SKU becomes obsolete and integrate the decision-making into the S&OP process 2. Determine business rules about the level of contribution an SKU should generate to be considered "active" 3. Implement quarterly review during S&OP meeting	1. Work with BU to define when an SKU becomes "Obsolete" (delisted) 2. Establish metrics (time, velocity, store presence) and obtain BU approval	1. Ensure that external partners (Finance, Accounting, CCO) are aware of actions and future plans 2. Create report to show which SKUs in inventory/marketplace are considered "obsolete"	1. Integrate business rules into S&OP process 2. Establish standard quarterly review to determine which SKUs are deactivated and manage outstanding inventory

Table 9.8 Reduce Excess Inventory

Team Members	Approach	Milestones		
		Short Term	Medium Term	Long Term
Marketing	1. Upfront promotion planning using CRM tool		X	
Sales	2. Improved Demand Planning process			
Communication	3. Establish weekly meetings to review production builds for new release product	X		X
Operations	a. Builds approved by BU			
Field Sales	b. Sales Planning & Forecasting to produce sales estimates nationally and by retailer			
Demand Planning	c. Demand Planning to produce sales estimated by store	X		
Creative	4. Establish weekly meetings to review production builds for catalog			
Retail Marketing	a. Builds approved by BU			
Accounts Payable	b. Operations to produce sales estimates and current on-hand inventory	X	X	
Legal	5. Establish policies for exclusive cut-out dates, one-way exclusives, liquidation, and destruction			
Business Decision Support (BDS)	6. Develop comprehensive reports			

Through a series of companywide announcements and city hall meetings the teams were recognized, and subsequently reorganized around a new set of CBR initiatives. It was also felt that the teams were reaching a plateau of effectiveness in solving problems—they needed tools for continuous improvement and optimization. To empower the teams with new tools, the consultant (author) was engaged to deliver a series of workshops on Lean Management processes. Derived heavily from six sigma body of knowledge, these tools were categorized into five process elements: define, measure, analyze, improve, and control. This initiative was collaboratively tailored and redesigned to fit the specific business needs of the studio by the consultant and the organizational effectiveness team from the studio (see Figure 9.4). Each session came with a set of tools—most common tools are project prioritization through impact charts, brainstorming, 5 why's analysis to identify root causes, pareto charting, design of experiments (to test hypotheses on product sales and related areas), SIPOC charting (suppliers, input, process, output, customers, and requirements), value stream analysis to identify value added versus non-value added processes, business case development with benefits template, X-Y matrix for prioritization, and others. The attendees were introduced to these tools with examples, and then each CBR team was asked to try and develop a plan on how they would apply these tools in their respective problems and challenges. Finally, the attendees presented back to the general audience their ideas on the tools.

The outcome of this phase was a much more enabled group of managers who had elevated competence sets and new skills and tools for better business optimization, and a renewed sense of urgency and enthusiasm. Additionally, since a year after this phase, the studio has accrued more than $100 million+ of savings and an unquantifiable amount of additional revenue.

Lessons Learned

When one looks back at the wide horizon of seven years, it is mind-boggling to see the vast and effective improvement at the studio through top leadership business acumen, foresight, support, strategy, and execution. Before the ship even hit an iceberg the senior management team began proactively preparing for saving the organization through a planned sequence of initiatives. While it is true that not all the steps were known ahead of time, management was confident about the general course of events and what needed to happen with time, and designed strategies accordingly.

Second, no great improvement can come without the committed involvement of leaders, managers, and frontline employees. Alignment of employees to a general common vision with a greater common good in perspective is essential for success and the workshop-based socialization approach to get such alignment proved to be successful (see Figure 9.5).

Third, hard work from all parties, along with rigor and an attention to detail was as important as the philosophy of consensus generation through socializing ideas. Change management ideas of pushing information out, pulling feedback in, and pushing execution plans out, in that sequence, was very effective, since it made frontline employees feel they were part of the decision-making process as opposed to the receiving end of it.

Finally, if such great results were achievable in such a rocket-speed fast-moving consumer goods environment with key dependencies on partners, much more powerful customers, and fickle-minded consumers who could choose substitute product in a commoditized market, we believe that all industries could learn from this experience. The authors of this article humbly propose that these experiences could serve as a "guidebook for companies facing decline in market."

Figure 9.4 Exhibit 1 - The Business Workflow of Home Entertainment Industry

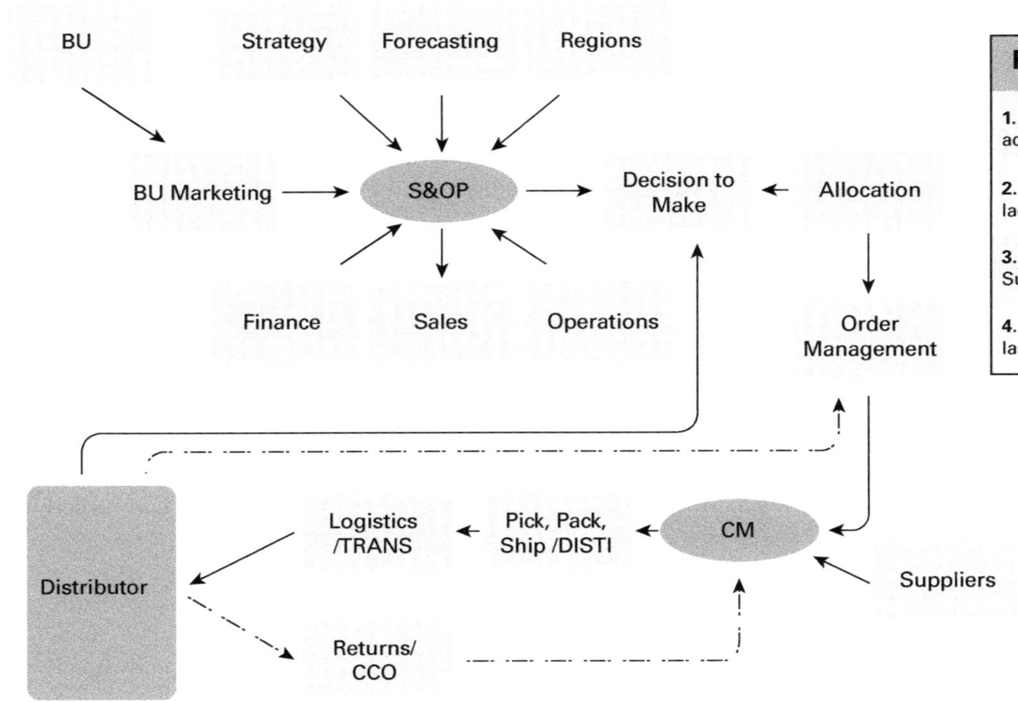

Root Causes	Metrics
1. Communications across functions	**1.** Perfect Order Fulfillment
2. Delay caused due to lack of documentation	**2.** Order Fulfillment Cycle Time
3. Long lead times at Suppliers	**3.** Upside Supply Chain Flexibility
4. Expedites due to last moment changes	**4.** Total Supply Chain Cost

Legend

Figure 9.5 Exhibit 2 - Organizational Layers and 360-degree coverage of ideas

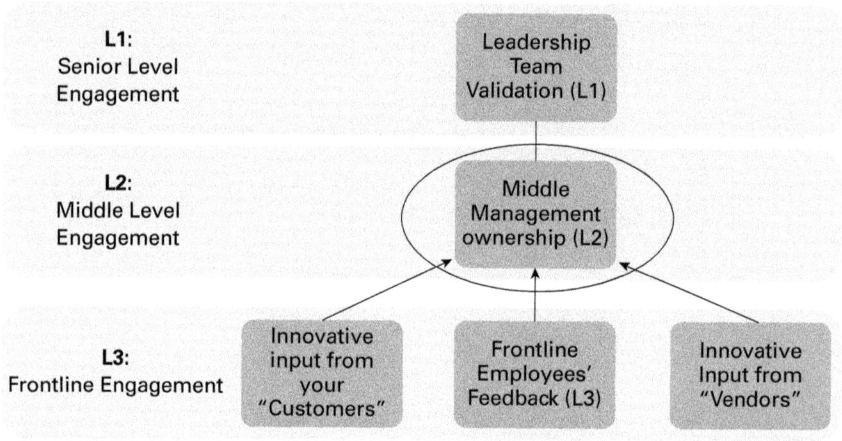

Figure 9.6 Exhibit 3 – Supply Chain Processes relevant to Home Entertainment

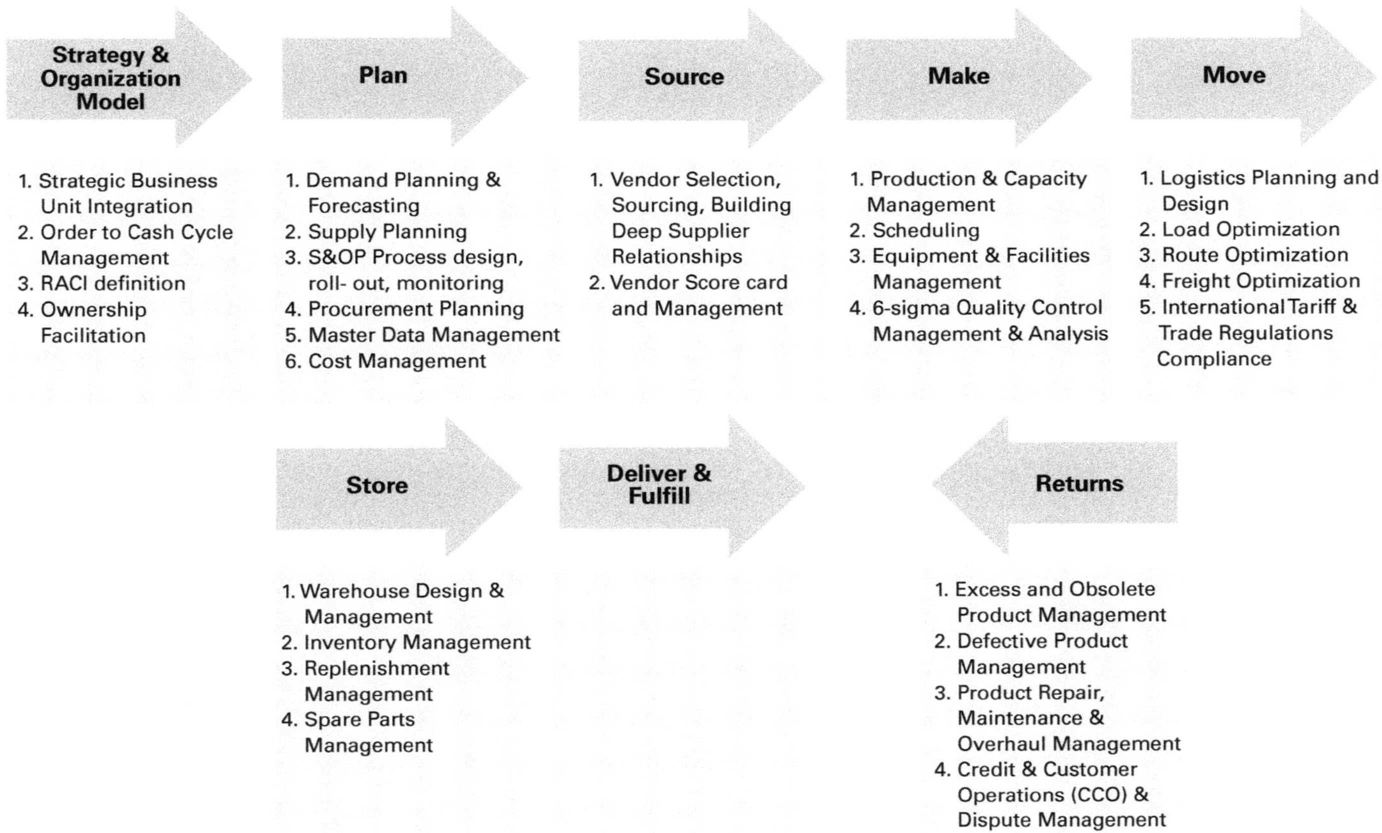

Lessons Learned from Three Supply Chain Network Design Case Studies 10

In the preceding chapters of this book, we've traced the contours of a supply chain landscape irrevocably altered by the global pandemic. This chapter pivots to a detailed exploration of transformation across different industry verticals, stitching together three distinct case studies that exemplify businesses' agility and innovative spirit in the face of adversity. Each case study serves as a narrative of the challenges and complications that companies encountered during and in the aftermath of the pandemic and the strategic pivots and tactical overhauls that have since defined their new normal.

We begin by setting the stage for each company—illuminating their pre-pandemic operations to appreciate the magnitude of the shift that was to come. As we delve into their stories, we trace the arc of disruption to recovery, examining how these organizations reimagined their supply chains through cultural realignment, mindset shifts, and sweeping organizational changes. The journey from grappling with unforeseen complications to implementing robust processes and cutting-edge technologies unfolds, providing a roadmap for transformation.

Concluding each narrative, we reflect on the tangible outcomes of these transformations. The results—from operational efficiencies to breakthroughs in service delivery—offer a testament to the resilience and ingenuity and distill valuable lessons for the future. These insights forge a blueprint for resilience, demonstrating how businesses can survive and thrive in a landscape forever changed by global events—"New Realties."

Case Study: COVID-19's Impact on the Global Protein Industry and the Role of Technology

Abstract

The Global Impact of COVID-19 on the protein food supply chain industry study aims to critically analyze the disruptions and adaptations within the protein supply chains, including meat and plant-based proteins, due to the COVID-19 pandemic. COVID-19 created a shockwave that affected everything: how we work, live, and source and consume goods and services. It also made us appreciate the role of global supply chains and its role in our lives. Although the impact was felt across many industries, an area with one of the most significant impacts was the food industry, especially meat. This case study will explore the impact of COVID-19 on meatpacking industries in regions around the world and the role of emerging technologies, such as traceability and regenerative meat, in helping mitigate future challenges within the food supply chain. Students will be asked to apply concepts used in the study to identify food supply chains critical to their region, list the main challenges that the regional and global meatpacking industries face today, and discuss how technology can help address them.

Learning Outcomes

- Describe the global impact of COVID-19 on the protein industry by region.
- Discuss the impact of technology on the meatpacking industry.
- Apply concepts used in the study to identify food supply chains that are critical to a specific region or country.

- The role of technologies to enhance agility and resiliency of the food supply chain. How can advanced network design concepts be integrated into the future of food supply chains?

Understanding the Protein Supply Chain (Meat and Alternative Protein Sources)

Understanding the protein supply chain involves a comprehensive look at the entire process, from production to consumption, for both traditional meat sources and alternative protein sources. Each has unique aspects, challenges, and considerations. The case study provides an in-depth analysis of both types of sources.

Background

The global protein market was valued at $23.24 billion in 2021 and is expected to grow at a compound annual growth rate (CAGR) of 3.59 percent to reach $27.73 billion by 2026. The demand for plant-based protein-rich alternatives is rapidly increasing, particularly in the food and beverage sector. Soy protein is still a popular option due to its cost-effectiveness and quality, but there is also a growing supply of plant proteins that mimic the texture of meat. Additionally, microbial proteins, especially algae protein, are experiencing fast growth due to innovation and new entrants.

In 2020, the meat- and dairy-alternatives industries accounted for a 31 percent share of the market by volume. This shows a significant shift in consumer preferences towards plant-based options. High protein content is a crucial factor for over 55 percent of households in North America when purchasing food, and 23 percent of Americans consume plant-based meat. Furthermore, 37 percent of Americans show interest in trying meat alternatives, indicating a substantial market opportunity.

The Middle East is expected to be the fastest-growing market, with a projected CAGR of 4.33 percent. This is due to the increasing demand for natural and sustainable ingredients, driven by rising health consciousness.

Lifecycle of Protein Supply Chain

- The protein supply chain has three main stages: production, processing, and distribution. Animal-based products go through breeding, feeding, and slaughtering, while plant-based products go through farming, harvesting, and processing. Both supply chains face unique challenges and opportunities. Due to environmental concerns, there is an increasing demand for plant-based protein. However, animal-based protein remains popular due to its nutritional value.

Alternative Protein Sources Supply Chain

- The supply chain of alternative protein sources comprises different stages such as source production, processing, product development, distribution and retail, and consumption.
- Plant-based proteins, including soy, peas, and other legumes, are grown using farming practices that are crucial and can vary widely. Processing these proteins requires significant effort to achieve the desired texture and flavor.
- Lab-grown meat is a form of cellular agriculture, where meat is grown from animal cells in a lab setting. This process is complex and expensive. Insect protein, such as that procured from crickets, is obtained through breeding, and harvesting insects rich in protein.
- Product development is a crucial stage that focuses on creating palatable products that appeal to consumers, often mimicking traditional meat textures and flavors. Distribution and retail of alternative proteins is like meat, but the marketing and placement can differ significantly, focusing on sustainability and health.
- Most importantly, consumer acceptance is vital for the success of alternative proteins. Education and awareness about the benefits of these proteins influence consumer choices.

Challenges on the Horizon

Meat production has a significant environmental footprint and requires a lot of resources. While alternative proteins are often promoted as more sustainable, their production, such as monoculture farming for plant-based proteins, also has environmental impacts.

Additionally, food safety and regulatory standards apply differently to these supply chains, particularly for lab-grown meats, as regulatory frameworks are still evolving. Costs are a significant factor, as alternative proteins often face higher production costs, impacting their market price and accessibility.

Cultural and dietary preferences also play a significant role in acceptance and adoption of alternative proteins, although growing awareness of health and environmental issues drive interest in these alternatives. Advancements in technology are vital in both sectors, with efficient and sustainable farming practices being important for meat and improving production processes and product quality being key for alternatives. Local and international trade policies, global demand, and geopolitical issues can also influence supply chains and global market dynamics.

The meat and alternative protein supply chains are complex and influenced by various factors, from production methods to consumer preferences. The future of protein supply will likely combine traditional and innovative sources, balancing nutritional needs with sustainability and ethical considerations.

The global protein market was valued at $23.24 billion in 2021 and is expected to grow at a compound annual growth rate (CAGR) of 3.59 percent to reach $27.73 billion by 2026.

Soy protein has been popular for its affordable cost and high quality. In recent years, there has been a surge in the availability of plant-based proteins that imitate the texture of meat, which has been particularly appealing to the food and beverage industry. There has also been significant growth in microbial proteins, such as algae protein, due to innovation and new players in the market.

As consumers increasingly sought protein-rich alternatives to meat and dairy, the industries for meat and dairy alternatives held a 31 percent share by volume in 2020. In North America, high protein content is a significant factor for over 55 percent of households when purchasing food. Additionally, about 23 percent of Americans consume plant-based meat, with 37 percent showing interest in trying them, indicating significant market potential for meat alternatives.

At the same time, the Middle East is expected to be the fastest-growing market for protein alternatives, with a projected CAGR of

4.33 percent. This growth is attributed to the rising demand for natural and sustainable ingredients driven by increasing health consciousness.

COVID-19 has impacted every part of our lives, from how we work to how we source and consume goods and services. This event has also made the world appreciate and evaluate regional and global supply-chain networks' role in our lives. The global meatpacking industry was one of the many industries impacted by disrupted supply chains. The overall impact was the same across countries in how it was disrupted in the initial days, but the deeper and the longer-term impact differed from region to region based on the response of the local Administration and the prevailing trade policies. The following is an analysis of the **region's impact of the pandemic**.

North America When the COVID-19 pandemic emerged, many businesses were forced to close. People needed to stay indoors for safety. Grocery stores were labeled critical businesses. Restaurants, classified as unessential and unsafe, were made to close, impacting the meatpacking industry from the demand side. In April 2020, President Trump signed an executive order allowing meatpacking plants to remain open as part of the Defense Production Act (DPA) (The Washington Post, 2020).

The meat supply in the United States relies primarily on four large conglomerate corporations: Cargill Meat Solutions, Sysco, JBS USA, and Tyson Foods. The industry's reliance on a few leading firms makes the food supply chain vulnerable to disruptions. These vulnerabilities were revealed during the pandemic when the government had to intervene to ensure that meat, a vital protein source, was available to the population.

Meat-processing plants were allowed to stay open, but without accompanying clear guidance on safety measures from the government, many plants were forced to close due to large COVID-19 outbreaks within the plants (NBC News). As illustrated in Figure 10.1, the concept of operation for the protein supply chain follows many labor-intensive steps performed in proximity.

Springdale, Arkansas–headquartered Tyson Foods, for example, which is responsible for 20 percent of the meat consumed by Americans, was forced to shut down one of its most giant pork plants in April 2020 (NBC News, 2020), causing a meat shortage due to slowed production. Additionally, all plants had to follow Center for Diseases Control guidelines for employees to stay six feet apart and wear personal protective equipment to keep them safe and keep the operations running. However, a meat-processing plant traditionally has employees working shoulder to shoulder, which ensures a quick and efficient assembly line for meat production. The lockdown restrictions, therefore, inevitably slowed meat production across the country. As a result, there was a meat shortage and increased meat prices in the United States.

As shown in Figure 10.2, between December 2020 and September 2021, beef prices rose by 14 percent, pork by 12.1 percent, and poultry by 6.6 percent. The shortage of products and increased demand due to panic buying for these three products caused a disruptive breakdown in the meat supply chain during the early months of the pandemic (Vox, 2020) and upward pressure on prices in the subsequent months.

Having learned from these price increases, the Biden Administration, and the United States Department of Agriculture (USDA) have since focused on addressing the reported anti-competitive practices (Farmers Weekly), enforcing antitrust laws, and bringing more transparency to the meat-processing industry. The administration is working on relieving small businesses impacted by the pandemic and creating a more competitive food supply chain. The government is also focused on assessing the effects of climate change on farmers and ranchers and the climate repercussions on how meat is processed from start to finish.

COVID-19 exposed the vulnerabilities of the meat and poultry supply chain. Direly, it revealed the consequences of a few companies dominating the meat industry. To address these vulnerabilities, as of January 3, 2022, the Biden Administration announced its commitment to creating a fairer and more competitive environment and a more resilient meat and poultry supply chain. Some of the measures taken by the Administration since then include the issuing of a proposed rule to stop prejudice, retaliation, and deception in the

Figure 10.1 US Beef, Pork, and Broiler Supply Chains

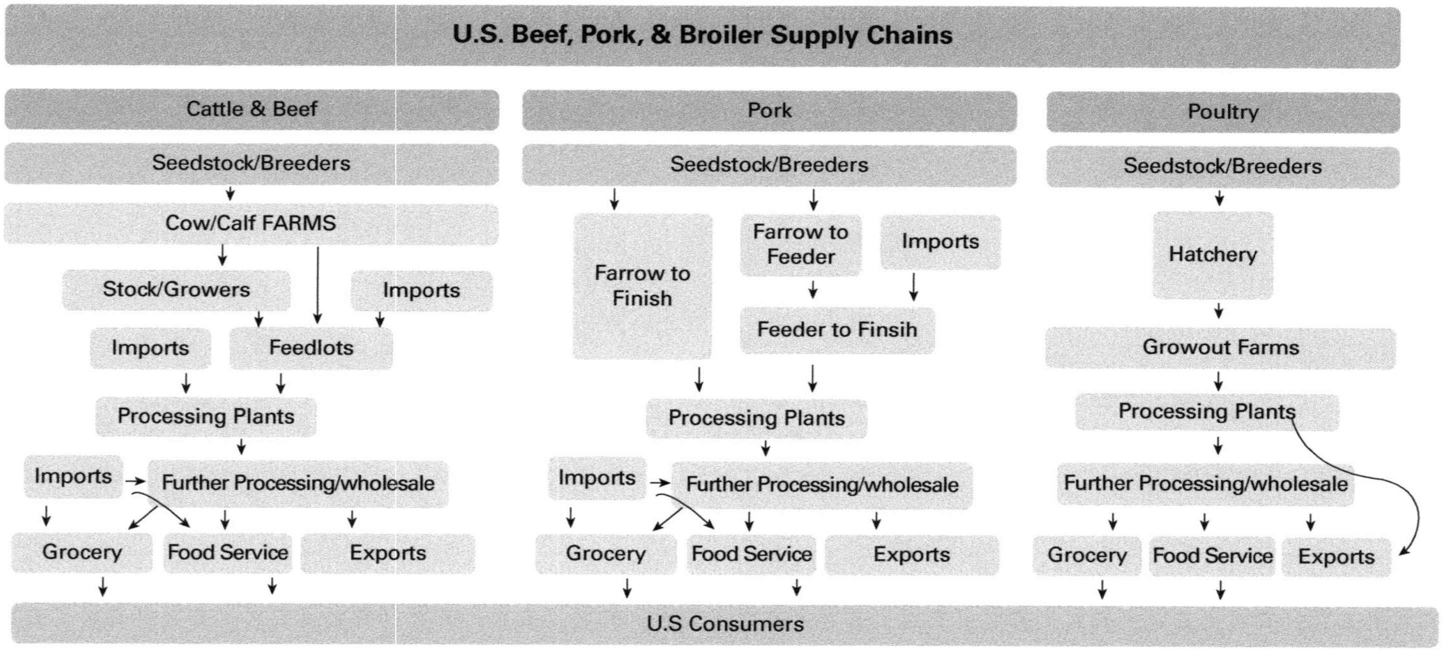

SOURCE Rural Migration News (Rural Migration News, 2022)

Figure 10.2 Prices of Major Food Items Spiked During the Pandemic

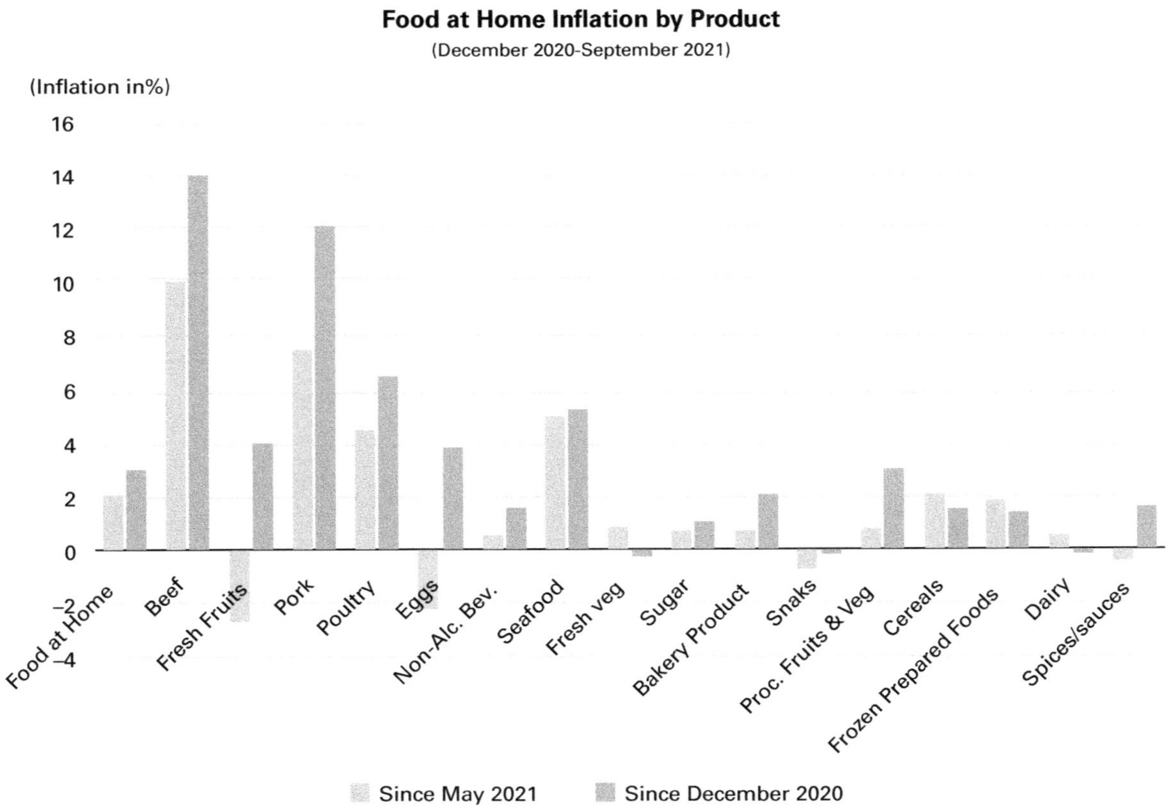

SOURCE The White House, 2021

meatpacking industry (USDA, 2022a), making available $215 million to the industry to strengthen the supply chain, and the launch of a complaint portal for reporting of anti-competitive practices (USDA, 2022b).

Africa A helpful observation can be drawn from how the pandemic affected the meat industry globally. South Africa, for example, has one of the biggest meat-producing industries in Africa and the world. COVID-19 caused several issues, ranging from hygiene to the non-availability of human resources. It also drew attention to the importance of food safety, which was intricately linked to the consumption of animal-resourced food.

On June 27, 2021, the South African government announced that the country would advance to a heightened level 4 lockdown in response to increased COVID-19 cases and hospital admissions. Although the agricultural sector is categorized as an essential service and, therefore, exempt from certain restrictions, segments of the agricultural industry were affected by the restrictions.

The lockdown restrictions affected the livestock industry directly, as people were prohibited from gathering for auctions. As a result, the in-person auctions were canceled or scheduled for online auctions. However, farmers were concerned that online auctions are not always practical or possible because of poor connectivity. Furthermore, restaurants and hotels were only allowed to sell takeaway food because dining at these establishments was restricted. This resulted in the closure of many restaurants and hotels, and a hit from tourism loss led to retrograde in poultry and beef.

The pandemic reduced US chicken imports into South Africa and other African countries and increased imports of certain beef products. In 2020, the United States exported 79,472 tons of poultry meat and products to South Africa, which represented a decrease of 11 percent from 2019. Furthermore, in 2020, the United States exported 20,235 tons of beef and beef products to South Africa at $12.6 million, which represented an increase of 9 percent from the prior year. The increase in beef imports results from the financial pressure that led consumers to switch from expensive beef cuts to beef livers as an alternative for protein. Edible beef livers contributed 89 percent of the US exports of beef and beef products to South Africa.

To stem this declining trend in the meat market, South Africa and other African countries created a forum to ensure a strong collaboration between governments, agribusinesses, and farmers. With this collaboration, Africa is building a post-pandemic food system architecture that is much more resilient.

Asia The complexity of supply chain network design for the meat industry in Asian countries like China, Japan, and South Korea, which are dominantly dependent on meat imports, has been affected by the COVID-19 pandemic in various ways. Asia had to face the pandemic-related disruptions in addition to the crisis of African swine fever. The combined effect of these two outbreaks caused a sharp drop in the meatpacking industry's capability and a steep increase in prices and dependency on pork imports, the most consumed animal protein in the region. However, unlike North America, Asia's meat industry did not face a protracted crisis due to early preventive measures.

As the largest importer of meat since 2019 and the first country to discover the COVID-19 outbreak, China has made a series of decisions in response to the outbreak. With the impact of factors such as COVID-19, African swine fever, and the decrease in the capacity of the meat industry in 2019, frozen and refrigerated food prices continued to run high in 2020.

According to the National Bureau of Statistics of China, food prices rose 10.6 percent over the same period in 2019, of which pork, beef, and lamb rose 49.7 percent, 14.4 percent, and 8.5 percent, respectively.

China's meat industry started relying more on imports to ensure an unhindered meat supply. According to data from the General Administration of Customs, in 2020, the country imported 9.911 million tons of meat, worth CNY 213.15 billion (CNY 1 is approximately USD 0.14). This quantity is an increase of 60.4 percent above the previous year, and the associated value is an increase of 60.2 percent. In terms of individual meat products, pork imports amounted to 5.73 million tons (an increase of 79.1 percent), worth CNY 103.10

billion (an increase of 120.9 percent), whereas beef imports amounted to 2.14 million tons (an increase of 27.0 percent), worth CNY 71.25 billion (a record increase of 23.7 percent).

With the continued spread of COVID-19, China's meat industry has been affected in the following three ways:

- **Imported food cold chain hit hard:** The Chinese government introduced a series of policies to strengthen food safety control during the pandemic. Many imported cold-chain food enterprises reported difficulties and crises such as container placement, batch inspection, repeated disinfection, inventory off the shelves, and market stagnation. Implementing these policies dramatically increased the operating costs of food enterprises, many of which have reported huge losses.
- **Decline in sales:** All businesses across the supply chain—restaurants, suppliers, distributors, wholesalers, and end consumer last-mile delivery operators—reported losses.
- **Human capital constraints:** The food industry is labor-intensive, and lockdown restrictions made it difficult for employees to return to work. The processing workstations are usually situated close to each other. Social distancing rules and other preventive measures are hard to implement in the industry. During the Spring Festival, frontline employees returned home early, and only about 50 percent of employees were reported to be working full-time. The shortage of staff led to severe capacity constraints. Overall, the pandemic created labor tensions in the industry.

Food Traceability and Transparency: The Role of Technology

COVID-19 has spotlighted how emerging technologies can provide solutions to traceability and transparency in the meat industry for improved response time, transportation, and facility and handling.

To understand how vital traceability is to businesses and consumers, McDonald's handling of the Avian Influenza outbreak is a crucial example. In the summer of 2015, Avian influenza killed almost 42 million hens across 15 states in the United States. This loss led McDonald's egg supply chain to lose about 46 percent of its suppliers' dedicated poultry stock. This impacted McDonald's supplies, causing a nationwide egg shortage for seven months with uncertainty about the future of the egg supply. However, McDonald's successfully navigated this outbreak, and in response to the egg shortage, it built its unique, more agile supply-chain system. As a result, all their suppliers are independently owned and operated today, for example. Because of their longstanding, strong relationship with McDonald's, all their suppliers prioritize egg supply to keep McDonald's egg supplies replenished.

To prevent the kind of disruptions in the supply chain that this pandemic has caused, food supply chains need to be more digitized, transparent, and easily accessible than they currently are. Since this pandemic caused a two-year-long consumer shift from eating out to cooking at home, consumers have become more concerned with what food they are buying, where it is sourced from, and how it is transported to their location.

The meat industry is an intricate ecosystem of various stakeholders still rooted in traditional ways of doing business globally. A typical meat-processing flow involves the supplier, the land manager, the ranching farmer, the processor, the warehouse where the meat is stored, and the logistics and retail players.

Companies that regard sustainability as a critical stakeholder deliverable have already toyed with using quick response (QR) codes on their products to trace them from farm to shelf.

Emerging technologies, such as blockchain, bring groundbreaking capabilities to food traceability. Examples of applications of blockchain to make food supply chains safer and more reliable include IBM's Food Trust (IBM), which has brought together food majors such as Nestle and Tyson Foods to develop a traceability system, and the use of a blockchain-based payment system by United Nations World Food Program (WFP) to help Syrian refugees pay for their food (WFP). In 2017, two pilot projects with IBM for addressing the risk in Walmart's supply chain for the Chinese pork industry to ensure speed, trust, reputation, and food safety.

Integrating decoupling points in the supply chain process makes the supply chain more resilient. Used widely for inventory management, decoupling points act as inventory-holding points and safety buffers in a distribution network. However, the concept can be applied at the level of global supply-chain management, where decoupling points can be used to connect different regionalized, customer-centric supply-chain networks. In a crisis, a decoupling can quickly redirect production and sourcing to other hubs, ensuring that operations in other parts of the supply chain continue undisrupted. This brings to light the role technology will play in our meat supply chain and the innovative ways businesses will use technology as it becomes more advanced.

Another instance that highlighted the importance of traceability and innovative technology was Chipotle's *E. coli* outbreaks between 2015 and 2018. These outbreaks caused more than 1,000 people to become ill and resulted in the hospitalization of a small percentage of them. The root cause of all these outbreaks was human error, wherein proper food safety procedures were not followed. Chipotle paid the Justice Department a $25 million fine for food adulteration. This example shows that strict adherence to safety guidelines to prevent human errors is an area that needs to be aided by technology for greater compliance.

This concept of bringing locally grown foods to restaurants has also gained popularity recently because locally sourced food is fresh for consumers and supports local farmers. Also, this trend toward local food provides a sustainable ecosystem for the farm-to-table concept, which can be traced end to end and supports a sustainable food supply chain. Additionally, it helps the environment since locally sourced food will leave a smaller carbon footprint.

Conclusion

The COVID-19 pandemic has changed people's lives and businesses functioning. The food sector, along with other critical industries, is vital to the well-being of people of any country. In the United States, the share of animal-based foods in per capita calorie consumption is over 30 percent, as per USDA estimates, among the highest in the world (USDA, 2016; World Economic Forum, 2018). In South Africa, where meat selling is auction-based, the government's rules of no in-person gatherings, combined with a sharp fall in imports, made purchasing meat difficult across the country (Food For Mzansi). As for

Asia, China was discussed because it is the most significant source and consumer of meat products. During the COVID-19 pandemic in China, prices skyrocketed, and imports plummeted. COVID-19 has illustrated how crucial efficient supply-chain processes are, and the examples of McDonald's and Chipotle have highlighted the importance of traceability in food supply chains. A deeper understanding of the supply chain and its various stakeholders is crucial not only for students of supply chain management but also for those involved in any aspect of decision-making in corporations and government institutions; the safety and reliability of food are matters of primary importance, both for us and the environment.

Case Study: Can the US Re-shore Its Lithium-ion Battery Supply Networks?

Abstract

More governments are taking actions to mitigate climate change. Replacing fossil fuels with alternative energy sources is increasingly important, as the transportation sector accounts for about 27 percent of total U.S. greenhouse gas (GHG) emissions, making it the largest contributor of US GHG emissions.[1] The market for electric vehicles (EVs) is growing fast, and among different battery types (lead acid, lithium-ion, nickel-metal hydride, nickel-cadmium), lithium-ion batteries (LIBs) seem to be most suitable for use in EVs due to their smaller size and lighter weight. This case study will focus on understanding whether re-shoring lithium-ion batteries domestically will improve its supply networks and sustainability.

Background

While EVs represented less than 0.5 percent of the world passenger vehicle fleet in 2019 and had sales of about 2 million units in 2018 (Scott and Ireland, 2020), the number of sold vehicles increased to about 7 million units in 2021 (Azevedo et al., 2022).

Haji and Slocum (2019) estimated that EV sales will account for 55 percent of all new car sales by 2040. They cited data estimating that if EVs accounted for all passenger vehicles, the demand for lithium, a main component in LIBs, would increase by 2900 percent. Kaunda (2020) stated that demand for LIBs more than tripled between 2015 and 2020 and is expected to grow by more than 500 percent by 2030.

Kaunda further estimated the projected annual sales of EVs to exceed 40 million vehicles by 2028, and the global demand for lithium to reach 1.3 million metric tons of lithium carbonate equivalent (LCE) by 2025.[2] Lithium carbonate is a lithium compound, used in the production of LIB. This increase in demand is also reflected in a recent price surge. According to the United States Geological Survey (USGS, 2020), the average price per metric ton of lithium carbonate from 2015 to 2019 was $12,000. While Azevedo et al. (2022) referenced prices in 2020 of lithium carbonate exceeding $75,000, and of lithium hydroxide exceeding $65,000.

Global lithium availability

According to the United Nations Conference on Trade and Development (UNCTAD, 2020), total world lithium resources[3] were estimated to be about 62 million tons in 2019, with about 50 percent of them located in the "lithium triangle" (Chile, Bolivia, and Argentina), while the world reserves[4] are estimated at 14 million tons. The major sources of lithium production are six mineral operations in Australia, two brine operations each in Argentina and Chile, and one brine and one mineral operation in China. In 2019, world production of lithium was 77,000 tons. Azevedo et al. (2022) estimated that in 2015, lithium demand was split as follows: 35 percent for ceramics and glasses, another over 35+ percent for greases, polymers, and other industrial uses, while less than 30 percent was for batteries. However, the authors projected that by 2030, batteries are expected to account for 95 percent of the demand for lithium, and that the demand for LCE will grow at an annual rate of 25-26 percent. Ongoing global initiatives are projected to supply annual growth of 20 percent, reaching about 2.7 million metric tons of LCE by 2030 (Azevedo et al., 2022). However, this leaves a gap of about 0.6–1.1 million metric tons that must be supplied from alternative sources, such as geothermal brines or recycling, as well as new technologies for direct lithium extraction (DLE) and direct lithium to product (DLP).

Lithium availability in the US

According to the USGS, total US lithium resources are estimated to be about 6.8 million tons[5], while the US reserves are estimated at 630,000 tons. Blair and Dunford Jr. (2022) discussed China's investments in the manufacturing of batteries and the assembly of EVs, as well as in the mining and processing of minerals needed for EVs. According to their article, as of 2020, Chinese firms controlled over 60 percent of the world's lithium and nickel refining and 70 percent of cobalt refining, the minerals necessary for EV battery production. At the same time, US companies accounted for only 4 percent of lithium, 1 percent of nickel, and 0 percent of cobalt refining. Establishing a domestic source of raw materials for LIBs is viewed by the US government as a critical step in moving to clean energy and mitigating climate change impacts.[6] To enable sustainable future production from local resources, the US needs to reduce the amount of lithium used in batteries and seek alternative local sources of lithium. While recycling is widely considered a potential alternative source of lithium, it would not be enough to fulfill such steep increases in demand.

U.S. lithium-ion battery (LIB) supply networks

FCAB, that brings together US Federal agencies interested in ensuring a domestic supply of lithium batteries, estimated in 2021 that worldwide sales of passenger EVs in 2040 will be around 56 million, of which about 9.6 million will be in the US market.[7] As the US auto industry historically contributed 5.5 percent of the total US gross domestic product[8], the country requires a robust supply network to produce EVs and batteries in quantities that can meet customer demand. After considering several EV demand-growth analyses by Avicenne, the Bank of Montreal, the Bloomberg New Energy Finance, Circular Energy Storage Research, Leiden University and the Argonne National Laboratory, Zhou et al. (2021) found continued growth of the global LIB market through 2030, although predictions vary: forecasts of annual LIB production for on-road vehicles ranged between

190 GWh and 1050 GWh by 2025, and between 700 GWh and 2500 GWh by 2030. When considering annual global LIB production capacity, the reports ranged from 500 GWh in 2020 to 1500 GWh in 2025 and 2500 GWh by 2030.

Sustainability Issues

There is a large use of toxic chemicals during lithium processing and large amounts of water per ton of lithium extracted. Berg and Sady-Kennedy (2021) estimated water consumption at 500,000 gallons per ton extracted in South America. Early (2020) estimated that hard rock lithium mining releases 15,000 kg of CO2 and requires 45,000 gallons of water per ton of lithium hydroxide monohydrate (LiOH·H2O), while obtaining lithium from brine releases 5,000 kg of CO2 and requires 125,000 gallons of water per ton of LiOH·H2O (Lithium hydroxide monohydrate, used to produce the cathode material of lithium-ion batteries).Under the assumption of 0.165 kg lithium obtained per one kilogram of LiOH·H2O, this implies emissions of about 91 (resp., 30.3) tons of CO2 and consumption of 273,000 (resp., 758,000) gallons of water per ton of lithium generated from rock mining (resp., from brine). This high-water consumption is even more significant when considering that some of these activities occur in areas with significant levels of water stress.[9]

Current US Supply Networks for Lithium Imports

The USGS (2020) listed US 2018 lithium imports at 3,420 tons, and estimated US 2019 lithium exports at 2,500 tons. Most of the imported lithium came from South America—53 percent from Argentina and 40 percent from Chile—and both locations rely on mining lithium from brine. The biggest source of lithium in South America is the so-called "lithium triangle," with main locations being La Negra and Solar de Atacama in Chile, and Solar del Hombre Muerto and Solar de Rincon in Argentina.

Lithium is traded most in the form of raw materials such as lithium carbonate (18.8 percent lithium content) and lithium hydroxide (29 percent lithium content).[10] In Table 10.1 we list the U.S. states that were biggest importers of lithium carbonate and lithium oxide and hydroxide in 2020. In each state we identify the origin country of imports, quantities[11], corresponding distances[12], and carbon

Table 10.1 The Biggest Importers of South American Lithium Carbonate and Lithium Oxide and Hydroxide by State and Corresponding Transportation Distances and Emissions

State	Country	SWT (tons)	Destination	Distance (n. miles)	Ocean CO_2 (kg/ton)	Rail Distance (miles)	Rail CO_2 (kg/ton)	Total CO_2 (kg)
Lithium Carbonates								
Delaware	Chile	1,350	Wilmington DE	4,092	63.66			85,939
Kentucky	Argentina	185	New York	4,136	64.34	1,062	15.75	14,817
Kentucky	Chile	646	New York	4,136	64.34	1,062	15.75	51,740
North Carolina	Argentina	109	Wilmington SC	3,773	58.70			6,398
North Carolina	Chile	1,807	Wilmington SC	3,773	58.70			106,063
South Carolina	Argentina	7,081	Charleston	3,724	57.93			410,227
South Carolina	Chile	78	Charleston	3,724	57.93			4,519
Lithium Oxide and Hydroxides								
Georgia	Chile	633	New Orleans	3,727	57.98			36,701
Total		11,889						716,405

emissions from the ocean freight[13]. In the case of Kentucky, which does not have ocean access, we assume that the cargo is shipped to New York by sea and then by rail to its final destination.[14]

Based on the abovementioned lithium content in the raw materials from Table 1, the total imported amount of lithium accounted for in this table was about 2,300 tons, implying manufacturing emissions of about 69,700 tons of CO_2, for a total (including transportation emissions) of 70,400 tons, or 30.61 tons of CO_2 per ton of lithium.

LIB Manufacturing in the US

The introduction of Chevrolet Volt, the first commercially available plug-in hybrid and Nissan Leaf, the first all-electric car to the US market in December of 2010 was a significant milestone in the evolution of the EVs. According to Zhou et al. (2021), annual plug-in electric vehicle (PEV) sales went from 18,000 in 2011 to over 330,000 in 2018 (with a 7 percent drop to 307,000 in 2020, as total sales of light-duty vehicles declined). Consequently, the battery capacity sold to the US market has grown over time. Panasonic and LG Chem are the largest battery cell suppliers for the US market supplying battery cells to 70.9 percent and 19 percent of vehicles sold in 2020 in the U.S., respectively. Tables 2 and 3 present battery cell and battery pack manufacturers' locations in the U.S. by make and model for battery electric vehicles (BEV) and plug-in hybrid electric vehicles (PHEV).

It is interesting to note that, primarily due to high sales of Tesla models, domestic production provides most of the battery packs for the US PEV market. Tesla's Gigafactory now accounts for 62 percent of total capacity for battery cells manufactured in the US between 2010 and 2020 (see Table 10.2). In terms of battery capacity, the share of U.S. battery cell production increased from 16 percent in 2017 to 60 percent in 2018, mainly due to sales of Tesla's Model 3. The total annual PEV battery cell capacity in 2020 was just above 18 GWh.

Many current US LIB producers are expected to increase their capacity soon. There are different estimates on how much lithium content a LIB uses per kWh—Greim et al. (2020) cite estimations between 111 g and 380 g per kWh, and use 130 g/kWh in their analysis; adopting

Table 10.2 BEV Battery Cell and Battery Pack Manufacturers Locations in the US by Make and Model (Zhou et al., 2021)

Vehicle Make	Vehicle Model	Calendar year	Cell and Pack OEM	Cell and Pack Production Location	Battery Size (kWh)	Cumulative sales (2010-2020)	Total MWh capacity
Chevrolet	Spark	2013-2014	A123	MI	19	1,700	32.30
Nissan	Leaf	2013-2020	AESC	TN	24-62	132,000	2,508.00
Chevrolet	Bolt	2019-2020	LG Chem	MI	60-66	28,900	1,820.70
Chevrolet	Spark	2015-2016	LG Chem	MI	19	5,700	108.30
Ford	Focus EV	2013-2018	LG Chem	MI	23-24	7,200	169.20
			Subtotal LG Chem				2,098.20
Tesla	Model 3	2017-2020	Panasonic	NV	54-75	355,700	3,734.85
Tesla	Model Y	2020	Panasonic	NV	75	58,200	4,365.00
			Subtotal Panasonic				8,099.85
Fiat	500e	2013-2020	Samsung	MI	24	14,000	336.00
			Total				13,074.35

Table 10.3 PHEV Battery Cell and Battery Pack Manufacturers Locations in the US by Make and Model (Zhou et al., 2021)

Vehicle Make	Vehicle Model	Calendar year	Cell and Pack OEM	Cell and Pack Production Location	Battery Size (kWh)	Cumulative sales (2010-2020)	Total MWh capacity
Cadillac	CT6	2017-2018	LG Chem	MI	18	500	9.0
Cadillac	ELR	2013-2016	LG Chem	MI	17	2,900	49.3
Chevrolet	Volt	2013-2019	LG Chem	MI	17-18	108,800	1,904.0
Chrysler	Pacifica Plug-in	2017-2020	LG Chem	MI	16	22,700	363.2
Jeep	Wrangler PHEV	2020	LG Chem	MI	17	100	1.7
Lincoln	Aviator Plug-in	2019-2020	LG Chem	MI	14	1,900	26.6
			Subtotal LG Chem				2,353.8
Ford	C-Max Energi	2012-2018	Panasonic	MI	8	42,200	337.6
Ford	Fusion Energi	2013-2020	Panasonic	MI	8	72,800	582.4
			Subtotal Panasonic				920.0
			Total				3,273.8

the same estimate, the U.S. LIB manufacturing will need an additional 44,590 tons of lithium at the current annually to ensure supply for these proposed facilities.

Geothermal Brine Lithium Recovery (GBLR)

GBLR provides a domestic source of lithium to the US Southern California's Imperial Valley is becoming known as Lithium Valley, thanks to numerous geothermal energy projects at the Salton Sea Geothermal Resource Area and the fact that the geothermal brine generated by the process is rich in lithium. Ventura et al. (2020) estimated typical lithium concentration in such brines at 211 parts per million (ppm), going up to 400 ppm in some cases.

It is estimated that Lithium Valley could produce more than 600,000 tons per year of LCE. Stringfellow and Dobson (2021) estimated the lithium reserves from the Salton Sea Geothermal field at about 2 million tons of lithium, corresponding to over 10 million tons of LCE. Thus, if the GBLR operates at full capacity, the supply would last for about 16 years. Stringfellow and Dobson (2021) referred to a dynamic model developed by Toba et al. (2021), which estimated that GBLR could reach approximately 70,000 tons LCE annually by 2030, corresponding to 13,160 tons of lithium. We will use this estimate in our model as an upper bound on GBLR capacity.

Cost and revenue estimates

Ventura et al. (2020) described a project focusing on coproduction of geothermal power and lithium carbonate in the Salton Sea area. The project's objective was to demonstrate a cost-effective extraction process for the GBLR. Based on the process design, a commercial-scale plant with 20,000 ton/year production of LCE (which would correspond to 3,760 tons of lithium) was designed to demonstrate process economics. The estimated production cost was less than $4,000 per ton of lithium carbonate[15], with a projected CAPEX of $52.3 million, OPEX of $76.9 M and revenue of $240 million for a price of $12,000 per ton of lithium carbonate.

Environmental impact

Co-producing lithium carbonate from geothermal fluids can also lead to a significant GHG emission reduction. According to Ventura et al. (2020), the 2010 CO_2 emissions of California geothermal power plants are estimated at 82 kg per MWh, while EPA estimated the average rate of CO_2 emissions for natural gas power plants at 515 kg/MWh. Thus, construction of lithium-recovery- enabled geothermal plants and displacement of natural-gas-powered power plants could lead to avoidance of about 433 kg of CO_2 emissions per MWh.

EV's LIB Recycling: Crucial for Sustainability

With the projected steep increase in EV manufacturing and limited global resources, recycling becomes a critical activity for ensuring lithium supply over the mid- to long-term horizon. Greim et al. (2020) considered 18 scenarios created by combining 8 demand-related variations with 4 supply conditions and found that supply and demand are well balanced in the short term (i.e., the first half of the century), but at the same time there is a strong need to establish efficient recycling systems for LIBs as lithium deposits could be depleted early in the second half of the century. They set lithium recycling efficiency to 95 percent based on recent technological development, and they set the collection rate to grow from 45 percent at present (based on global data) to 99 percent by 2050, implying that 94 percent of lithium could eventually be recovered.

Steward et al. (2019) discussed four main recycling methods to recover battery materials from LIBs—mechanical processes, hydrometallurgy, pyrometallurgy, and direct recycling. Lithium can be recovered by all methods except pyrometallurgy, with direct recycling being the most environmentally friendly. The current known U.S. LIB recycling capacity is 23,000 tons LIB/year, with planned additional capacity of 125,000 tons/year (Kendall et al., 2022). LIBs can have a very different ratio of total weight to lithium content. Tesla S battery has capacity of 85 kWh and weighs 540 kg[16], with about 157 Wh/kg, while vW e-Golf has capacity of 32 kWh and weighs 349 kg[17], with about 92 Wh/kg. If we assume lithium content of 130 g/kWh, Tesla S battery would contain 20.5 g of lithium per kg, and e-Golf would have 12 g per. Dai et al. (2019) developed a model for battery recycling cost and environmental impact, EverBatt. The EverBatt model assumes that recycling 1 ton of battery at an efficiency of 90 percent would generate 23.4 kg of lithium, and we will use this estimate in our analysis. This would imply that current U.S. recycling capacity can generate 538 tons of lithium annually, with projected additional capacity of 2,925 tons.

Cost and revenue estimates

Lander et al. (2021) presented an analysis of the recycling process for EV LIBs, which considers product design, transportation cost, volume, etc. They concluded, among other things, that in-country recycling can reduce the cost by up to 70 percent (as transportation cost can contribute more than 60 percent to the recycling cost), and that direct recycling achieves the highest profits, while pyrometallurgical generates the lowest. Direct recycling leads to higher profits compared to pyro- and hydrometallurgical (which is most commonly used in the U.S. recycling facilities as of 2020) processes, as more material can be recovered (revenues are generated from all materials, including cobalt, nickel, copper, etc.), and is estimated to be able to go up to \$21.91/kWh (in countries with low labor costs such as China), with values between \$5 and \$12 for recycling in the US.

Environmental impact

Steward et al. (2019) estimated that recycling can reduce the cost of raw materials by 38–43 percent, and that CO_2 emissions can be reduced by 5–11 kg per kg of material compared to the use of virgin raw materials. Gaines et al. (2021) estimated that direct recycling reduces GHG emissions by 68 percent and water consumption by 69 percent compared to the use of virgin materials in production of NMC111 (lithium oxide) batteries.

EverBatt[18] estimated that 3 gallons of water are used per 1 kg of battery recycled and that 23.4 kg of lithium are generated per ton of battery recycled. This corresponds to consumption of 128,000 gallons of water per ton of lithium, compared with 758,000 gallons used to obtain lithium from Chilean brine.[19]

Local Supply Network Models for Proposed US LIB Plants

As mentioned above, the main LIB plant locations in the US are currently in Michigan, Nevada, and Tennessee, with additional LIB plants planned for building or expansion in California, Georgia, Kentucky, and Ohio. California and Nevada are the only two locations in the Western US, and they are also the locations closest to the Salton Sea. Therefore, using lithium obtained through GBLR would be cheaper for them compared with locations in Central and Eastern US In the rest of the paper, we omit California and Nevada locations and focus on the remaining proposed new LIB plants and their capacities, as summarized in Table 10.4. Table 10.4 also provides electricity related GHG emissions and electricity cost for each location.

Table 10.5 provides data for each pair of GBLR plant and LIB plant—transportation emissions (in kg CO_2 per 20 ft container) and shipping costs, along with the lead time (in days) for road transportation (we conducted a limited analysis for rail transportation and obtained similar results, so we omit that analysis). Notice that the lead times across locations range between 4–5 days and recall that in Section 2, we indicated the shipping time from Antofagasta to the U.S. East coast ranged between 16–18 days. Thus, GBLR can reduce the lead time for lithium received by U.S. LIB plants by more than two weeks, leading to higher responsiveness and lower inventory cost.

We will consider three scenarios—low (10 percent), medium (50 percent), and high (94 percent) level of recycling, which will be denoted by $\alpha_l = 0.10$, $\alpha_m = 0.50$, and $\alpha_h = 0.94$. We will also consider three

Table 10.4 Proposed LIB plants and their capacity

Proposed plant	Capacity (GWh)	kg CO_2MWh	c/kWh
Holland (MI)	23	523	12.63
Lordstown (OH)	30	447	10.54
Spring Hill (TN1)	40	246	11.41
Stanton (TN2)	43	246	11.41
Commerce (GA)	21	254	12.72
Glendale (KY)	86	291	11.88
Total	243		

Table 10.5 Transportation Emission Rates, Costs, and the Number of Days for Full Truckload Shipping of a 20 ft Container

Holland (MI)	508	7,034	5
Lordstown (OH)	581	8,049	5
Spring Hill (TN1)	481	6,661	4
Stanton (TN2)	440	6,098	4
Commerce (GA)	541	7,494	5
Glendale (KY)	498	6,892	4

SOURCE http://railrates.com

possible values of the recycling profit per ton—the lower bound of the recycling profit per ton (excluding electricity cost), r_l = 63, 712, the higher bound of the of the recycling profit per ton (excluding electricity cost), r_h = 117, 562, and its mid-range value, r_m = 90, 637. Finally, in our analysis we consider three possible carbon costs—E_c = 0, E_c = 20, and E_c = 100—giving us a total of 27 scenarios. While the model details are given in the Appendix, our results are given in Table 6.

First, we note that the only cases in which we can meet all the demand (and thus maximize profit) are the ones with high recycling capacity. In addition, if the recycling profit per ton is high and medium, we always utilize all recycling capacity. Thus, increasing recycling capacity in the US is a necessary first step in redesigning the US lithium supply networks. Although the cases with medium and low recycling capacity exhibit full utilization of all lithium sources (as we cannot supply all the demand), we observe a difference in GHG emissions, which comes from different allocation of lithium sources among plants. For instance, when recycling profit is high and there is no emission penalty, GBLR is used for GA plant, otherwise it is used for MI. Plants most likely to receive reduced or zero supply are Holland (MI), Commerce (GA), and Lordstown (OH), followed by Glendale (KY).

With limited recycling capacity, sourcing allocation depends only on the emission cost. However, we can observe that in almost all cases (exceptions are the cases with high recycling capacity and high or medium recycling profit per ton) there is no difference between low emission penalty (E_c = 20) and no emission penalty (E_c = 0) results. Thus, to see a meaningful impact on carbon emissions, legislation should impose higher carbon penalties. A comparison of European

Table 10.6 Optimal solutions under different scenarios

	Ec = 0					Ec = 20					Ec = 100				
	Profit(in '000 USD)	GHGemis sions (tons CO2)	Li from GBLR (tons)	Li from recycling tons)	Total Li (tons)	Profit(in '000 USD)	GH Gemissions (tons CO2)	Li from GBLR (tons)	Li from recycling (tons)	Total Li (tons)	Profit (in '000 USD)	GH Gemissions (tons CO2)	Li from GBLR (tons)	Li from recycling (tons)	Total Li (tons)
m_h; α_η	2,866,655	2,047,221	1,895	29,695	31,590	2,827,565	1,937,736	1,895	29,695	31,590	2,672,546	1,937,736	1,895	29,695	31,590
m_h; α_m	2,291,581	1,173,087	13,160	15,795	28,955	2,268,119	1,173,087	13,160	15,795	28,955	2,175,999	1,042,453	13,160	15,795	28,955
m_h; α_l	1,115,613	462,933	13,160	3,159	16,319	1,106,354	462,933	13,160	3,159	16,319	1,077,026	326,590	13,160	3,159	16,319
m_m; α_h	2,067,128	2,047,221	1,895	29,695	31,590	2,028,531	1,828,095	2,990	28,600	31,590	1,905,749	1,207,113	13,160	18,430	31,590
m_m; α_m	1,866,301	1,173,087	13,160	15,795	28,955	1,842,839	1,173,087	13,160	15,795	28,955	1,750,718	1,042,453	13,160	15,795	28,955
m_m; α_l	1,030,557	462,933	13,160	3,159	16,319	1,021,298	462,933	13,160	3,159	16,319	991,970	326,590	13,160	3,159	16,319
m_l; α_h	1,541,622	1,337,743	13,160	18,430	31,590	1,514,867	1,337,743	13,160	18,430	31,590	1,409,521	1,207,113	13,160	18,430	31,590
m_l; α_m	1,441,020	1,173,087	13,160	15,795	28,955	1,417,559	1,173,087	13,160	15,795	28,955	1,325,438	1,042,453	13,160	15,795	28,955
m_l; α_l	945,501	462,933	13,160	3,159	16,319	936,242	462,933	13,160	3,159	16,319	906,914	326,590	13,160	3,159	16,319

and California Carbon Credit Markets[20] reveals that on April 19, 2023, carbon price in the EU was €94.39 per ton of CO_2, while in California the price was $28.99. If California wants to achieve a higher impact through its carbon policies, it should lower the caps in its cap-and-trade market to increase the carbon price, while the EU should already be able to see some impact of its cap-and-trade policy.

In Section 2, we estimated emissions from imported lithium at 30.61 kg of CO_2 per ton of lithium. Table 7 reveals that local lithium sourcing achieves lower emissions only in the case of low recycling capacity, as recycling generates highest emissions among all processes. However, in our analysis we allocated all emissions from both methods (GBLR and recycling) entirely to lithium generation; in reality, only a portion of the emissions should be allocated to lithium for recycling, as we can retrieve other elements during the process. Consequently, carbon emissions attributed to locally sourced lithium could be significantly lower. For instance, EverBatt[21] analyzed lithium cobalt oxide (LCO) batteries under direct recycling model and they used mass allocation of 28.5 percent and economic value allocation of 48.4 percent for lithium, while the rest was shared across other materials. Table 8 shows the results if we attribute to lithium only 48.4 percent of emissions from recycling and reveals that the average emissions across all categories fall below the emissions for imported lithium.

If we look at the detailed results, we can observe that there are only two scenarios in which emissions per ton exceed the emissions from imported lithium, and they both occur when there is no emission penalty: when we have high recycling capacity and high or medium recycling profit per ton, emissions are 31.87 kg of CO_2 per ton

Table 10.7 Average carbon emissions per ton under different scenarios (in tons CO2)

Recycling capacity	Ec = 0	Ec = 20	Ec = 100
High	57.32	53.85	45.92
Medium	40.51	40.51	36.00
Low	28.37	28.37	20.01

Table 10.8 Average carbon emissions per ton under different scenarios assigning 48.4 percent of recycling emissions to lithium

Recycling capacity	Ec = 0	Ec = 20	Ec = 100
High	29.00	27.36	24.21
Medium	22.64	22.46	20.38
Low	18.78	18.78	14.74

of lithium. Thus, imposing even a low emission penalty would reduce emissions from local lithium sourcing compared to imported lithium.

If we consider high recycling capacity and medium recycling profit per ton, higher emission penalty shifts sourcing from recycled lithium to GBLR lithium, as recycling generates more GHG emissions. More precisely, when $E_c = 0$, we use all of the recycled lithium capacity and only 14 percent of potential lithium obtained from GBLR; when $E_c = 20$, we use 96 percent of recycled lithium capacity and 23 percent of potential lithium obtained from GBLR. Finally, when $E_c = 100$, we use only 62 percent of potential recycled lithium capacity and all of the potential lithium obtained from GBLR. This has a significant impact on emission reduction, as it changes from 64.81 (resp., 31.87 with lower allocation of emissions to lithium) to 38.21 (resp., 21.25) tons of CO_2 per ton of lithium, a reduction of over 40 percent (resp., 33 percent) in average emissions per ton.

As we discussed earlier, each ton of lithium imported into US from South America implies consumption of about 2,900 m^3 of water during its production, often in areas already experiencing high water-stress level. EnergySource estimates[22] water depletion from geothermal brine lithium mining at 50 m^3 per ton of $LiOH{\cdot}H_20$, corresponding to about 300 m^3 per ton of lithium, a reduction of 90 percent compared to imports from South America, while EverBatt estimates LIB recycling water usage at 128,000 gallons (or 485 m^3) per ton of lithium, a reduction of about 83 percent.

Conclusion

The fragility of global supply chains is motivating countries to turn their attention to domestic manufacturing and supplies of raw materials. As more countries are increasing the use of energy efficient vehicles such as EVs, establishing a domestic source of lithium and facilities for LIB manufacturing is becoming ever more critical, especially meeting the demand for recycling capacity. Our analysis also reveals that higher carbon penalty leads to lower emissions, while low carbon penalty of \$20 per ton of CO_2 leads to results that are often identical to scenarios with no carbon penalty whatsoever. Our model for re-shoring lithium supply networks also has a positive impact on water use, as both GBLR and LIB recycling use significantly less water (83–90 percent) than traditional lithium mining processes.

In summary, the approach for re-shoring lithium supply networks proposed above helps countries to locally source an element critical for green energy generation, to reduce their dependence on global partners, and to strengthen their supply networks. From a sustainability perspective, it reduces the environmental impact compared to traditional lithium mining both in terms of CO_2 generation and water consumption.

Case Study: How a leading American discount retailer Designed and Implemented an Omnichannel Supply Chain

This leading American discount retailer has over 1,900 stores across the United States. The company has pioneered omnichannel retailing, offering customers a seamless shopping experience across its physical and digital channels. In 2017, this retailer was ranked first in the "Top 50 Omni-Channel Retailers" by Digital Commerce 360.

Their omnichannel success is partly due to its well-designed and implemented omnichannel supply chain. The company's supply chain is designed to support a variety of fulfillment options, including in-store pickup, buy online, pickup in-store (BOPIS), and ship-from-store (SFS). They also invested heavily in technology to enable real-time data sharing and visibility across its supply chain network.

Omnichannel Supply Chain Design

This retailer's omnichannel supply chain is designed to be flexible, efficient, and scalable. The company's distribution centers, and store network are strategically located to serve customers quickly and efficiently. They also use a variety of transportation modes, including trucks, rail, and air, to move products between its facilities.

The company's supply chain is also designed to be data driven. The company uses real-time data to optimize its inventory levels, fulfillment processes, and transportation routes. This data helps ensure that products are always in stock and available to customers when and where they want them.

Omnichannel Supply Chain Implementation

The retailer has implemented its omnichannel supply chain in a phased approach. The company first focused on integrating its physical and digital channels. This involved implementing a single view of inventory across all channels and enabling customers to make purchases online and pick them up in stores.

They also invested in several new technologies to support its omnichannel supply chain. Creating a comprehensive technology footprint for an omnichannel retail transformation involves integrating various technologies to create a branded customer experience, grow sales, and increase efficiencies in the supply chain. Below is an outline of the technology stack required, along with a brief description of how each component contributes to the overall strategy.

1. Customer Relationship Management (CRM) System

- Function: Manages customer data, interactions, and personalization.
- Contribution: Enhances customer experience through personalized communication and targeted marketing.

2. Enterprise Resource Planning (ERP) System

- Function: Integrates all the core business processes, including inventory management, order processing, and finance.
- Contribution: Streamlines operations and provides a unified view of business performance.

3. E-Commerce Platform

- Function: Manages online sales, including website management, online catalog, and customer portal.
- Contribution: Acts as the central hub for online sales, offering a seamless customer experience.

4. Point of Sale (POS) System

- Function: Manages in-store transactions.
- Contribution: Ensures a smooth in-store customer experience and integrates sales data with the CRM and ERP systems.

5. Supply Chain Management (SCM) System

- Function: Oversees logistics, inventory distribution, and supplier relationships.
- Contribution: Optimizes inventory levels and distribution, reducing costs and improving delivery times.
    - **Warehouse automation:** The company has automated its warehouses to improve efficiency and accuracy.
    - **Transportation management systems (TMS):** The company uses TMS to optimize transportation routes and reduce costs.

6. Data Analytics and Business Intelligence (BI) Tools

- Function: Analyzes data from various sources to provide actionable insights.

– Contribution: Drives decision-making based on customer behavior, sales trends, and supply chain performance.

7. Marketing Automation Tools

– Function: Automates marketing campaigns across various channels.

– Contribution: Increases sales through targeted marketing efforts and consistent branding.

8. Customer Service Tools

– Function: Manages customer interactions and support across various channels.

– Contribution: Improves customer satisfaction and loyalty through efficient service.

9. Mobile Application

– Function: Provides a mobile platform for shopping and brand interaction.

– Contribution: Enhances customer engagement and sales through a convenient mobile experience.

10. Internet of Things (IoT) and Smart Devices

– Function: Collects real-time data from various sources, including in-store sensors and smart inventory systems.

– Contribution: Improves inventory tracking, customer in-store experience, and collects valuable customer data.

- **RFID tags:** The company has tagged its products with RFID tags to track their movement throughout the supply chain.

11. Cloud Computing Infrastructure

- Function: Hosts applications, data storage, and computing power.
- Contribution: Offers scalability, reliability, and flexibility in managing IT resources.

12. Cybersecurity Solutions

- Function: Protects against data breaches and cyber threats.
- Contribution: Ensures the security of customer and business data, maintaining trust and compliance.

13. Artificial Intelligence and Machine Learning

- Function: Powers advanced analytics, personalization, and automation.
- Contribution: Enhances customer experience, optimizes supply chain operations, and drives innovation.

This comprehensive technology footprint ensures a seamless omnichannel experience for customers, drives sales, and creates efficiencies across the supply chain. When designing the architecture, it's crucial to ensure that these systems are well-integrated, allowing for data flow and insights across the entire retail operation.

Results

The company's omnichannel supply chain has had several positive results. These results include:

- **Increased sales:** The company's omnichannel sales have grown significantly recently. In 2020, omnichannel sales accounted for over 10% of the company's total sales.
- **Improved customer satisfaction:** The company's customers are more satisfied with their shopping experience. The company's Net Promoter Score (NPS) has increased steadily recently.
- **Reduced costs:** The company has reduced its supply chain costs by implementing its omnichannel strategy.

Organizational and Cultural Considerations

In addition to the factors mentioned above, the company's omnichannel success can also be attributed to the following:

- **A strong company culture:** The company has a strong culture focused on innovation and customer service. This culture has helped the company to embrace change and implement new technologies.
- **A commitment to omnichannel:** The company is committed to omnichannel retailing. The company has made significant investments in omnichannel initiatives and has a team of dedicated omnichannel experts.
- **A focus on data:** The company is a data-driven company. The company uses data to make informed decisions about its omnichannel strategy.

Conclusion

The company's omnichannel supply chain is a critical competitive advantage. The company's well-designed and implemented supply chain has helped it grow significantly and improve customer satisfaction. The company's omnichannel success is a model for other retailers looking to implement omnichannel strategies. Overall, the company's omnichannel supply chain is a success story. The company has been able to achieve significant growth and improve customer satisfaction by implementing a well-designed and implemented omnichannel supply chain.

Endnotes

1 EPA. Carbon Pollution from Transportation | US EPA. US EPA, May 19, 2022, www.epa.gov/transportation-air-pollution-and-climate-change/carbon-pollution-transportation (archived at https://perma.cc/88WG-GZLU).

2 M Azevedo et al. Lithium Mining: How New Production Technologies Could Fuel the Global EV Revolution | McKinsey. April 12, 2022, www.mckinsey.com/industries/metals-and-mining/our-insights/lithium-mining-how-new-production-technologies-could-fuel-the-global-ev-revolution (archived at https://perma.cc/7JUR-VFKF).
3 United Nations Conference on Trade and Development. COMMODITIES at a GLANCE Special Issue on Strategic Battery Raw Materials. February 2020.
4 US Geological Survey. Lithium. USGS, January 2023, pubs.usgs.gov/ (archived at https://perma.cc/GJS7-ZJWJ)
5 US Geological Survey. Lithium. USGS, January 2023, pubs.usgs.gov/periodicals/mcs2023/mcs2023-lithium.pdf (archived at https://perma.cc/5AM7-NX2V).
6 Federal Consortium for Advanced Batteries. NATIONAL BLUEPRINT for LITHIUM BATTERIES EXECUTIVE SUMMARY, 2021.
7 Federal Consortium for Advanced Batteries. NATIONAL BLUEPRINT for LITHIUM BATTERIES EXECUTIVE SUMMARY, 2021.
8 Alliance for Automotive Innovation. Driving US Economy and Innovation | Alliance for Automotive Innovation, 2020, www.autosinnovate.org/initiatives/the-industry (archived at https://perma.cc/MXQ9-6WNS).
9 European Environment Agency. Water Stress — European Environment Agency. www.eea.europa.eu/help/glossary/eea-glossary/water-stress#:~:text=Water%20stress%20occurs%20when%20the (archived at https://perma.cc/SA2C-6V23)
10 Molecular Weight and Molar Mass for Chemistry Problems. Convertunits.com, 2019, www.convertunits.com/molarmass (archived at https://perma.cc/477U-8J3Z).
11 Bureau, US Census. 2020 Census. Census.gov, 2020, www.census.gov/programs-surveys/decennial-census/decade/2020/2020-census-main.html (archived at https://perma.cc/SY7M-JYLS).
12 Sea-Distancing. Distances, 2023 www.Sea-Distances.org (archived at https://perma.cc/98L4-CPN6)
13 The European Chemical Transport Association (2011) estimated GHG emissions to be 8.4 g CO2e/ton-km for deep-sea container shipping. One nautical mile corresponds to 1.852 km.-need support finding this citation from Professor Greys
14 Railrates. Distances and emissions are estimated using information www.railrates.com.siteindices.com/ (archived at https://perma.cc/6XJG-BKNN)

15 P Greim, A Solomon and C Breyer. Assessment of lithium criticality in the global energy transition and addressing policy gaps in transportation. Nature Communications 11 (2020): Article 4570.
16 B Onyango. How Much Does a Tesla Car Battery Weigh? (Model S, Model 3, Model X, and Model Y) - Car, Truck and Vehicle How to Guides - Vehicle Freak. Vehicle Freak, May 31, 2022, vehiclefreak.com/how-much-does-a-tesla-car-battery-weigh-model-s-model-3-model-x-and-model-y/ (archived at https://perma.cc/6XJG-zzzz).
17 L Pedro. Comparison of Different EV Batteries in 2020 (Update). PushEVs, April 4, 2020, pushevs.com/2020/04/04/comparison-of-different-ev-batteries-in-2020/ (archived at https://perma.cc/C8PH-J7N8).
18 EverBatt. Argonne National Laboratory. Www.anl.gov, 2023, www.anl.gov/amd/everbatt-download (archived at https://perma.cc/4HA4-7ZWL).
19 ATLiS. EnergySourceMinerals, 2023, www.esminerals.com/atlis (archived at https://perma.cc/ZP2C-LAKF).
20 CarbonCredits.com. Live Carbon Prices Today. Carbon Credits, August 5,2021, carboncredits.com/carbon-prices-today/ (archived at https://perma.cc/GY9D-FZ96).
21 EverBatt. Argonne National Laboratory. Www.anl.gov, 2023, www.anl.gov/amd/everbatt-download (archived at https://perma.cc/2UZE-63NC).
22 ATLiS. EnergySourceMinerals,September 2023, www.esminerals.com/atlis (archived at https://perma.cc/SY3T-9EEM).

APPENDIX

Model parameters and variables

We will denote the set of locations of future LIB plants in the U.S. by Plants,

$$\text{Plants} = \{\text{MI, OH, TN1, TN2, GA, KY}\},$$

where MI denotes the plant in Holland, OH the plant in Lordstown, TN1 the plant in Spring Hill, TN2 the plant in Stanton, GA the plant in Commerce, and KY the plant in Glendale, as illustrated in Table 10.4. In Table 11.1, we introduce relevant parameters and variables. We use the notation from Table 11.1 to develop the profit function and constraints for our model. In profit calculation, we consider logistics cost, manufacturing profit, and environmental impact cost.

Cost function—Logistics

The first set of costs to consider is logistics costs, and in our analysis, we consider both transportation and pipeline inventory costs. Table 10.5 provides costs of shipping a full truckload/20- ft container and lead times (in days) for any combination of GBLR plant and LIB plant. Each container can carry up to 28 tons. Thus, s_j can be obtained by dividing appropriate numbers from Table 10.5 by 28.

For GBLR, the annual transportation cost to LIB plant j is $s_j y_j$. We assume local recycling, so we do not consider transportation cost for recycled lithium.

To obtain the pipeline inventory cost, we assume that the inventory cost represents 20 percent of the product cost; the current lithium price is estimated to be \$83.5/kg[1]. As the lead times d_j are expressed in days, the annual pipeline-inventory cost incurred when y_j tons of lithium is shipped from Salton Sea to LIB plant j can be expressed as

$$0.20 \cdot 83.5 \cdot d_j \cdot 1000/365 \cdot y_j = 45.753425 \cdot d_j y_j.$$

Table 11.1 Parameters and Variables Required to Evaluate the Optimization Model

Variable/Parameter	Description
e_j, j Plants	electricity emissions (in kg CO_2/MWh) at plant j (Table 10.4)
c_j, i Plants	electricity cost (in c/kWh) at plant j (Table 10.4)
y_j, j Plants	the quantity of lithium (in tons) produced by GBLR supplying LIB plant j
s_j, j Plants	cost (in USD) of shipping a ton of lithium produced by GBLR to LIB plant j (Table 10.5)
d_j, j Plants	shipping length (in days) for lithium produced by GBLR to LIB plant j (Table 10.5)
e_t , j Plants	emissions generated by shipping a ton of lithium produced by GBLR to LIB plant j (in kg of CO_2) (Table 10.5)
z_j, j Plants	the quantity of locally recycled lithium (in tons) supplying LIB plant j
$r_l = 63,712$	low profit (in USD) per ton of recycled lithium (excluding electricity cost)
$r_h = 90,637$	middle-range profit (in USD) per ton of recycled lithium (excluding electricity cost)
$r_h = 117,562$	high profit (in USD) per ton of recycled lithium (excluding electricity cost)
C_j, $j \in$ Plants	capacity of LIB plant j in GWhs (Table 10.4)

We assume local recycling, so we do not consider pipeline inventory for recycled lithium.

Profit function—Manufacturing

In addition to the transportation and inventory costs, we consider the profit generated through manufacturing.

In Section 4 we mentioned cost estimate of \$4,000/ton of lithium carbonate from GBLR, corresponding to \$21,277/ton lithium. Thus, profit from recovering y_j tons of lithium from geothermal brine and supplying it to LIB plant j can be written as

$$(83,500 - 21,277) \cdot y_j = 62,223 \cdot y_j.$$

We discussed how possible profit from LIB recycling in the U.S. can be estimated in the range \$5–\$12 per kWh, and that we assume lithium content of 130 g/kWh. As a result, profit generated when 1 kg of lithium is obtained through recycling ranges between \$38.46–\$92.31. Dai et al. (2019) estimate that direct recycling of 1 kg of LCO battery requires 18.089 MJ of electricity, corresponding to 5.0247 kWh. If we use their assumption discussed in Section 5, that 1 ton of battery corresponds to 23.4 kg of lithium, we need 214.73 kWh of electricity to generate 1 kg of lithium through recycling, corresponding to \$25.252/kg at a rate of 11.76 c/kWh. In order to get estimates for local recycling in which we use state-dependent electricity rates, we will add the electricity cost based on average electricity rates to profit estimates from Section 5 and subtract electricity cost based on local rates. In other words, we will express profit generated when z_j tons of lithium is obtained through direct local recycling and used at LIB plant j as $(r_k - 2,147.3 \cdot c_j) \cdot z_j$,where k = l denotes the lower bound of the recycling profit per ton (excluding electricity cost), $r_l = 38,460 + 25,252 = 63,712$, k = h denotes the higher bound of the of the recycling profit per ton (excluding electricity cost), $r_h = 92,310 + 25,252 = 117,562$, and $r_m = 90,637$ denotes its mid-range value.

Cost function—Environmental impact costs

An important element of our analysis is the environmental impact of local lithium supply networks, as moving goods incur transportation emissions, and for manufacturing we, in general, consider energy emissions. In our model, we are replacing imported lithium with local lithium supplies, so we expect transportation emissions to decrease. In terms of manufacturing emissions, as imported lithium mostly comes from south American locations that mine it from brine using evaporation ponds, we may see an increase in emissions.

Table 10.5 provides emissions generated by shipping a full truckload for any combination of GBLR location and LIB plant. Assuming that a truckload carries 28 tons, coefficients e^t_{ij} and e^t_j can be obtained by dividing appropriate numbers from Table 10.5 by 28. As mentioned earlier, we assume local battery recycling, so we assume no transportation emissions for recycling.

GBLR is still in its early stages and different technologies are being considered. Abovementioned Energy Source's project ATLiS[2] estimated that their process generates 2 tons of CO_2 per ton of $LiOH \cdot H_2O$, implying 12.12 tons CO_2 per ton of lithium under the assumption of 0.165 kg lithium per 1 kg of $LiOH \cdot H_2O$.[3] As a result, the cost of the environmental impact when y_j tons of lithium generated through GBLR supply LIB plan j can be expressed as

$$E_c(e^t + 12, 120) \cdot y_j/1000.$$

For recycling of LCO batteries, using the EverBatt assumption that recycling 1 ton of battery would generate 23.4 kg of lithium, we need 214.73 MWh of electricity to process 1 ton of lithium. Consequently, the total emissions cost attributed to recycling when z_j tons of locally recycled lithium is supplied to LIB plant j can be expressed as

$$E_c \cdot 214.73 \cdot e_j \cdot z_j/1000.$$

Constraints

We stated that we estimate 130 g of lithium per 1 kWh of LIB power (equivalent to 130 tons/GWh), and that C_j is capacity (in GWhs) of LIB plant j. Our demand constraint for LIB plant j can, therefore, be written as $y_j + z_j \leq 130 \cdot C_j$.

We discussed capacity issues for GBLR by considering the overall capacity in the Salton Sea area and the realistic annual extraction capacity in near future, so we introduce capacity constraint $\sum_{j \in Plants} y_j \leq 13{,}160$.

The potential total new LIB plant capacity of 243 GWh corresponds to 31,590 tons of lithium, and we will consider three scenarios— low (10 percent), medium (50 percent), and high (94 percent) level of recycling. The corresponding constraint is:

$$\sum_{j \in Plants} z_j \leq \alpha_k \cdot 31{,}590,$$

where $\alpha l = 0.10$, $\alpha_m = 0.50$, and $\alpha_h = 0.94$.

Local Supply Network Models for Proposed U.S. Lithium Plants

By combining all the elements developed above, our model under Scenario m; α can be written as

$$\max \sum_{j \in Plants} \left[62{,}223 - s_j - 45.753425 d_j - \frac{E_c \left(e_j^t + 12{,}120 \right)}{1000} \right] y_j + \sum_{j \in Plants} \left[r - 2{,}147.3 c_j - \frac{E_c 214.73 e_j}{1000} \right] z_j$$

s.t.

$$\sum_{j \in Plants} y_j \leq 13{,}160,$$

$$\sum_{j \in Plants} z_j \leq \alpha \quad 31{,}590,$$

$$y_j, z_j \geq 0, \; j \in Plants$$

where $\alpha \in \{\alpha_l, \alpha_m, \alpha_h\}$ and $r \in \{r_l, r_m, r_h\}$.

Abbreviations

Acronym	Description
BEV	battery electric vehicle
CO_2	carbon dioxide
DLE	direct lithium extraction
DLP	direct lithium to product
EV	electric vehicle
GBLR	geothermal brine lithium recovery
GHG	greenhouse gas
LCE	lithium carbonate equivalent
LCO	lithium cobalt oxide
Li	lithium

LiOH H_2O	lithium hydroxide monohydrate
LLTO	$Li_{0.33}La_{0.56}TiO_3$
LIB	lithium-ion battery
PEV	plug-in electric vehicle
PHEV	plug-in hybrid electric vehicle
SLM	seawater lithium mining

Endnotes

1 Wikipedia (2024) Prices of chemical elements. en.wikipedia.org/wiki/Prices_of_chemical_elements (archived at https://perma.cc/P8QM-9BFV)

2 EnergySource Minerals (2023) Smallest environmental impact in the world. www.esminerals.com/atlis (archived at https://perma.cc/5HKP-FGXQ)

3 Savannah Resources (2023) Lithium Overview www.savannahresources.com/lithium/lithium-overview/ (archived at https://perma.cc/ZWT3-8T8F)

REFERENCES

Amazon. Amazon FBA's Official Page. www.amazon.com/fulfillmentbyamazon (archived at perma.cc/F3XJ-V7AG).

Amazon. Amazon Seller Central. sellercentral.amazon.com (archived at https://perma.cc/TH5F-2EFN).

Amato, A et al. Challenges for sustainable lithium supply: A critical review." Journal of Cleaner Production, 300 (2021): Article 126954.

Amazon. Amazon Fulfillment Engine. amazonemancipatory.com/afe-amazon-fulfillment-engine (archived at https://perma.cc/8DGK-3WU3).

APICS. Supply chain sustainability uncovering the triple bottom line apics insights and innovations. 2016 www.apics.org/docs/default-source/industry-content/sustainability-report_short.pdf?sfvrsn=0 (archived at https://perma.cc/S5DV-YN5J).

Aronow, S. The biggest factors affecting supply chains in 2022. Gartner, January 27, 2022. www.gartner.com/en/articles/supply-chain-pressures-will-dominate-2022-but-equilibrium-is-coming (archived at https://perma.cc/H9K7-2EFE)

Associated Press. Tyson Foods suspends its largest pork plant amid Iowa outbreak. NBC News, April 19, 2020. www.nbcnews.com/news/us-news/tyson-foods-suspends-its-largest-pork-plant-amid-iowa-outbreak-n1189566 (archived at https://perma.cc/3WQY-LDH5).

Azevedo, M, Baczynska, M, Hoffman, K and Krauze, A. Lithium mining: How new production technologies could fuel the global EV revolution. McKinsey & Company Insights, 2022. www.mckinsey.com/industries/metals-and-mining/our-insights/lithium-mining-how-new-production-technologies-could-fuel-the-global-ev-revolution (archived at https://perma.cc/7FB8-DAZX).

Ball, J. Six Products, Six Carbon Footprints. Wall Street Journal (2009). online.wsj.com/news/articles/SB122304950601802565 (archived at https://perma.cc/SZF4-H4BL).

Bardi, U. Extracting Minerals from Seawater: An Energy Analysis. Sustainability 2 (2010): 980–992.

Berg, R.C, and Sady-Kennedy, T. A. South America's Lithium Triangle: Opportunities for the Biden Administration. Commentary, Center for Strategic and International Studies, 2021. www.csis.org/analysis/south-americas-lithium-triangle-opportunities-biden-administration (archived at https://perma.cc/6GRT-7FLX).

Bhutada, G. Visualizing 25 Years of Lithium Production, by Country. Elements, December 23, 2022. elements.visualcapitalist.com/25-years-of-lithium-production-by-country/ (archived at https://perma.cc/VBJ4-5KAC).

Biswas, S et al. Performance enhancement of renewable based deregulated system using distributed power flow controller, Redox flow battery, and Tesla power wall battery. International Journal of Green Energy, 2022. hdoi.org/10.1080/15435075.2022.2078164 (archived at https://perma.cc/H77Z-zzzz)

Blair, D. C, and Dunford Jr. J.F. The West's Delusion of Energy Independence. New York Times, 2022. www.nytimes.com/2022/02/22/opinion/russia-ukraine-energy-conflict.html (archived at https://perma.cc/56WD-EL4F).

Bogage, J, Kindy, K and Telford, T. Trump orders meat plants to stay open in pandemic. The Washington Post, April 28, 2020. www.washingtonpost.com/business/2020/04/28/trump-meat-plants-dpa/. (archived at https://perma.cc/E79P-6WH2)

Bookbinder, J. Supply Chain Network Design: Applying Optimization and Analytics to the Global Supply Chain. Interfaces 44, no. 3 (2014): 348+. link.gale.com/apps/doc/A372553505/AONE?u=anon~34bc8a29&sid=googleScholar&xid=8f6676db. (archived at https://perma.cc/P8LC-VTG2)

Borowski, S. The Dust Bowl: A wake-up call in environmental practices. American Association for the Advancement of Science, 2012. www.aaas.org/dust-bowl-wake-call-environmental-practices (archived at https://perma.cc/7FB5-MRZW).

Boulding, K. E. The Economics of the Coming Spaceship Earth. In Environmental Quality in a Growing Economy, Resources for the Future, edited by H. Jarrett, 3–14. Baltimore, MD: Johns Hopkins University Press, 1966. arachnid.biosci.utexas.edu/courses/THOC/Readings/Boulding_SpaceshipEarth.pdf (archived at https://perma.cc/J66X-4MYV).

Bradsher, K, and Forsythe, M. Why a Chinese Company Dominates Electric Car Batteries. New York Times, 2021. www.nytimes.com/2021/12/22/business/china-catl-electric-car-batteries.html (archived at https://perma.cc/U7W4-SVKE).

Brown, M. Last-mile deliveries need both old and new solutions. Retrieved from Supply Chain Management Review, January 23, 2023. www.scmr.com/article/last_mile_deliveries_need_both_old_and_new_solutions/third_party_logistics (archived at https://perma.cc/CG46-J3FG).

Buholtz, T et al. Electrifying Freight: Pathways to Accelerating the Transition. Electrification Coalition, 2023. electrificationcoalition.org/wp-content/uploads/2020/11/Electrifying-Freight-Pathways-to-Accelerating-the-Transition.pdf (archived at https://perma.cc/8AN9-UNSP).

Burstein, M. Fashion Supply Chain Transparency Takes Center Stage. Forbes, April 7, 2023. www.forbes.com/sites/forbestechcouncil/2023/04/07/fashion-supply-chain-transparency-takes-center-stage/?sh=36c6ab2865d6 (archived at https://perma.cc/UX87-AGWG).

Cascone, J. Mitigating Compliance Risk for Global Supply Chain, Deloitte United States, www2.deloitte.com/us/en/pages/consumer-business/articles/mitigating-compliance-risk-for-global-supply-chain.html (archived at https://perma.cc/YXP3-VALB)

Choi, T. Y et al.Coronavirus is a wake-up call for supply chain management. Harvard Business Review (2019). Coronavirus Is a Wake-Up Call for Supply Chain Management (hbr.org).

CIPS. 'Almost all' firms nearshoring supply chains amid geopolitical tensions. 2023. www.cips.org/supply-management/news/2023/january/almost-all-firms-nearshoring-supply-chains-following-geopolitical-tensions/ (archived at https://perma.cc/WA2N-DB2S).

Claire, G. (2021) Designing a Sustainable Supply Chain Based on the Triple Bottom Line. www.allthingssupplychain.com/designing-a-sustainable-supply-chain-based-on-the-triple-bottom-line-of-people-planet-profit/ (archived at https://perma.cc/VBF5-WAMS).

Computer Security Division, Information Technology Laboratory. NIST Risk Management Framework | CSRC | CSRC. CSRC | NIST, November 20, 2016. csrc.nist.gov/Projects/risk-management#:~:text=The%20NIST%20Risk%20Management%20Framework (archived at https://perma.cc/DNJ4-UQXC).

Comte, M. How to manage supply chain risk during geopolitical unrest, PwC, March 18, 2022, www.pwc.com/us/en/services/consulting/business-transformation/library/supply-chain-geopolitical-unrest.html (archived at https://perma.cc/WP32-VCST)

Council of the European Union. Council Directive 75/442/EEC of 15 July 1975 on waste. EUR-Lex. eur-lex.europa.eu/legal-content/EN/TXT/?uri=CELEX:31975L0442 (archived at https://perma.cc/9LDG-G3GM).

Coy, P. Making Water More Liquid. BusinessWeek, August 6, 2015. www.bloomberg.com/news/articles/2015-08-06/to-ease-california-s-drought-make-water-easier-to-trade (archived at https://perma.cc/BZA4-SSS4).

Dai, et al. EverBatt: A Closed-loop Battery Recycling Cost and Environmental Impacts Model, Argonne National Laboratory, ANL-19/16. (2019).

Denend, L, and Plambeck, E (2007). Walmart's Sustainability Strategy, Stanford GSB case study OIT-71A. www.gsb.stanford.edu/faculty-research/case-studies/wal-marts-sustainability-strategy (archived at https://perma.cc/R6H7-NF8D).

Early, C. The new 'gold rush' for green lithium. BBC, 2020. www.bbc.com/future/article/20201124-how-geothermal-lithium-could-revolutionise-green-energy (archived at https://perma.cc/6VPE-LJE9).

EasyShip. USPS vs. UPS vs. FedEx: Who Has Better Rates in 2022? Retrieved from EasyShip, February 8, 2022. www.easyship.com/blog/usps-vs-ups-vs-fedex.(archived at perma.cc/YW6L-8DE3)

Eke, J et al. The global status of desalination: An assessment of current desalination T technologies, plants and capacity. Desalination, 495 (2020): Article 114633.

EPA. National Recycling Strategy: Part One of a Series on Building a Circular Economy for All. EPA, 2021. www.epa.gov/system/files/documents/2021-11/final-national-recycling-strategy.pdf (archived at https://perma.cc/GK9N-7SNR).

EPA. Draft National Strategy to Prevent Plastic Pollution. EPA, 2023. www.epa.gov/circulareconomy/draft-national-strategy-prevent-plastic-pollution (archived at https://perma.cc/45CX-XTUR).

ERI. How are Tesla batteries recycled? [blog] ERI, May 22, 2022, eridirect.com/blog/2022/05/how-are-tesla-batteries-recycled/ (archived at https://perma.cc/KC4B-MJ58)

European Chemical Transport Association. Guidelines for Measuring and Managing CO2 Emission from Freight Transport Operation. European Chemical Transport Association, 2011. www.ecta.com. (archived at https://perma.cc/FPK9-MZ4N)

European Commission. Proposal for a Directive of the European Parliament and of the Council amending Directive 2008/98/EC on waste. European Commission, 2023. August 16, 2023. environment.ec.europa.eu/system/files/2023-07/Proposal%20for%20a%20DIRECTIVE%20OF%20THE%20EUROPEAN%20PARLIAMENT%20AND%20OF%20THE%20COUNCIL%20amending%20Directive%20200898EC%20on%20waste%20COM_2023_420.pdf (archived at https://perma.cc/YN7F-7DJQ).

EY. C-suite Insights: Sustainability and ESG Trends Index. EY, 2023. assets.ey.com/content/dam/ey-sites/ey-com/en_us/topics/sustainability/ey-c-suite-insights-sustainability-and-esg-trends-index.pdf (archived at https://perma.cc/96DX-DBSK).

FCAB. National Blueprint for Lithium Batteries, Federal Consortium for Advanced Batteries. FCAB, 2021. www.energy.gov/sites/default/files/2021-06/FCAB%20National%20Blueprint%20Lithium%20Batteries%200621_0.pdf (archived at https://perma.cc/5NK9-W78R).

FCAB. National Blueprint for Lithium Batteries. FCAB, 2021. www.energy.gov/sites/default/files/2021-06/FCAB%20National%20Blueprint%20Lithium%20Batteries%200621_0.pdf (archived at https://perma.cc/6CDM-S6F7).

Gaines, L et al. Direct Recycling R&D at the ReCell Center. *Recycling* 6, no. 3 (2021). doi.org/10.3390/recycling6020031 (archived at https://perma.cc/54RY-8J2Q).

Gilmore, D. Insights from Unilever's perfect logistics network exercise. Supply Chain Digest, July 25, 2014. www.scdigest.com/assets/FirstThoughts/14-07-25.php?cid=8321 (archived at https://perma.cc/U7XW-BXHJ)

Global Newswire. Third Party Logistics (3PL) Market Size is projected to reach USD 2018.22 Billion by 2030, growing at a CAGR of 8.58%: Straits Research. www.globenewswire.com/en/news-release/2022/10/03/2527160/0/en/Third-Party-Logistics-3PL-Market-Size-is-projected-to-reach-USD-2018-22-Billion-by-2030-growing-at-a-CAGR-of-8-58-Straits-Research.html (archived at https://perma.cc/8K8X-Z6YW).

GlobeScan and BSR. The State of Sustainable Business 2015. Org, 2015. www.bsr.org/reports/BSR_GlobeScan_State_of_Sustainable_Business_2015.pdf (archived at https://perma.cc/5TDY-V689).

GlobeScan and BSR. The State of Sustainable Business 2016. Org, 2016. www.bsr.org/reports/BSR_GlobeScan_State_of_Sustainable_Business_Survey_2016.pdf (archived at https://perma.cc/E7HX-KJ4S).

GlobeScan and BSR. The State of Sustainable Business 2018. Org, 2018. www.bsr.org/reports/BSR_Globescan_State_of_Sustainable_Business_2018.pdf (archived at https://perma.cc/83T5-88K4).

GlobeScan and BSR. The State of Sustainable Business 2019. Org, 2019. globescan.wpenginepowered.com/wp-content/uploads/2019/11/BSR-GlobeScan-State-of-Sustainable-BusinessSurvey-FinalReport-12Nov2019.pdf (archived at https://perma.cc/KKW4-ERGF).

Goodman, P. S, and Chokshi, N. How the World Ran out of Everything. The New York Times, June 1, 2021, www.nytimes.com/2021/06/01/business/coronavirus-global-shortages.html (archived at https://perma.cc/X5PJ-Q4BF)

Grand View Research. Reclaimed Lumber Market Size, Share & Trends Analysis Report By Application (Flooring, Beams & Boards, Furniture), By End-use (Residential, Commercial), By Region (Asia Pacific, Europe), And Segment Forecasts, 2021 – 2028. Report ID GVR-2-68038-802-2, 2021. www.grandviewresearch.com/industry-analysis/reclaimed-lumber-market (archived at https://perma.cc/VM3H-NBV8).

Greim, P, Solomon, A, and Breyer, C. Assessment of lithium criticality in the global energy transition and addressing policy gaps in transportation. Nature Communications 11 (2020): Article 4570.

Gupta, V (2017) Blockchain's Impact on Supply Chains. Harvard Business Review, 2017. hbr.org/2017/03/the-promise-of-blockchain-is-a-world-without-middlemen. (archived at https://perma.cc/7D7P-MRL9)

Hahu Zone. (2020) Interim Financial Reporting. Hahu Zone. hahuzone.com/interim-financial-reporting (archived at https://perma.cc/8ZAJ-TDBV).

Harapko, S. How COVID-19 impacted supply chains and what comes next. EY, 2023. www.ey.com/en_us/supply-chain/how-covid-19-impacted-supply-chains-and-what-comes-next#:~:text=The%20pandemic%20continues%20to,disrupting%20manufacturing%20as%20a%20result (archived at https://perma.cc/3YU4-GZTY).

Hardin, G. The Tragedy of the Commons. Science 162, no. 3859 (1968): 1243–48. www.jstor.org/stable/1724745 (archived at https://perma.cc/4Y95-2G62).

Heim, T. The Indigenous Origins of Regenerative Agriculture. National farmers Union Blog, 2020. nfu.org/2020/10/12/the-indigenous-origins-of-regenerative-agriculture/ (archived at https://perma.cc/K9FF-5DQE).

Henderson, S (2022) NIST Updates Cybersecurity Guidance for Supply Chain Risk Management. NIST, www.nist.gov/news-events/news/2022/05/nist-updates-cybersecurity-guidance-supply-chain-risk-management.

Hernandez, S. (2022) Information Technology (IT) System Supply Chain Risk Management (SR) Standard, https://www2.ed.gov/fund/contract/about/acs/2022-sr-supply-chain-risk-management.pdf (archived at https://perma.cc/VL8F-382Y)

Hoffman, A. J. (2015) How Culture Shapes the Climate Change Debate. Stanford Briefs, Stanford University Press.

Hooper, A. Cost of Congestion to the Trucking Industry: 2018 Update. American Transportation Research Institute, 2018. https://protect2.fireeye.com/v1/url?k=31323334-501d0a38-31357b2d-454441504e31-d2ab704dcd329968&q=1&e=504de458-2b9d-42ad-94e7-1d207aa4eec7&u=https%3A%2F%2F truckingresearch.org%2Fatri-research%2Ftraffic-incident-management%2F (archived at https://perma.cc/AA97-VL43) Traffic Incident Management (truckingresearch.org) http://www.doi.org/the-identifier/resources/handbook/ (archived at https://perma.cc/QTR9-DFZA) www.doi.org/the-identifier/resources/handbook/ (archived at https://perma.cc/QTR9-DFZA)

IBM. (2021) What Is Supply Chain Optimization? www.ibm.com, 2021, www.ibm.com/topics/supply-chain-optimization (archived at https://perma.cc/Z8A7-FSZG)

IEA. Global Supply Chains of EV Batteries, 2022, iea.blob.core.windows.net/assets/4eb8c252-76b1-4710-8f5e-867e751c8dda/GlobalSupplyChainsofEVBatteries.pdf (archived at https://perma.cc/B3VJ-84VE)

IEA. (2023) Global EV Outlook 2023, iea.blob.core.windows.net/assets/dacf14d2-eabc-498a-8263-9f97fd5dc327/GEVO2023.pdf (archived at https://perma.cc/B3VJ-84VE)

IKEA. (2023) Sustainability Report FY222, 2023, gbl-sc9u2-prd-cdn.azureedge.net/-/media/aboutikea/newsroom/publications/documents/ikea-sustainability-report-fy22.pdf (archived at https://perma.cc/W2G8-XCBM)

Ivanov, D. Predicting the impacts of epidemic outbreaks on global supply chains: A simulation-based analysis on the coronavirus outbreak (COVID-19/SARS-CoV-2) case. Transportation Research Part E: Logistics and Transportation Review, 136 (2020).

Janjevic, M, Merchán, D, and Winkenbach, M. Designing Multi-Tier, Multi-Service-Level, and Multi-Modal Last-Mile Distribution Networks for Omni-Channel Operations. European Journal of Operational Research 294, no. 3 (2021): 1059–1077. www.doi.org/the-identifier/resources/handbook/ (archived at https://perma.cc/QTR9-DFZA) Journal of Operational Research.

Jones, E, et al. The state of desalination and brine production: A global outlook. Science of The Total Environment 657 (2019): 1343–1356.

Kaunda, R. B. Potential environmental impacts of lithium mining. Journal of Energy & Natural Resources Law 38, no. 3 (2020): 237–244.

Kendall, A et al. Lithium-ion Car Battery Recycling Advisory Group Final Report, March 16, 2022. calepa.ca.gov/wp-content/uploads/sites/6/2022/05/2022_AB-2832_Lithium-Ion-Car-Battery-Recycling-Advisory-Goup-Final-Report.pdf (archived at https://perma.cc/VKC9-GSR3)

Lander, L et al. Financial viability of electric vehicle lithium-ion battery recycling. iScience 24 (2021): 102787.

Lopienski, K. ShipBob's Analytics Tool: How Fast-Growing DTC Brands Use Fulfillment Data. ShipBob, January 20, 2020. www.shipbob.com/blog/new-free-analytics-reporting-tool/ (archived at https://perma.cc/HCF7-YNAJ).

Ludwig, C. Controlling destinies in GM's supply chain, August 4, 2023. Automotive Logistics, 2023. www.automotivelogistics.media/supply-chain-management/investing-in-the-long-term-interview-series-with-gms-jeff-morrison-vp-global-purchasing-and-supply-chain/44480.article (archived at https://perma.cc/49P4-DWTY).

Makower, J. et al. State of Green Business 2023. GreenBiz, 2023. info.greenbiz.com/rs/211-NJY-165/images/State_of_Green_Business_2023_Report.pdf?mkt_tok=MjExLU5KWS0xNjUAAAGM0QUQs5wWih-3YoFLEGfx0IIWmmcPitTu_lE-eQUsO4wLfar67cgVZP7UYRf3AOaQ78_L1K_-OQ63IZV9ajCi9KjISB-DHZtoGvCZHXjUTjdLgH4 (archived at https://perma.cc/2UHG-B3Y3).

Mawet, P, and Webb T. Micro-Fulfillment Centers (MFCs): How retailers can deliver on same-day expectations. Supply Chain Management Review, January 5, 2023. www.scmr.com/article/micro_fulfillment_centers_mfcs_how_retailers_can_deliver_on_same_day_expect. (archived at https://perma.cc/RJ99-2RA3)

McGillivray, G. An Expert Explains: What COVID Did to Global Supply Chains. World Economic Forum, July 30, 2021. www.weforum.org/agenda/2021/07/covid-19-pandemic-global-supply-chains/ (archived at https://perma.cc/7SFU-MHA8)

McKinsey & Company. How companies capture the value of sustainability: Survey findings. 2021. www.mckinsey.com/capabilities/sustainability/our-insights/how-companies-capture-the-value-of-sustainability-survey-findings (archived at https://perma.cc/DRW8-VC9X).

McKinsey and Company. Consumers care about sustainability—and back it up with their wallets" 2021. www.mckinsey.com/industries/consumer-packaged-goods/our-insights/consumers-care-about-sustainability-and-back-it-up-with-their-wallets#/ (archived at https://perma.cc/2WLD-YHZA).

Miller, K. The triple bottom line: What it is & why it's important. [blog] Harvard Business School Online, December 8, 2020. online.hbs.edu/blog/post/what-is-the-triple-bottom-line (archived at https://perma.cc/3WUL-PDAQ)

Murodjon, S., et al. Lithium Recovery from Brines Including Seawater, Salt Lake Brine, Underground Water and Geothermal Water. In Thermodynamics and Energy Engineering, edited by P. Vizureanu. Place: Intech Open, 2020. http://dx.doi.org/10.5772/intechopen.90371 (archived at https://perma.cc/QAQ8-V9NZ).

National Credit Union Association. Supply Chain Risk Management (SCRM), National Credit Union Association, October 28, 2021. ncua.gov/regulation-supervision/regulatory-compliance-resources/cybersecurity-resources/supply-chain-risk-management-scrm (archived at https://perma.cc/C83Y-48U5).

Neumann, J, et al. Recycling of Lithium-Ion Batteries—Current State of the Art, Circular Economy, and Next Generation Recycling. Advanced Energy Materials 12, no. 17 (2022): 2102917 doi.org/10.1002/aenm.202102917 (archived at https://perma.cc/5UW7-NG22).

Nike. Sustainable business performance summary, FY12/13. Nike, 2014. ungc-production.s3.us-west-2.amazonaws.com/attachments/81781/original/FY12-13_NIKE_Inc_CR_Report.pdf?1400276890 (archived at https://perma.cc/Z2W4-FQ2D).

Nike. Introducing the Nike Re-Creation Program, Turning Locally Collected Nike Products into New Designs. Nike, 2022. about.nike.com/en/newsroom/releases/nike-re-creation-program (archived at https://perma.cc/E38V-XQF4).

Nike. FY22 Impact Report. Nike, 2023. about.nike.com/en/newsroom/reports/fy22-nike-inc-impact-report (archived at https://perma.cc/9H8T-BJVP).

Nunez, C. Beyond 'Green': The Empire State Building Retrofit. National Geographic, August 20, 2011. www.nationalgeographic.com/environment/article/beyond-green-the-empire-state-building-retrofit (archived at https://perma.cc/75US-VNBU).

Obrecht, M et al. Conceptualizing a new circular economy feature – storing renewable electricity in batteries beyond EV end-of-life: The case of Slovenia International Journal of Productivity and Performance Management, vol. ahead-of-print, no. ahead-of-print, 4 June 2021, https://doi.org/10.1108/ijppm-01-2021-0029 (archived at https://perma.cc/6KCN-R3WS).

O'Connor, T. How is same-day delivery becoming a viable strategy for U.S. retailers? Supply Chain Management Review, May 2, 2022. www.scmr.com/article/how_is_same_day_delivery_becoming_a_viable_strategy_for_u.s._retailers/third_party_logistics (archived at https://perma.cc/483L-4KKQ)

'Once-in-a-century disruption' reverberates across global supply chains (yahoo.com)

o9 Solutions. o9 takes big steps in augmenting its industry-leading integrated planning platform with generative AI capabilities, August 17, 2023, o9solutions.com/news/o9-takes-big-steps-in-augmenting-its-industry-leading-integrated-planning-platform-with-generative-ai-capabilities?utm_campaign=PR.Product&utm_medium=linkedin_o9&utm_source=marketing_social (archived at https://perma.cc/46W9-S5LU)

Patil, P, et al. 'Plastic roads' made from waste: A path worth paving for South Asia? World Bank Blogs, 2021. blogs.worldbank.org/endpovertyinsouthasia/plastic-roads-made-waste-path-worth-paving-south-asia (archived at https://perma.cc/W2ZJ-4AXX).

Paton, E. Burberry to Stop Burning Clothing and Other Goods It Can't Sell. The New York Times September 6, 2018. www.nytimes.com/2018/09/06/business/burberry-burning-unsold-stock.html (archived at https://perma.cc/5N35-H8AJ).

Penn, I, and Lipton, E. The Lithium Gold Rush: Inside the Race to Power Electric Vehicles. New York Times. www.nytimes.com/2021/05/06/business/lithium-mining-race.html (archived at https://perma.cc/5C7D-4GV2).

Pierce, D. W and Turner R. K. Economics of Natural Resources and the Environment. Baltimore, MD: Johns Hopkins University Press, 1989.

Potting, J et al. Circular economy: Measuring innovation in the product chain. The Hague, 2016. www.pbl.nl/sites/default/files/downloads/pbl-2016-circular-economy-measuring-innovation-in-product-chains-2544.pdf (archived at https://perma.cc/HK6H-UEV6).

Rockel, N. Don't get lost in the cloud: How to manage multiple providers. Fortune Magazine, November 8, 2022. fortune.com/2022/11/08/business-multi-cloud-providers/. (archived at https://perma.cc/R6QS-FGKZ)

Rogers, C. Nike may run out of Vietnamese sneakers as COVID-19 accelerates. S&P Global Market Intelligence, July 19, 2021. www.spglobal.com/marketintelligence/en/news-insights/latest-news-headlines/nike-may-run-out-of-vietnamese-sneakers-as-covid-19-accelerates-65536921. (archived at https://perma.cc/635M-7HHC)

Roser, C. The inner workings of the amazon fulfillment centers part, AllAboutLean.com. October 22, 2019. www.allaboutlean.com/amazon-fulfillment-1/ (archived at https://perma.cc/ZM6N-WPXB)

Rowsell, J. How Nike transformed supply chains to survive Covid. Chartered Institute of Procurement & Supply, January 21, 2022. www.cips.org/supply-management/news/2022/january/how-nike-transformed-supply-chains-to-survive-covid/. (archived at https://perma.cc/WQ2H-V6SC)

Rural Migration News. Meat: Covid, concentration, and automation. Rural Migration News, January 19, 2022. migration.ucdavis.edu/rmn/blog/post/?id=2696. (archived at https://perma.cc/T4MB-BTKA)

Saberi, S., et al. Blockchain technology and its relationships to sustainable supply chain management. International Journal of Production Research 57, no. 7(2019): 2117–2135.

Save the Children (2023). Child Rights Risks in Global Supply Chains: Why a 'Zero Tolerance' Approach is not Enough. www.savethechildren.de/fileadmin/user_upload/Downloads_Dokumente/Berichte_Studien/2023/save-the-children-child-rights-risks-in-global-supply-chains-2023.pdf (archived at https://perma.cc/K88V-CLYK).

Scott, S. and Ireland, R. Lithium-Ion Battery Materials for Electric Vehicles and their Global Value Chains. U.S. International Trade Commission, Office of Industries, Working paper ID-068, 2020. www.usitc.gov/publications/332/working_papers/gvc_overview_scott_ireland_508_final_061120.pdf (archived at https://perma.cc/34VG-UZZD)

Seric, A et al. Managing COVID-19: How the pandemic disrupts global value chains. World Economic Forum, 27 April 2020. www.weforum.org/agenda/2020/04/covid-19-pandemic-disrupts-global-value-chains/ (archived at https://perma.cc/KLW4-X697)

Sethuraman, V. Supply chain industry trends to watch out for in 2023. Economic Times, January 5, 2023. economictimes.indiatimes.com/small-biz/sme-sector/supply-chain-industry-trends-to-watch-out-for-in-2023/articleshow/96754309.cms?utm_source=contentofinterest&utm_medium=text&utm_campaign=cppst (archived at https://perma.cc/A886-PEFG)

Shipfinex. Blog. Stay Informed about ownership updates www.shipfinex.com/blog (archived at https://perma.cc/93X8-C4N4).

Simchi-Levi, D, Timmermans, K. A Simpler Way to Modernize Your Supply Chain. Harvard Business Review. Last accessed July 28, 2023. https://hbr.org/2021/09/a-simpler-way-to-modernize-your-supply-chain (archived at https://perma.cc/QMG5-S5MV).

Stahel, W. R. The product life factor. An Inquiry into the Nature of Sustainable Societies: The Role of the Private Sector (Series: 1982 Mitchell Prize Papers), NARC, 74–96.

Stamatis, D. H. (2003) Failure mode and effect analysis: FMEA from theory to execution. Milwaukee: ASQ Quality Press, 2003.

Stelloh, T. Meat processing plant ordered to shut down after COVID-19 outbreak." NBC News, November 9, 2020. www.nbcnews.com/news/us-news/meat-processing-plant-ordered-shut-down-after-covid-outbreak-company-n1247189 (archived at https://perma.cc/88Q2-RBED).

Steward, D. et al. Economics and Challenges of Li-Ion Battery Recycling from End-of-Life Vehicles. Procedia Manufacturing 33 (2019): 272–279.

Stringfellow, W.T., and Dobson, P.F. Technology for the Recovery of Lithium from Geothermal Brines. Energies 14 (2021): 6805. www.mdpi.com/1996-1073/14/20/6805 (archived at https://perma.cc/8X73-DPNS).

Syverson, S (2021) Everything You Need to Know About Supply Chain Optimization, 2021 www.warehouseanywhere.com/resources/supply-chain-optimization/ (archived at https://perma.cc/9L6R-SCPW).

Tibco. What Is Supply Chain Optimization? TIBCO Software, www.tibco.com/reference-center/what-is-supply-chain-optimization (archived at https://perma.cc/4NNB-5ALU).

Toba, A et al. U.S. lithium resources from geothermal and extraction feasibility. Resources, Conservation and Recycling 169 (2021): Article 105514.

Torkornoo, D. OPS Rules Blog: Insights into Supply Chain and Operations Strategy. When is it a good time for supply chain network design? OPS Rules Blog, August 4, 2014. web.archive.org/web/20160925195356/http:/www.opsrules.com/supply-chain-optimization-blog/bid/342858/When-is-it-a-good-time-for-supply-chain-network-design (archived at https://perma.cc/76TG-CJ9E).

Trivedi, S. Triple Bottom Line Elements of Sustainable Supply Chain. August 23, 2022 managemententhusiast.com/triple-bottom-line-elements-of-sustainable-supply-chain-measures-to-make-supply-chain-sustainable/ (archived at https://perma.cc/GW4Y-BLDS).

The White House. Food prices for American families. Briefing, September 8, 2021. www.whitehouse.gov/briefing-room/blog/2021/09/08/addressing-concentration-in-the-meat-processing-industry-to-lower-food-prices-for-American-families/. (archived at https://perma.cc/TN5G-8PN8)

UNCTAD. Commodities at a glance - Special issue on strategic battery raw materials. United Nations Conference on Trade and Development (UNCTAD), 2020. unctad.org/system/files/official-document/ditccom2019d5_en.pdf (archived at https://perma.cc/VVS8-RKN3).

U.S. Census Bureau. Reports: State Imports by HS commodities. USA Trade Online, 2021. Source: U.S. Import and Export Merchandise trade statistics. https://usatrade.census.gov/index.php (archived at https://perma.cc/G9TU-G355).

U.S. Mission Russia. Europe moves away from Russia's oil and gas. May 12, 2023. Accessed July 19, 2023. ru.usembassy.gov/europe-moves-away-from-russias-oil-and-gas/ (archived at https://perma.cc/AG7B-XH79).

USGS. Mineral Commodity Summaries 2020. U.S. Geological Survey, 2020. pubs.usgs.gov/periodicals/mcs2020/mcs2020.pdf (archived at https://perma.cc/UD5E-D5ST).

USITC. Lithium-Ion Battery Materials for Electric Vehicles and their global Value Chains. U.S. International Trade Commission, 2020. Accessed December 9, 2021. https://www.usitc.gov/publications/332/working_papers/gvc_overview_scott_ireland_508_final_061120.pdf (archived at https://perma.cc/B3VC-BT2B).

Ventura, S, et al. Selective Recovery of Lithium from Geothermal Brines. California Energy Commission, CEC- 500-2020-020, 2020.

Vyas, N. USC Global Supply Chain Management Institute Effective Supply Chain in an Era of Decoupling. SCOPE Virtual Summit, June 13–17, 2022. uscsupplychain.com (archived at https://perma.cc/4GTH-BF55).

Vyas, N. Supply chains: Agility, not fragility, was the goal – let's not blame lean. enterprise viewpoint, July 25, 2022. enterpriseviewpoint.com/supply-chains-agility-not-fragility-was-the-goal-lets-not-blame-lean/ (archived at https://perma.cc/EE3P-BXJ9)

Vyas, N. Five Questions on How Coronavirus Will Impact the Global Supply Chain USC Today, March 13, 2020. today.usc.edu/coronavirus-global-supply-chain-economy-nick-vyas-usc-marshall/ (archived at https://perma.cc/BX8X-AEF6).

Vyas N. Supply-Chain-Management-c2-1.pdf thenickvyas.com (archived at https://perma.cc/6R7B-B49Y)

Vyas, N. Strenghening Global Supply Chains in the Wake of COVID-19. The Ripon Society, May 20, 2021. riponsociety.org/article/strengthening-global-supply-chains-in-the-wake-of-covid-19/ (archived at https://perma.cc/F7A9-2SYH)

Vyas, N and Weiss, J. Effective supply chain management in an era of decoupling, January 2021. www.steptoe.com/a/web/211420/Supply-Chain-Management.pdf (archived at https://perma.cc/TJ2K-74T8)

Wack, P. Scenarios: uncharted waters ahead. Harvard Business Review 63, no. 5 (1985): 73–89.

Walmart. Supplier Requirements for Supply Chain Traceability, 2022. one.walmart.com/content/dam/responsiblesourcing/supplier_expectations/Resource_Traceability_ENG.pdf (archived at https://perma.cc/6C82-NNDP).

Wissen, M. Category Archive for 'Organizations.' www.militaer-wissen.de/category/organizations/?lang=en (archived at https://perma.cc/6TKQ-78UC).

Wlodarcyzk, N. Geopolitics: Growing Politically Driven Decision Making Impacting Supply Chains in 2022. www.spglobal.com, April 6, 2022. www.spglobal.com/marketintelligence/en/news-insights/research/geopolitics-growing-politically-driven-decision-making-impacting-supply-chains-in-2022 (archived at https://perma.cc/9WY8-VCNZ).

World Economic Forum. Global Risks Report 2021. World Economic Forum, 2021. www.weforum.org/reports/the-global-risks-report-2021 (archived at https://perma.cc/78T6-AS9E).

Xu, Z. et al. (2020) Impacts of COVID-19 on global supply chains: Facts and perspectives, IEEE Engineering Management Review, 2020, 48 (3), 153–166

Yaksic, A., and Tilton, J.E. Using the cumulative availability curve to assess the threat of mineral depletion: The case of lithium. Resources Policy 34 (2009): 185–194.

Yanatma, S. Europe's 'energy war' in data: How have EU imports changed since Russia's invasion of Ukraine? Euronews, February 24, 2023. www.euronews.com/green/2023/02/24/europes-energy-war-in-data-how-have-eu-imports-changed-since-russias-invasion-of-ukraine#:~:text=Russia%20was%20the%20largest%20supplier,Algeria%20(8.2%20per%20cent) (archived at https://perma.cc/9CLU-QKGD). Accessed July 19, 2023.

Zhou, Y, et al. Lithium-ion Battery Supply Chain for E-Drive Vehicles in the Unites States: 2010-2020. Argonne National Library, 2021. publications.anl.gov/anlpubs/2021/04/167369.pdf (archived at https://perma.cc/TR65-BT22).

INDEX

Note: Page numbers in *italics* refer to tables or figures.

Printed in the USA
CPSIA information can be obtained
at www.ICGtesting.com
LVHW061227050524
779261LV00024B/188

9 781398 614918